SEVEN SEAS ENTERTAINMENT PRESENTS

Magia the Ninth vol.2

story and art by **ICHIYA SAZANAMI**   script editor by **HIROKI HORIE**

TRANSLATION
Adrienne Beck

ADAPTATION
Janet Houck

LETTERING AND RETOUCH
Erika Terriquez

LOGO DESIGN
Meaghan Tucker

COVER DESIGN
Nicky Lim

PROOFREADER
Katherine Bell

PRODUCTION MANAGER
Lissa Pattillo

EDITOR-IN-CHIEF
Adam Arnold

PUBLISHER
Jason DeAngelis

MAGIA THE NINTH VOL. 2
© Ichiya Sazanami 2015, © Hiroki Horie 2015
First published in Japan in 2015 by KADOKAWA CORPORATION, Tokyo.
English translation rights reserved by Seven Seas Entertainment, LLC.
under the license from KADOKAWA CORPORATION, Tokyo.

Seven Seas books may be purchased in bulk for promotional, educational, or
business use. Please contact your local bookseller or the Macmillan Corporate
and Premium Sales Department at 1-800-221-7945, extension 5442, or by
e-mail at MacmillanSpecialMarkets@macmillan.com.

Seven Seas and the Seven Seas logo are trademarks of
Seven Seas Entertainment, LLC. All rights reserved.

ISBN: 978-1-

Printed in Ca

First Printing

10 9 8 7 6

D0004206

FOLLOW US ONLINE: *www.gomanga.com*

READING DIRECTIONS

This book reads from *right to left*, Japanese style.
If this is your first time reading manga, you start
reading from the top right panel on each page and
take it from there. If you get lost, just follow the
numbered diagram here. It may seem backwards at
first, but you'll get the hang of it! Have fun!!

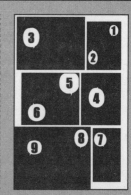

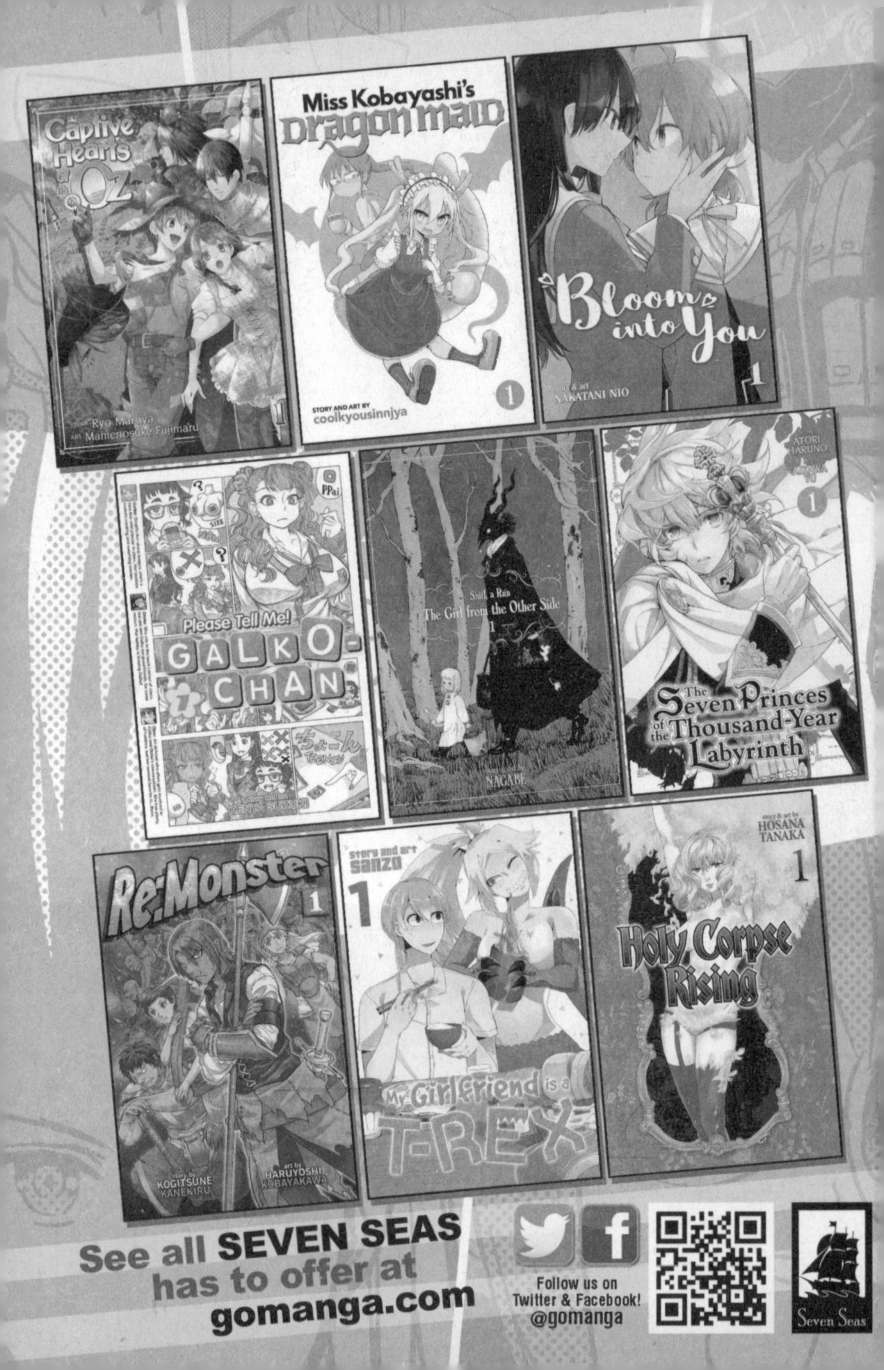
Captive Hearts of Oz
Story: Ryo Maruya
Art: Mamenosuke Fujimaru
Miss Kobayashi's Dragon Maid
1
Story and art by coolkyousinnjya
Bloom into You
1
Story & art NAKATANI NIO
Please Tell Me! GALKO-CHAN
Story and art KENYA SUZUKI
The Girl from the Other Side
1
NAGABE
The Seven Princes of the Thousand-Year Labyrinth
1
Re:Monster
1
story by KOGITSUNE KANEKIRU
art by HARUYOSHI KOBAYAKAWA
story and art SANZO
1
My Girlfriend is a T-REX
story & art by HOSANA TANAKA
1
Holy Corpse Rising
See all SEVEN SEAS has to offer at gomanga.com
Follow us on Twitter & Facebook! @gomanga
Seven Seas

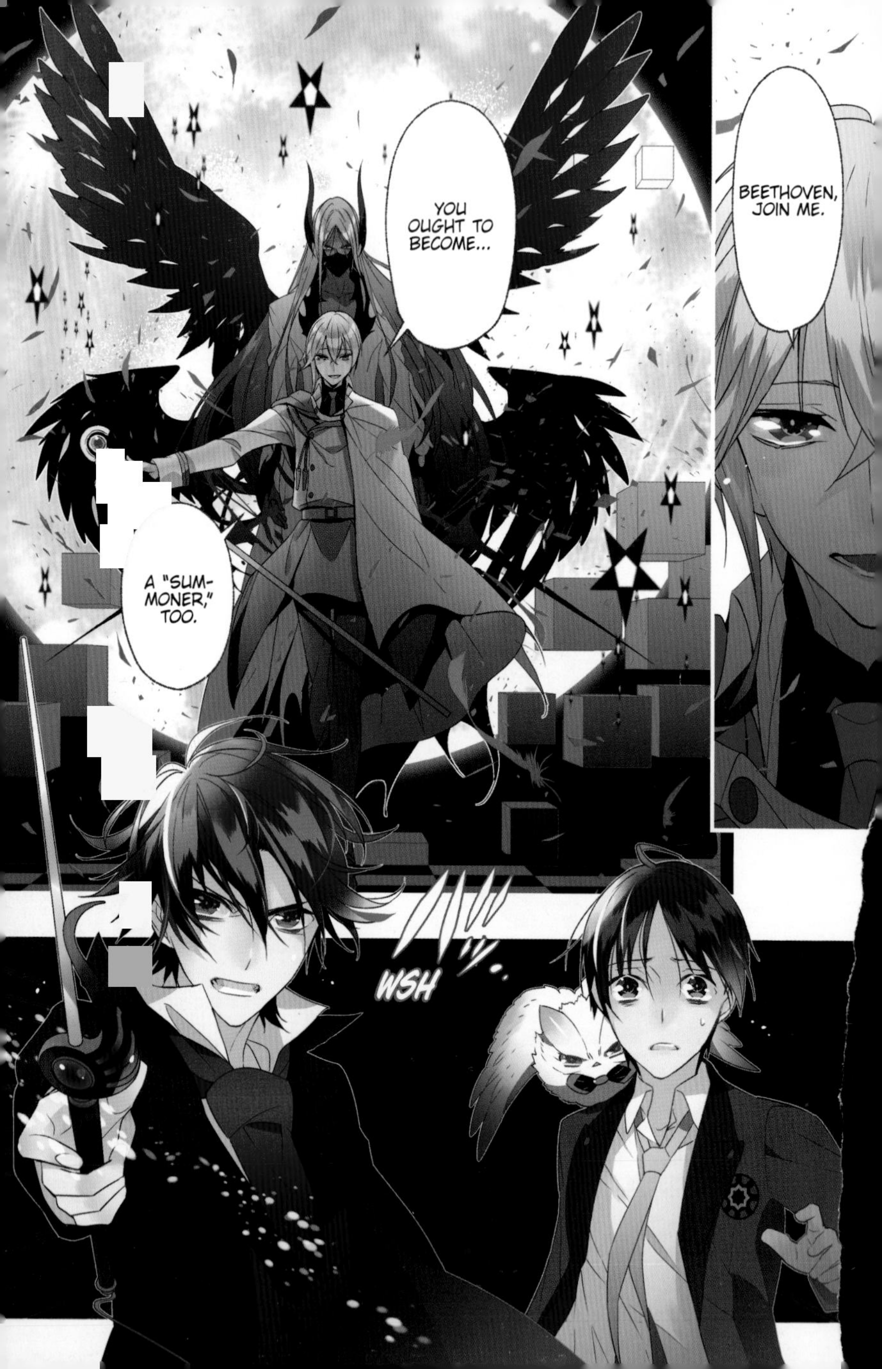
BEETHOVEN, JOIN ME.
YOU OUGHT TO BECOME...
A "SUM-MONER," TOO.
WSH

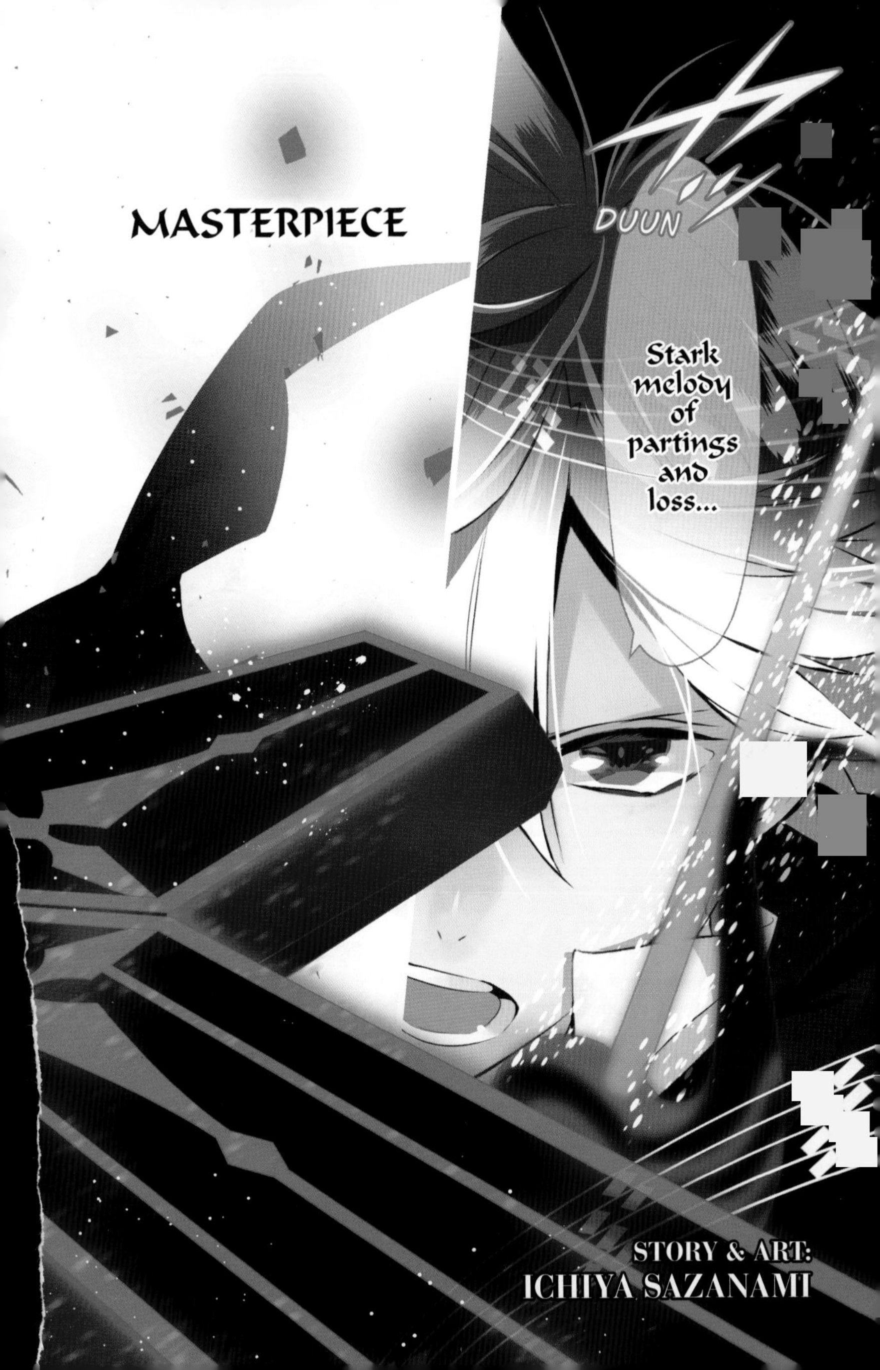
MASTERPIECE
DUUN
Stark melody of partings and loss...
STORY & ART:
ICHIYA SAZANAMI

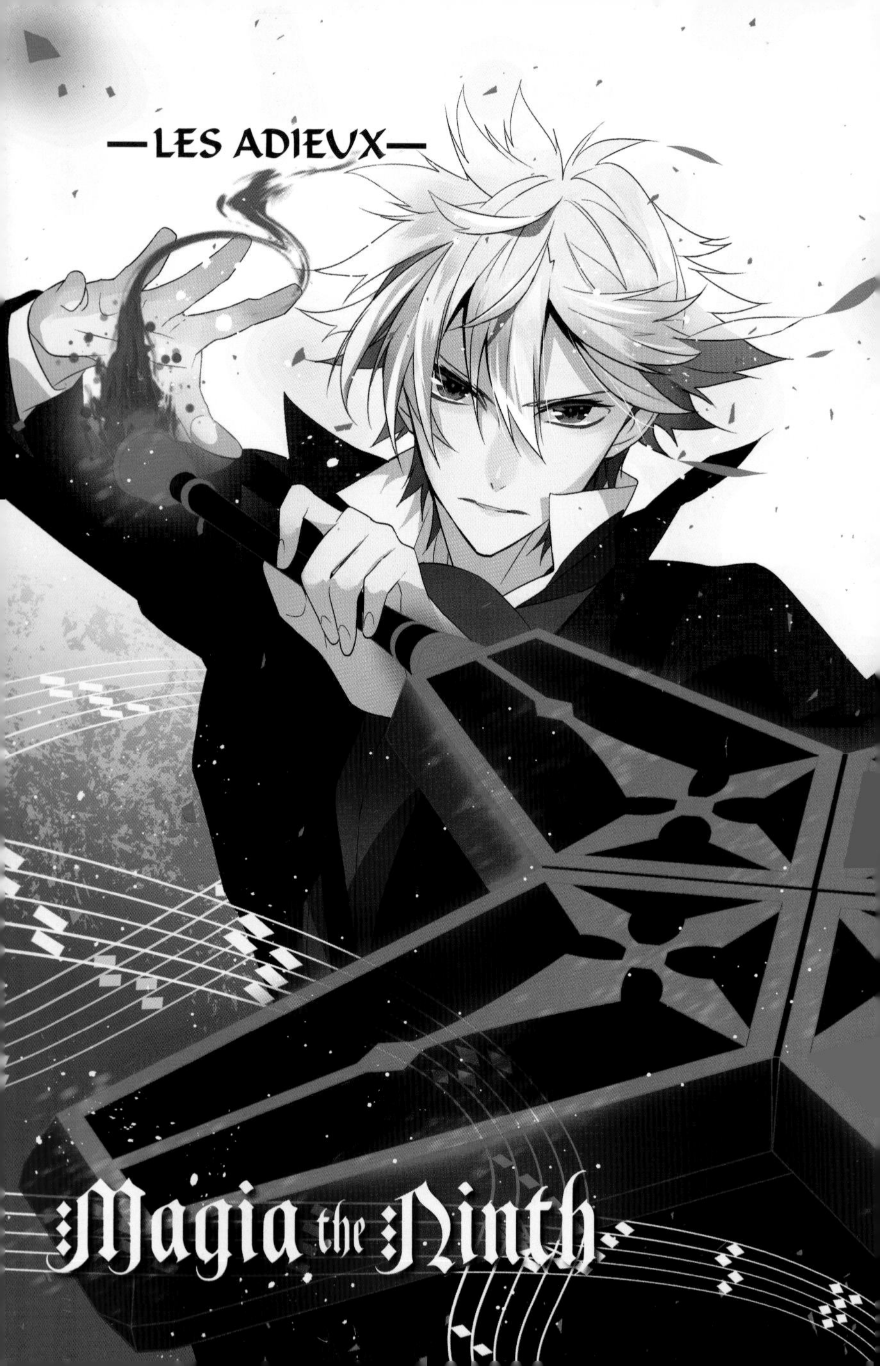
—LES ADIEUX—
Magia the Ninth

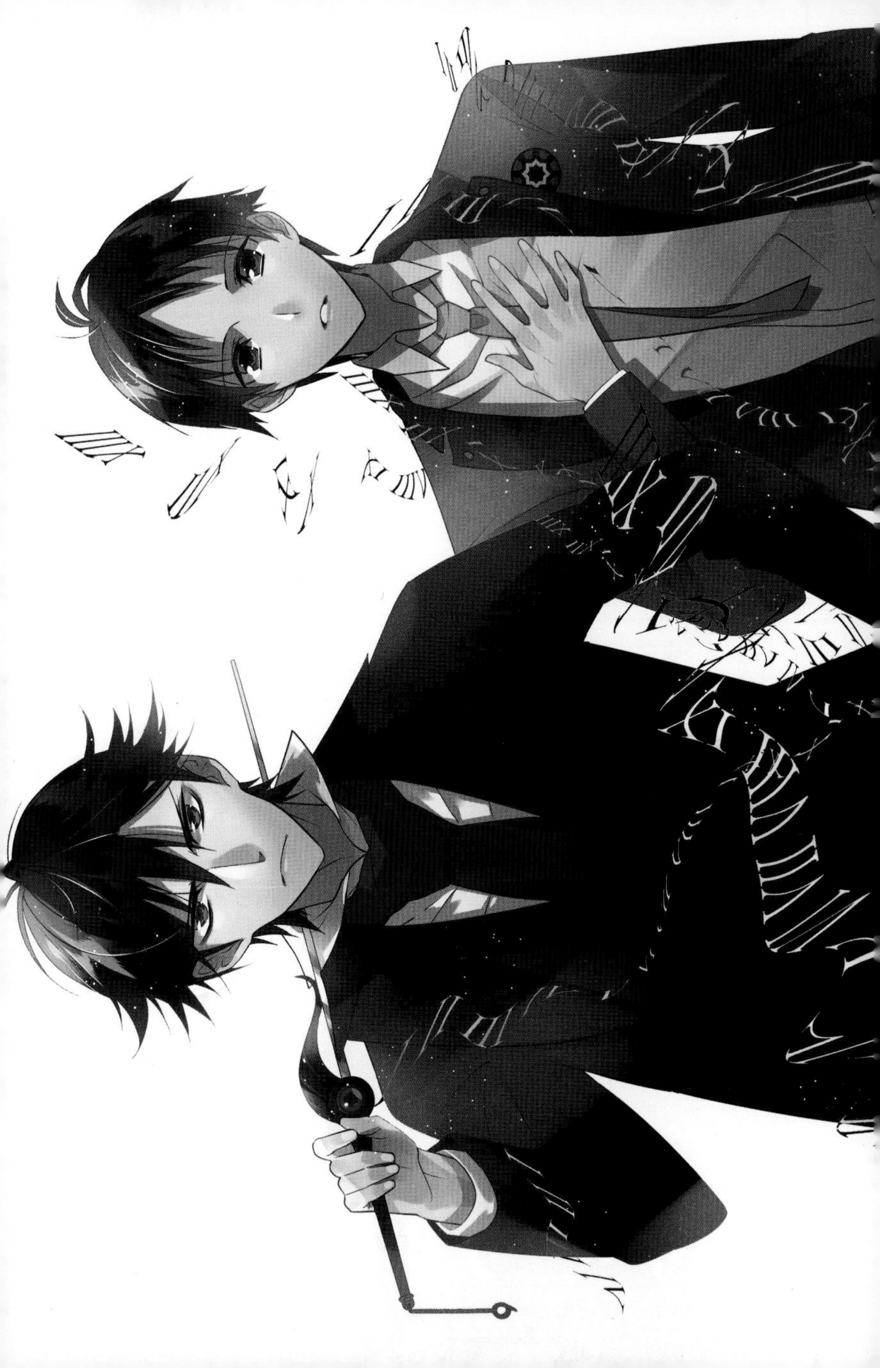

#6. Les Adieux

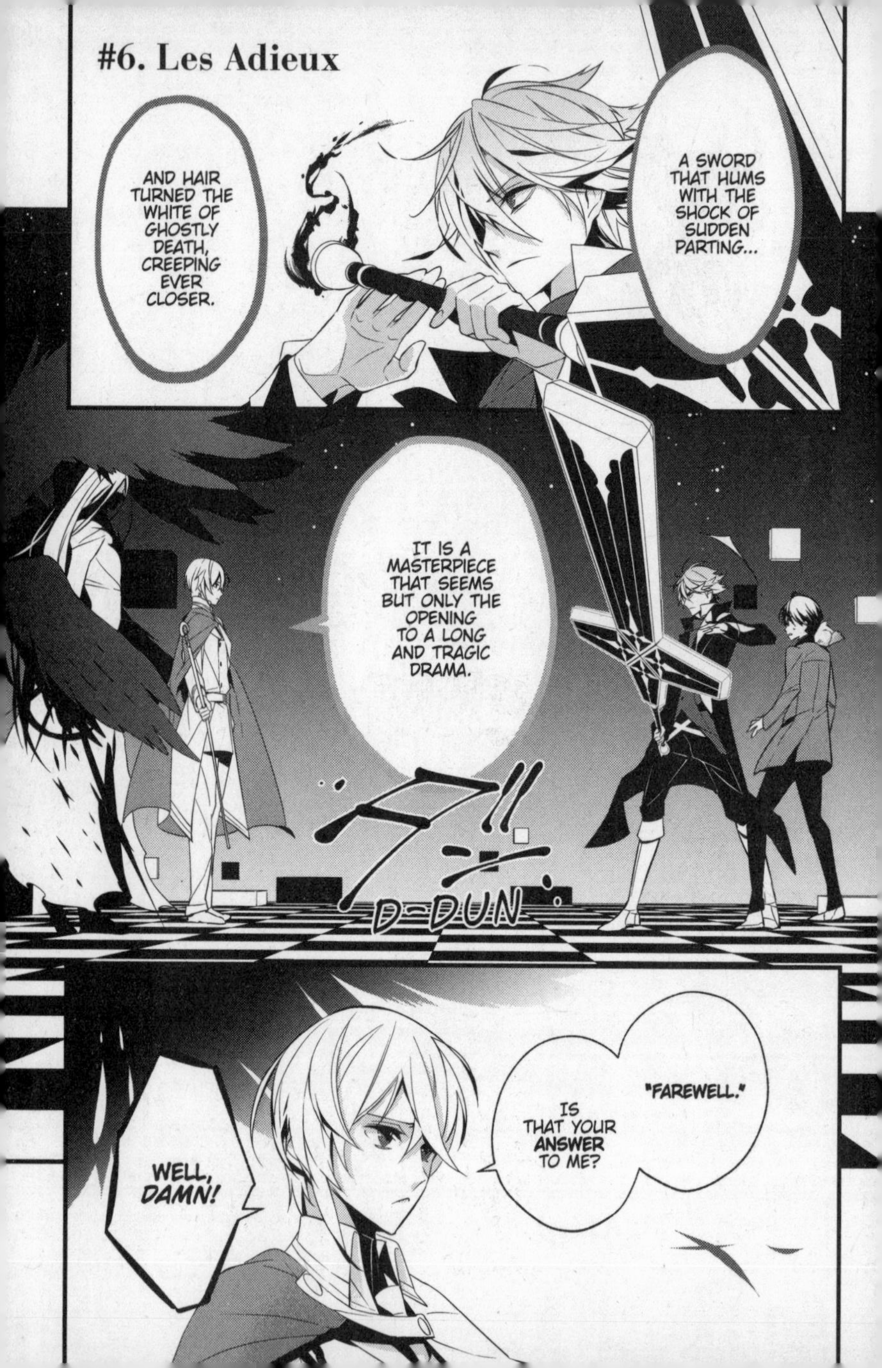
A SWORD THAT HUMS WITH THE SHOCK OF SUDDEN PARTING...
AND HAIR TURNED THE WHITE OF GHOSTLY DEATH, CREEPING EVER CLOSER.
IT IS A MASTERPIECE THAT SEEMS BUT ONLY THE OPENING TO A LONG AND TRAGIC DRAMA.
D-DUN
"FAREWELL."
IS THAT YOUR ANSWER TO ME?
WELL, DAMN!

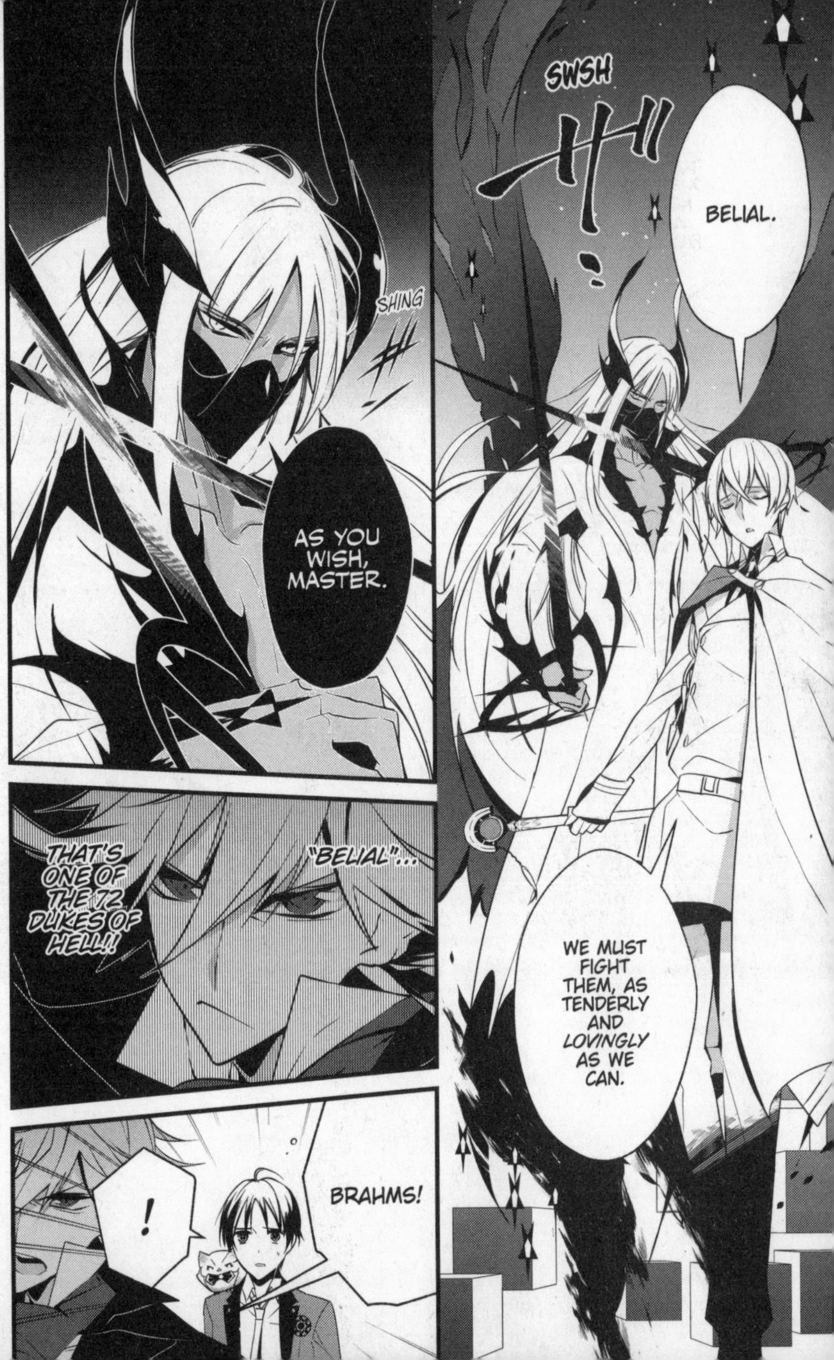
SWSH
BELIAL.
WE MUST FIGHT THEM, AS TENDERLY AND LOVINGLY AS WE CAN.
SHING
AS YOU WISH, MASTER.
"BELIAL"...
THAT'S ONE OF THE 72 DUKES OF HELL!!
BRAHMS!
!

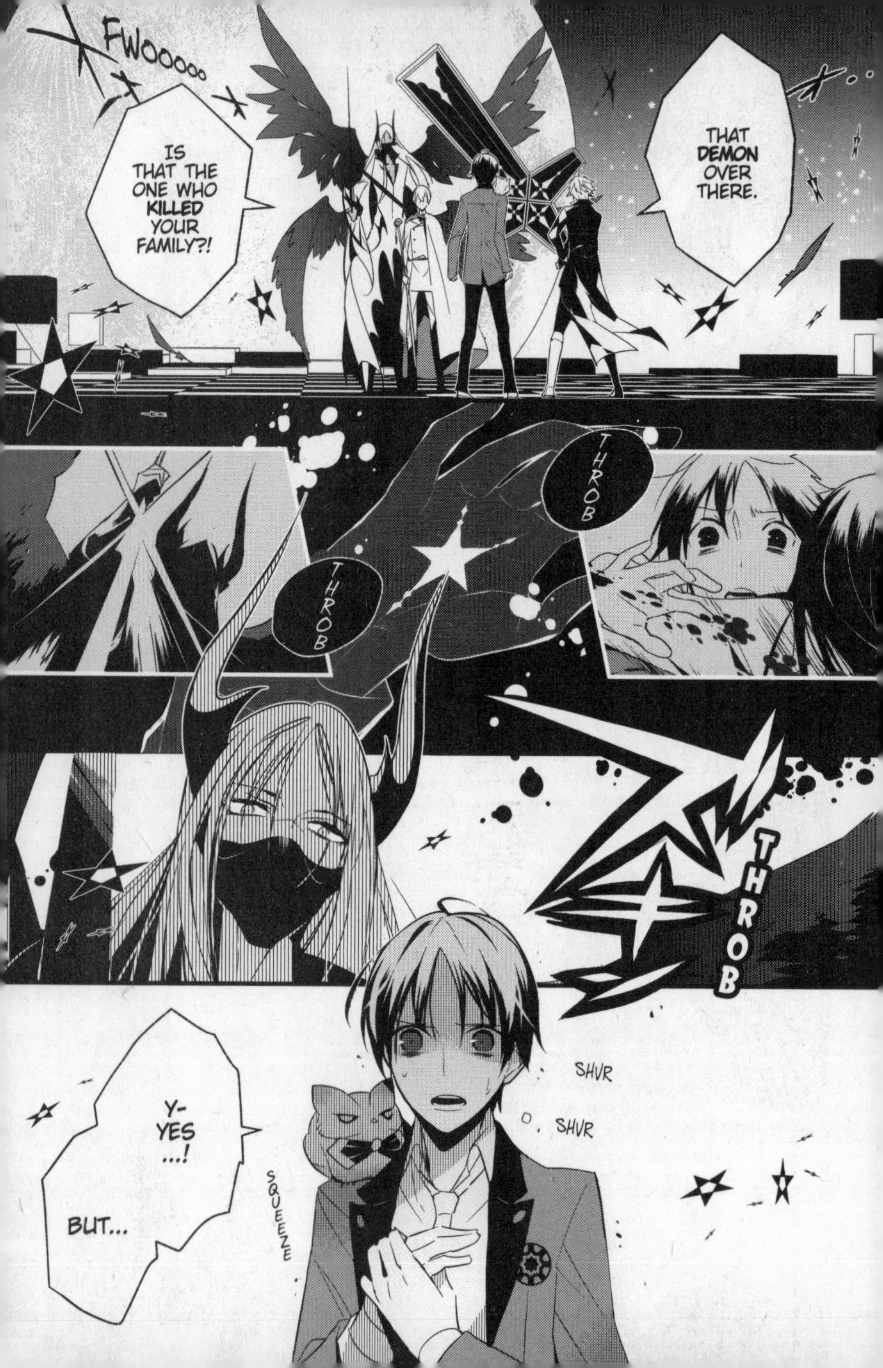
THAT DEMON OVER THERE.
FWOOOOO
IS THAT THE ONE WHO KILLED YOUR FAMILY?!
THROB
THROB
THROB
SHVR
SHVR
Y-YES ...!
BUT...
SQUEEZE

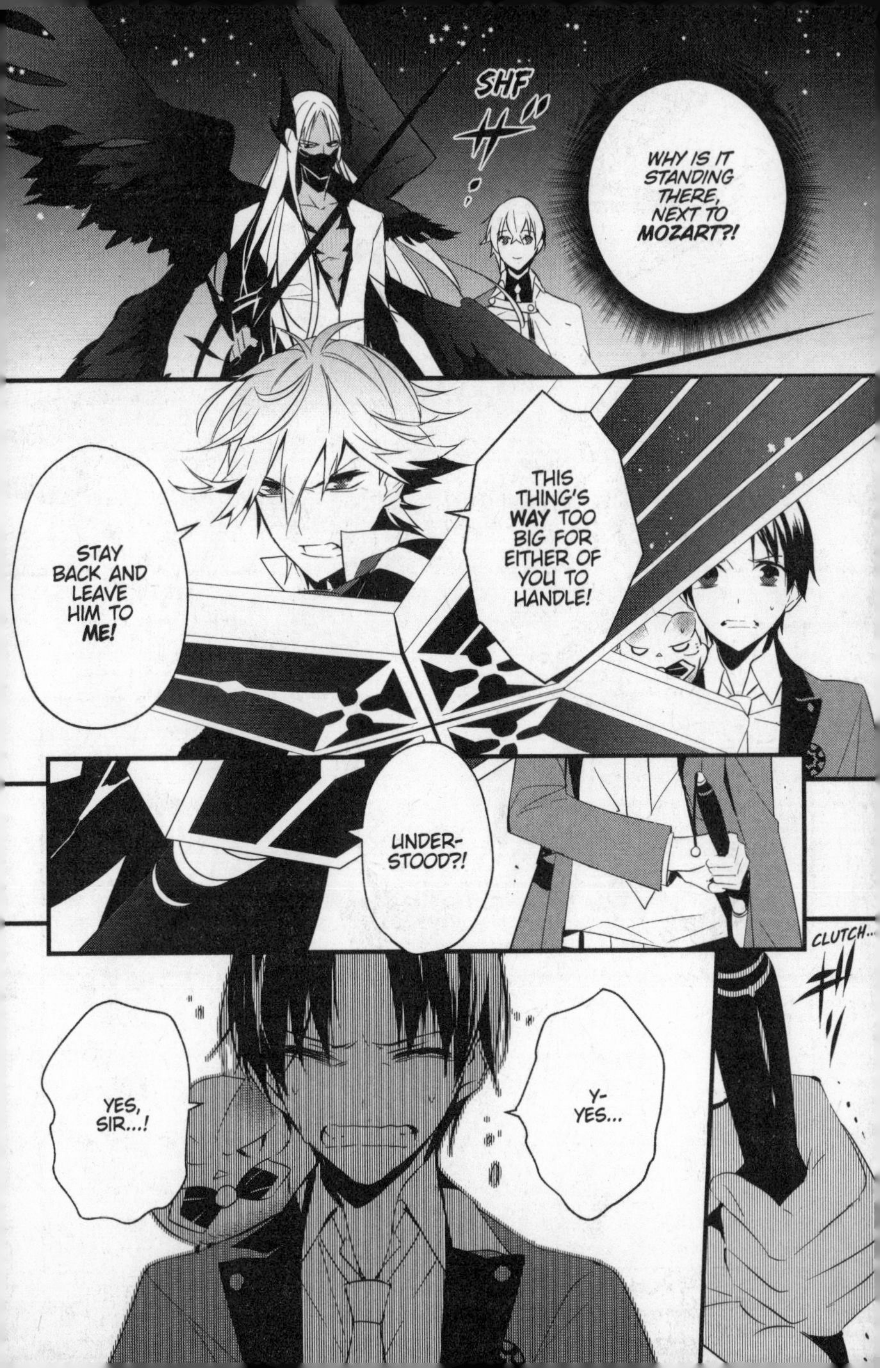
WHY IS IT STANDING THERE, NEXT TO MOZART?!
SHF
THIS THING'S WAY TOO BIG FOR EITHER OF YOU TO HANDLE!
STAY BACK AND LEAVE HIM TO ME!
CLUTCH...
UNDER-STOOD?!
Y-YES...
YES, SIR...!

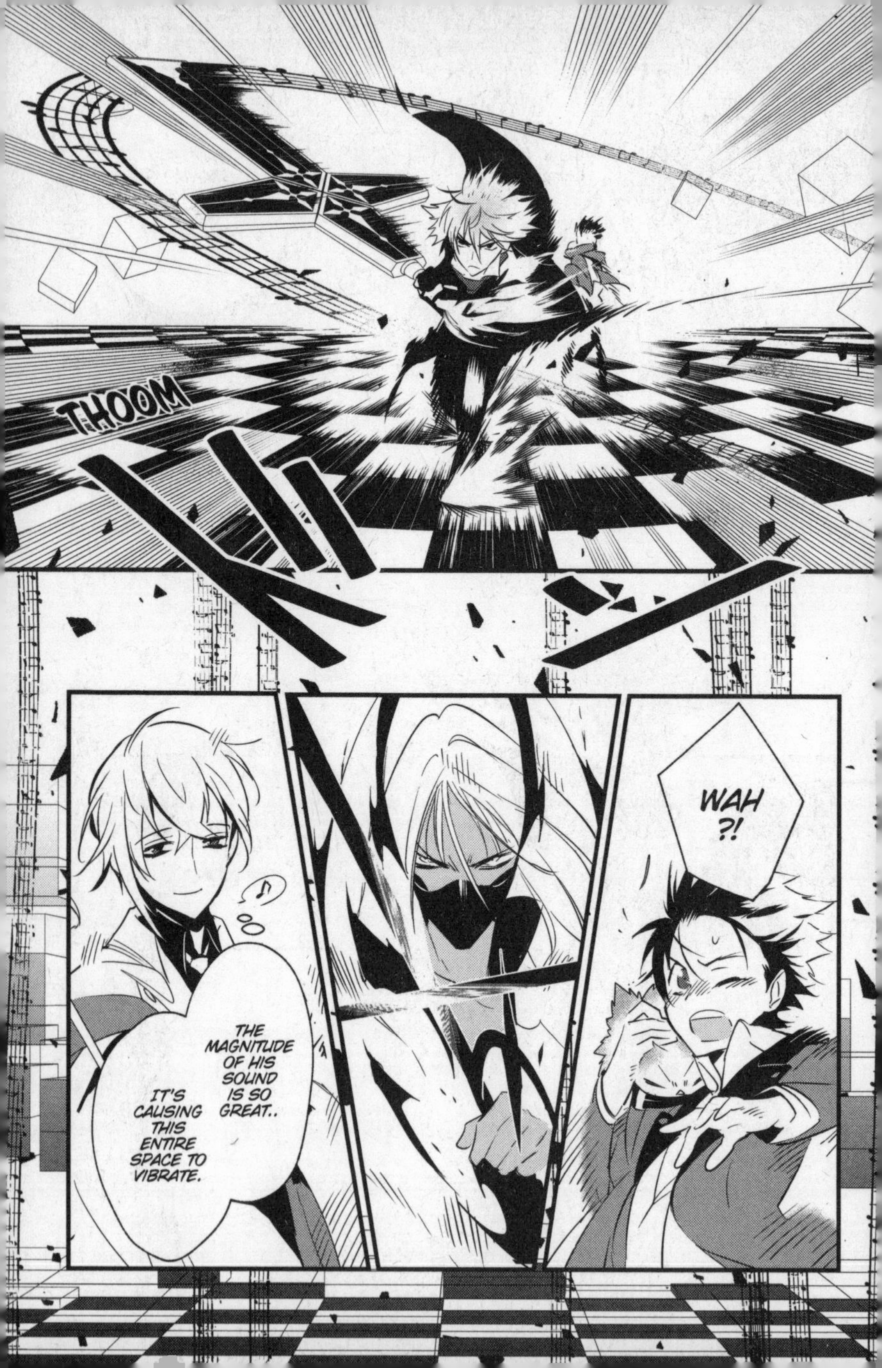
THOOM
WAH ?!
THE MAGNITUDE OF HIS SOUND IS SO GREAT..
IT'S CAUSING THIS ENTIRE SPACE TO VIBRATE.

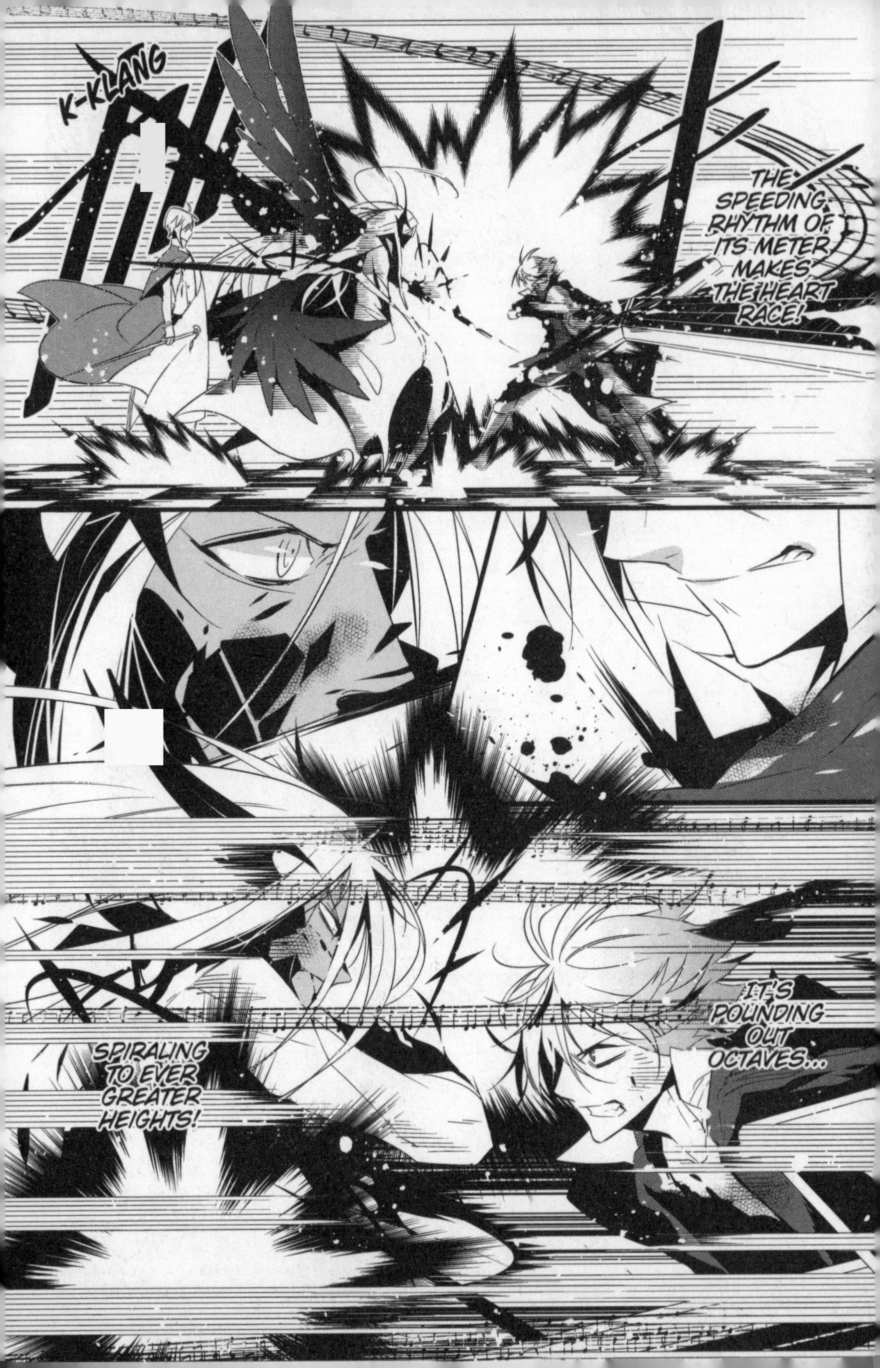
THE SPEEDING RHYTHM OF ITS METER MAKES THE HEART RACE!
K-KLANG
IT'S POUNDING OUT OCTAVES...
SPIRALING TO EVER GREATER HEIGHTS!

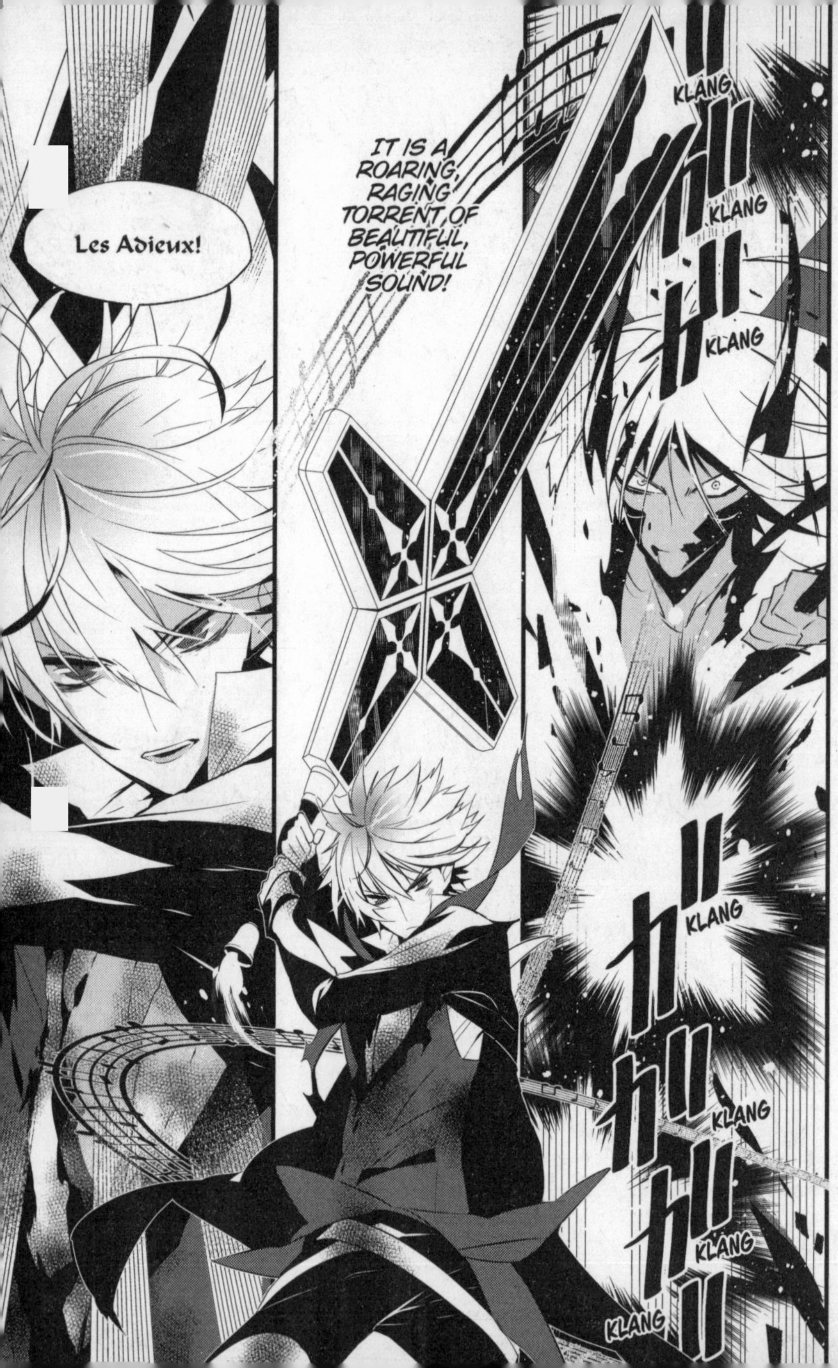
KLANG
KLANG
KLANG
KLANG
KLANG
KLANG
KLANG
IT IS A ROARING, RAGING TORRENT OF BEAUTIFUL, POWERFUL SOUND!
Les Adieux!

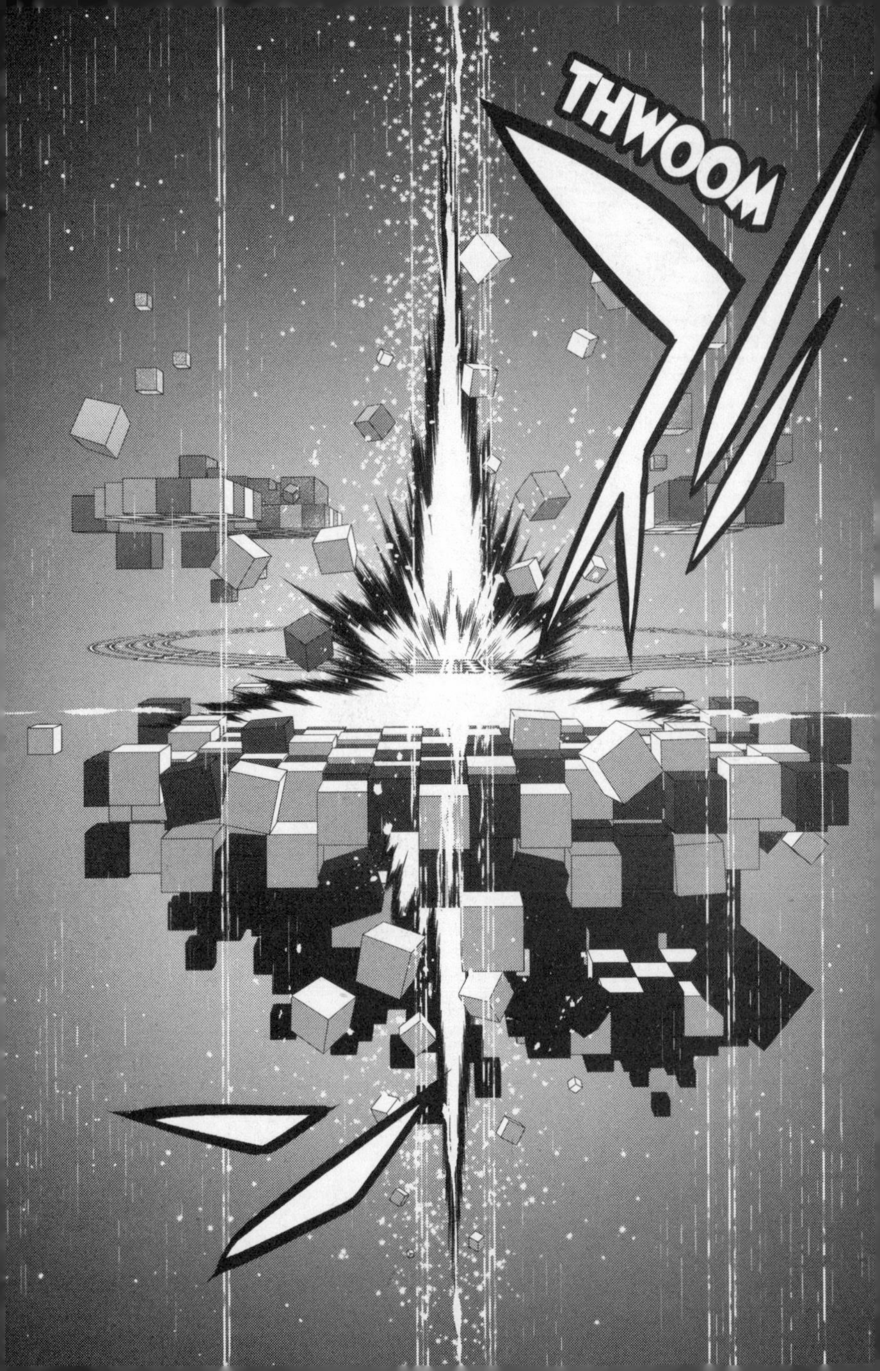
THWOOM

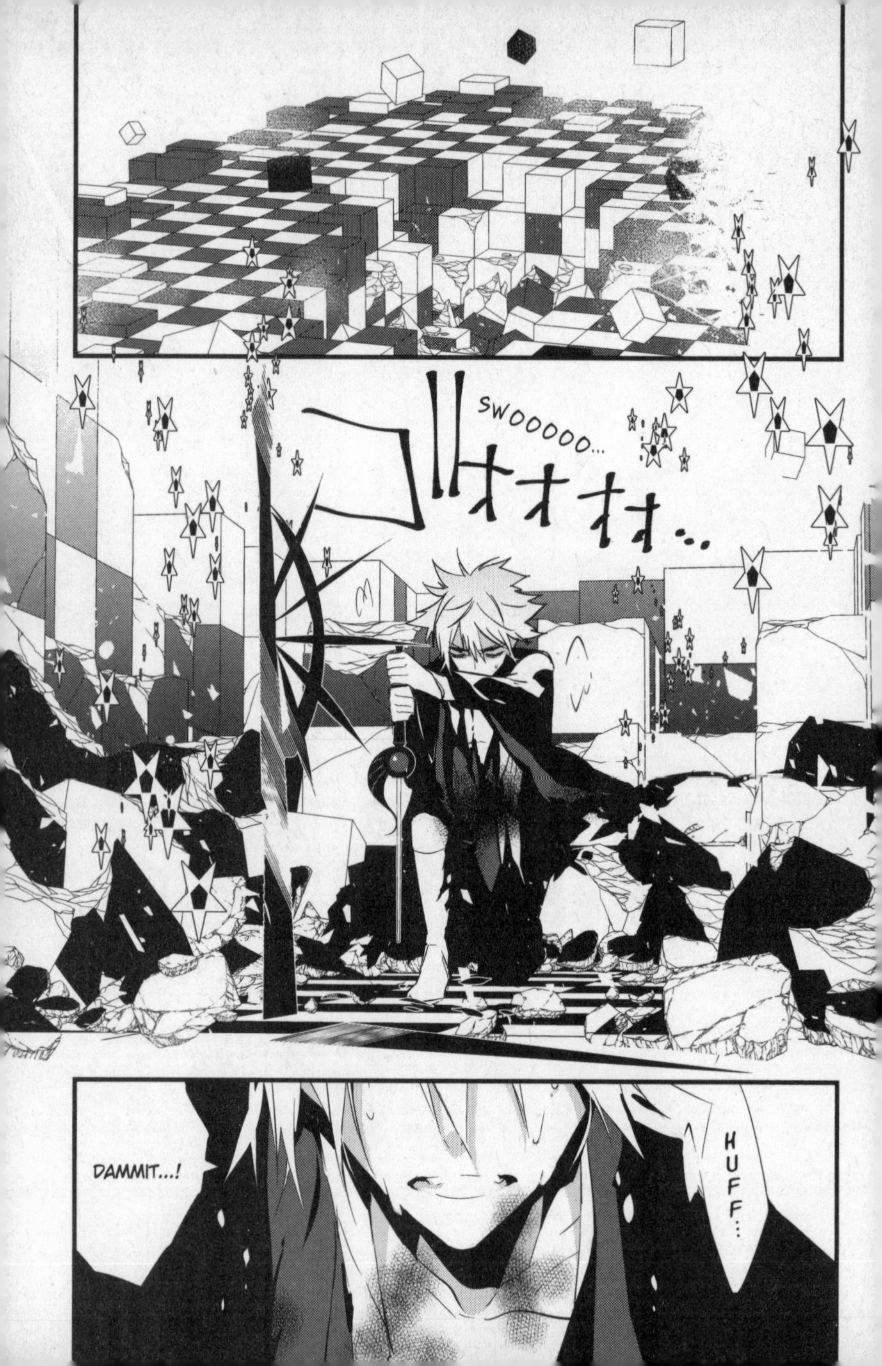
ゴォォォ…
SWOOOOOO...
HUFF...
DAMMIT...!

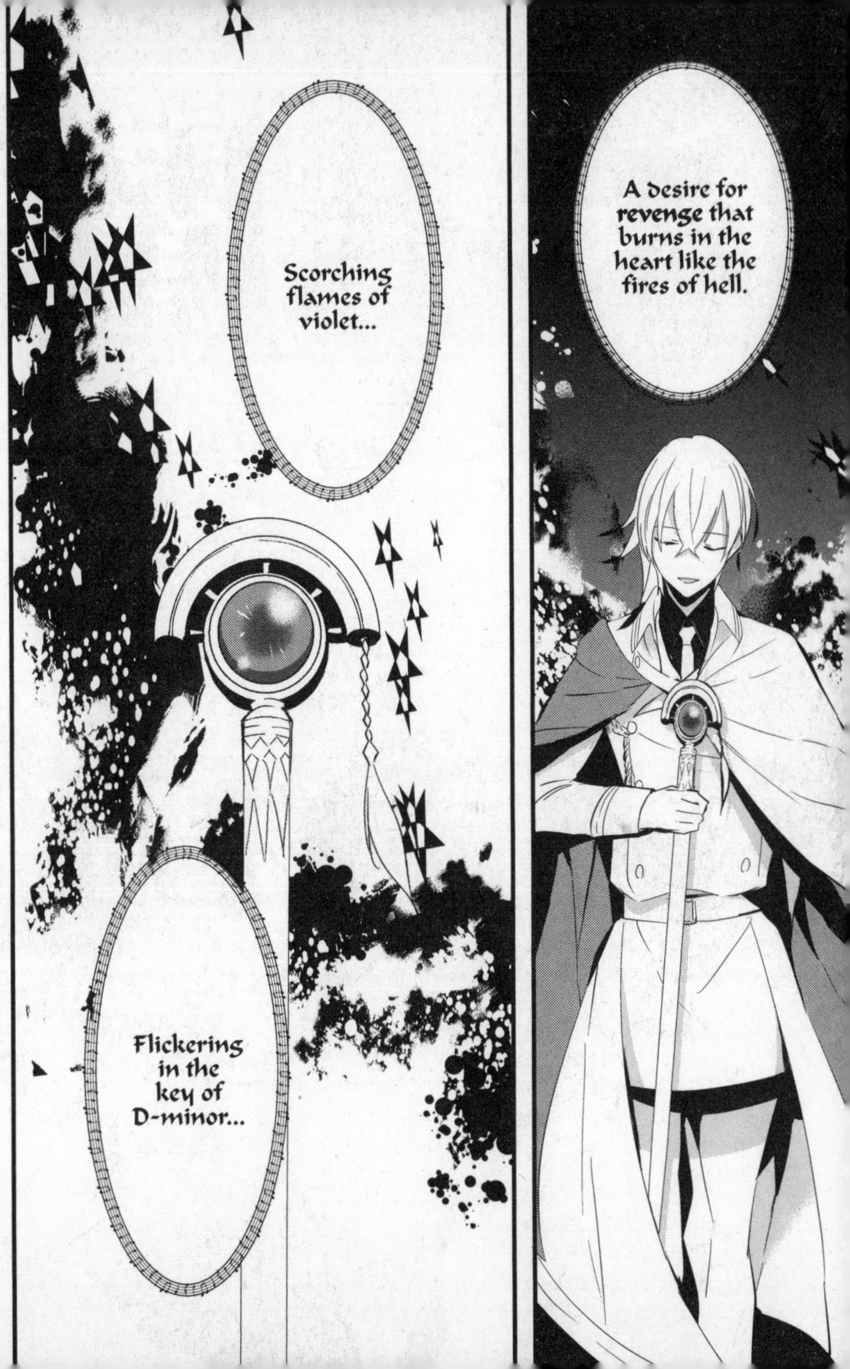
A desire for revenge that burns in the heart like the fires of hell.
Scorching flames of violet...
Flickering in the key of D-minor...

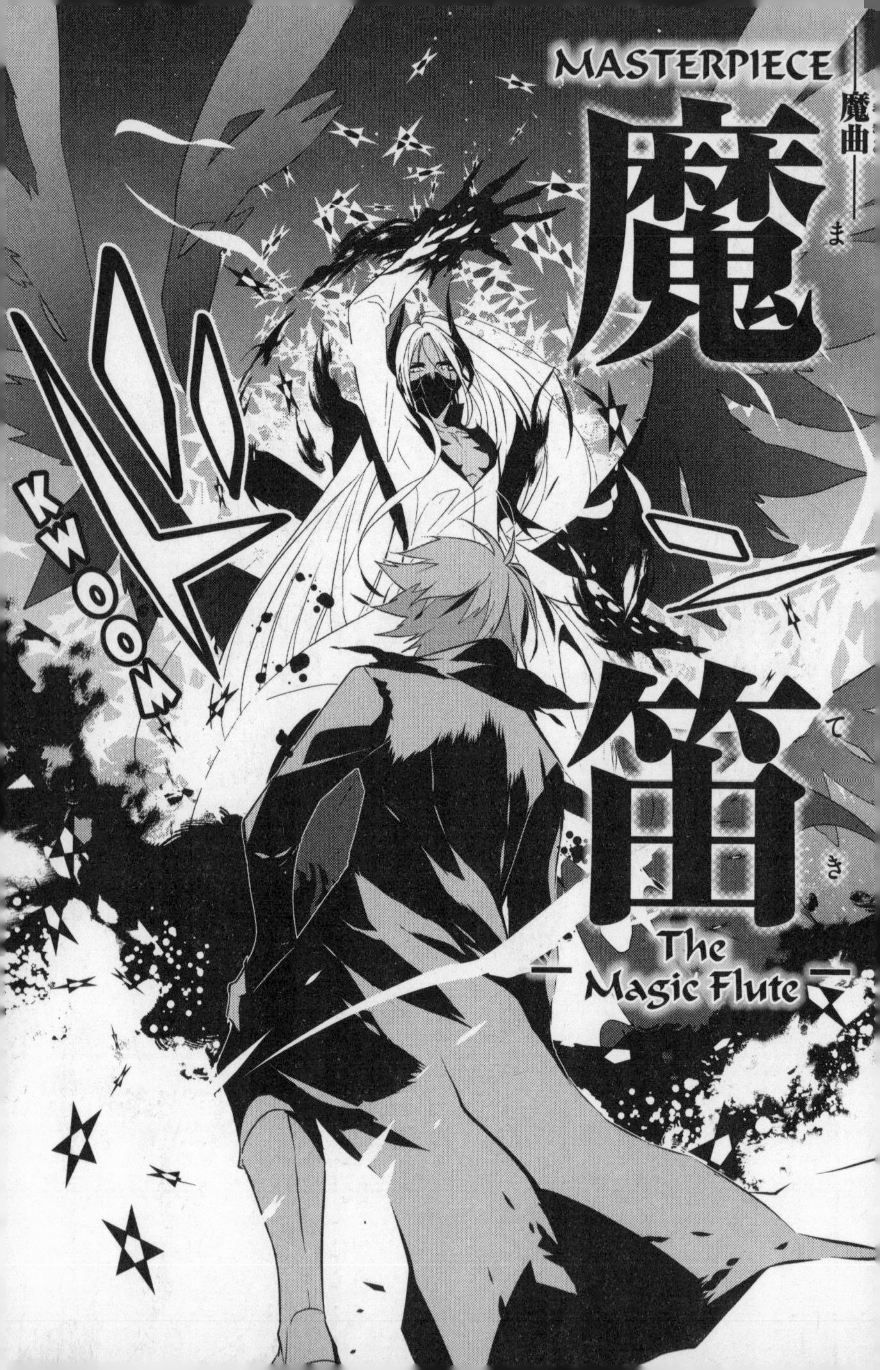
MASTERPIECE
—魔曲—
魔笛
—The Magic Flute—
KWOOOM

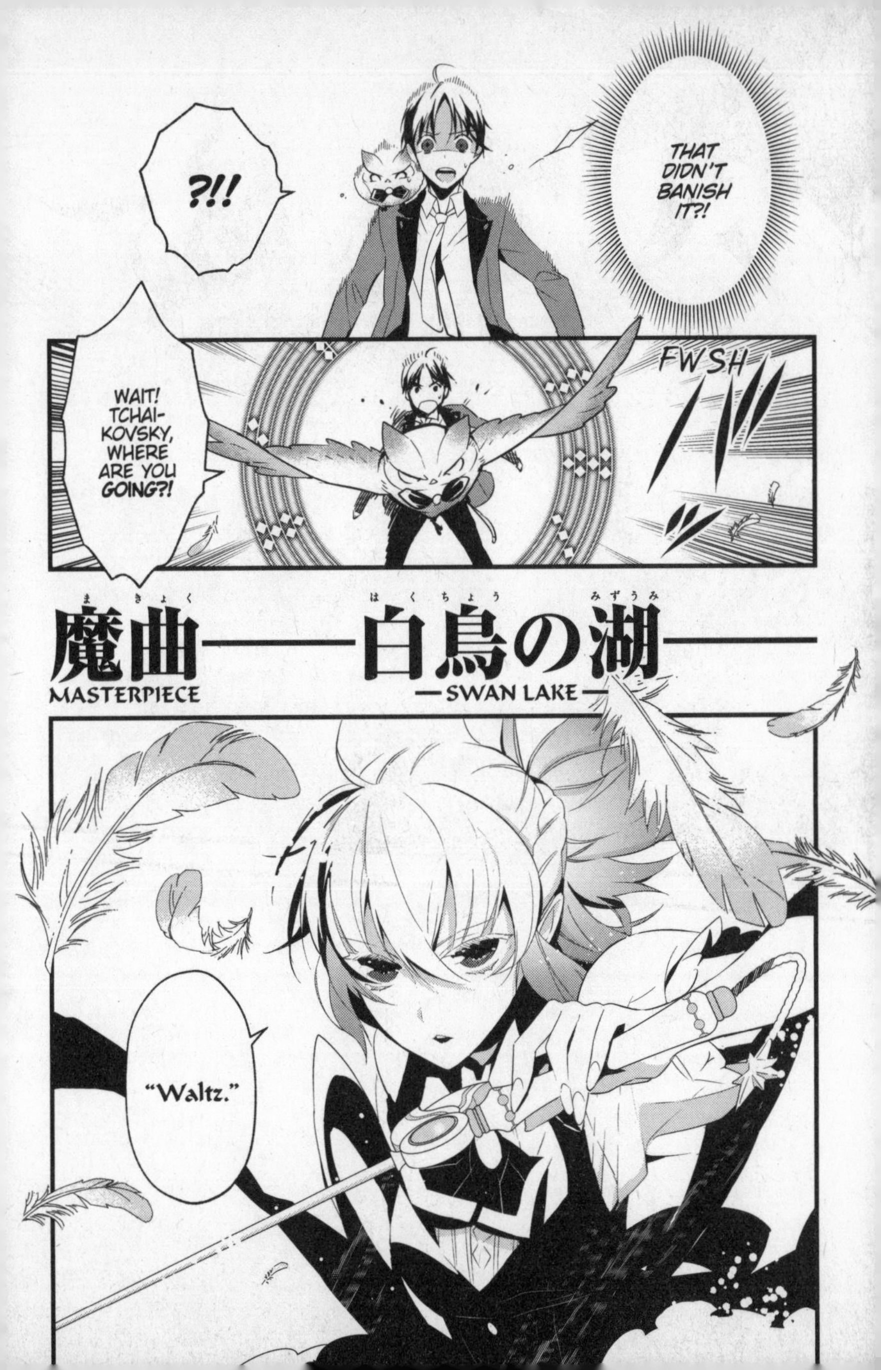
THAT DIDN'T BANISH IT?!
?!!
FWSH
WAIT! TCHAI-KOVSKY, WHERE ARE YOU GOING?!
魔曲——白鳥の湖——
MASTERPIECE
—SWAN LAKE—
"Waltz."

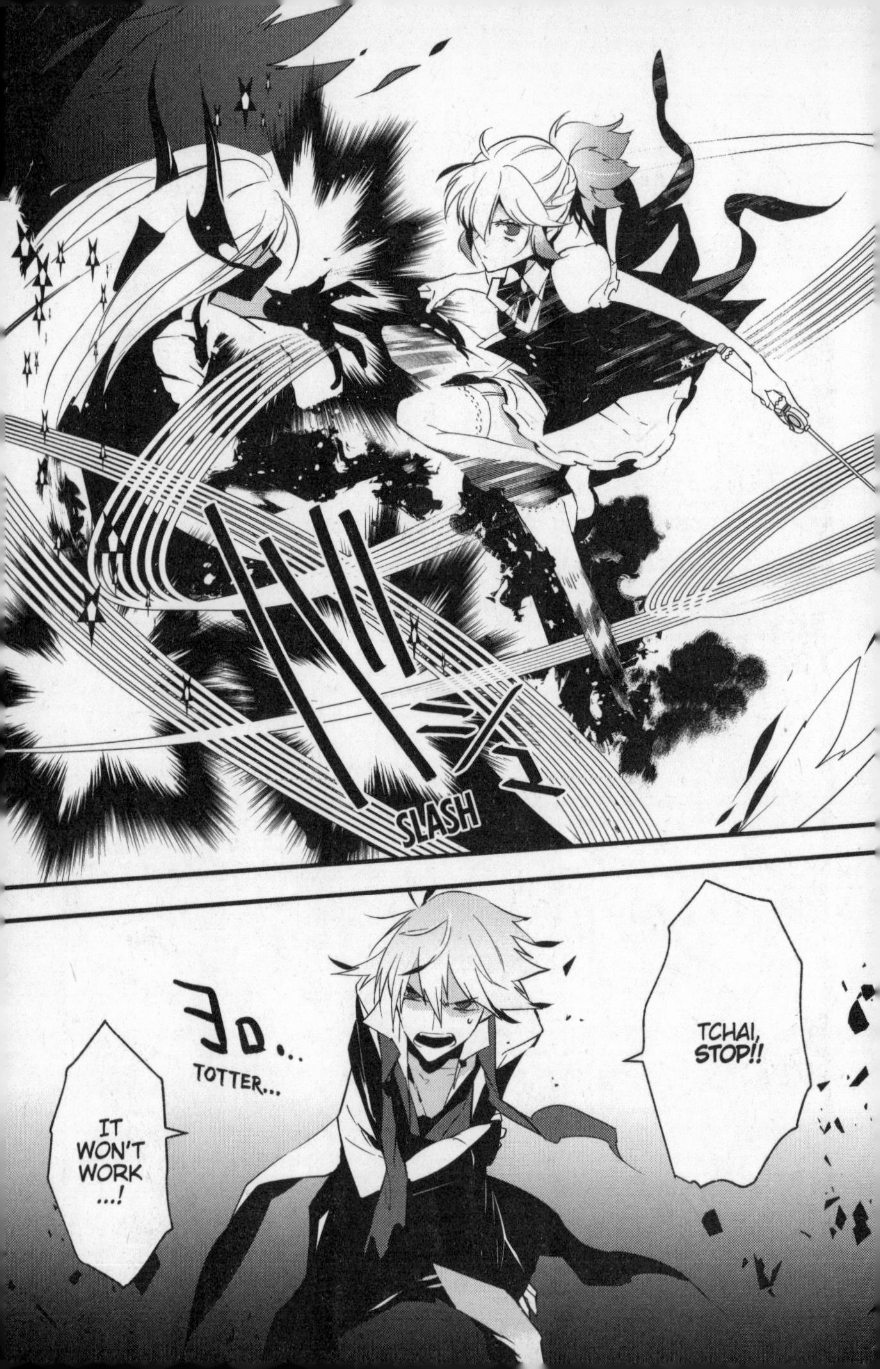
SLASH
TCHAI, STOP!!
ヨロ...
TOTTER...
IT WON'T WORK ...!

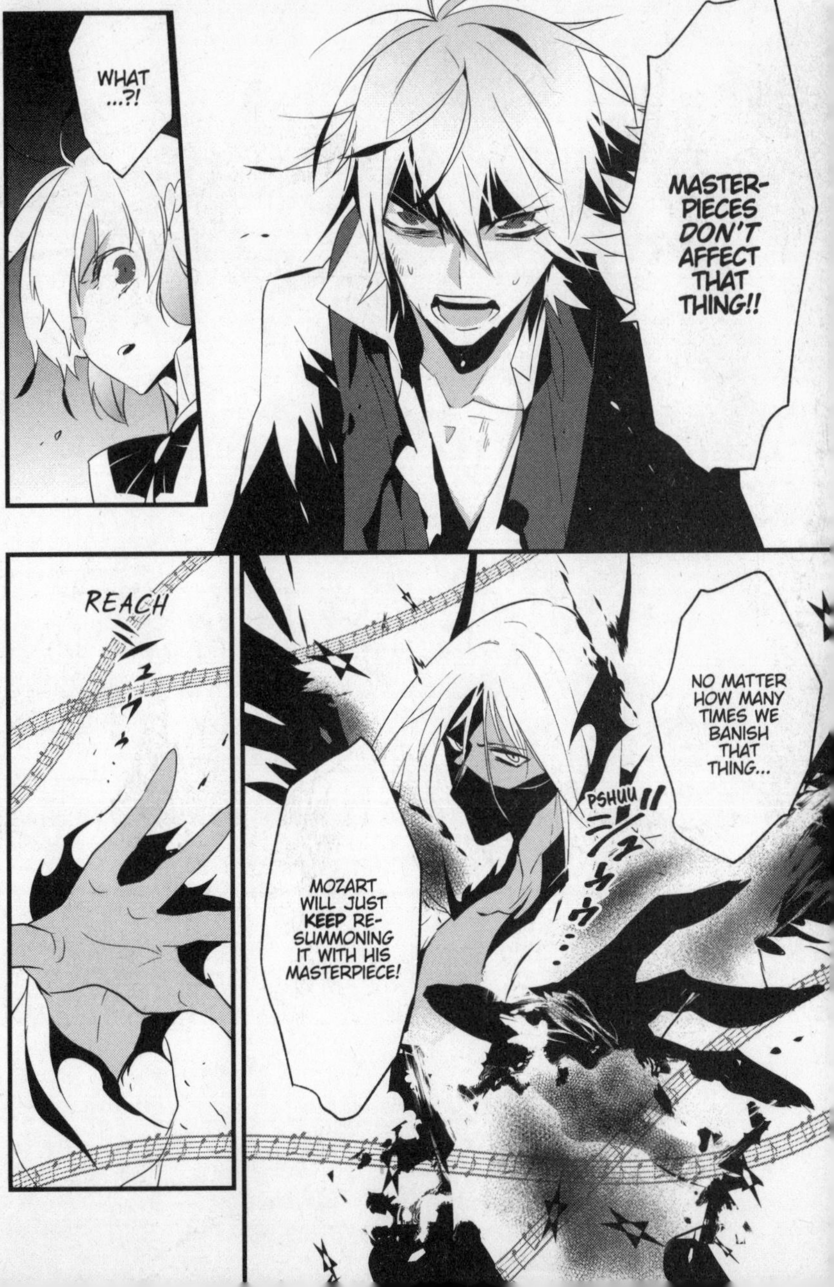
MASTER-PIECES DON'T AFFECT THAT THING!!
WHAT ...?!
NO MATTER HOW MANY TIMES WE BANISH THAT THING...
PSHUU
MOZART WILL JUST KEEP RE-SUMMONING IT WITH HIS MASTERPIECE!
REACH

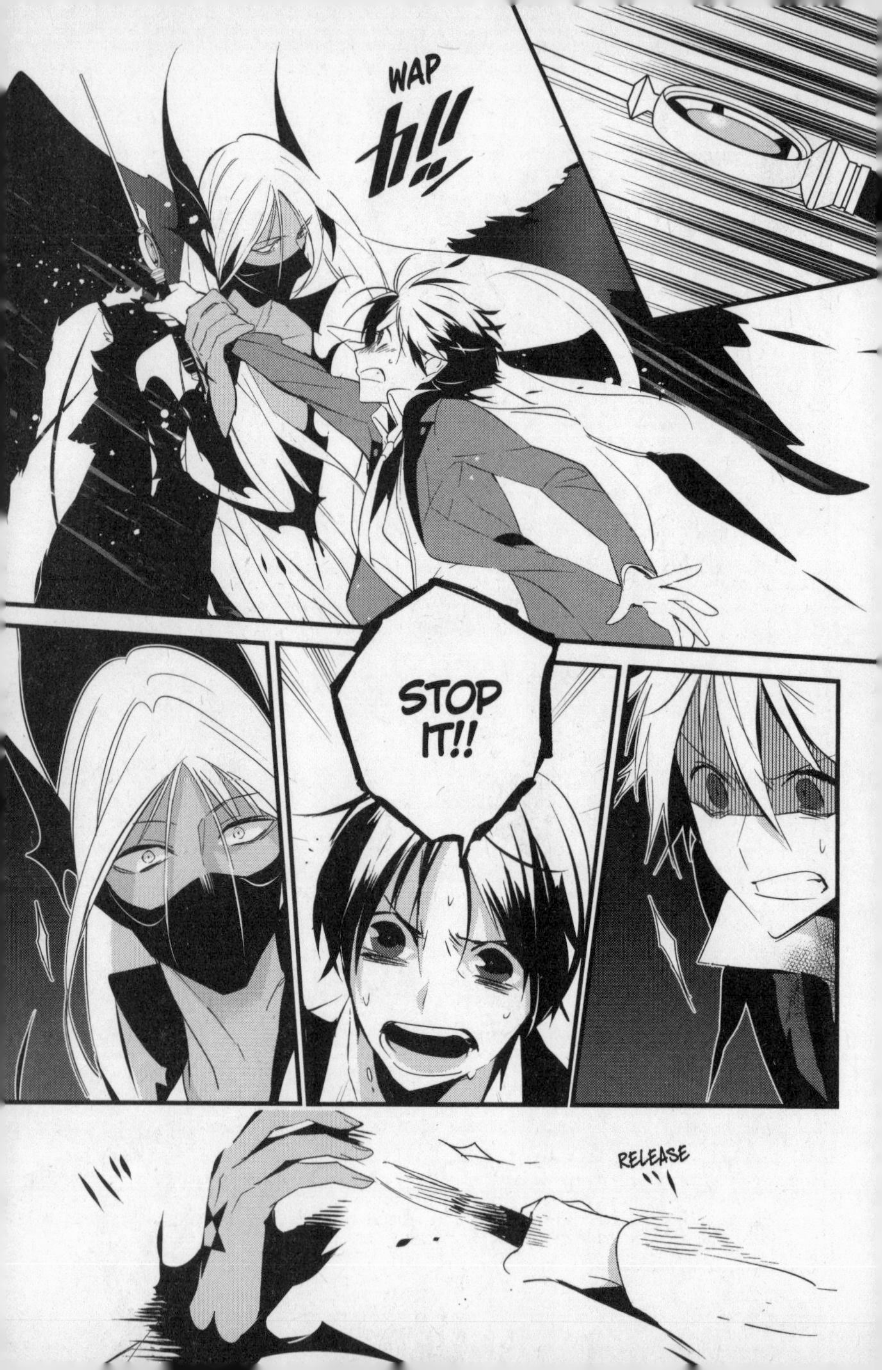
WAP
STOP IT!!
RELEASE

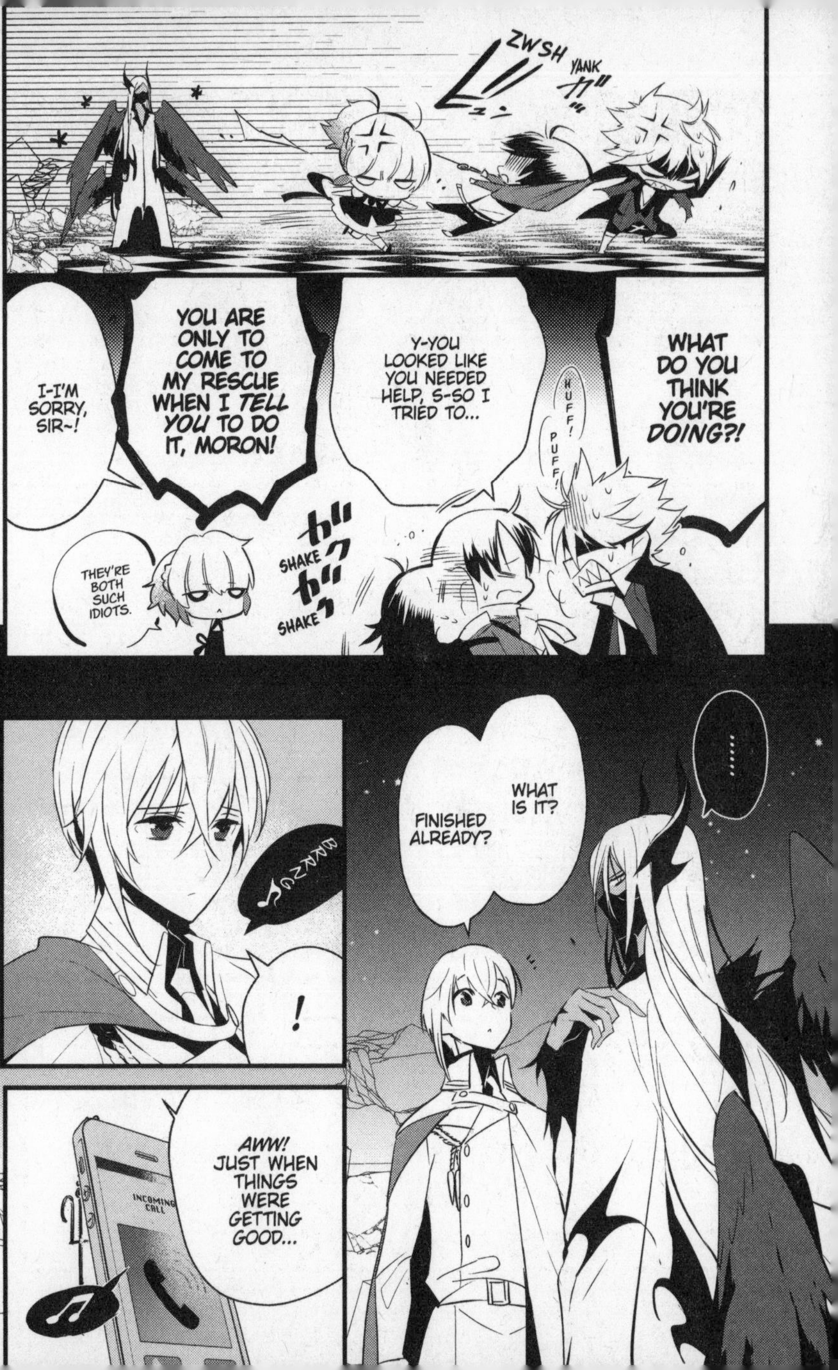
ZWSH
YANK
WHAT DO YOU THINK YOU'RE DOING?!
HUFF! PUFF!
Y-YOU LOOKED LIKE YOU NEEDED HELP, S-SO I TRIED TO...
YOU ARE ONLY TO COME TO MY RESCUE WHEN I TELL YOU TO DO IT, MORON!
I-I'M SORRY, SIR~!
SHAKE SHAKE
THEY'RE BOTH SUCH IDIOTS.
......
WHAT IS IT?
FINISHED ALREADY?
BRRING
!
AWW! JUST WHEN THINGS WERE GETTING GOOD...
INCOMING CALL

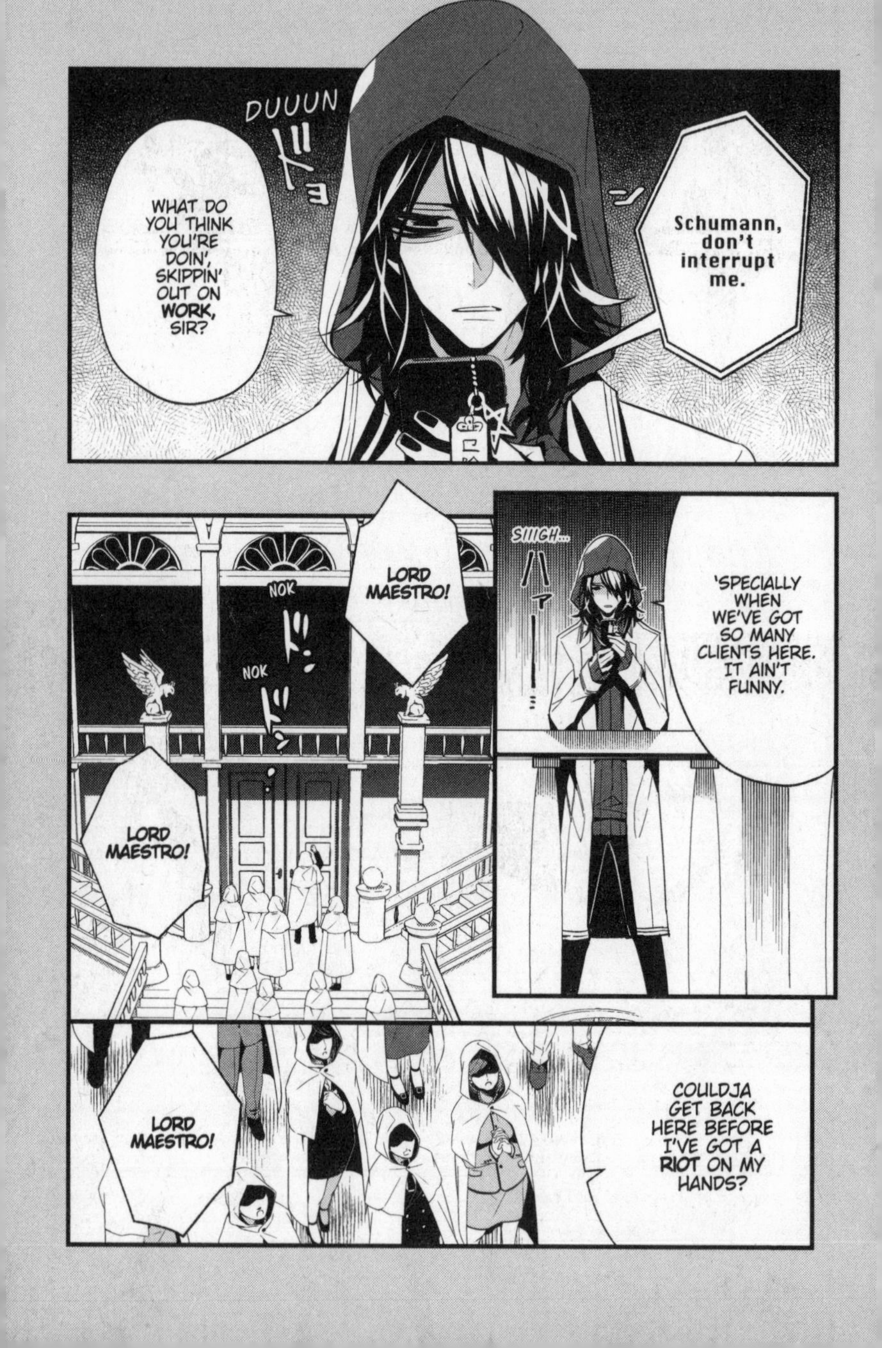
DUUUN
Schumann, don't interrupt me.
WHAT DO YOU THINK YOU'RE DOIN', SKIPPIN' OUT ON **WORK**, SIR?
SIIIGH...
'SPECIALLY WHEN WE'VE GOT SO MANY CLIENTS HERE. IT AIN'T FUNNY.
LORD MAESTRO!
NOK
NOK
LORD MAESTRO!
COULDJA GET BACK HERE BEFORE I'VE GOT A **RIOT** ON MY HANDS?
LORD MAESTRO!

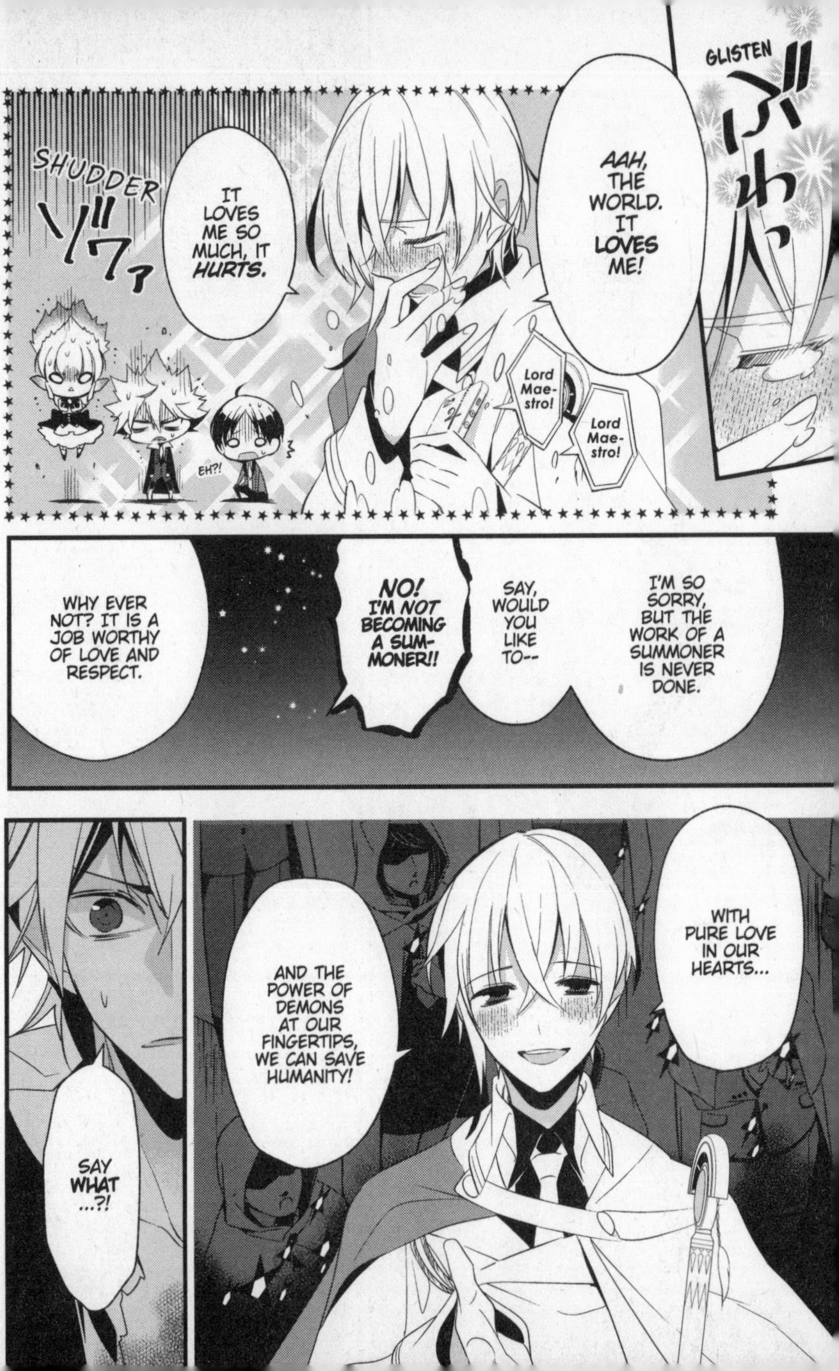
GLISTEN
ぶわっ
AAH, THE WORLD. IT LOVES ME!
Lord Maestro!
Lord Maestro!
IT LOVES ME SO MUCH, IT HURTS.
SHUDDER
ゾワァ
EH?!
I'M SO SORRY, BUT THE WORK OF A SUMMONER IS NEVER DONE.
SAY, WOULD YOU LIKE TO--
NO! I'M NOT BECOMING A SUMMONER!!
WHY EVER NOT? IT IS A JOB WORTHY OF LOVE AND RESPECT.
WITH PURE LOVE IN OUR HEARTS...
AND THE POWER OF DEMONS AT OUR FINGERTIPS, WE CAN SAVE HUMANITY!
SAY WHAT ...?!

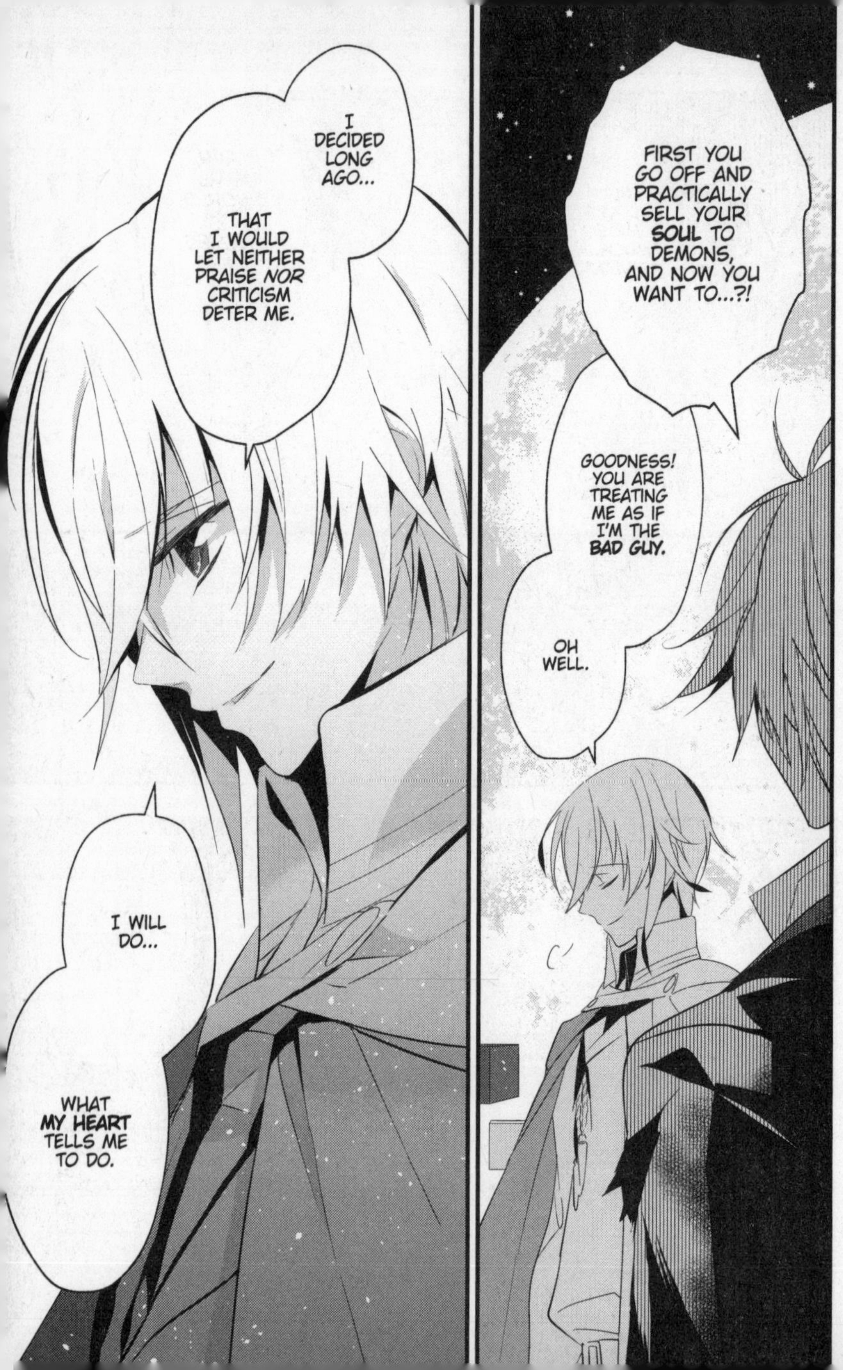
FIRST YOU GO OFF AND PRACTICALLY SELL YOUR **SOUL** TO DEMONS, AND NOW YOU WANT TO...?!
GOODNESS! YOU ARE TREATING ME AS IF I'M THE **BAD GUY.**
OH WELL.
I DECIDED LONG AGO...
THAT I WOULD LET NEITHER PRAISE *NOR* CRITICISM DETER ME.
I WILL DO...
WHAT **MY HEART** TELLS ME TO DO.

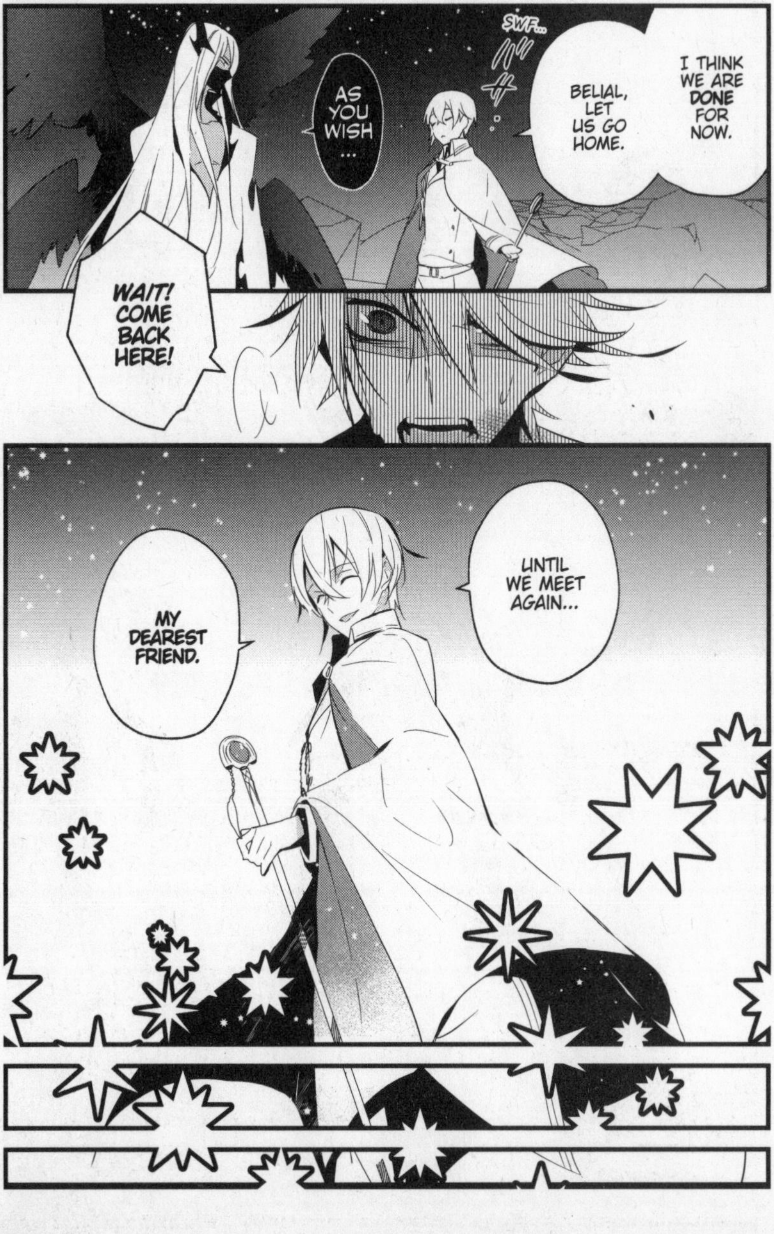
I THINK WE ARE DONE FOR NOW.
BELIAL, LET US GO HOME.
SWF...
AS YOU WISH ...
WAIT! COME BACK HERE!
UNTIL WE MEET AGAIN...
MY DEAREST FRIEND.

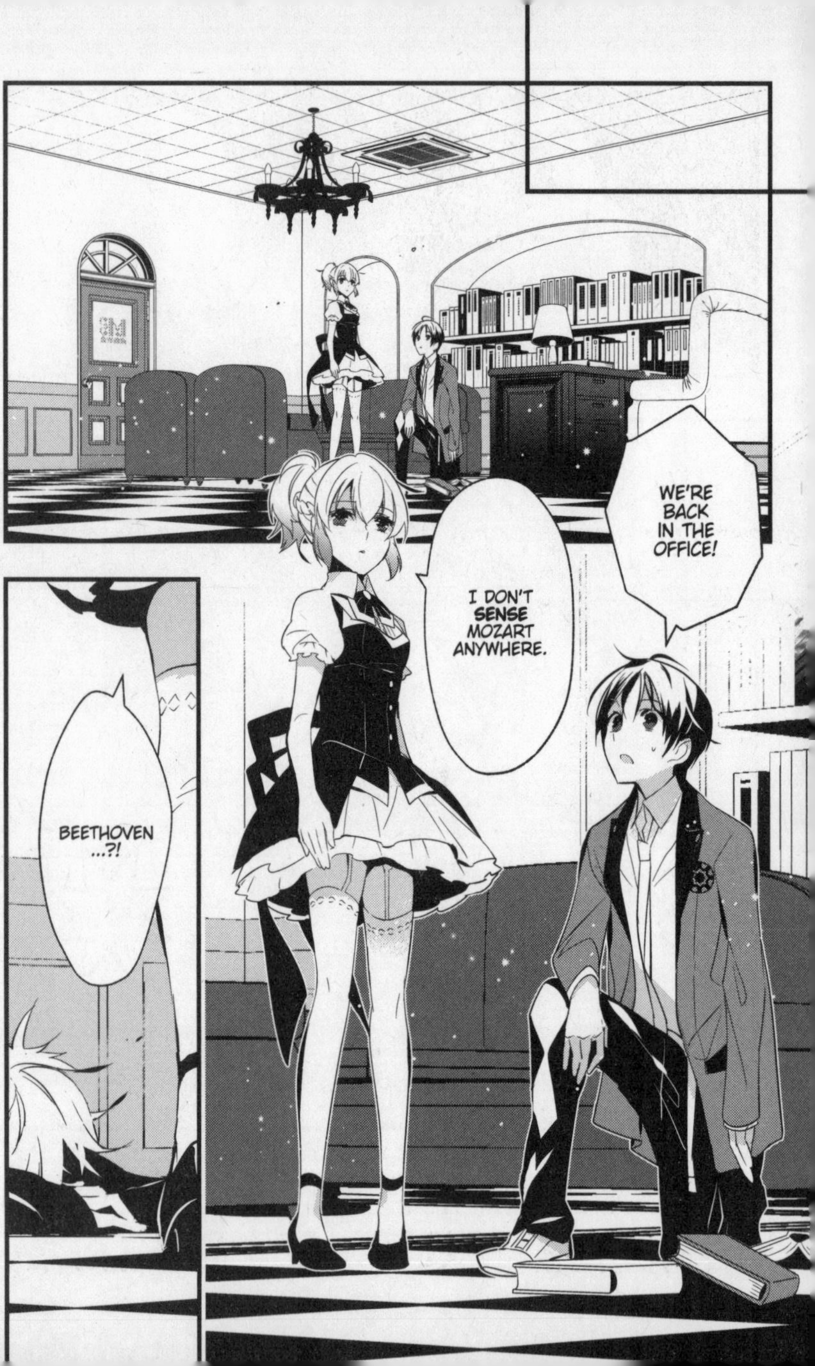
WE'RE BACK IN THE OFFICE!
I DON'T SENSE MOZART ANYWHERE.
BEETHOVEN ...?!

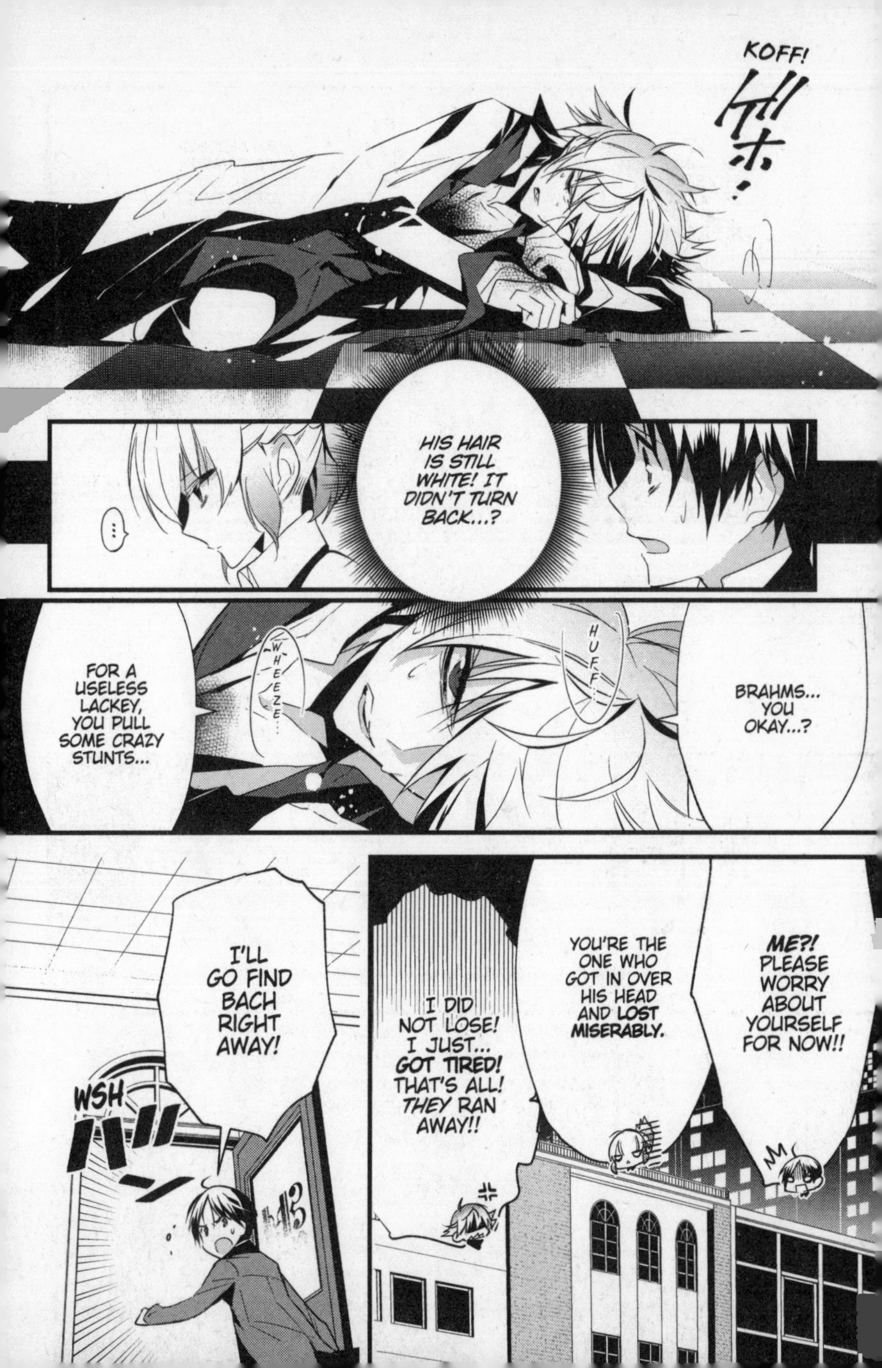
KOFF!
HIS HAIR IS STILL WHITE! IT DIDN'T TURN BACK...?
...
BRAHMS... YOU OKAY...?
HUFF...
WHEEZE...
FOR A USELESS LACKEY, YOU PULL SOME CRAZY STUNTS...
ME?! PLEASE WORRY ABOUT YOURSELF FOR NOW!!
YOU'RE THE ONE WHO GOT IN OVER HIS HEAD AND LOST MISERABLY.
I DID NOT LOSE! I JUST... GOT TIRED! THAT'S ALL! THEY RAN AWAY!!
I'LL GO FIND BACH RIGHT AWAY!
WSH

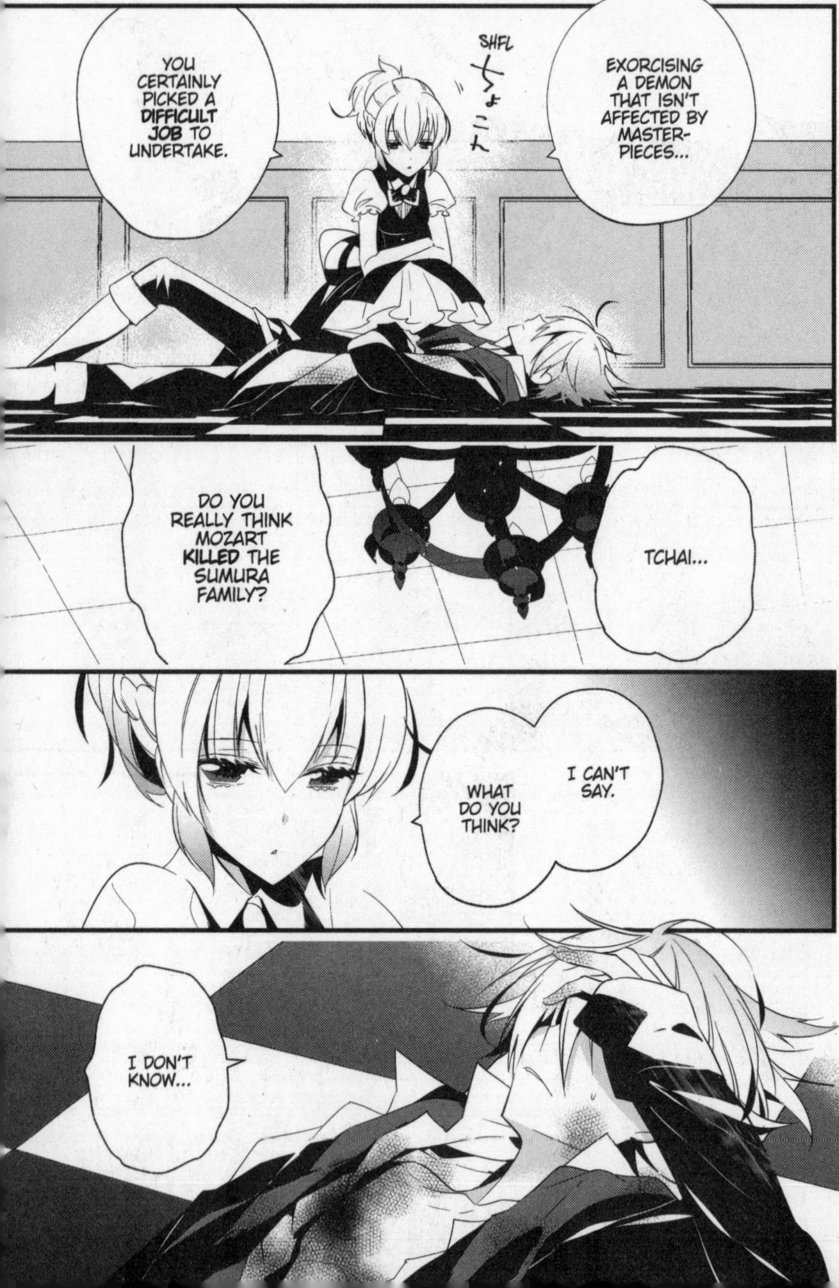
EXORCISING A DEMON THAT ISN'T AFFECTED BY MASTER-PIECES...
SHFL
ちょこん
YOU CERTAINLY PICKED A **DIFFICULT JOB** TO UNDERTAKE.
TCHAI...
DO YOU REALLY THINK MOZART **KILLED** THE SUMURA FAMILY?
I CAN'T SAY.
WHAT DO YOU THINK?
I DON'T KNOW...

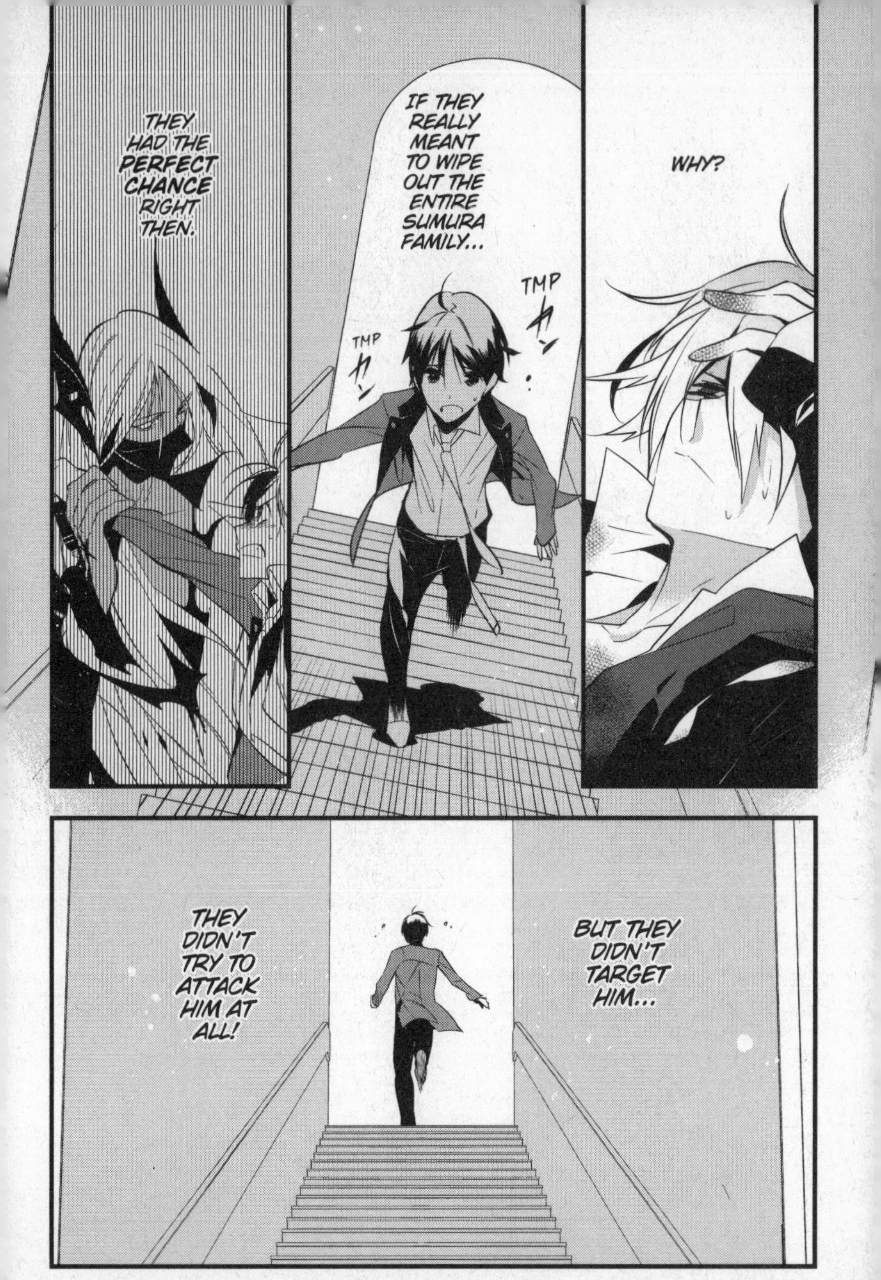
WHY?
IF THEY REALLY MEANT TO WIPE OUT THE ENTIRE SUMURA FAMILY...
TMP
TMP
THEY HAD THE PERFECT CHANCE RIGHT THEN.
BUT THEY DIDN'T TARGET HIM...
THEY DIDN'T TRY TO ATTACK HIM AT ALL!

Magia the Ninth

Magia the Ninth

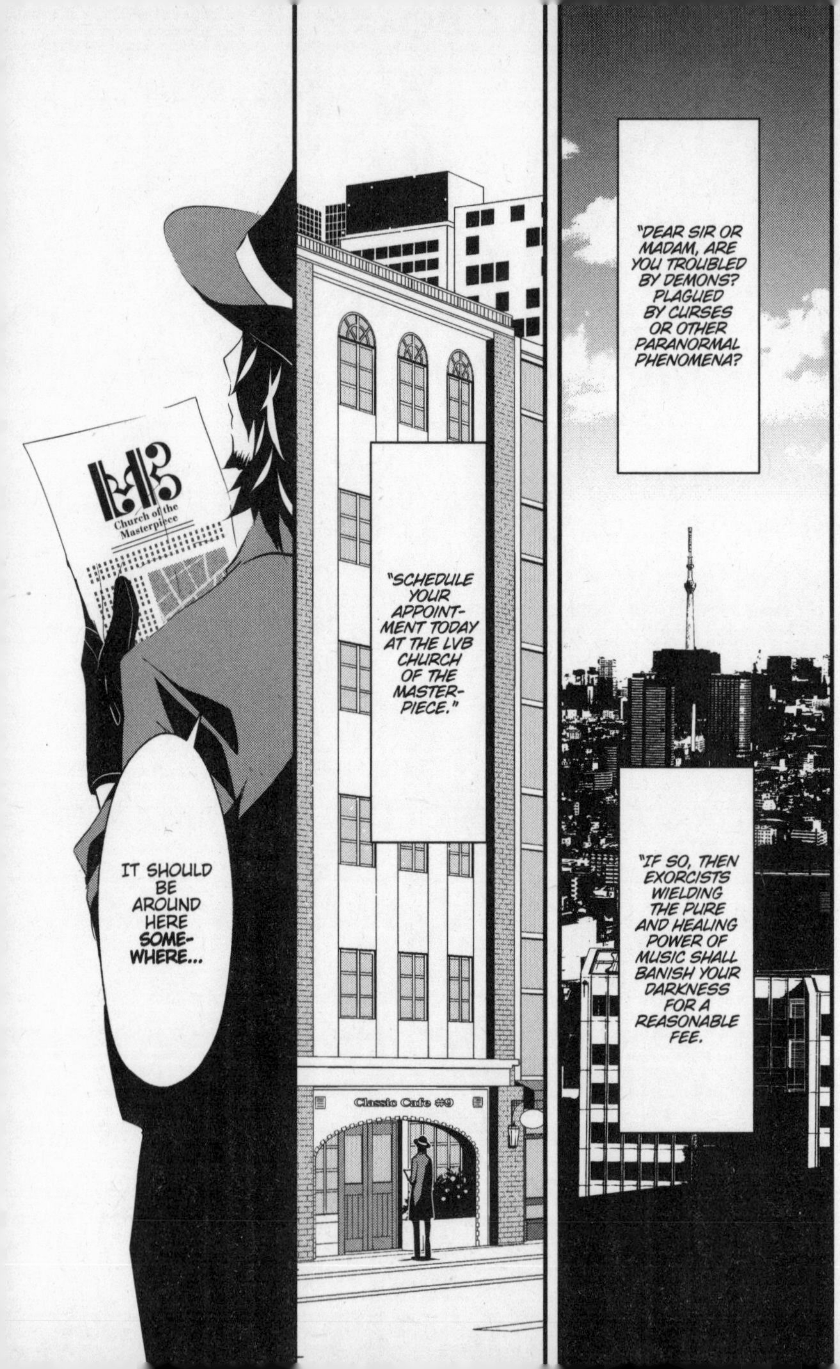
"DEAR SIR OR MADAM, ARE YOU TROUBLED BY DEMONS? PLAGUED BY CURSES OR OTHER PARANORMAL PHENOMENA?
"IF SO, THEN EXORCISTS WIELDING THE PURE AND HEALING POWER OF MUSIC SHALL BANISH YOUR DARKNESS FOR A REASONABLE FEE.
"SCHEDULE YOUR APPOINTMENT TODAY AT THE LVB CHURCH OF THE MASTERPIECE."
Classic Cafe #9
Church of the Masterpiece
IT SHOULD BE AROUND HERE **SOME-WHERE**...

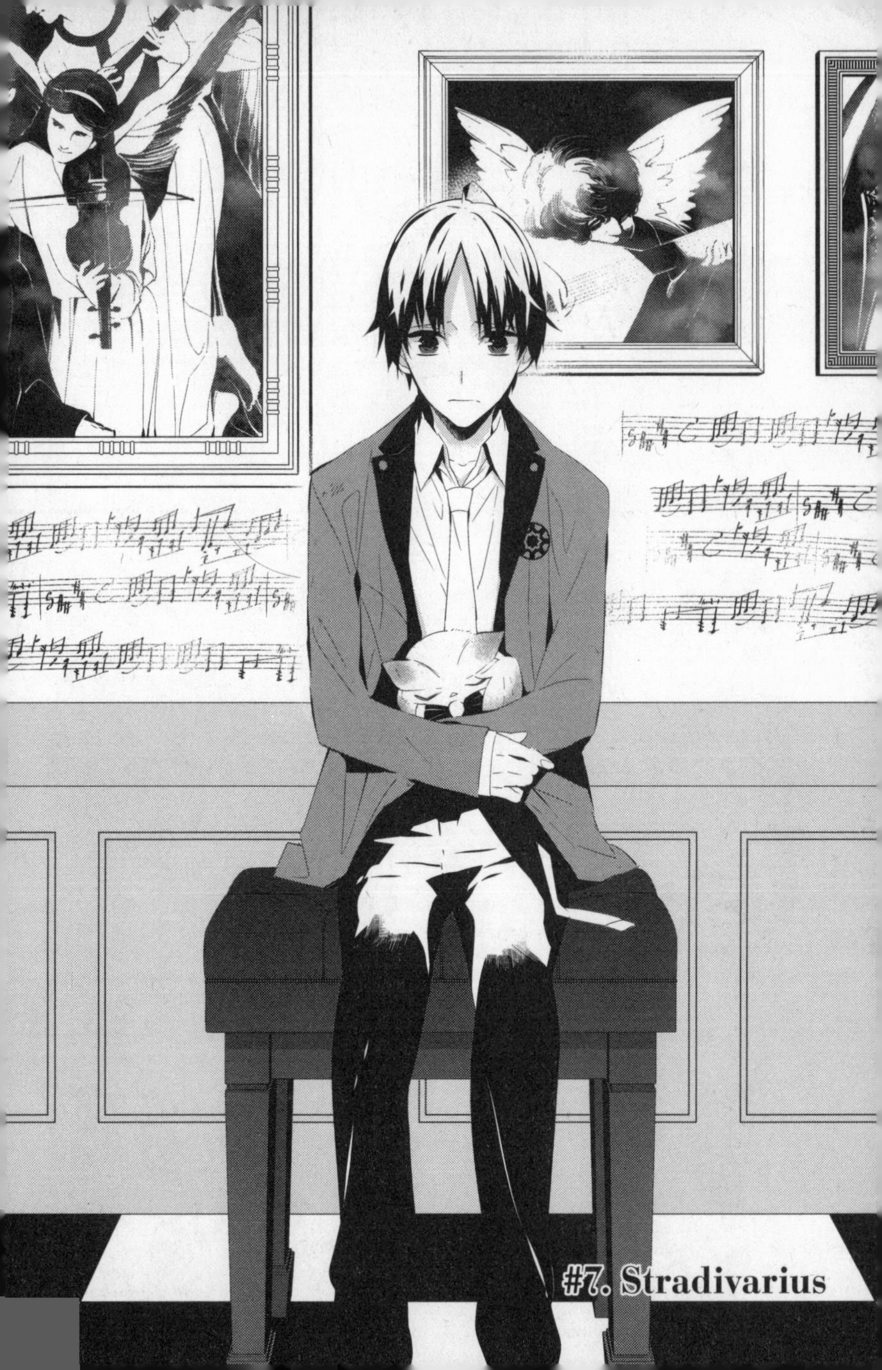
#7. Stradivarius

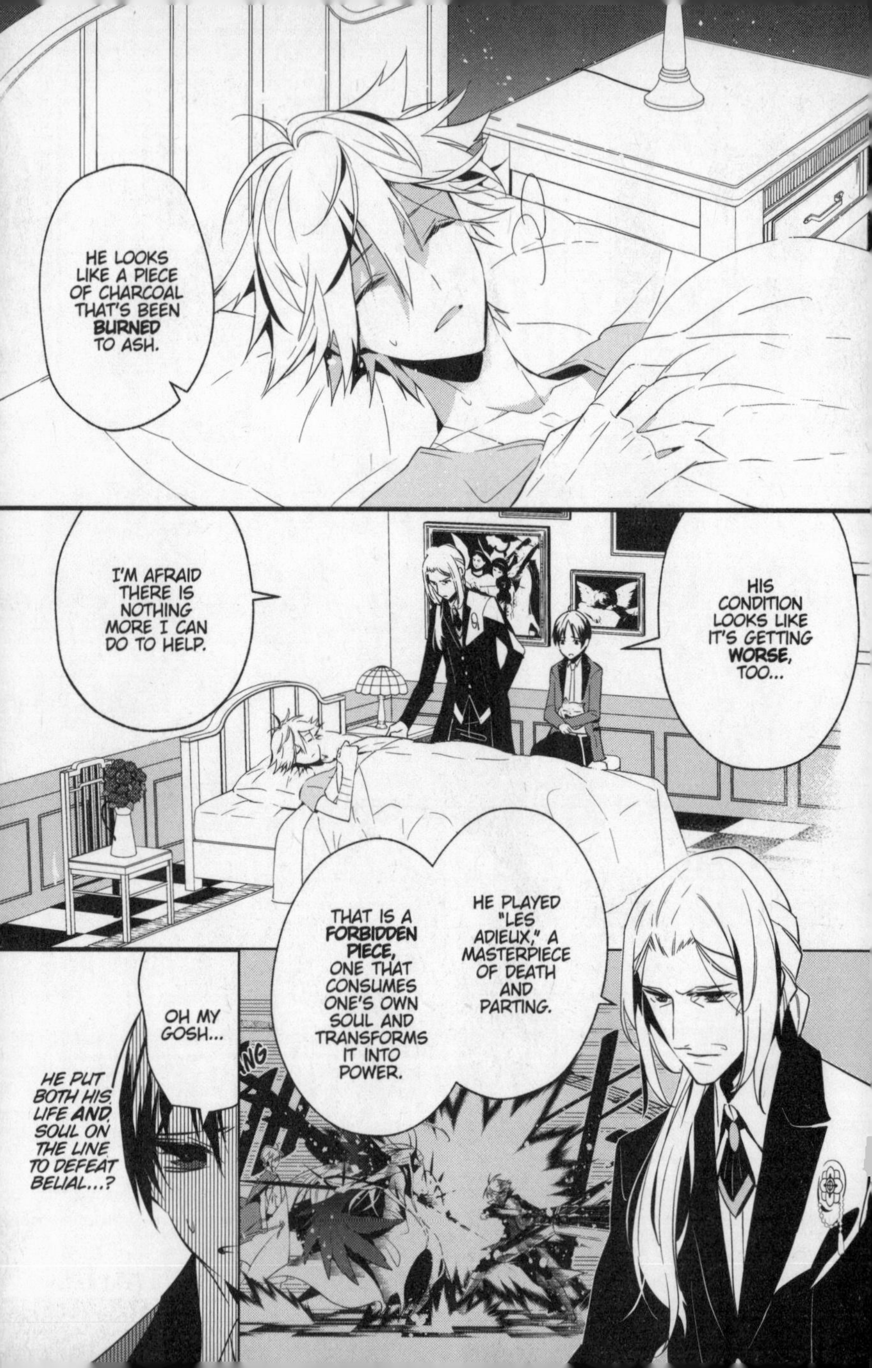
HE LOOKS LIKE A PIECE OF CHARCOAL THAT'S BEEN BURNED TO ASH.
HIS CONDITION LOOKS LIKE IT'S GETTING WORSE, TOO...
I'M AFRAID THERE IS NOTHING MORE I CAN DO TO HELP.
HE PLAYED "LES ADIEUX," A MASTERPIECE OF DEATH AND PARTING.
THAT IS A FORBIDDEN PIECE, ONE THAT CONSUMES ONE'S OWN SOUL AND TRANSFORMS IT INTO POWER.
OH MY GOSH...
HE PUT BOTH HIS LIFE AND SOUL ON THE LINE TO DEFEAT BELIAL...?

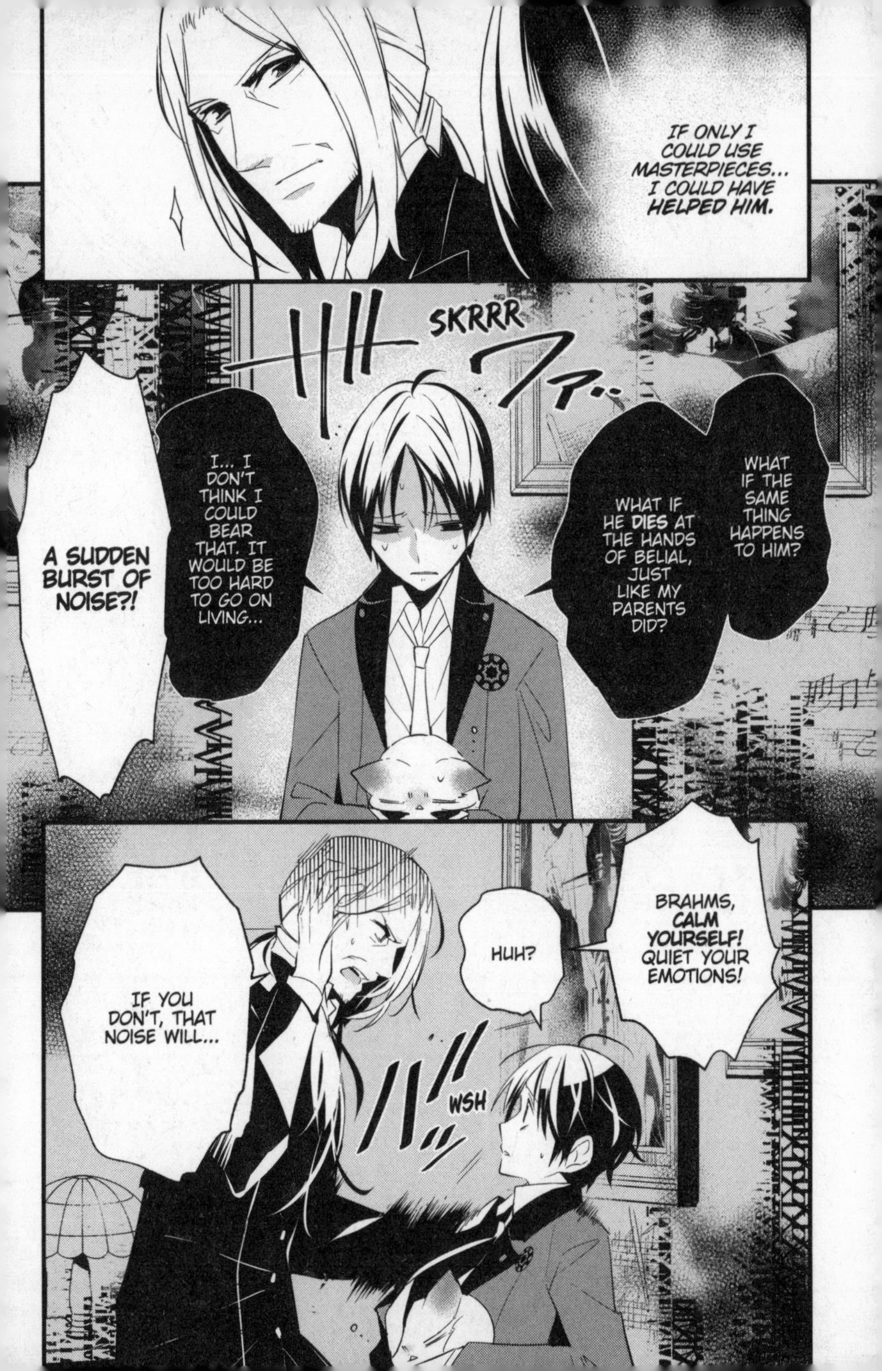
IF ONLY I COULD USE MASTERPIECES... I COULD HAVE HELPED HIM.
SKRRR
WHAT IF THE SAME THING HAPPENS TO HIM?
WHAT IF HE DIES AT THE HANDS OF BELIAL, JUST LIKE MY PARENTS DID?
I... I DON'T THINK I COULD BEAR THAT. IT WOULD BE TOO HARD TO GO ON LIVING...
A SUDDEN BURST OF NOISE?!
BRAHMS, CALM YOURSELF! QUIET YOUR EMOTIONS!
HUH?
IF YOU DON'T, THAT NOISE WILL...
WSH

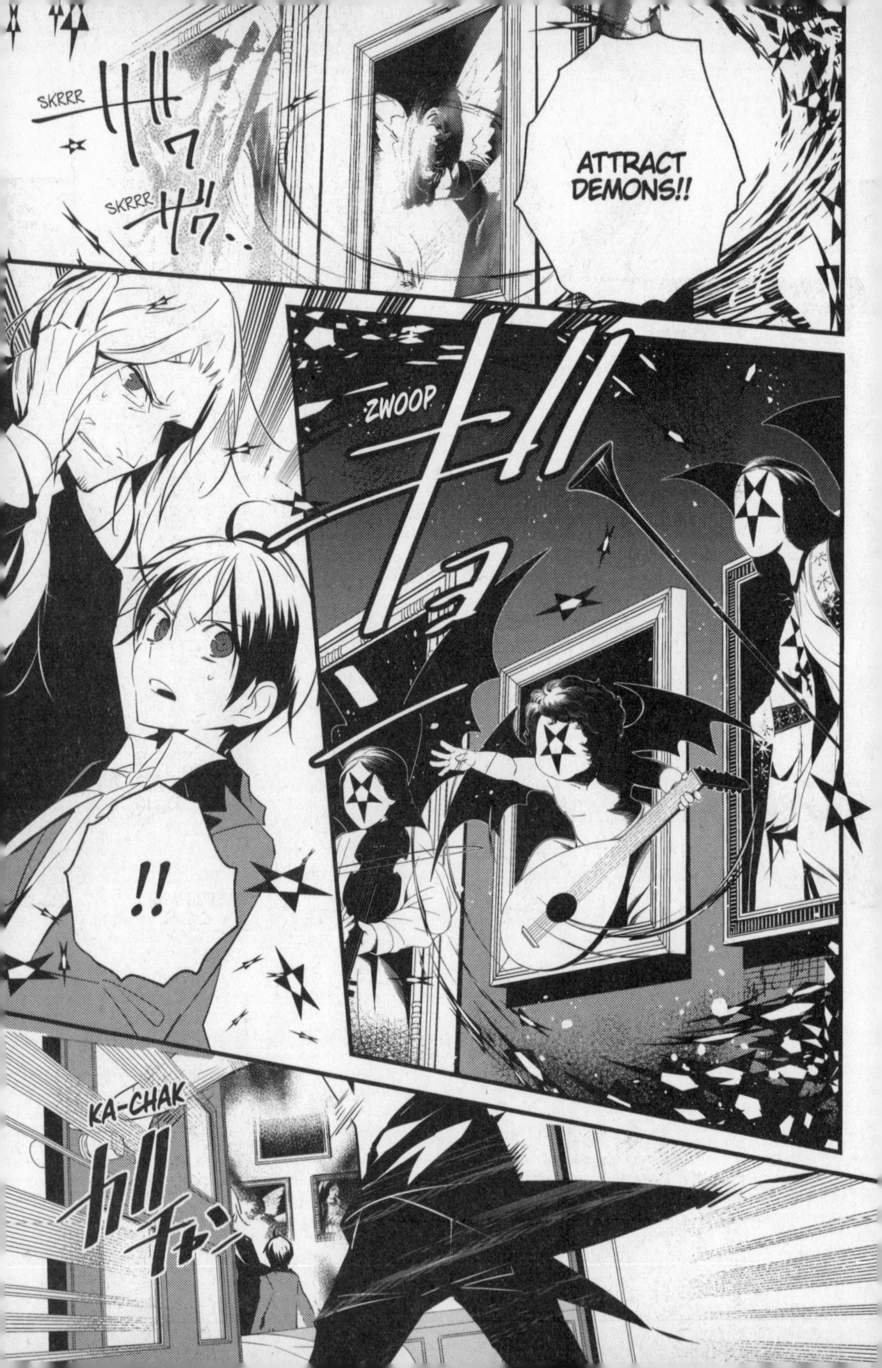
ATTRACT DEMONS!!
SKRRR
SKRRR
ZWOOP
!!
KA-CHAK

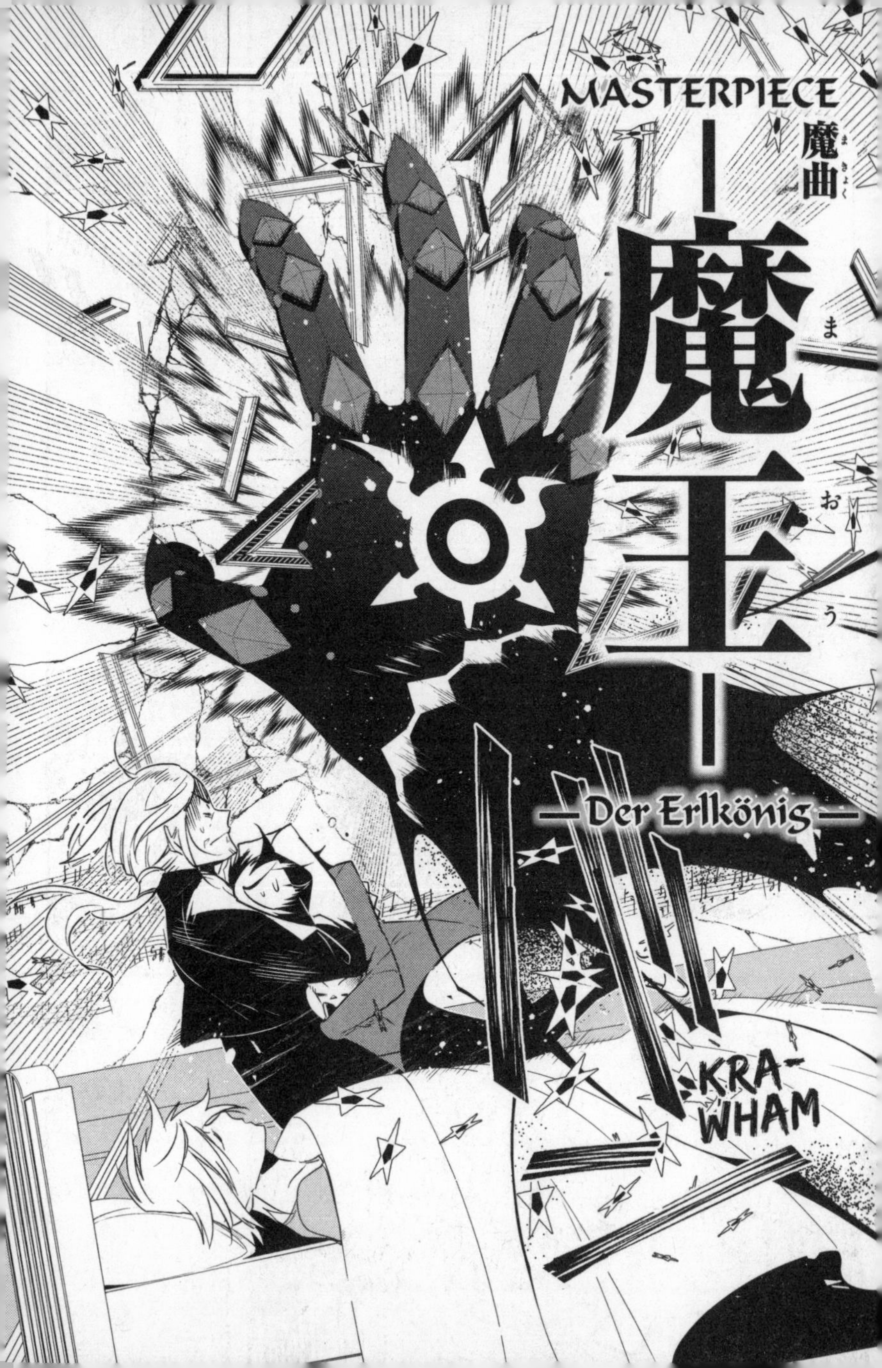
MASTERPIECE
魔曲(まきょく)
魔王(まおう)
—Der Erlkönig—
KRA-WHAM

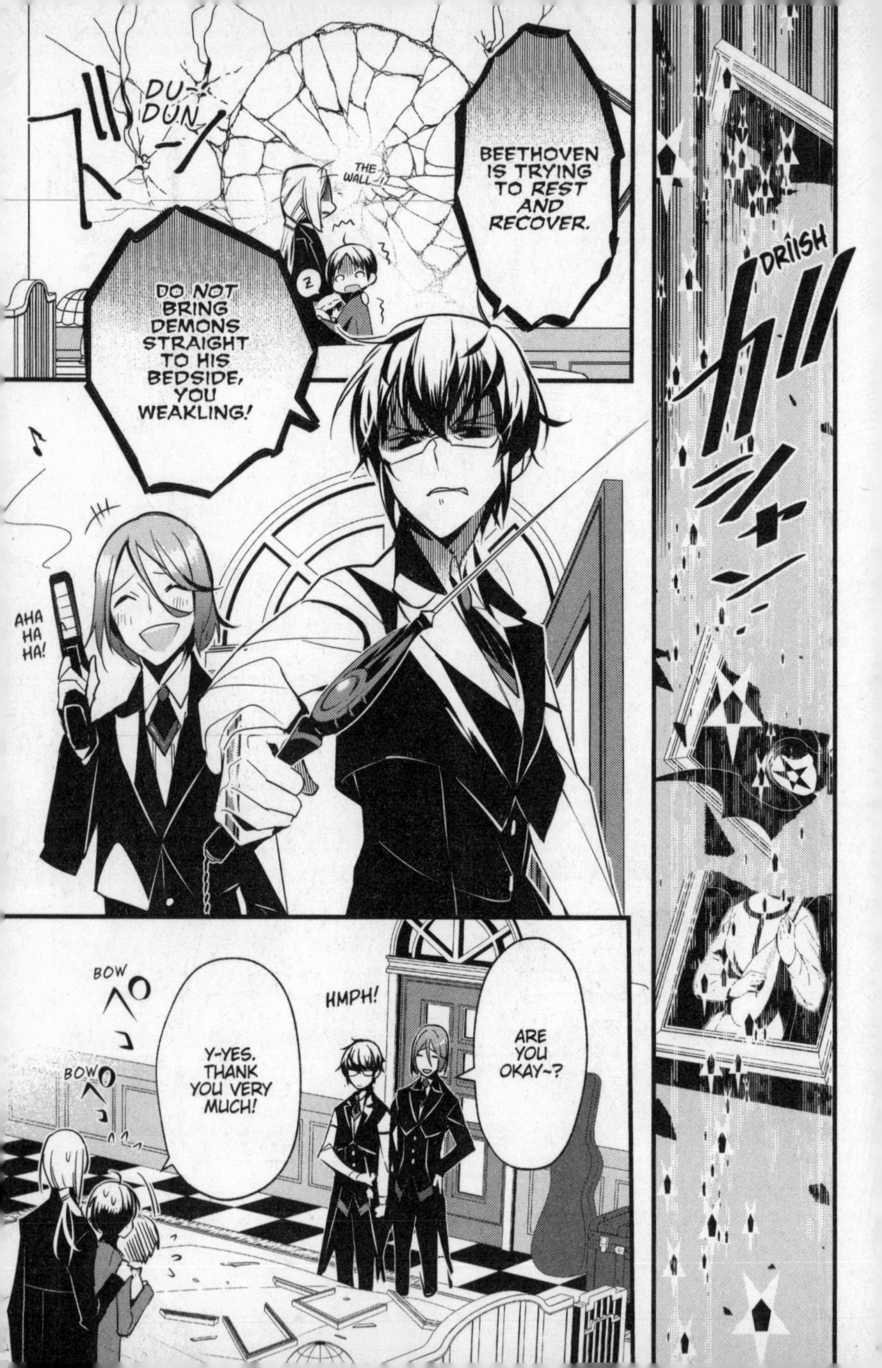
DRÎISH
BEETHOVEN IS TRYING TO REST AND RECOVER.
THE WALL...
DU-DUN
DO NOT BRING DEMONS STRAIGHT TO HIS BEDSIDE, YOU WEAKLING!
AHA HA HA!
ARE YOU OKAY~?
HMPH!
Y-YES. THANK YOU VERY MUCH!
BOW
BOW

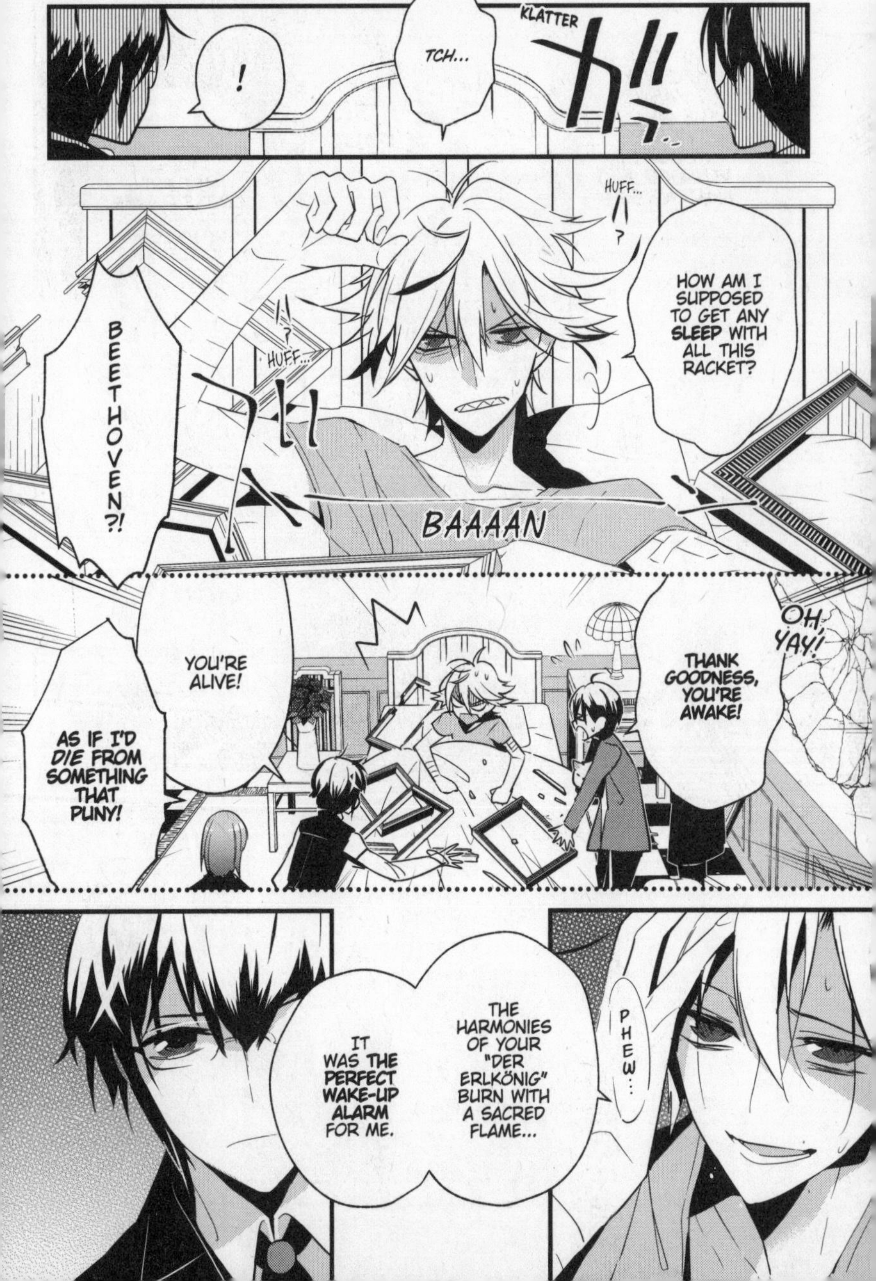
KLATTER
TCH...
!
HUFF...
HOW AM I SUPPOSED TO GET ANY SLEEP WITH ALL THIS RACKET?
HUFF...
BEETHOVEN?!
BAAAAN
OH, YAY!
THANK GOODNESS, YOU'RE AWAKE!
YOU'RE ALIVE!
AS IF I'D DIE FROM SOMETHING THAT PUNY!
PHEW...
THE HARMONIES OF YOUR "DER ERLKÖNIG" BURN WITH A SACRED FLAME...
IT WAS THE PERFECT WAKE-UP ALARM FOR ME.

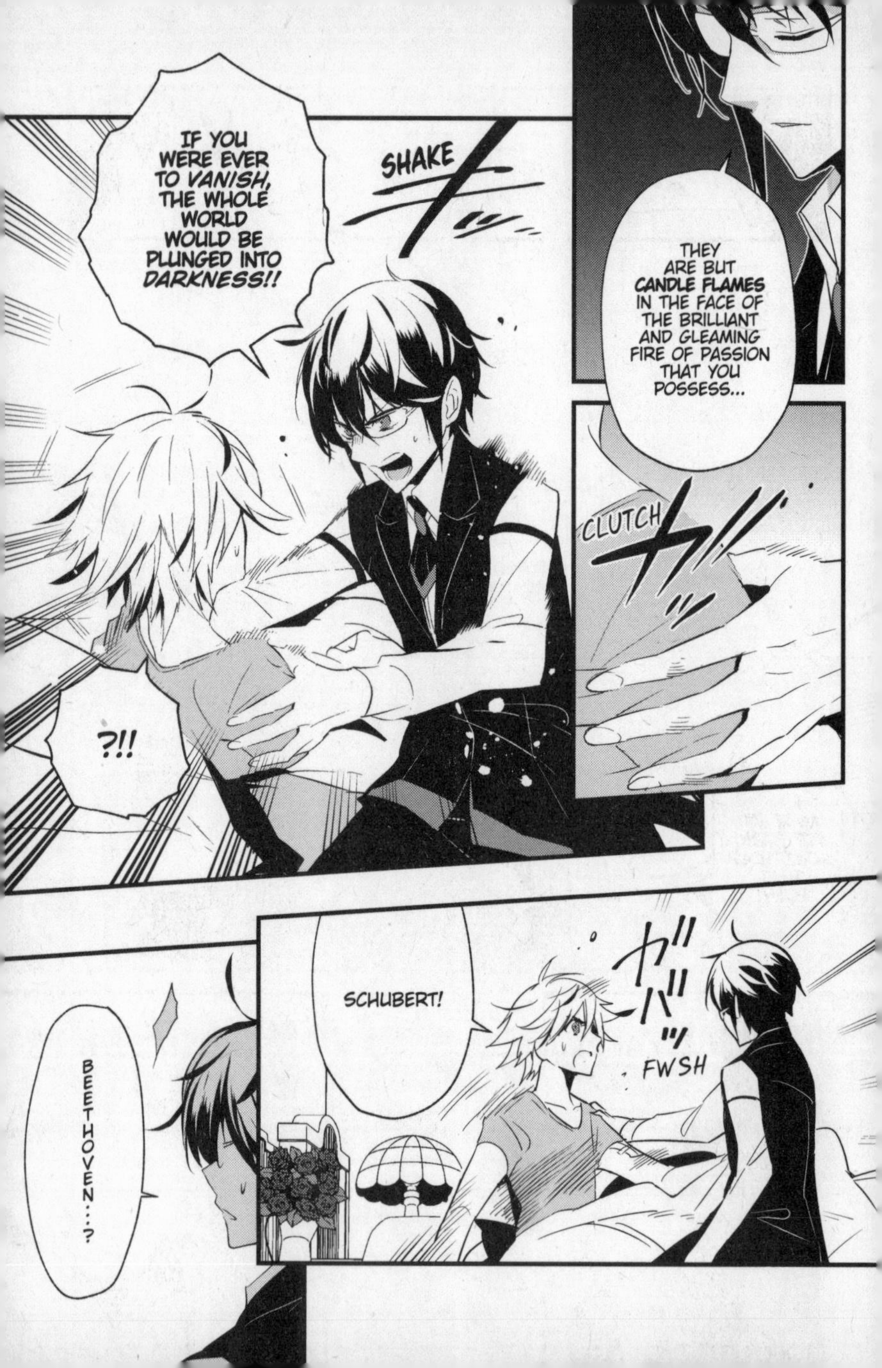
THEY ARE BUT CANDLE FLAMES IN THE FACE OF THE BRILLIANT AND GLEAMING FIRE OF PASSION THAT YOU POSSESS...
CLUTCH
SHAKE
IF YOU WERE EVER TO VANISH, THE WHOLE WORLD WOULD BE PLUNGED INTO DARKNESS!!
?!!
FWSH
SCHUBERT!
BEETHOVEN...?

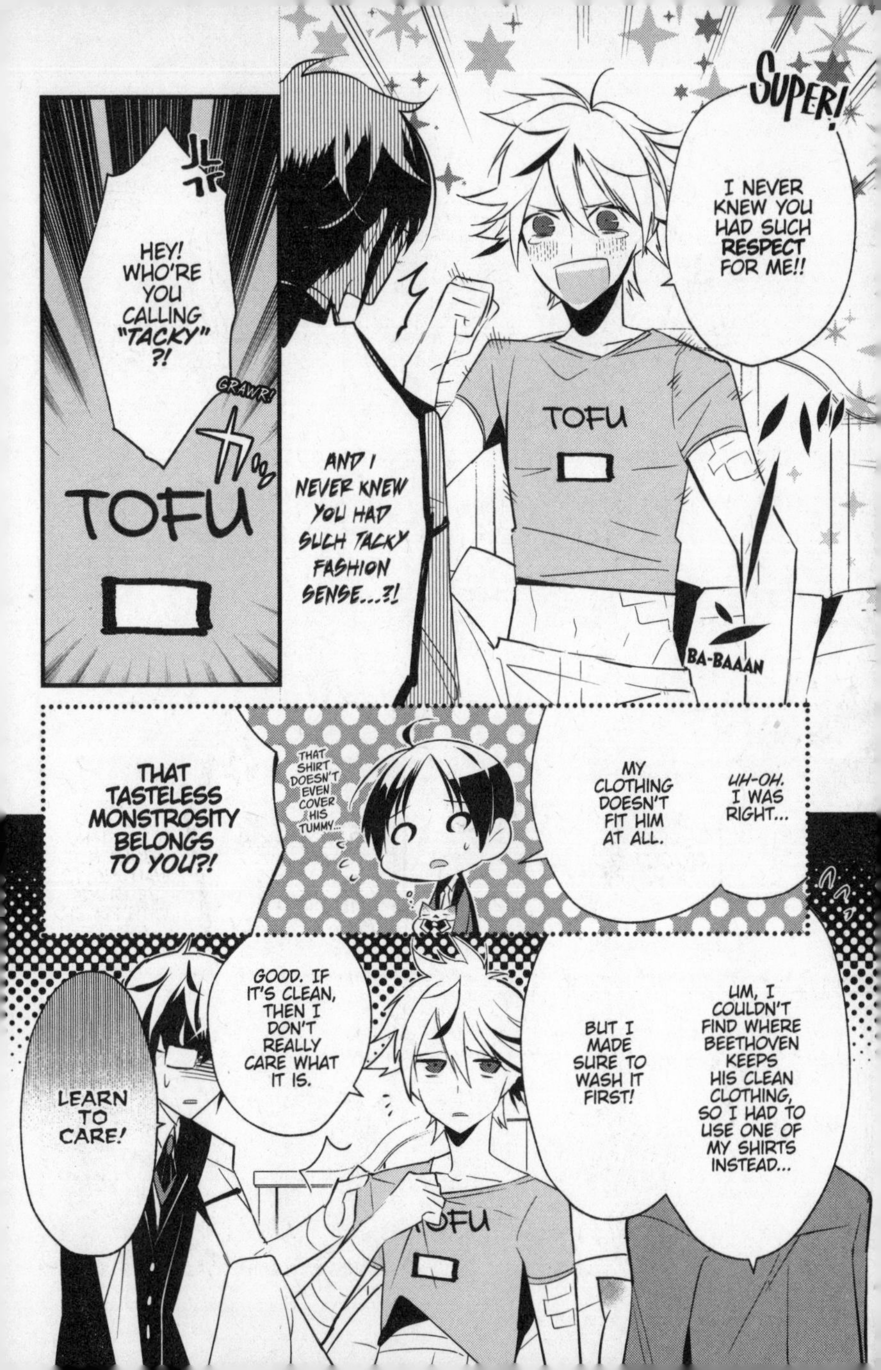
SUPER!
I NEVER KNEW YOU HAD SUCH RESPECT FOR ME!!
TOFU
BA-BAAAN
AND I NEVER KNEW YOU HAD SUCH TACKY FASHION SENSE...?!
HEY! WHO'RE YOU CALLING "TACKY"?!
GRAWR!
TOFU
UH-OH. I WAS RIGHT...
MY CLOTHING DOESN'T FIT HIM AT ALL.
THAT SHIRT DOESN'T EVEN COVER HIS TUMMY...
THAT TASTELESS MONSTROSITY BELONGS TO YOU?!
UM, I COULDN'T FIND WHERE BEETHOVEN KEEPS HIS CLEAN CLOTHING, SO I HAD TO USE ONE OF MY SHIRTS INSTEAD...
BUT I MADE SURE TO WASH IT FIRST!
GOOD. IF IT'S CLEAN, THEN I DON'T REALLY CARE WHAT IT IS.
TOFU
LEARN TO CARE!

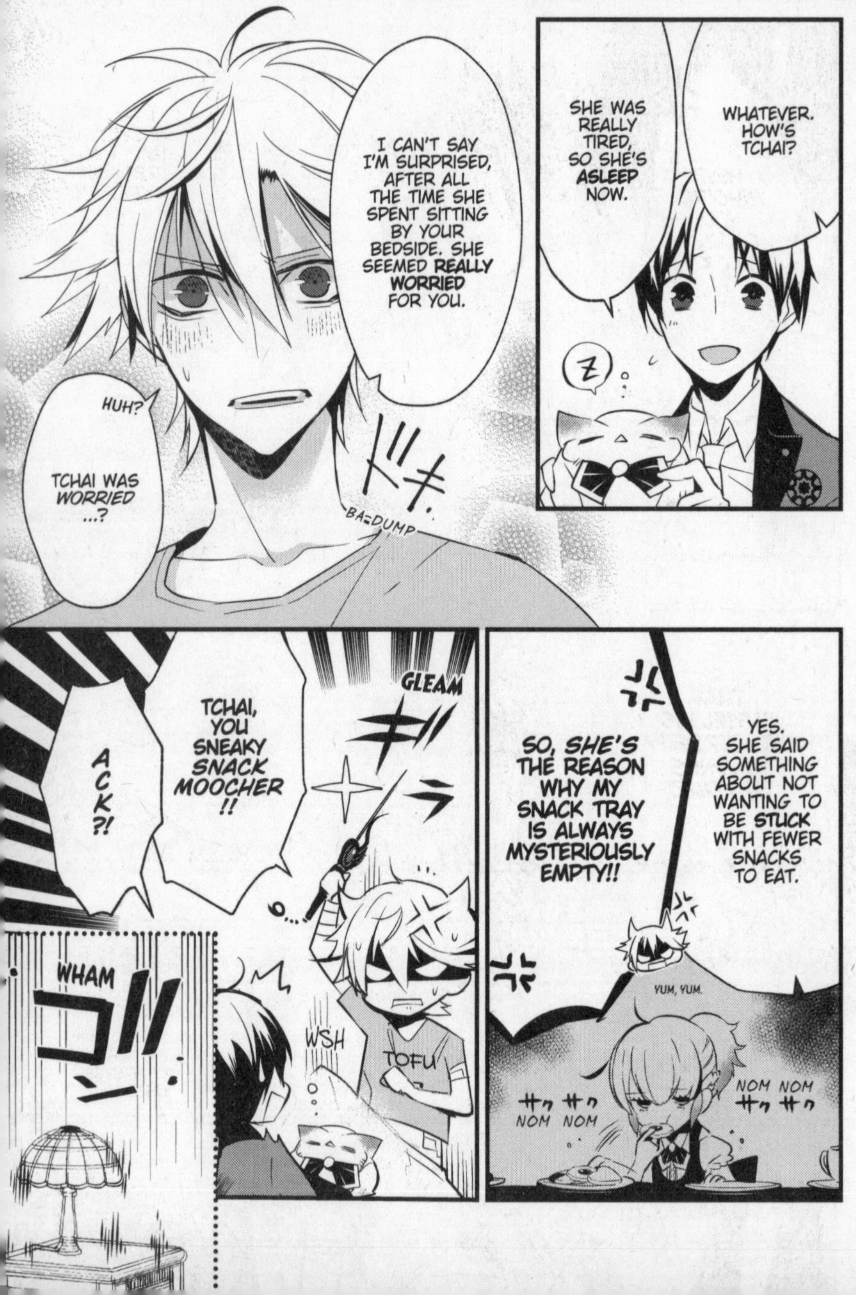
WHATEVER. HOW'S TCHAI?
SHE WAS REALLY TIRED, SO SHE'S ASLEEP NOW.
I CAN'T SAY I'M SURPRISED, AFTER ALL THE TIME SHE SPENT SITTING BY YOUR BEDSIDE. SHE SEEMED REALLY WORRIED FOR YOU.
BA-DUMP
HUH?
TCHAI WAS WORRIED ...?
YES. SHE SAID SOMETHING ABOUT NOT WANTING TO BE STUCK WITH FEWER SNACKS TO EAT.
SO, SHE'S THE REASON WHY MY SNACK TRAY IS ALWAYS MYSTERIOUSLY EMPTY!!
YUM, YUM.
NOM NOM
NOM NOM
GLEAM
TCHAI, YOU SNEAKY SNACK MOOCHER!!
ACK?!
WSH
TOFU
WHAM

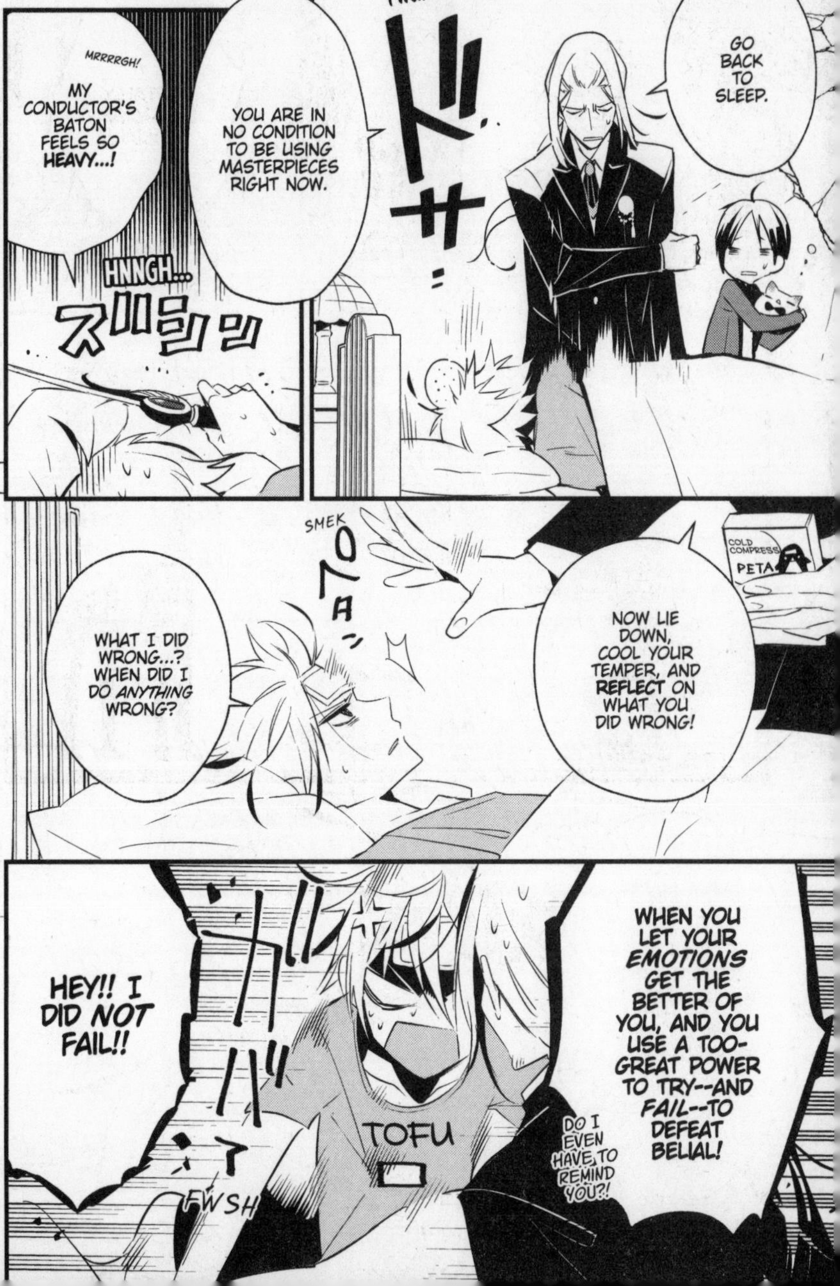
GO BACK TO SLEEP.
FWUMP...
YOU ARE IN NO CONDITION TO BE USING MASTERPIECES RIGHT NOW.
MRRRRGH!
MY CONDUCTOR'S BATON FEELS SO HEAVY...!
HNNGH...
COLD COMPRESS
PETA
NOW LIE DOWN, COOL YOUR TEMPER, AND REFLECT ON WHAT YOU DID WRONG!
SMEK
WHAT I DID WRONG...? WHEN DID I DO ANYTHING WRONG?
WHEN YOU LET YOUR EMOTIONS GET THE BETTER OF YOU, AND YOU USE A TOO-GREAT POWER TO TRY--AND FAIL--TO DEFEAT BELIAL!
DO I EVEN HAVE TO REMIND YOU?!
HEY!! I DID NOT FAIL!!
TOFU
FWSH

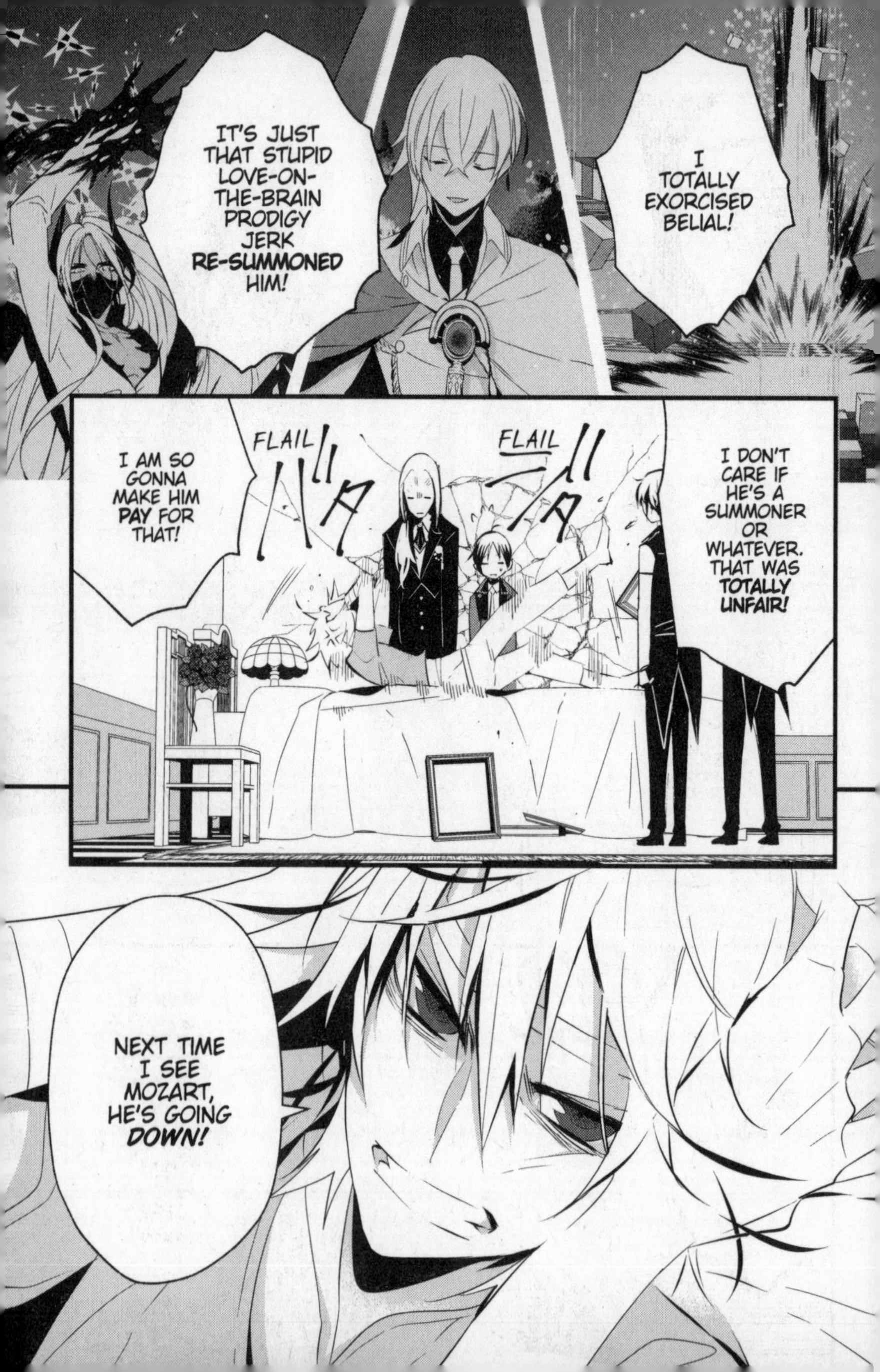
I TOTALLY EXORCISED BELIAL!
IT'S JUST THAT STUPID LOVE-ON-THE-BRAIN PRODIGY JERK RE-SUMMONED HIM!
I DON'T CARE IF HE'S A SUMMONER OR WHATEVER. THAT WAS TOTALLY UNFAIR!
FLAIL
FLAIL
I AM SO GONNA MAKE HIM PAY FOR THAT!
NEXT TIME I SEE MOZART, HE'S GOING DOWN!

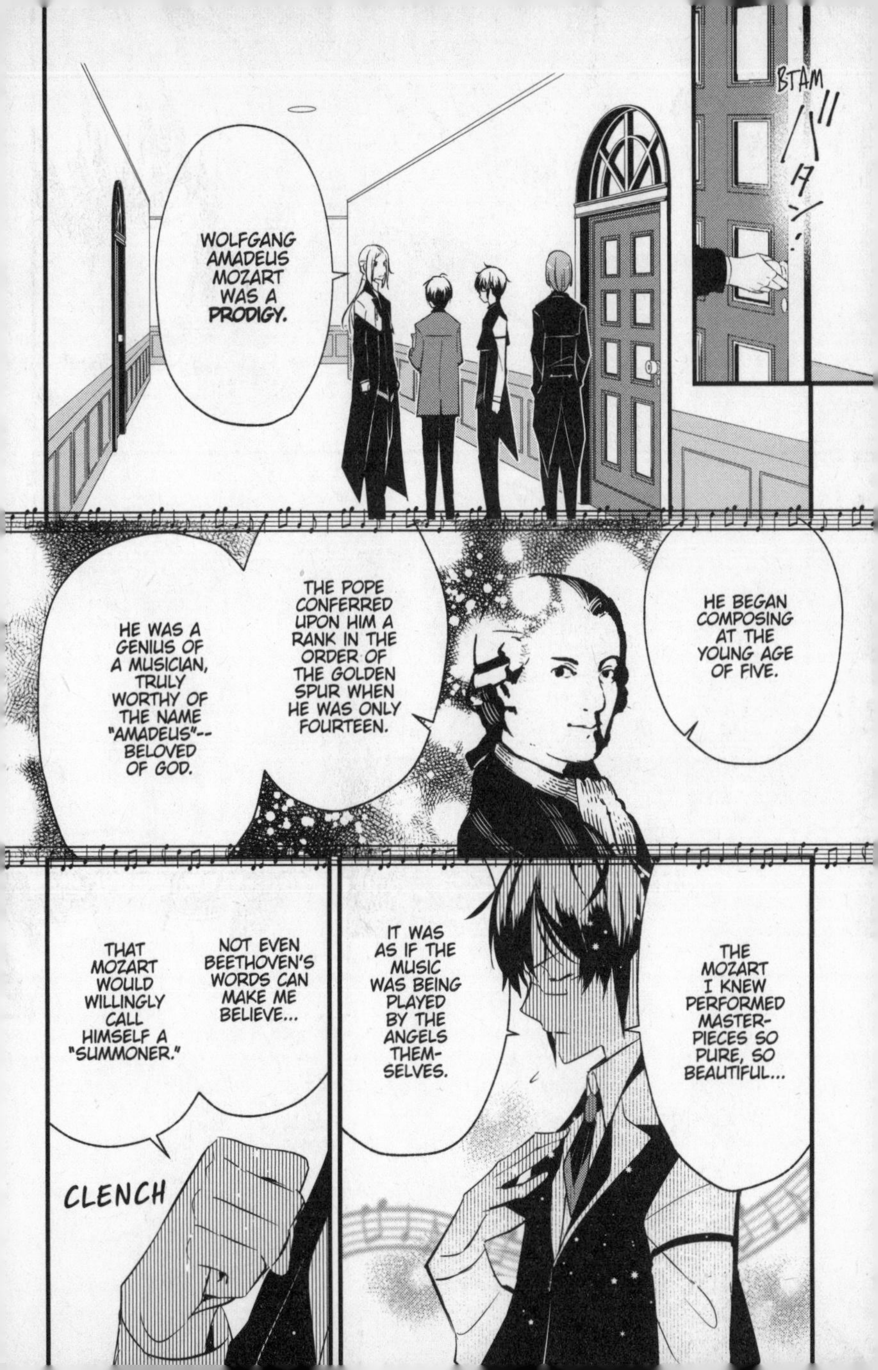
BTAM
WOLFGANG AMADEUS MOZART WAS A PRODIGY.
HE BEGAN COMPOSING AT THE YOUNG AGE OF FIVE.
THE POPE CONFERRED UPON HIM A RANK IN THE ORDER OF THE GOLDEN SPUR WHEN HE WAS ONLY FOURTEEN.
HE WAS A GENIUS OF A MUSICIAN, TRULY WORTHY OF THE NAME "AMADEUS"--BELOVED OF GOD.
THE MOZART I KNEW PERFORMED MASTER-PIECES SO PURE, SO BEAUTIFUL...
IT WAS AS IF THE MUSIC WAS BEING PLAYED BY THE ANGELS THEM-SELVES.
NOT EVEN BEETHOVEN'S WORDS CAN MAKE ME BELIEVE...
THAT MOZART WOULD WILLINGLY CALL HIMSELF A "SUMMONER."
CLENCH

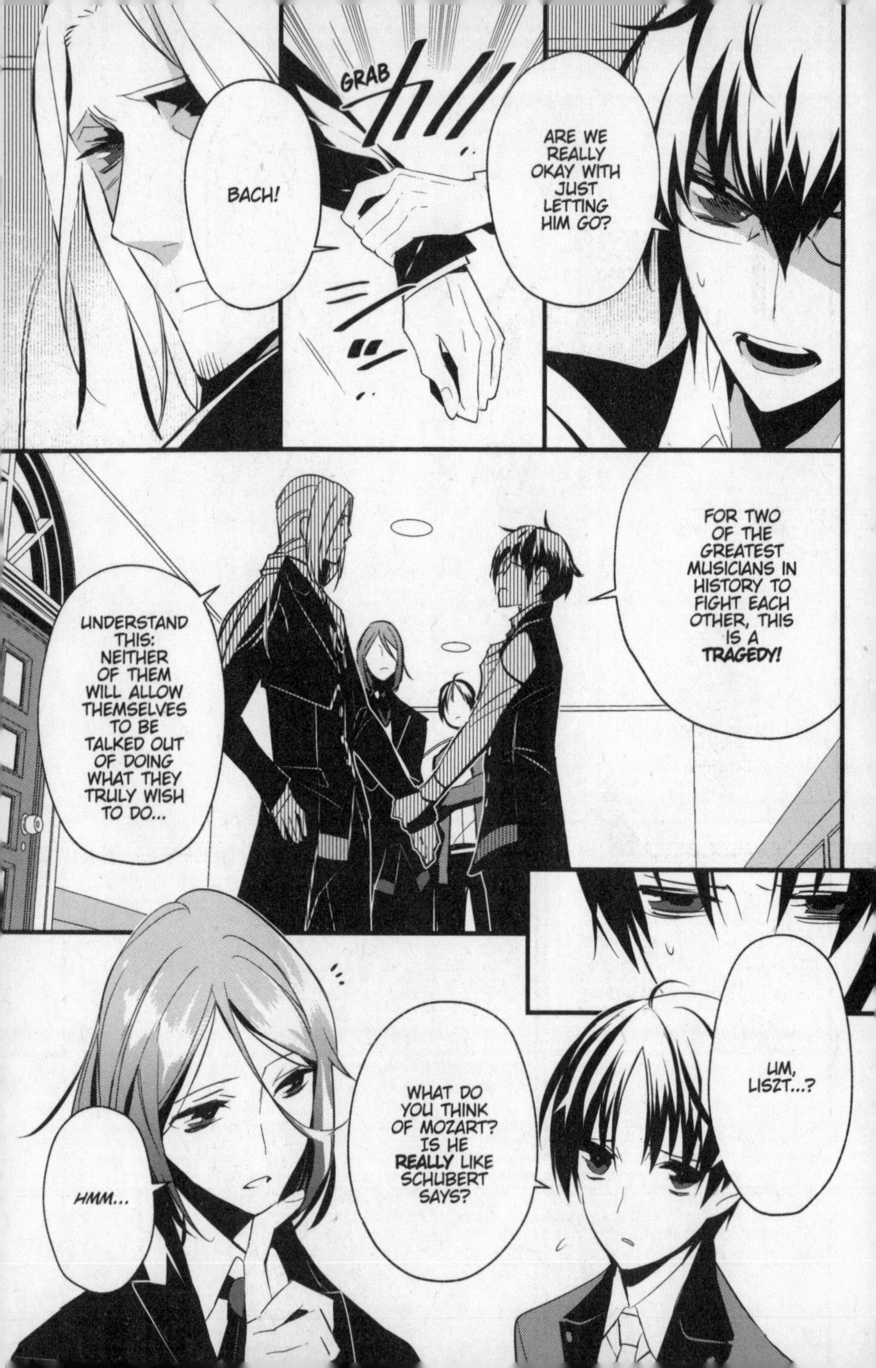
ARE WE REALLY OKAY WITH JUST LETTING HIM GO?
GRAB
BACH!
FOR TWO OF THE GREATEST MUSICIANS IN HISTORY TO FIGHT EACH OTHER, THIS IS A **TRAGEDY!**
UNDERSTAND THIS: NEITHER OF THEM WILL ALLOW THEMSELVES TO BE TALKED OUT OF DOING WHAT THEY TRULY WISH TO DO...
UM, LISZT...?
WHAT DO YOU THINK OF MOZART? IS HE **REALLY** LIKE SCHUBERT SAYS?
HMM...

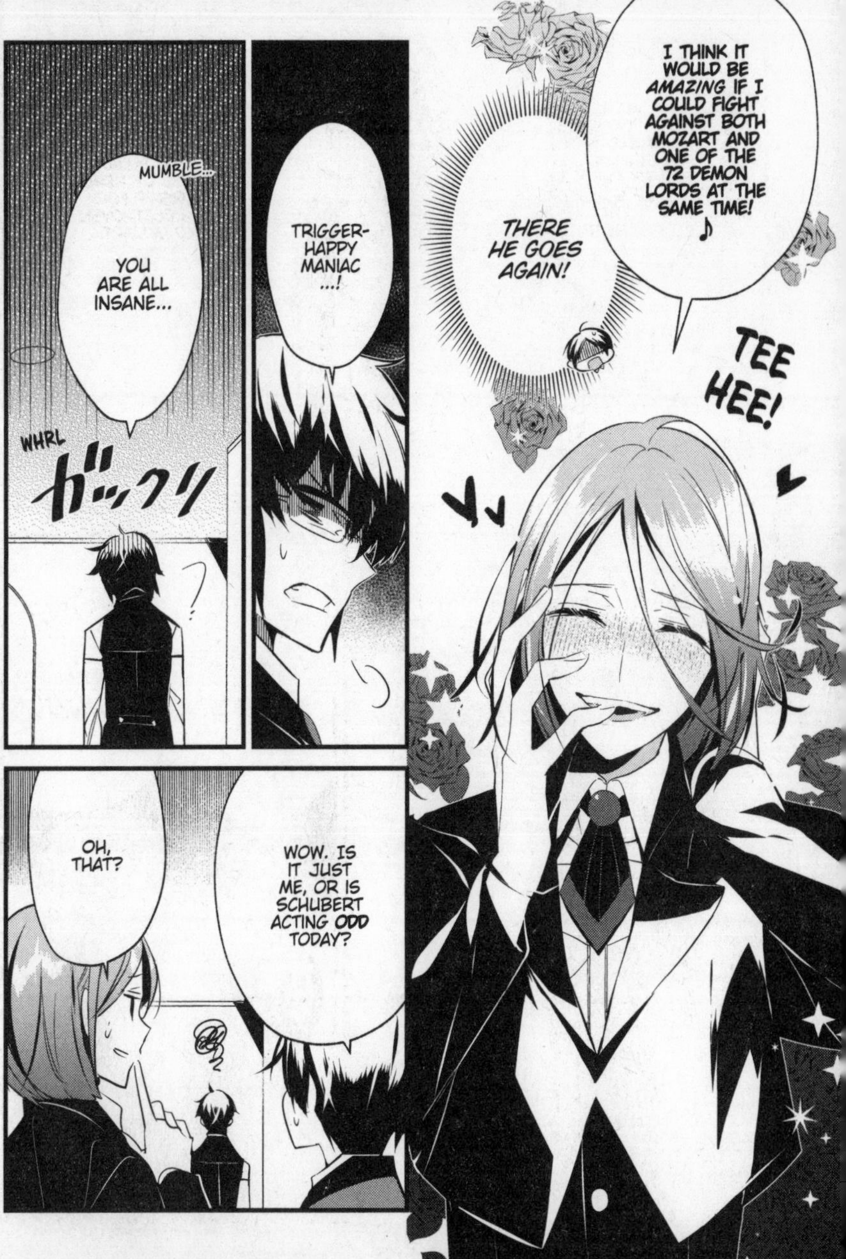
I THINK IT WOULD BE AMAZING IF I COULD FIGHT AGAINST BOTH MOZART AND ONE OF THE 72 DEMON LORDS AT THE SAME TIME! ♪
THERE HE GOES AGAIN!
TEE HEE!
TRIGGER-HAPPY MANIAC ...!
MUMBLE...
YOU ARE ALL INSANE...
WHRL
ガックリ
WOW. IS IT JUST ME, OR IS SCHUBERT ACTING ODD TODAY?
OH, THAT?

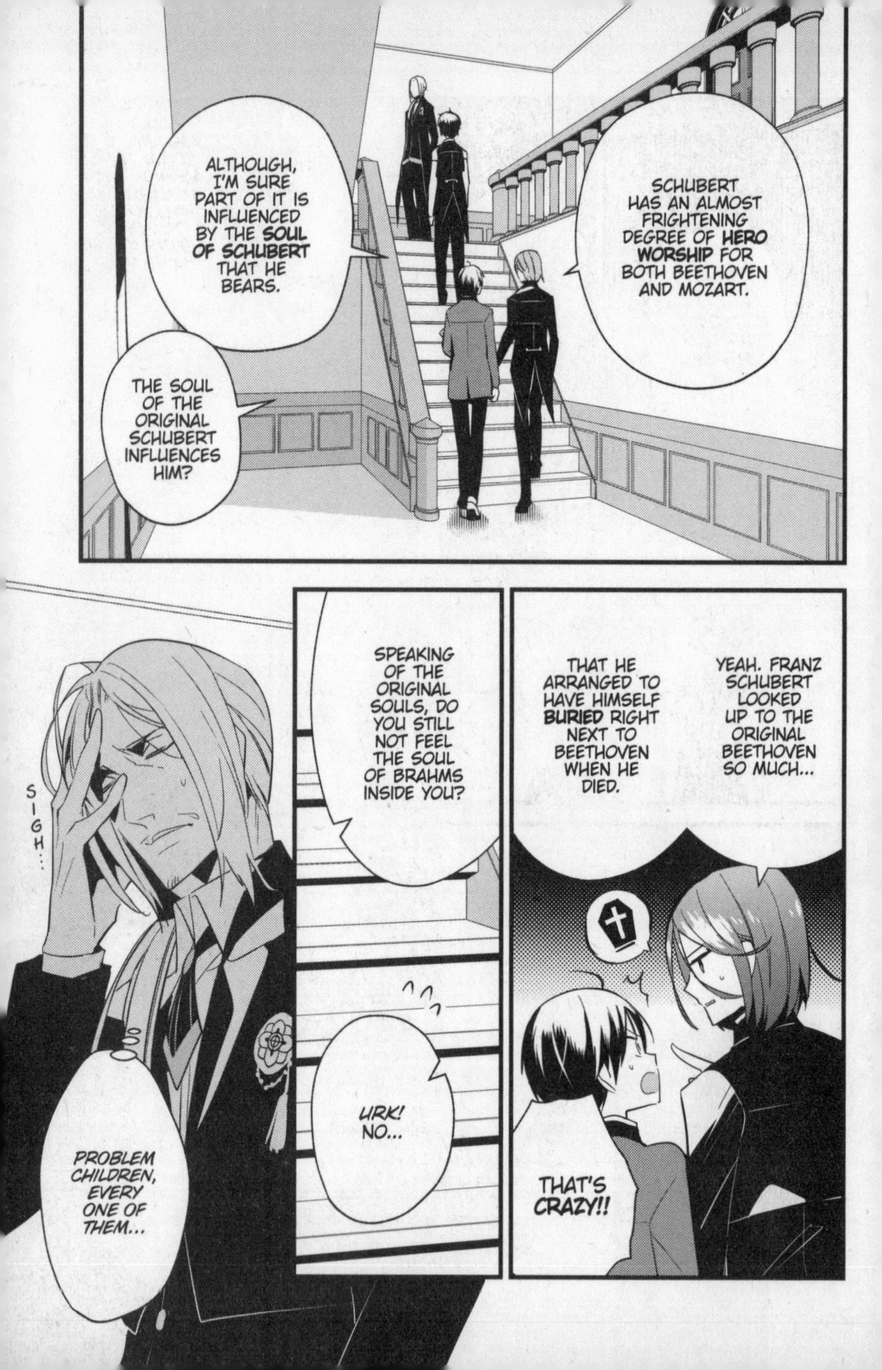
SCHUBERT HAS AN ALMOST FRIGHTENING DEGREE OF **HERO WORSHIP** FOR BOTH BEETHOVEN AND MOZART.
ALTHOUGH, I'M SURE PART OF IT IS INFLUENCED BY THE **SOUL OF SCHUBERT** THAT HE BEARS.
THE SOUL OF THE ORIGINAL SCHUBERT INFLUENCES HIM?
YEAH. FRANZ SCHUBERT LOOKED UP TO THE ORIGINAL BEETHOVEN SO MUCH...
THAT HE ARRANGED TO HAVE HIMSELF **BURIED** RIGHT NEXT TO BEETHOVEN WHEN HE DIED.
THAT'S **CRAZY!!**
SPEAKING OF THE ORIGINAL SOULS, DO YOU STILL NOT FEEL THE SOUL OF BRAHMS INSIDE YOU?
URK! NO...
SIGH...
PROBLEM CHILDREN, EVERY ONE OF THEM...

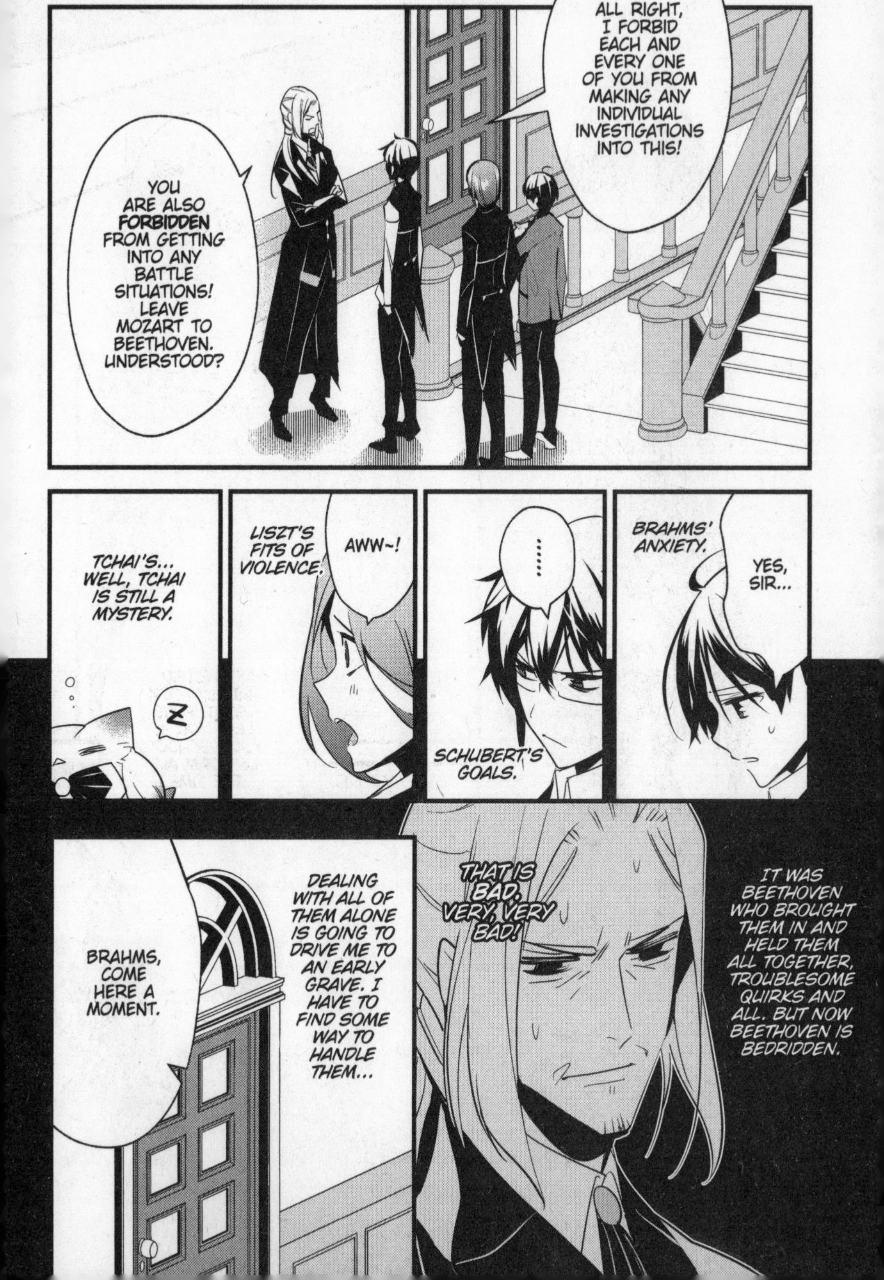
ALL RIGHT, I FORBID EACH AND EVERY ONE OF YOU FROM MAKING ANY INDIVIDUAL INVESTIGATIONS INTO THIS!
YOU ARE ALSO **FORBIDDEN** FROM GETTING INTO ANY BATTLE SITUATIONS! LEAVE MOZART TO BEETHOVEN. UNDERSTOOD?
BRAHMS' ANXIETY.
YES, SIR...
......
SCHUBERT'S GOALS.
AWW~!
LISZT'S FITS OF VIOLENCE.
TCHAI'S... WELL, TCHAI IS STILL A MYSTERY.
Z
IT WAS BEETHOVEN WHO BROUGHT THEM IN AND HELD THEM ALL TOGETHER, TROUBLESOME QUIRKS AND ALL. BUT NOW BEETHOVEN IS BEDRIDDEN.
THAT IS BAD. VERY, VERY BAD!
DEALING WITH ALL OF THEM ALONE IS GOING TO DRIVE ME TO AN EARLY GRAVE. I HAVE TO FIND SOME WAY TO HANDLE THEM...
BRAHMS, COME HERE A MOMENT.

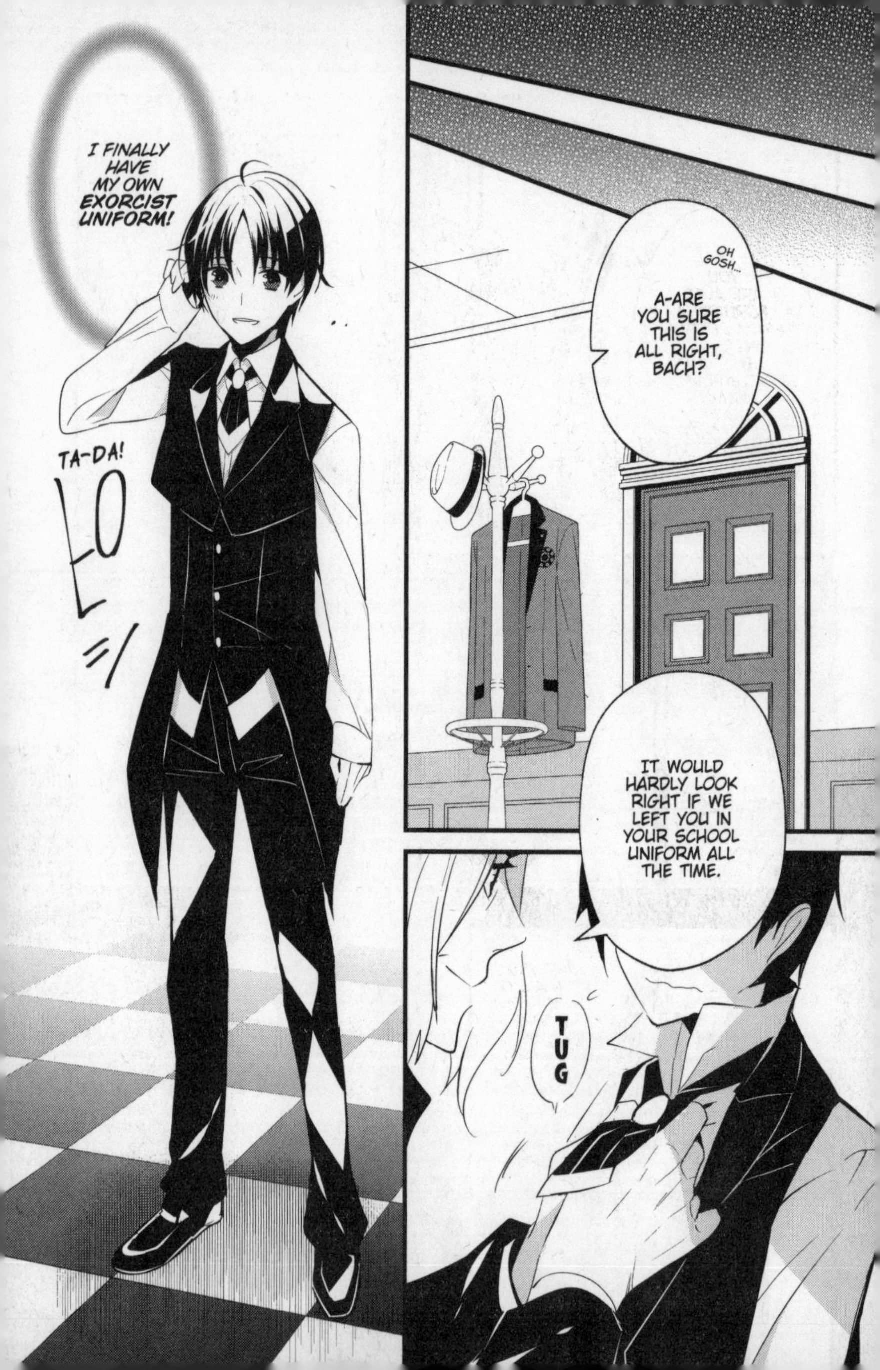
OH GOSH...
A-ARE YOU SURE THIS IS ALL RIGHT, BACH?
IT WOULD HARDLY LOOK RIGHT IF WE LEFT YOU IN YOUR SCHOOL UNIFORM ALL THE TIME.
TUG
I FINALLY HAVE MY OWN EXORCIST UNIFORM!
TA-DA!

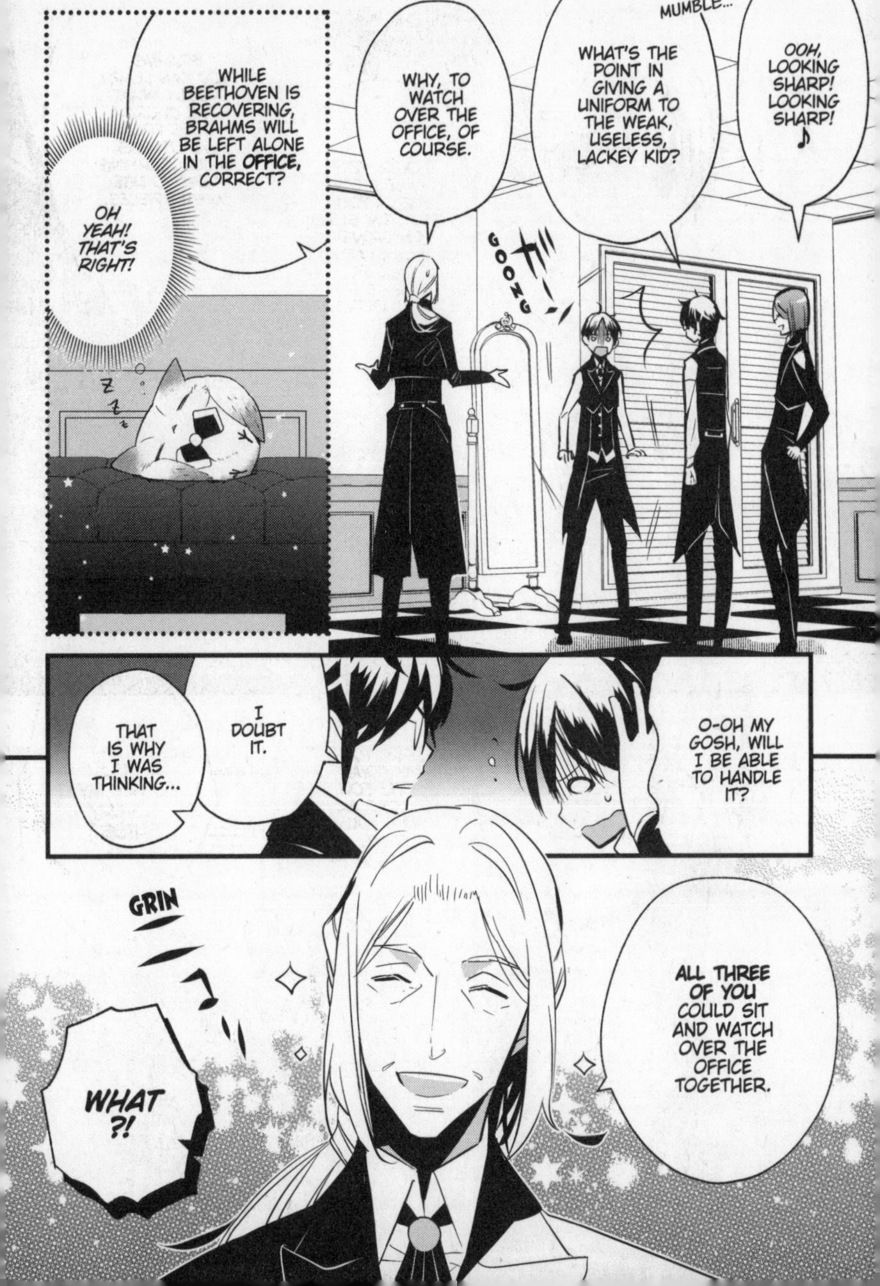
OOH, LOOKING SHARP! LOOKING SHARP! ♪
MUMBLE...
WHAT'S THE POINT IN GIVING A UNIFORM TO THE WEAK, USELESS, LACKEY KID?
GOONG
WHY, TO WATCH OVER THE OFFICE, OF COURSE.
WHILE BEETHOVEN IS RECOVERING, BRAHMS WILL BE LEFT ALONE IN THE OFFICE, CORRECT?
OH YEAH! THAT'S RIGHT!
ZZZ
O-OH MY GOSH, WILL I BE ABLE TO HANDLE IT?
I DOUBT IT.
THAT IS WHY I WAS THINKING...
ALL THREE OF YOU COULD SIT AND WATCH OVER THE OFFICE TOGETHER.
GRIN
WHAT?!

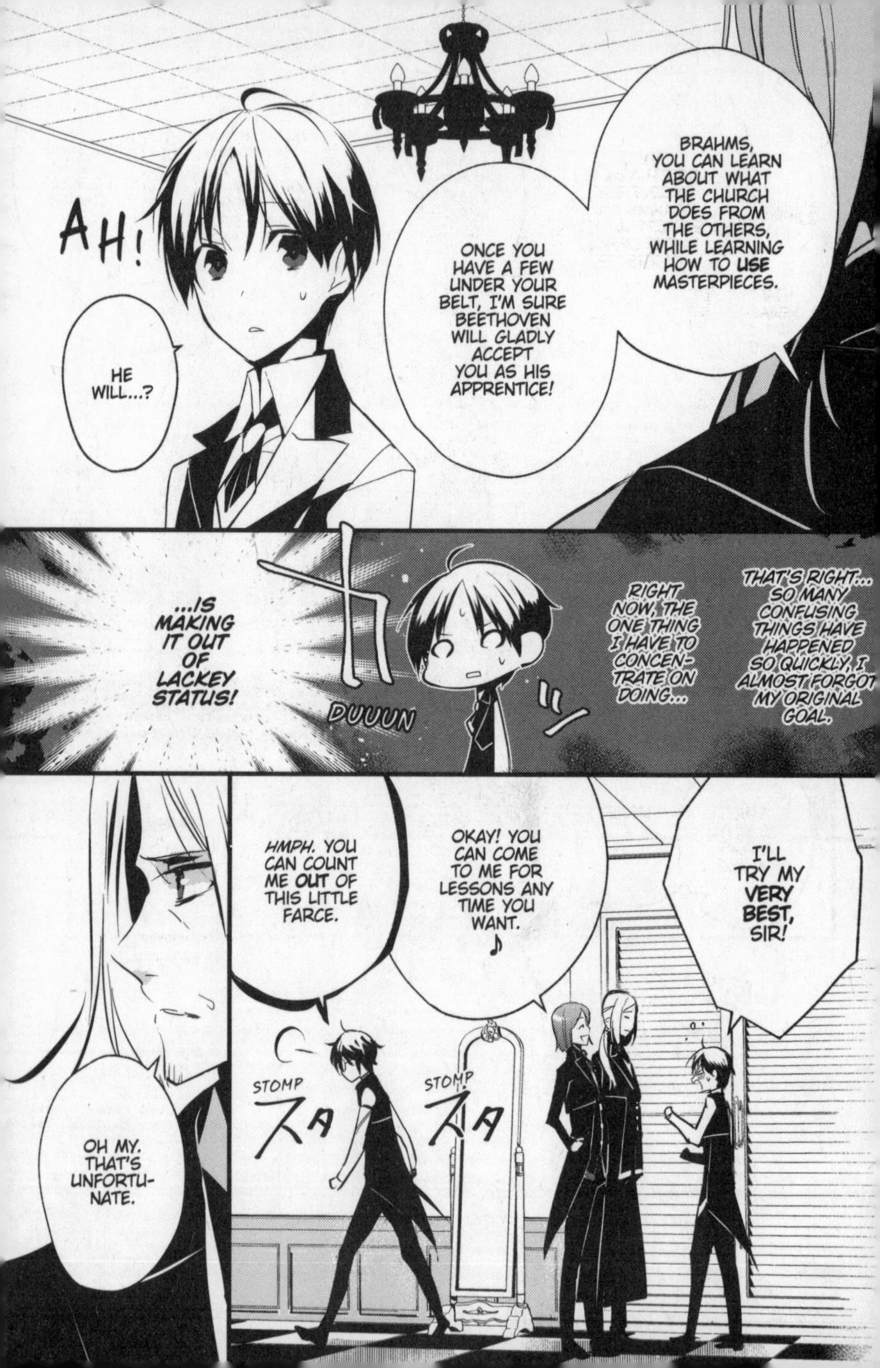
BRAHMS, YOU CAN LEARN ABOUT WHAT THE CHURCH DOES FROM THE OTHERS, WHILE LEARNING HOW TO USE MASTERPIECES.
ONCE YOU HAVE A FEW UNDER YOUR BELT, I'M SURE BEETHOVEN WILL GLADLY ACCEPT YOU AS HIS APPRENTICE!
AH!
HE WILL...?
THAT'S RIGHT... SO MANY CONFUSING THINGS HAVE HAPPENED SO QUICKLY, I ALMOST FORGOT MY ORIGINAL GOAL.
RIGHT NOW, THE ONE THING I HAVE TO CONCENTRATE ON DOING...
DUUUN
...IS MAKING IT OUT OF LACKEY STATUS!
I'LL TRY MY VERY BEST, SIR!
OKAY! YOU CAN COME TO ME FOR LESSONS ANY TIME YOU WANT. ♪
HMPH. YOU CAN COUNT ME OUT OF THIS LITTLE FARCE.
STOMP
STOMP
OH MY. THAT'S UNFORTUNATE.

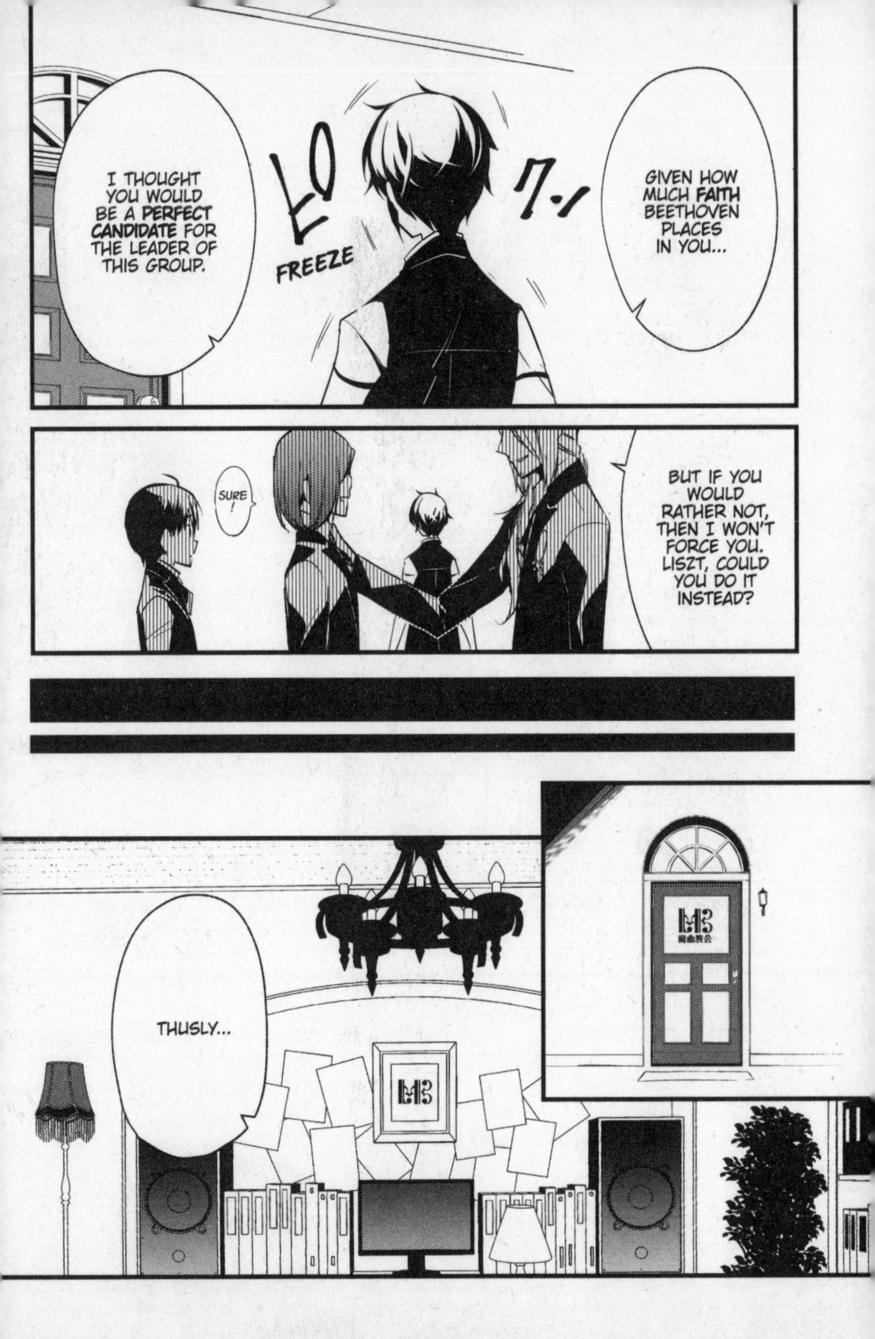
GIVEN HOW MUCH FAITH BEETHOVEN PLACES IN YOU...
FREEZE
I THOUGHT YOU WOULD BE A PERFECT CANDIDATE FOR THE LEADER OF THIS GROUP.
BUT IF YOU WOULD RATHER NOT, THEN I WON'T FORCE YOU. LISZT, COULD YOU DO IT INSTEAD?
SURE!
魔曲教会
THUSLY...

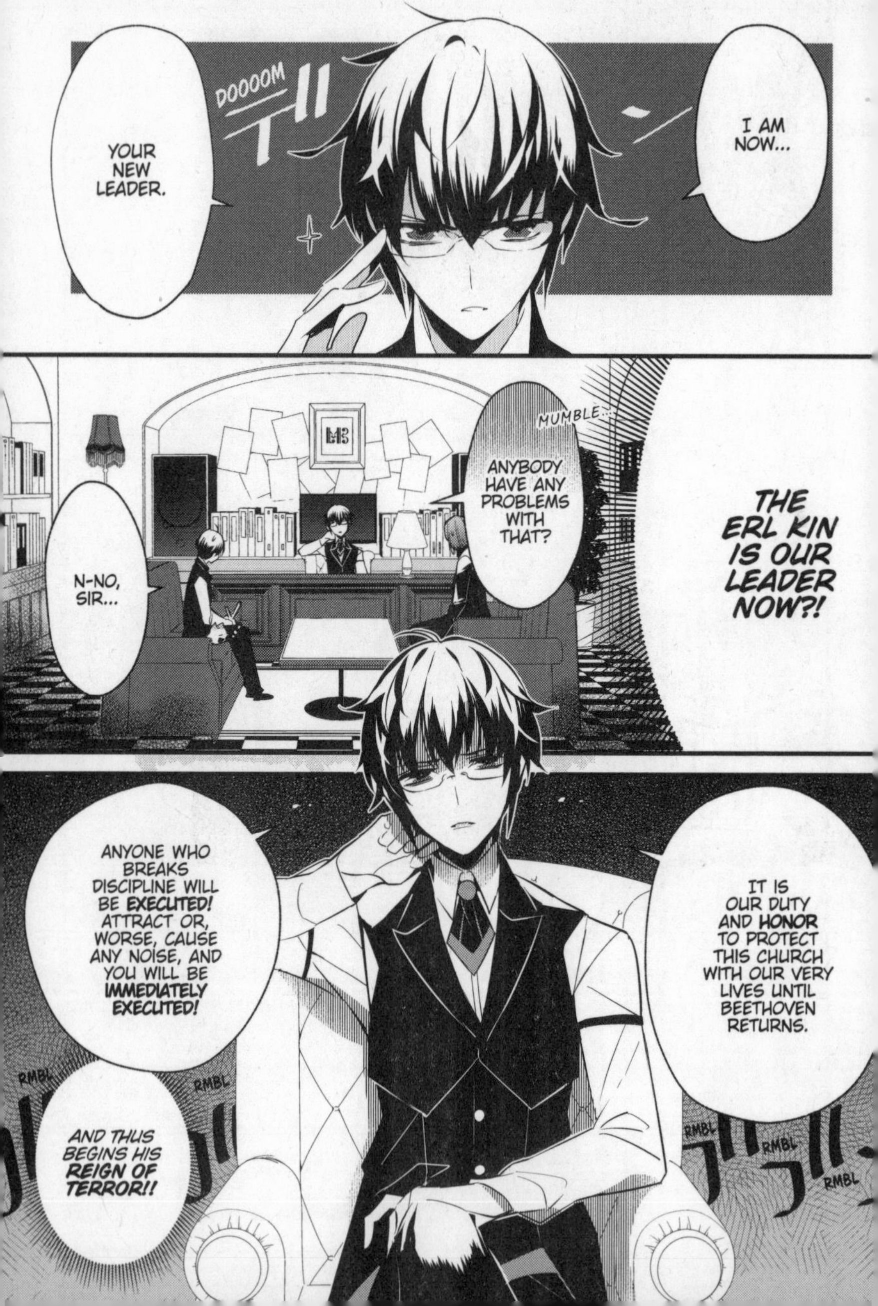
I AM NOW...
DOOOOM
YOUR NEW LEADER.
THE ERL KIN IS OUR LEADER NOW?!
MUMBLE...
ANYBODY HAVE ANY PROBLEMS WITH THAT?
N-NO, SIR...
IT IS OUR DUTY AND HONOR TO PROTECT THIS CHURCH WITH OUR VERY LIVES UNTIL BEETHOVEN RETURNS.
ANYONE WHO BREAKS DISCIPLINE WILL BE EXECUTED! ATTRACT OR, WORSE, CAUSE ANY NOISE, AND YOU WILL BE IMMEDIATELY EXECUTED!
RMBL RMBL RMBL
RMBL RMBL
AND THUS BEGINS HIS REIGN OF TERROR!!

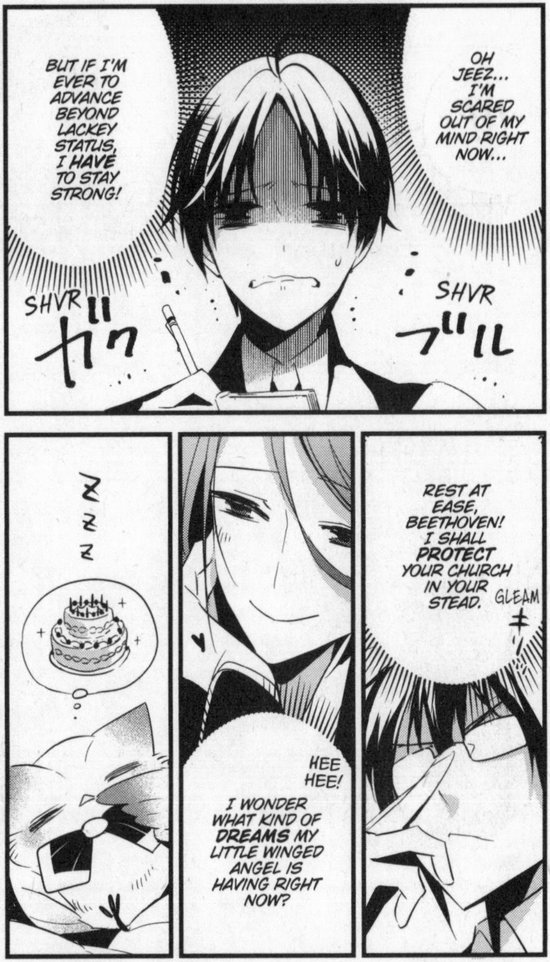
OH JEEZ... I'M SCARED OUT OF MY MIND RIGHT NOW...
BUT IF I'M EVER TO ADVANCE BEYOND LACKEY STATUS, I HAVE TO STAY STRONG!
SHVR
ブル
SHVR
ガク
REST AT EASE, BEETHOVEN! I SHALL PROTECT YOUR CHURCH IN YOUR STEAD.
GLEAM
キ
HEE HEE!
I WONDER WHAT KIND OF DREAMS MY LITTLE WINGED ANGEL IS HAVING RIGHT NOW?
Z Z Z
SHEESH...
...
I HOPE THIS WILL TEACH THEM TO WORK TOGETHER, AT LEAST FOR A SHORT TIME...

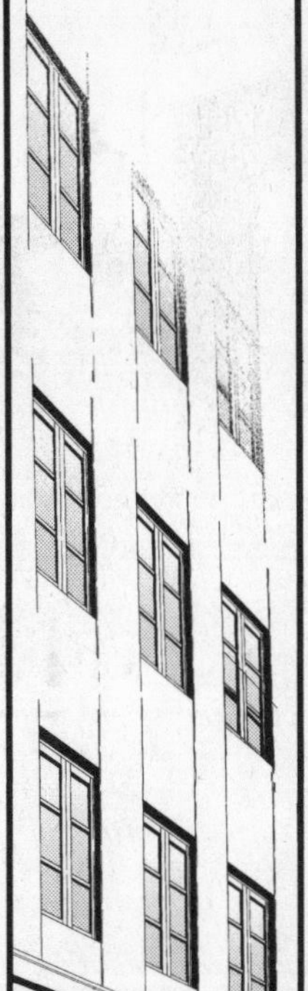
Classic Cafe #9

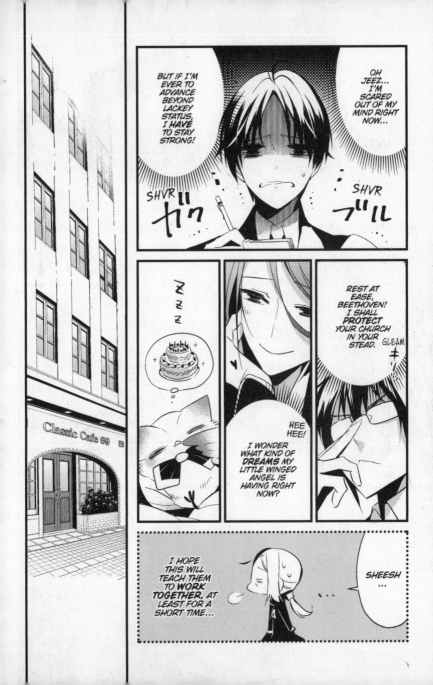

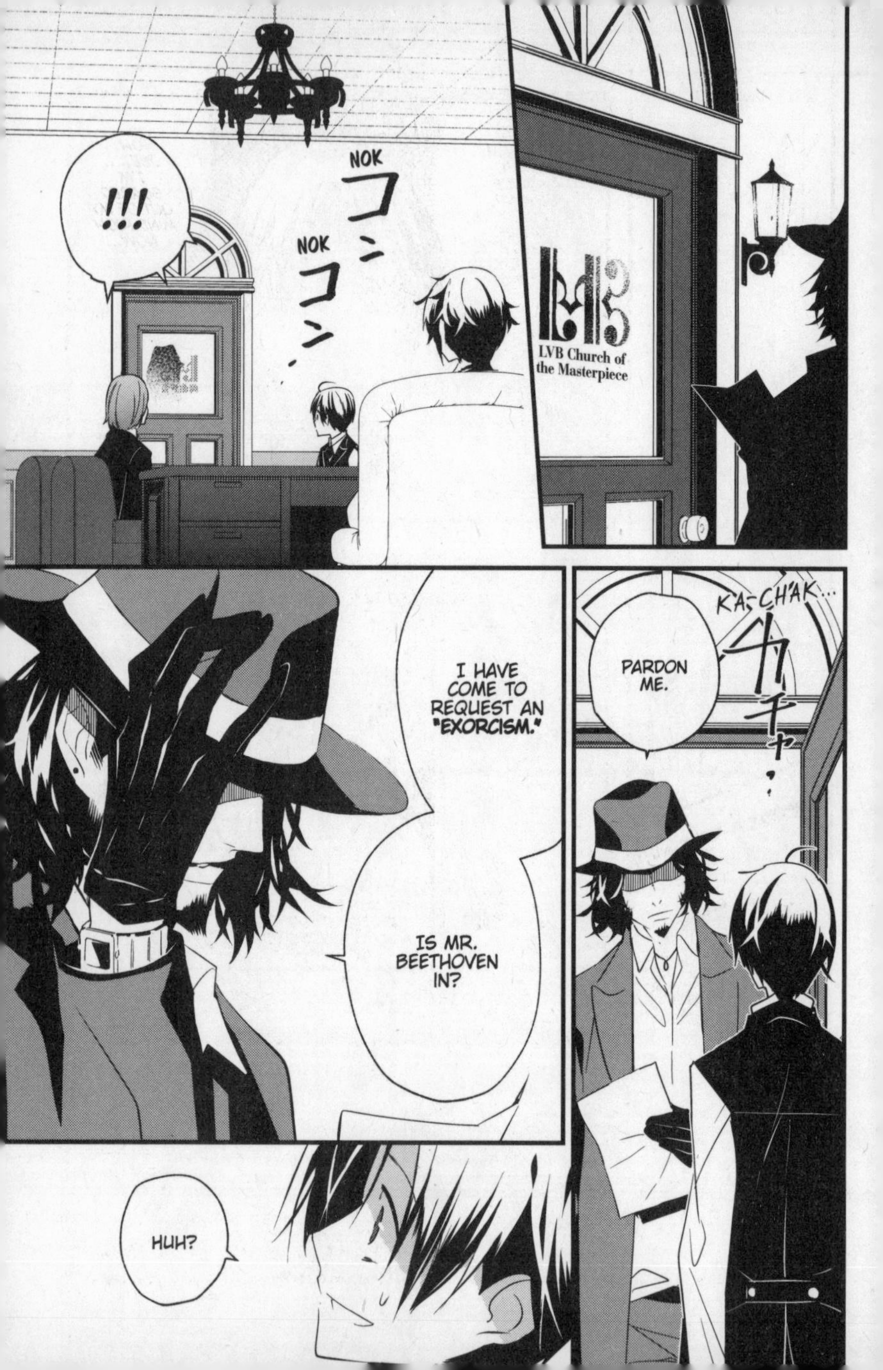
LVB Church of the Masterpiece
NOK NOK
コンコン
!!!
KA-CH'AK...
カチャ
PARDON ME.
I HAVE COME TO REQUEST AN "EXORCISM."
IS MR. BEETHOVEN IN?
HUH?

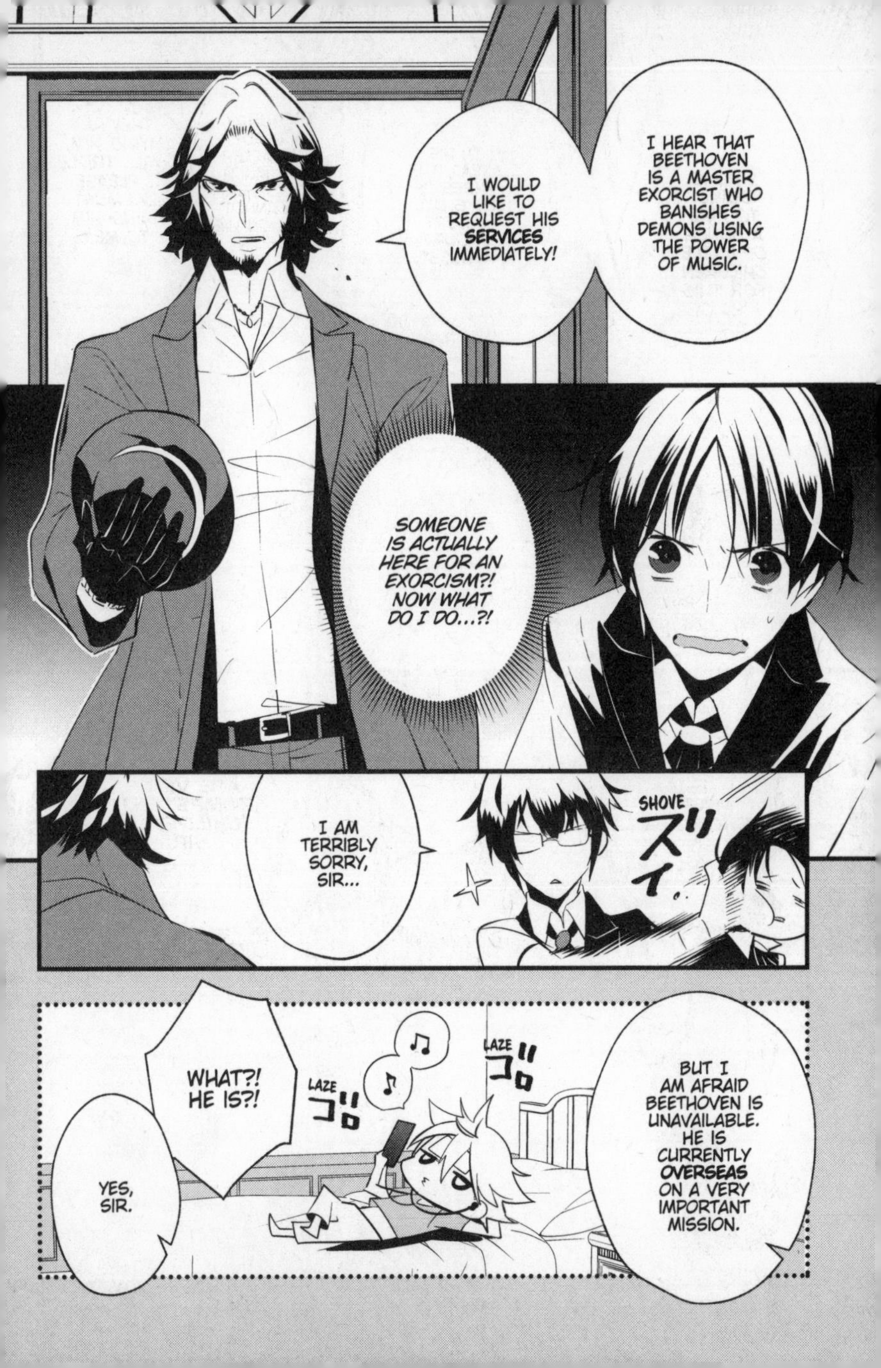
I HEAR THAT BEETHOVEN IS A MASTER EXORCIST WHO BANISHES DEMONS USING THE POWER OF MUSIC.
I WOULD LIKE TO REQUEST HIS SERVICES IMMEDIATELY!
SOMEONE IS ACTUALLY HERE FOR AN EXORCISM?! NOW WHAT DO I DO...?!
SHOVE
ズリイ
I AM TERRIBLY SORRY, SIR...
BUT I AM AFRAID BEETHOVEN IS UNAVAILABLE. HE IS CURRENTLY OVERSEAS ON A VERY IMPORTANT MISSION.
LAZE
ゴロ
LAZE
ゴロ
WHAT?! HE IS?!
YES, SIR.

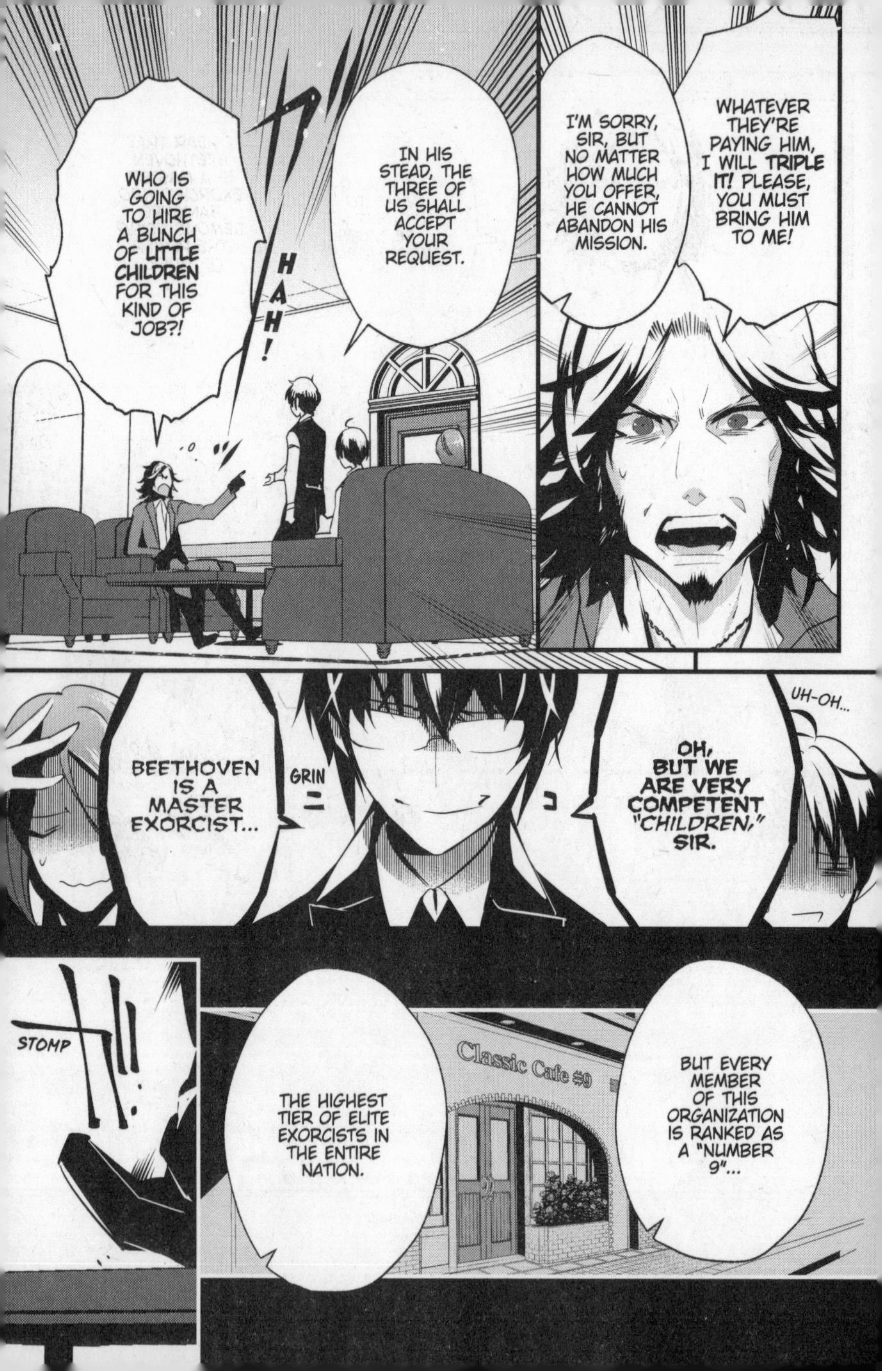
WHATEVER THEY'RE PAYING HIM, I WILL TRIPLE IT! PLEASE, YOU MUST BRING HIM TO ME!
I'M SORRY, SIR, BUT NO MATTER HOW MUCH YOU OFFER, HE CANNOT ABANDON HIS MISSION.
IN HIS STEAD, THE THREE OF US SHALL ACCEPT YOUR REQUEST.
HAH!
WHO IS GOING TO HIRE A BUNCH OF LITTLE CHILDREN FOR THIS KIND OF JOB?!
UH-OH...
OH, BUT WE ARE VERY COMPETENT "CHILDREN," SIR.
GRIN
BEETHOVEN IS A MASTER EXORCIST...
BUT EVERY MEMBER OF THIS ORGANIZATION IS RANKED AS A "NUMBER 9"...
Classic Cafe #9
THE HIGHEST TIER OF ELITE EXORCISTS IN THE ENTIRE NATION.
STOMP

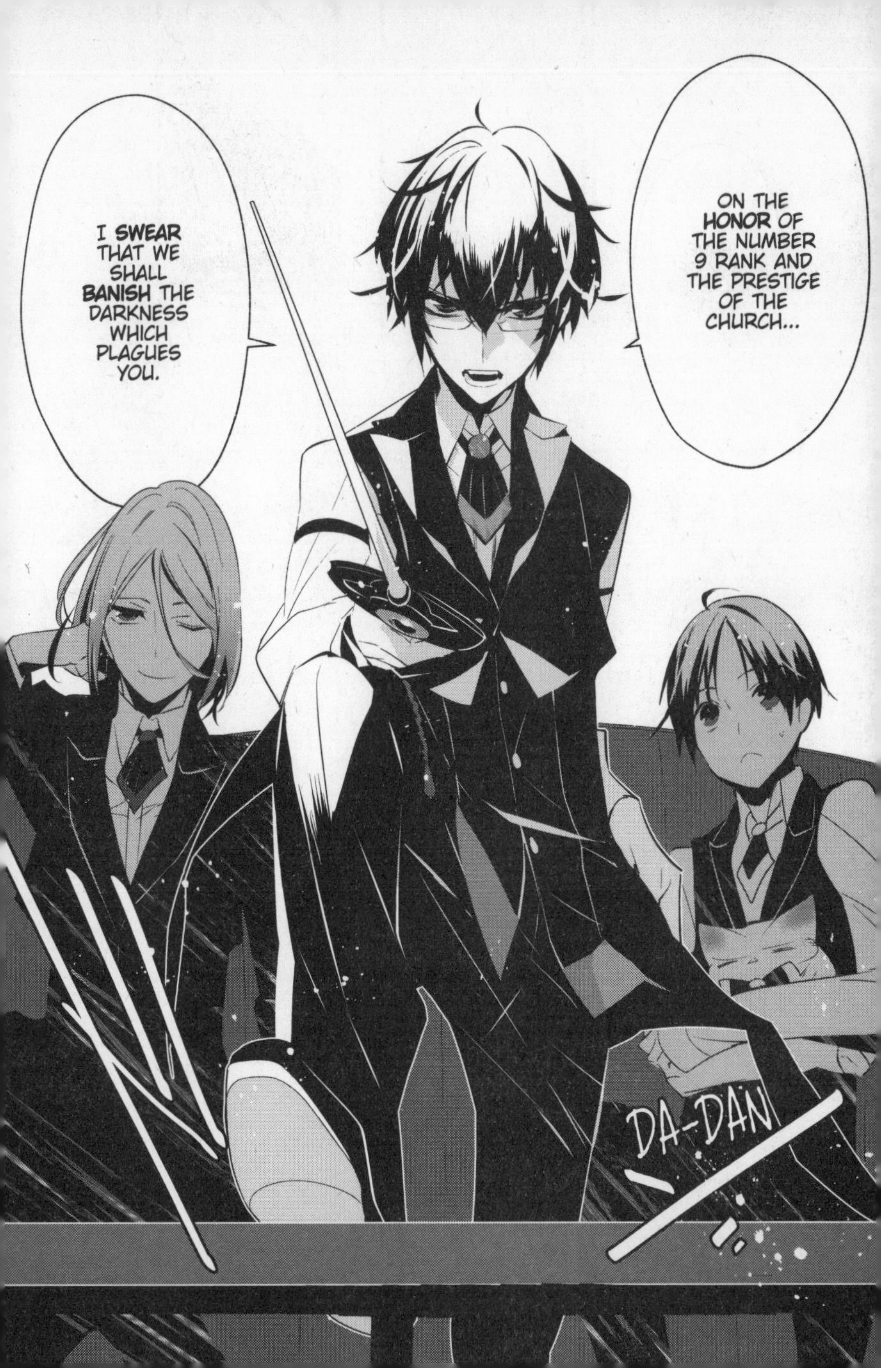
ON THE HONOR OF THE NUMBER 9 RANK AND THE PRESTIGE OF THE CHURCH...
I SWEAR THAT WE SHALL BANISH THE DARKNESS WHICH PLAGUES YOU.
DA-DAN

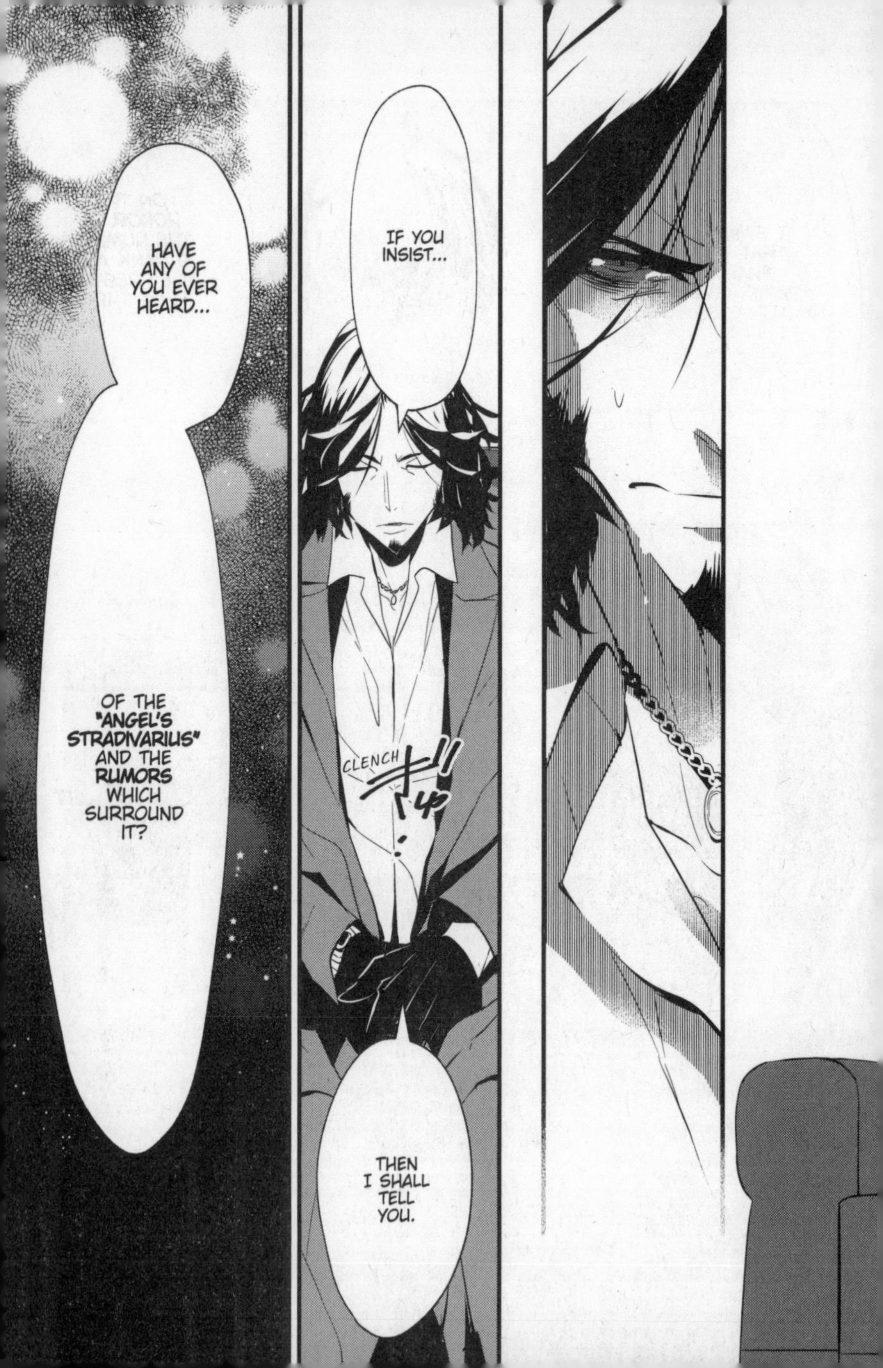
IF YOU INSIST...
CLENCH
THEN I SHALL TELL YOU.
HAVE ANY OF YOU EVER HEARD...
OF THE "ANGEL'S STRADIVARIUS" AND THE RUMORS WHICH SURROUND IT?

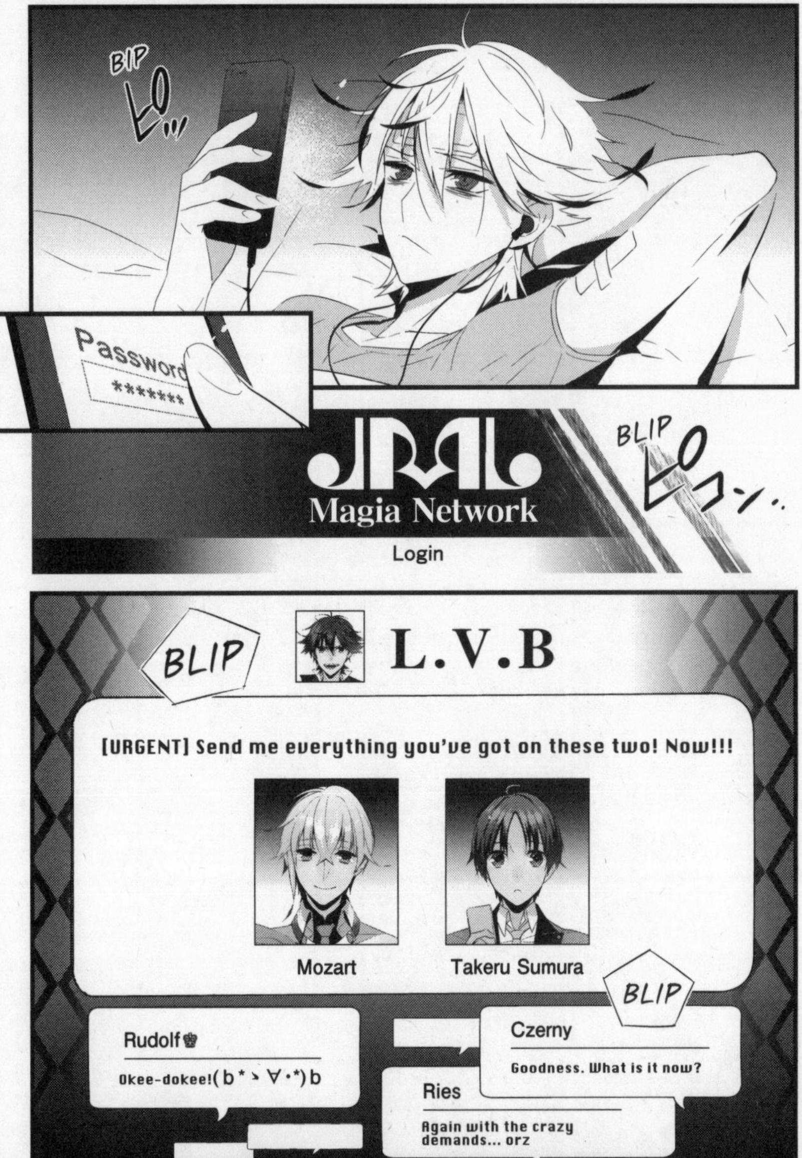

BIP
Password
****
BLIP
Magia Network
Login
L.V.B
BLIP
[URGENT] Send me everything you've got on these two! Now!!!
Mozart
Takeru Sumura
BLIP
Czerny
Goodness. What is it now?
Rudolf♛
Okee-dokee!(b * ゝ ∀ ･*) b
Ries
Again with the crazy demands... orz

Magia the Ninth

#8. Angela

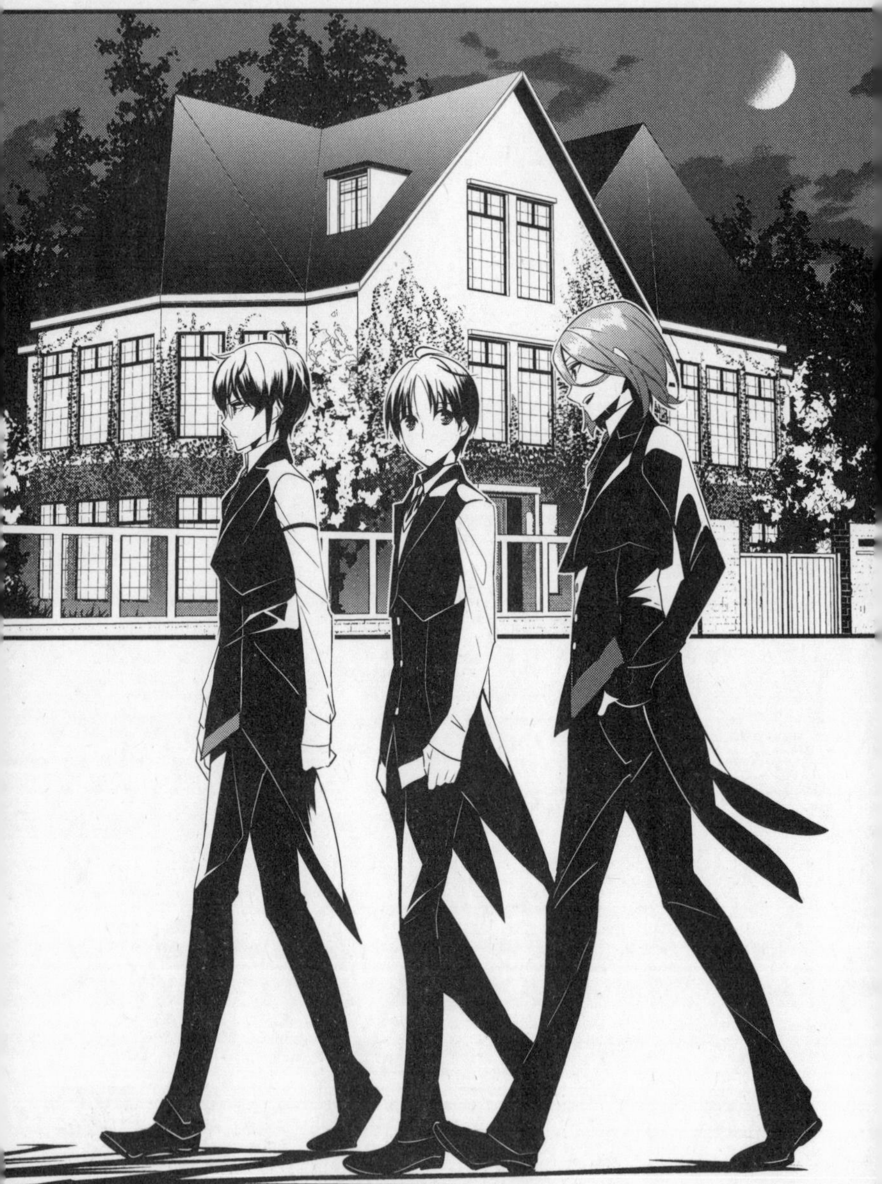

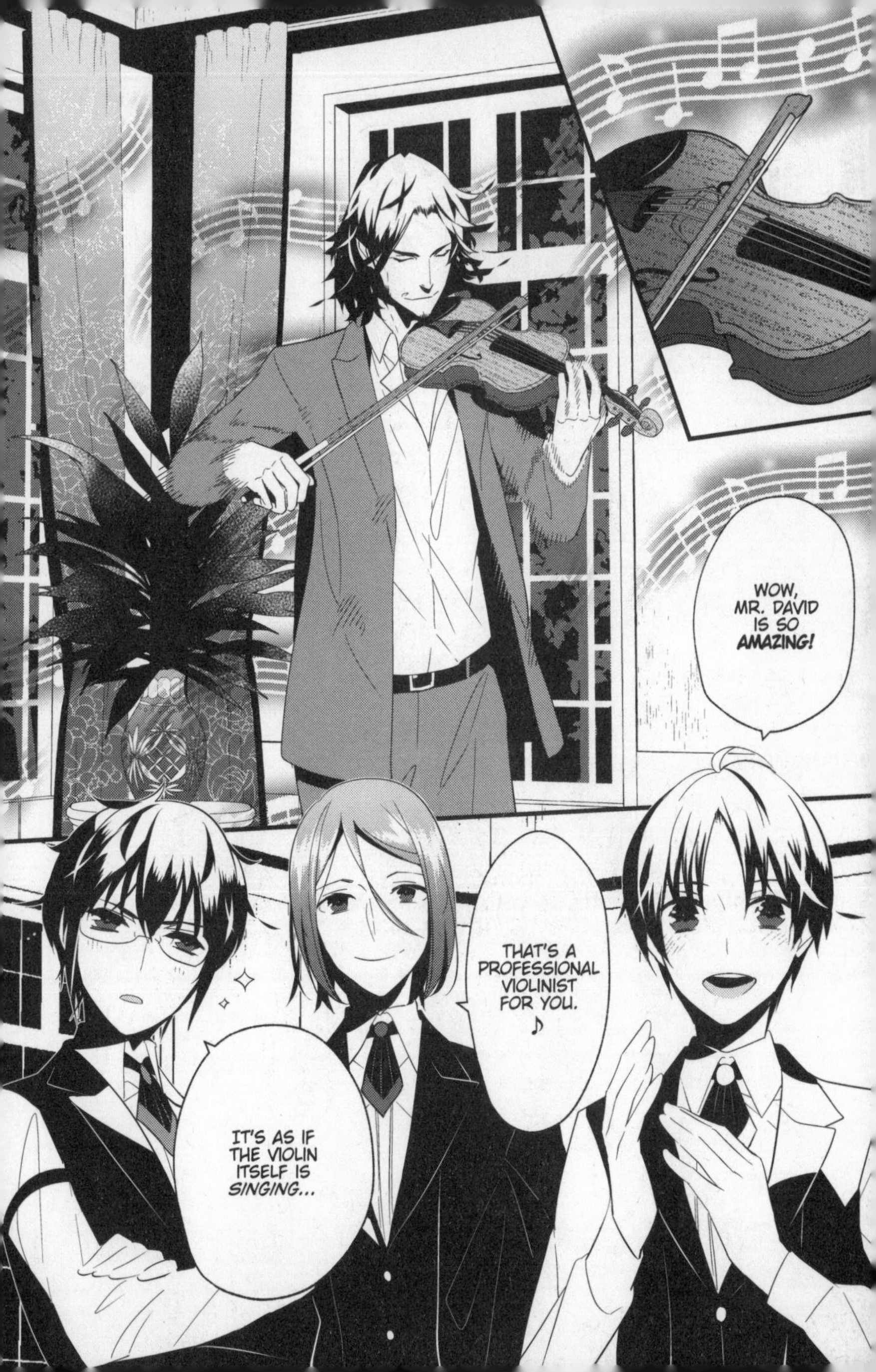
WOW, MR. DAVID IS SO AMAZING!
THAT'S A PROFESSIONAL VIOLINIST FOR YOU. ♪
IT'S AS IF THE VIOLIN ITSELF IS SINGING...

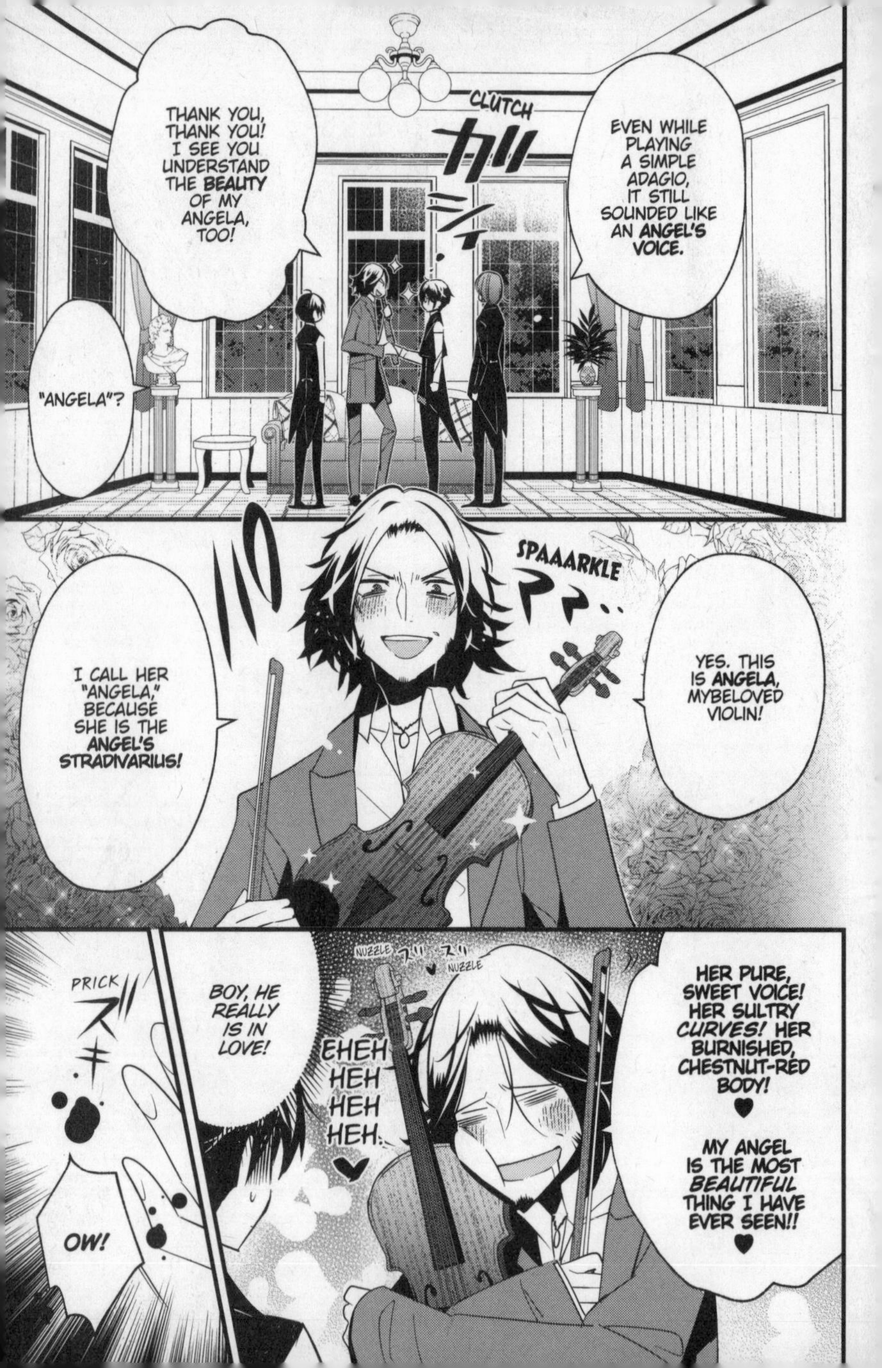

EVEN WHILE PLAYING A SIMPLE ADAGIO, IT STILL SOUNDED LIKE AN ANGEL'S VOICE.
CLUTCH
THANK YOU, THANK YOU! I SEE YOU UNDERSTAND THE BEAUTY OF MY ANGELA, TOO!
"ANGELA"?
SPAAARKLE
YES. THIS IS ANGELA, MYBELOVED VIOLIN!
I CALL HER "ANGELA," BECAUSE SHE IS THE ANGEL'S STRADIVARIUS!
HER PURE, SWEET VOICE! HER SULTRY CURVES! HER BURNISHED, CHESTNUT-RED BODY!
MY ANGEL IS THE MOST BEAUTIFUL THING I HAVE EVER SEEN!!
NUZZLE
NUZZLE
EHEH HEH HEH HEH
BOY, HE REALLY IS IN LOVE!
PRICK
OW!

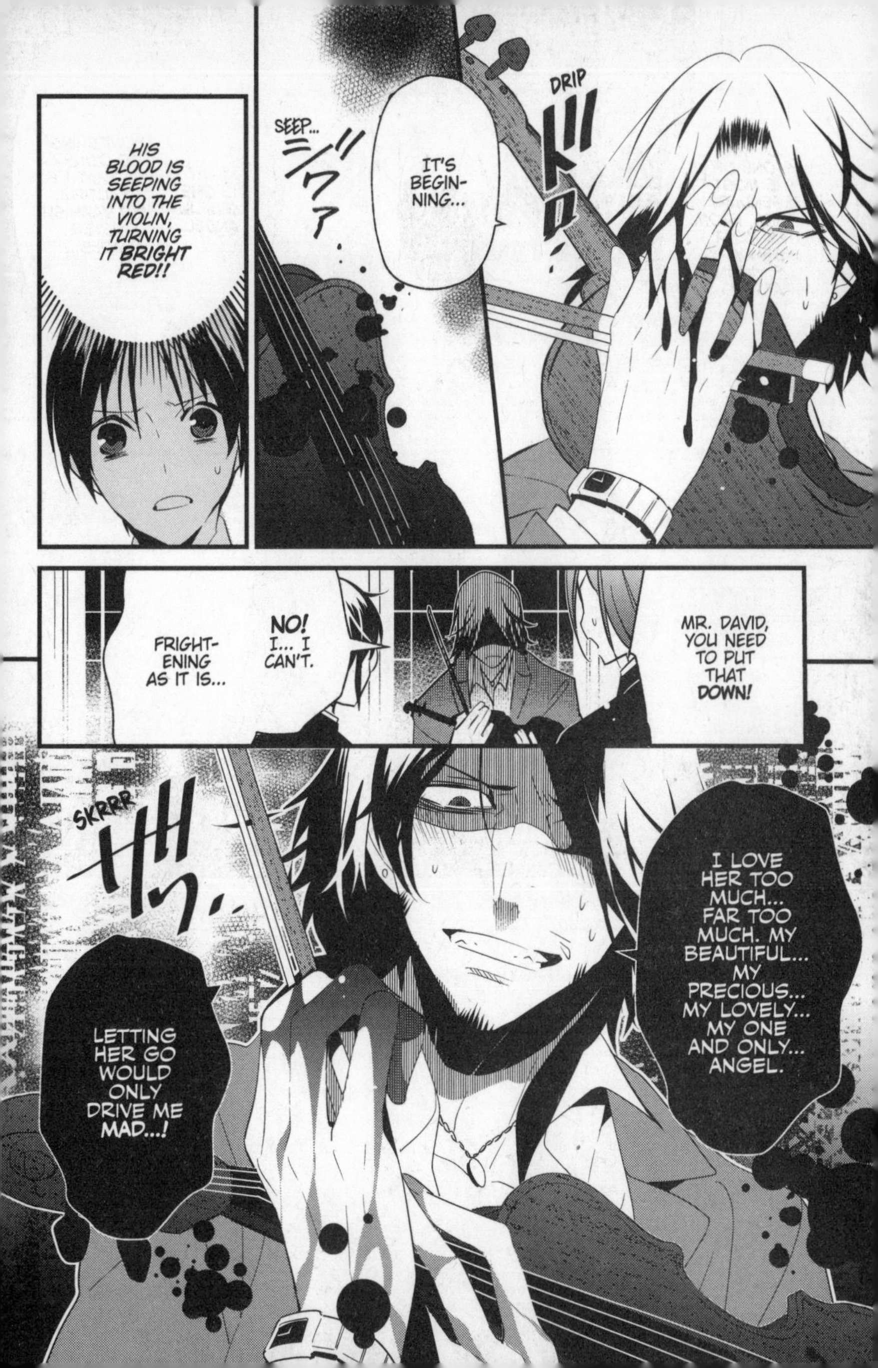
DRIP
ドロ
IT'S BEGIN- NING...
SEEP...
ジワァ
HIS BLOOD IS SEEPING INTO THE VIOLIN, TURNING IT BRIGHT RED!!
MR. DAVID, YOU NEED TO PUT THAT DOWN!
NO! I... I CAN'T.
FRIGHT- ENING AS IT IS...
I LOVE HER TOO MUCH... FAR TOO MUCH. MY BEAUTIFUL... MY PRECIOUS... MY LOVELY... MY ONE AND ONLY... ANGEL.
SKRRR
ザリッ
LETTING HER GO WOULD ONLY DRIVE ME MAD...!

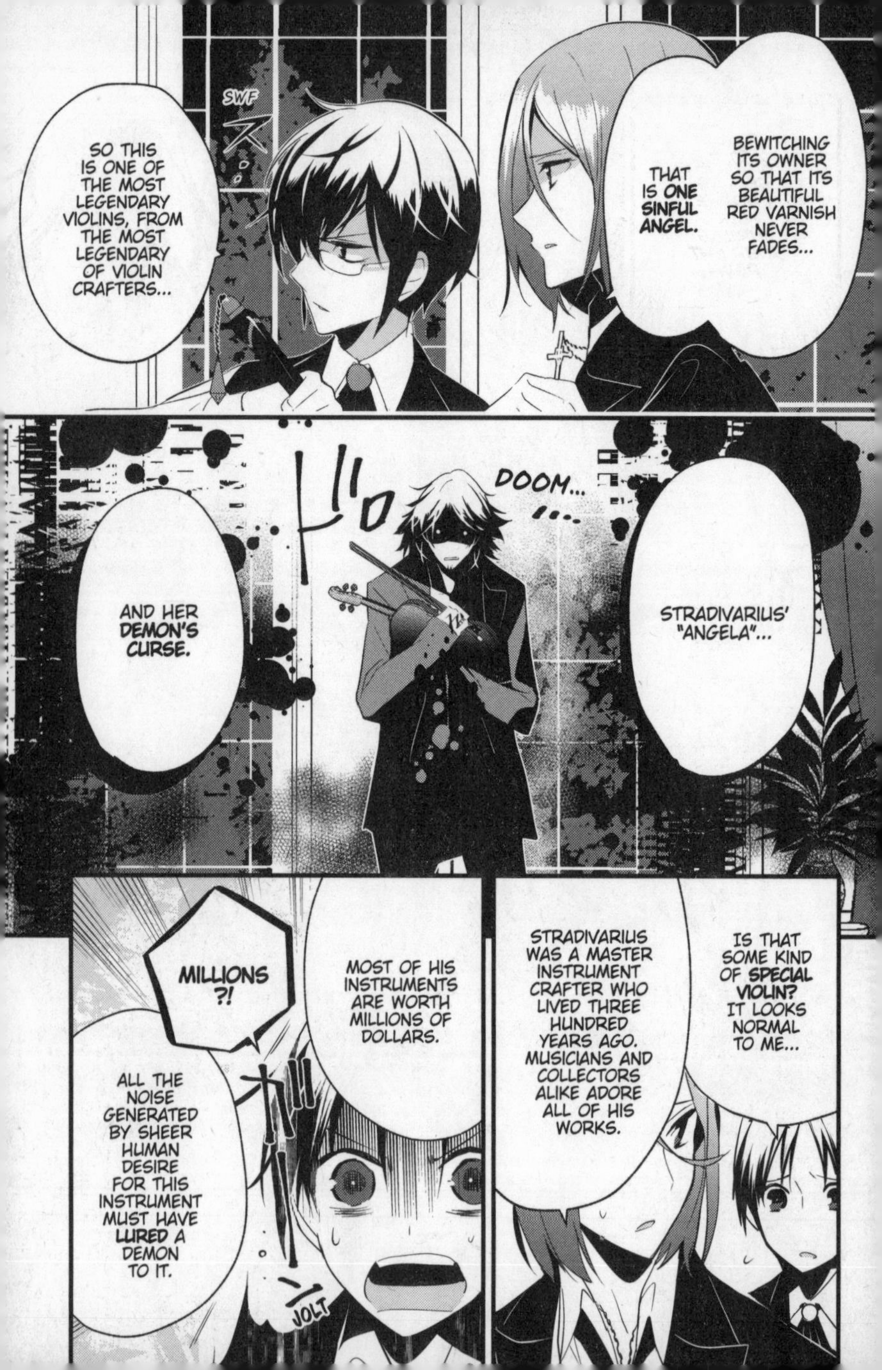
BEWITCHING ITS OWNER SO THAT ITS BEAUTIFUL RED VARNISH NEVER FADES...
THAT IS ONE SINFUL ANGEL.
SWF
SO THIS IS ONE OF THE MOST LEGENDARY VIOLINS, FROM THE MOST LEGENDARY OF VIOLIN CRAFTERS...
STRADIVARIUS' "ANGELA"...
DOOM...
AND HER DEMON'S CURSE.
IS THAT SOME KIND OF SPECIAL VIOLIN? IT LOOKS NORMAL TO ME...
STRADIVARIUS WAS A MASTER INSTRUMENT CRAFTER WHO LIVED THREE HUNDRED YEARS AGO. MUSICIANS AND COLLECTORS ALIKE ADORE ALL OF HIS WORKS.
MOST OF HIS INSTRUMENTS ARE WORTH MILLIONS OF DOLLARS.
MILLIONS ?!
JOLT
ALL THE NOISE GENERATED BY SHEER HUMAN DESIRE FOR THIS INSTRUMENT MUST HAVE LURED A DEMON TO IT.

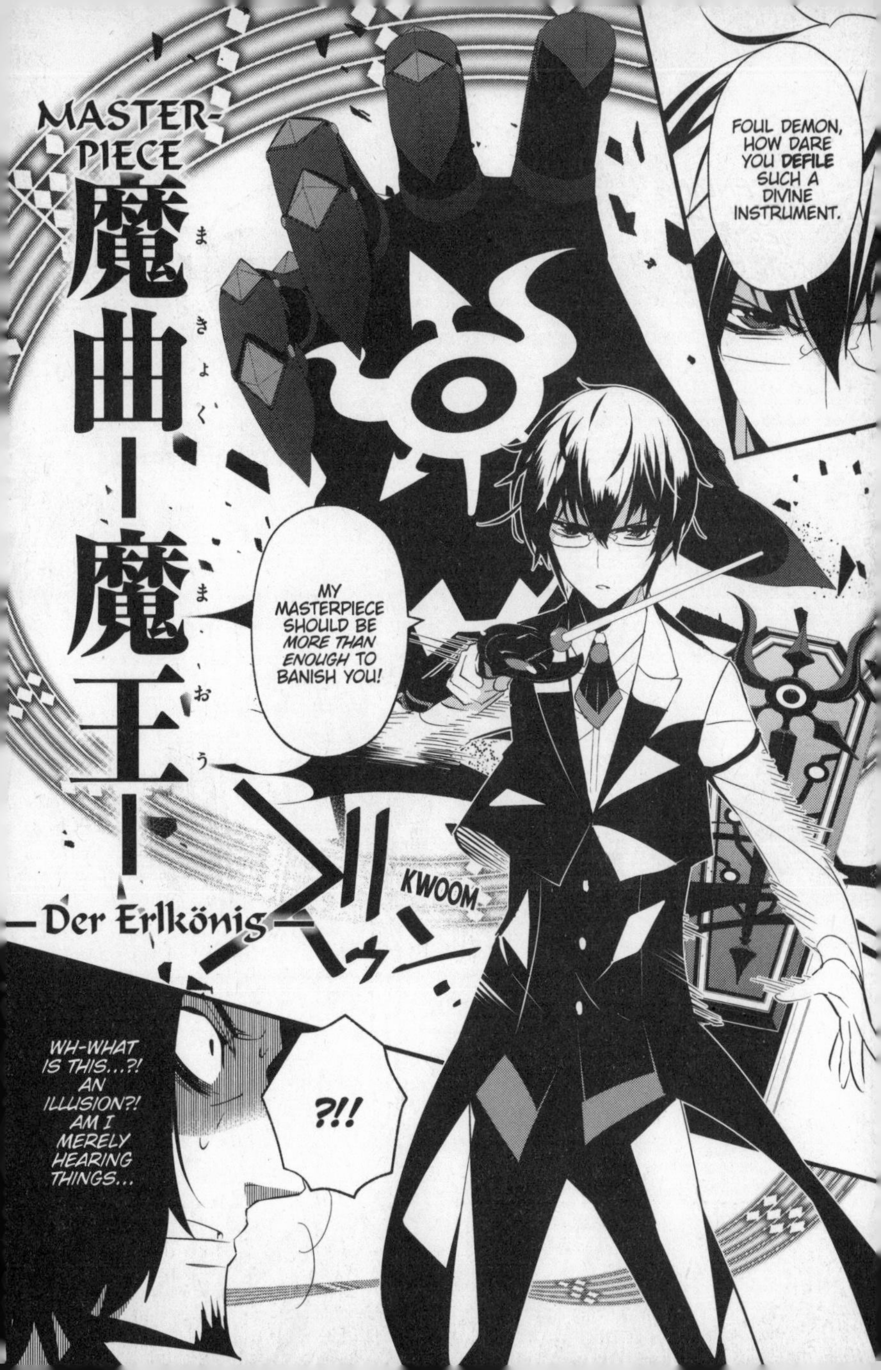
FOUL DEMON, HOW DARE YOU DEFILE SUCH A DIVINE INSTRUMENT.
MASTER-PIECE
魔曲ー魔王ー
まきょく まおう
—Der Erlkönig—
MY MASTERPIECE SHOULD BE MORE THAN ENOUGH TO BANISH YOU!
KWOOM
?!!
WH-WHAT IS THIS...?! AN ILLUSION?! AM I MERELY HEARING THINGS...

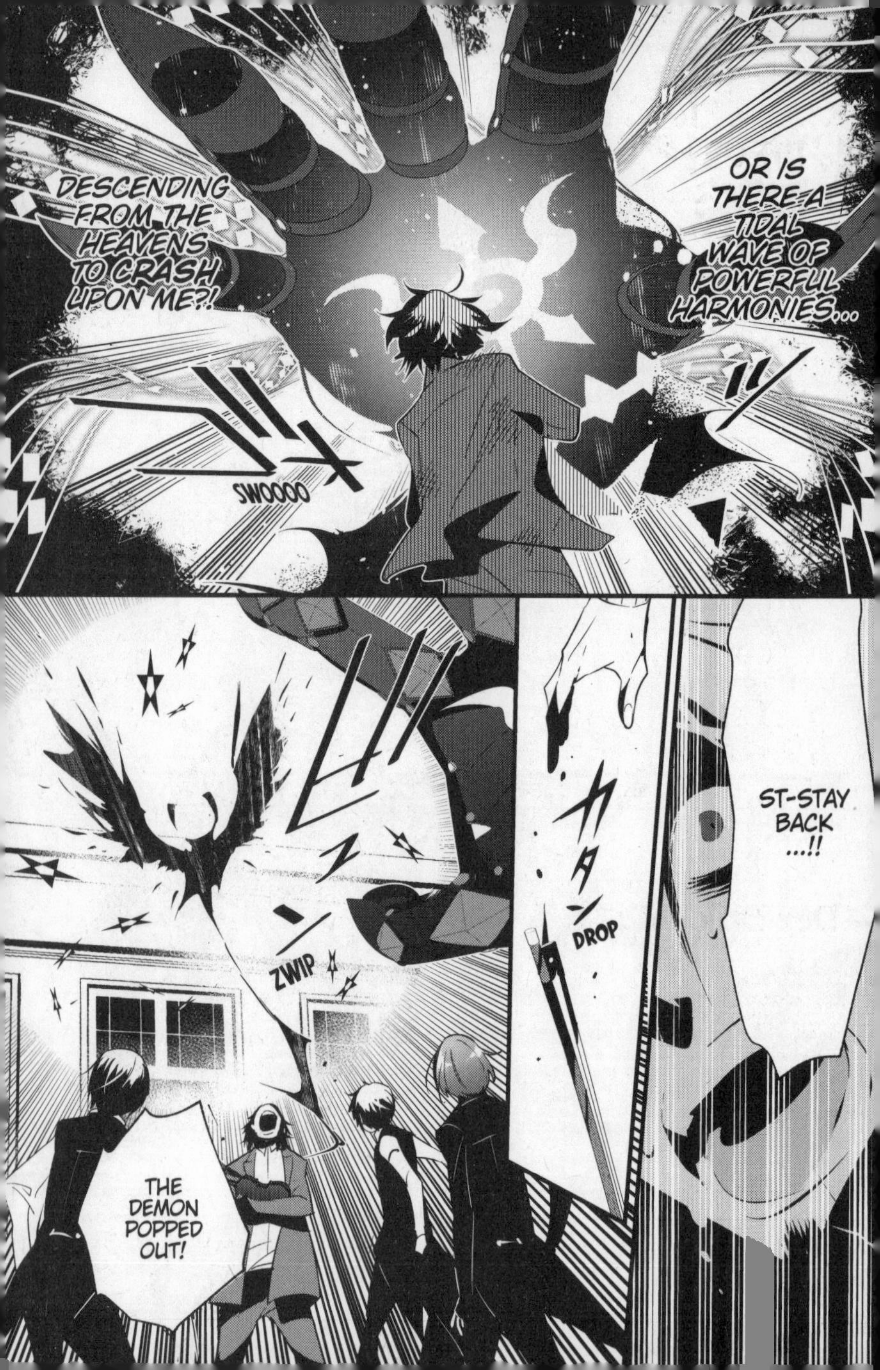
OR IS THERE A TIDAL WAVE OF POWERFUL HARMONIES...
DESCENDING FROM THE HEAVENS TO CRASH UPON ME?!
SWOOOO
ST-STAY BACK ...!!
DROP
ZWIP
THE DEMON POPPED OUT!

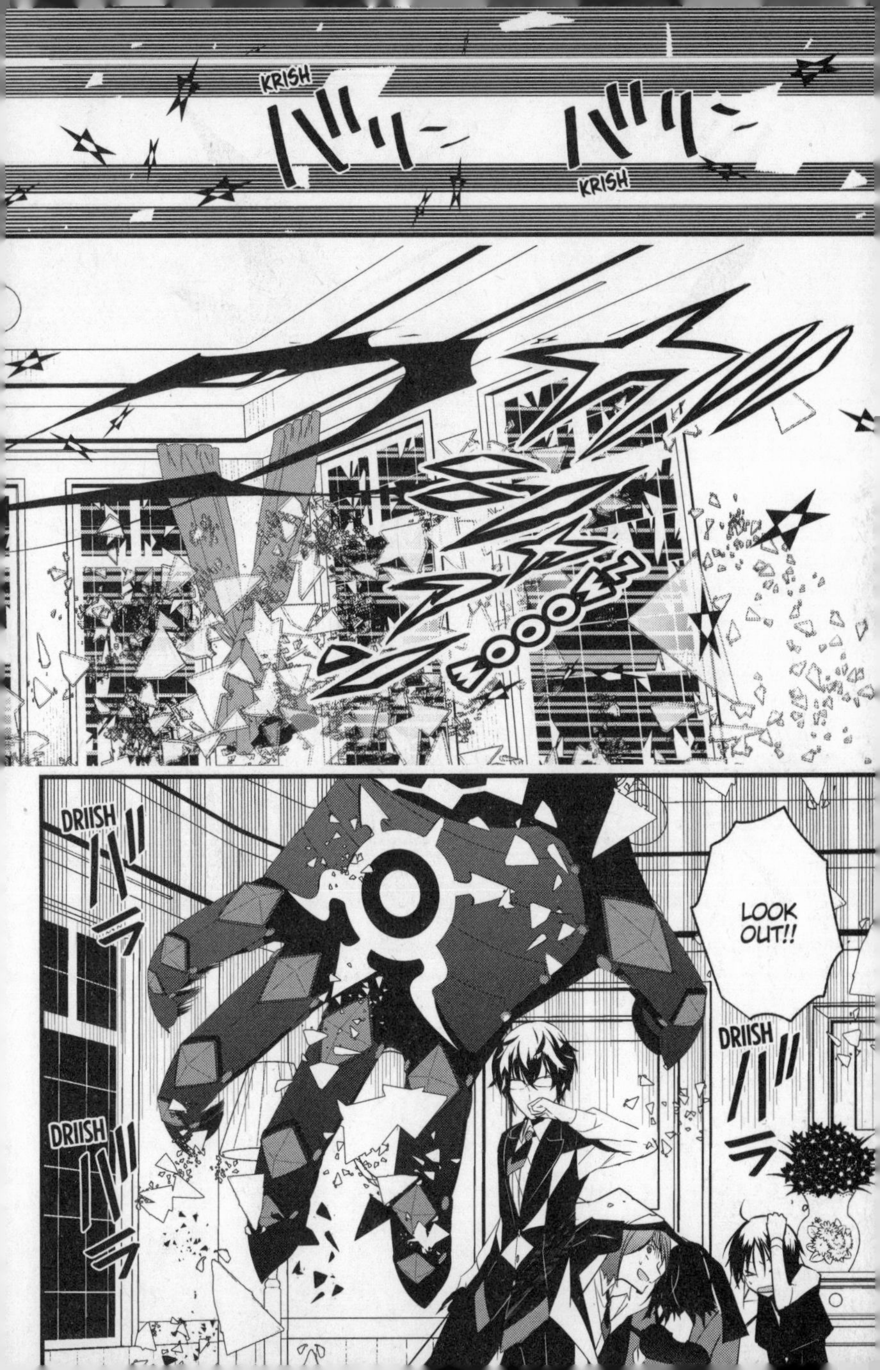
バリーン
KRISH
バリーン
KRISH
WOOOM!!
LOOK OUT!!
DRIISH
バラ
DRIISH
バラ
DRIISH
バラ

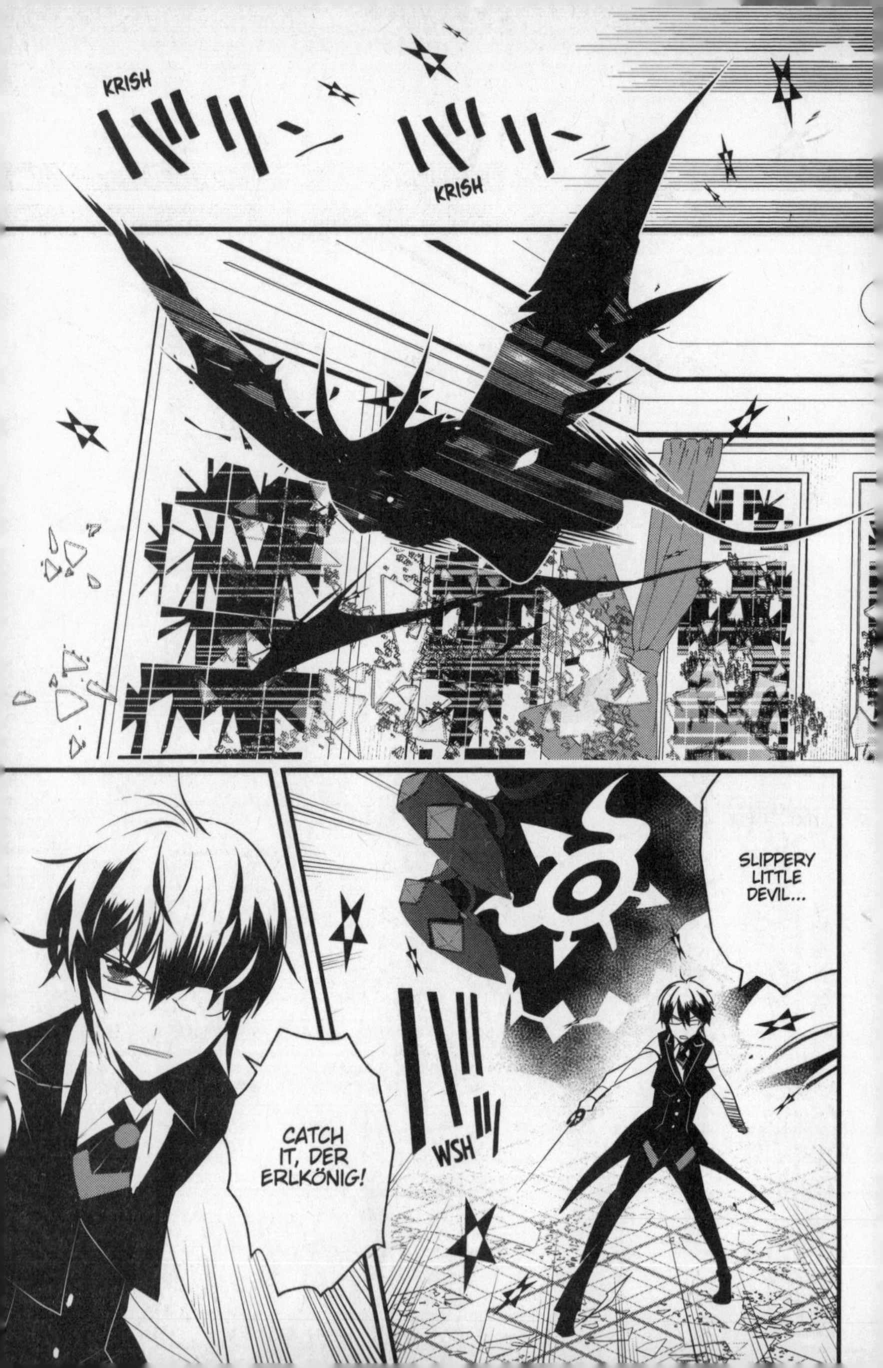
KRISH
KRISH
SLIPPERY LITTLE DEVIL...
WSH
CATCH IT, DER ERLKÖNIG!

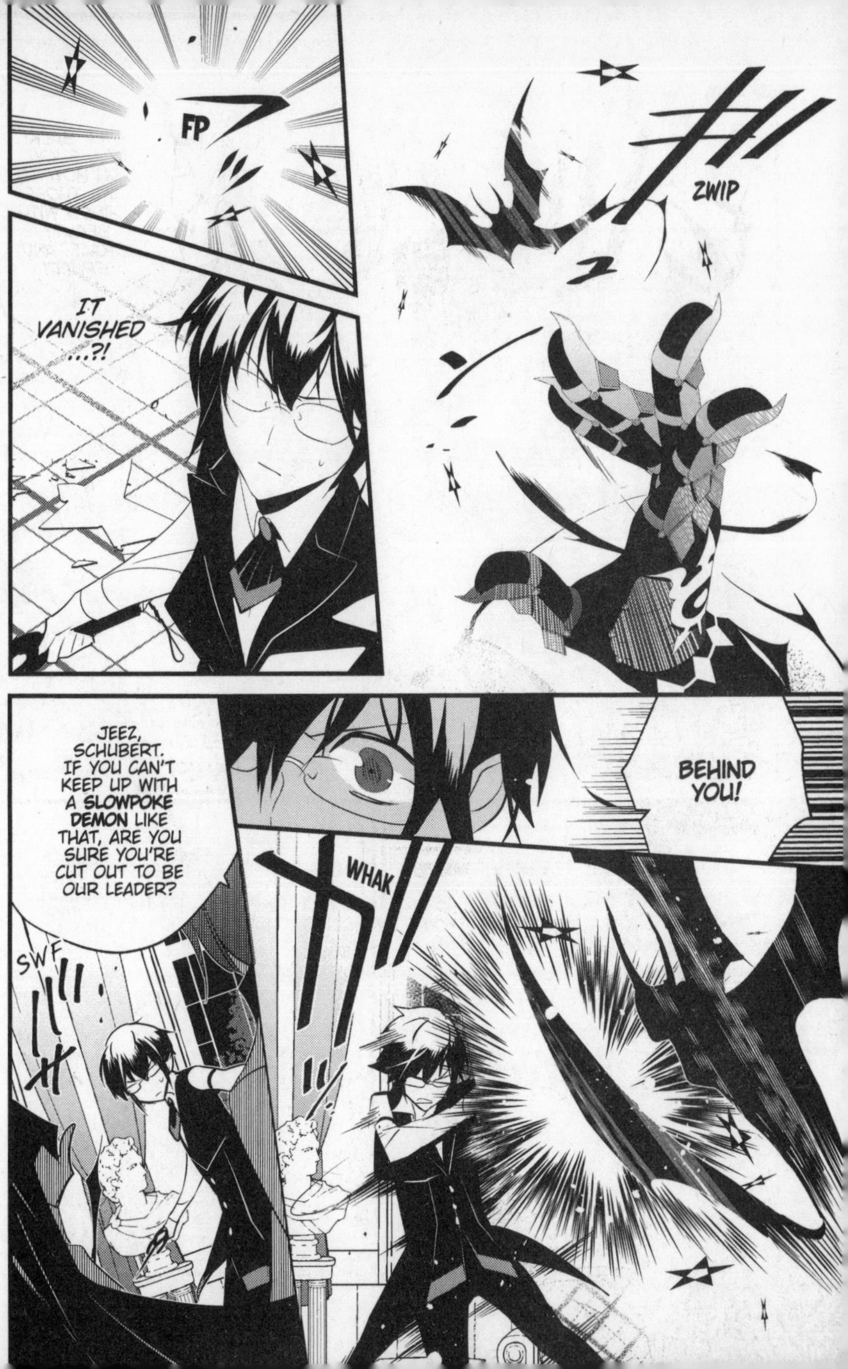
ZWIP
FP
IT VANISHED ...?!
BEHIND YOU!
WHAK
JEEZ, SCHUBERT. IF YOU CAN'T KEEP UP WITH A **SLOWPOKE DEMON** LIKE THAT, ARE YOU SURE YOU'RE CUT OUT TO BE OUR LEADER?
SWF

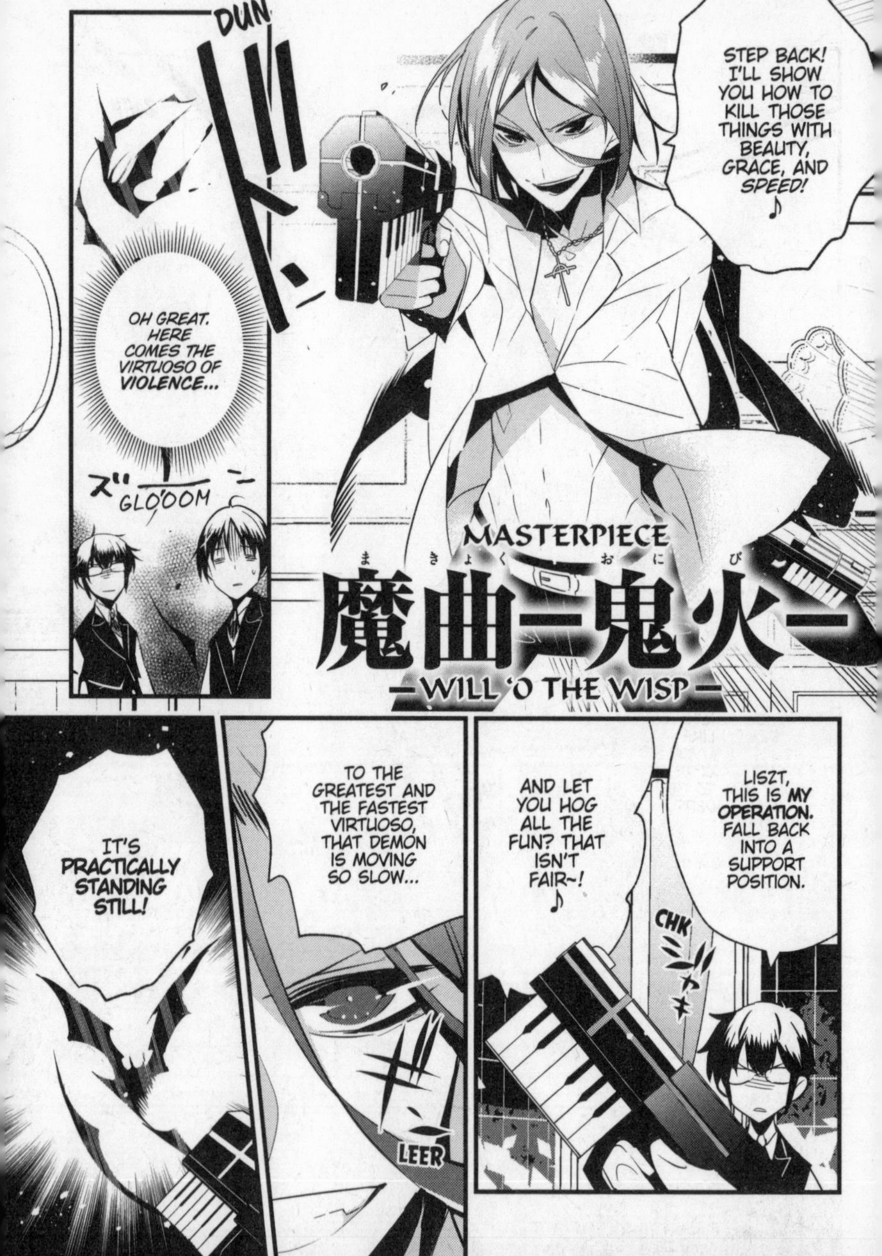
STEP BACK! I'LL SHOW YOU HOW TO KILL THOSE THINGS WITH BEAUTY, GRACE, AND SPEED! ♪
MASTERPIECE
まきょくおにび
魔曲ニ鬼火
—WILL 'O THE WISP—
DUN
ドン
OH GREAT. HERE COMES THE VIRTUOSO OF VIOLENCE...
ズーン
GLOOOM
LISZT, THIS IS MY OPERATION. FALL BACK INTO A SUPPORT POSITION.
AND LET YOU HOG ALL THE FUN? THAT ISN'T FAIR~! ♪
CHK
ジャキ
TO THE GREATEST AND THE FASTEST VIRTUOSO, THAT DEMON IS MOVING SO SLOW...
LEER
IT'S PRACTICALLY STANDING STILL!

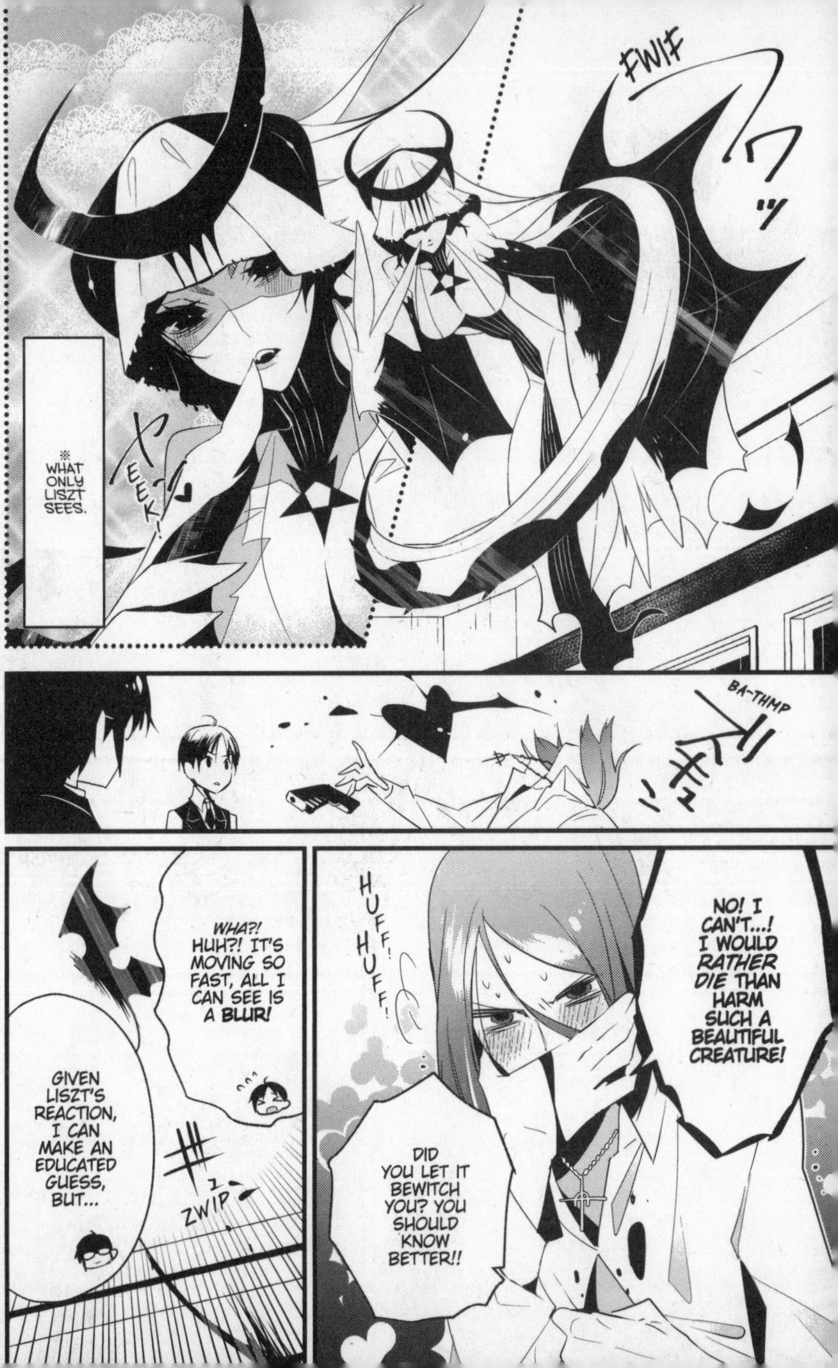
FWIF
EEK!
※ WHAT ONLY LISZT SEES.
BA-THMP
NO! I CAN'T...! I WOULD *RATHER DIE* THAN HARM SUCH A BEAUTIFUL CREATURE!
HUFF! HUFF!
DID YOU LET IT BEWITCH YOU? YOU SHOULD KNOW BETTER!!
WHA?! HUH?! IT'S MOVING SO FAST, ALL I CAN SEE IS A **BLUR**!
GIVEN LISZT'S REACTION, I CAN MAKE AN EDUCATED GUESS, BUT...
ZWIP

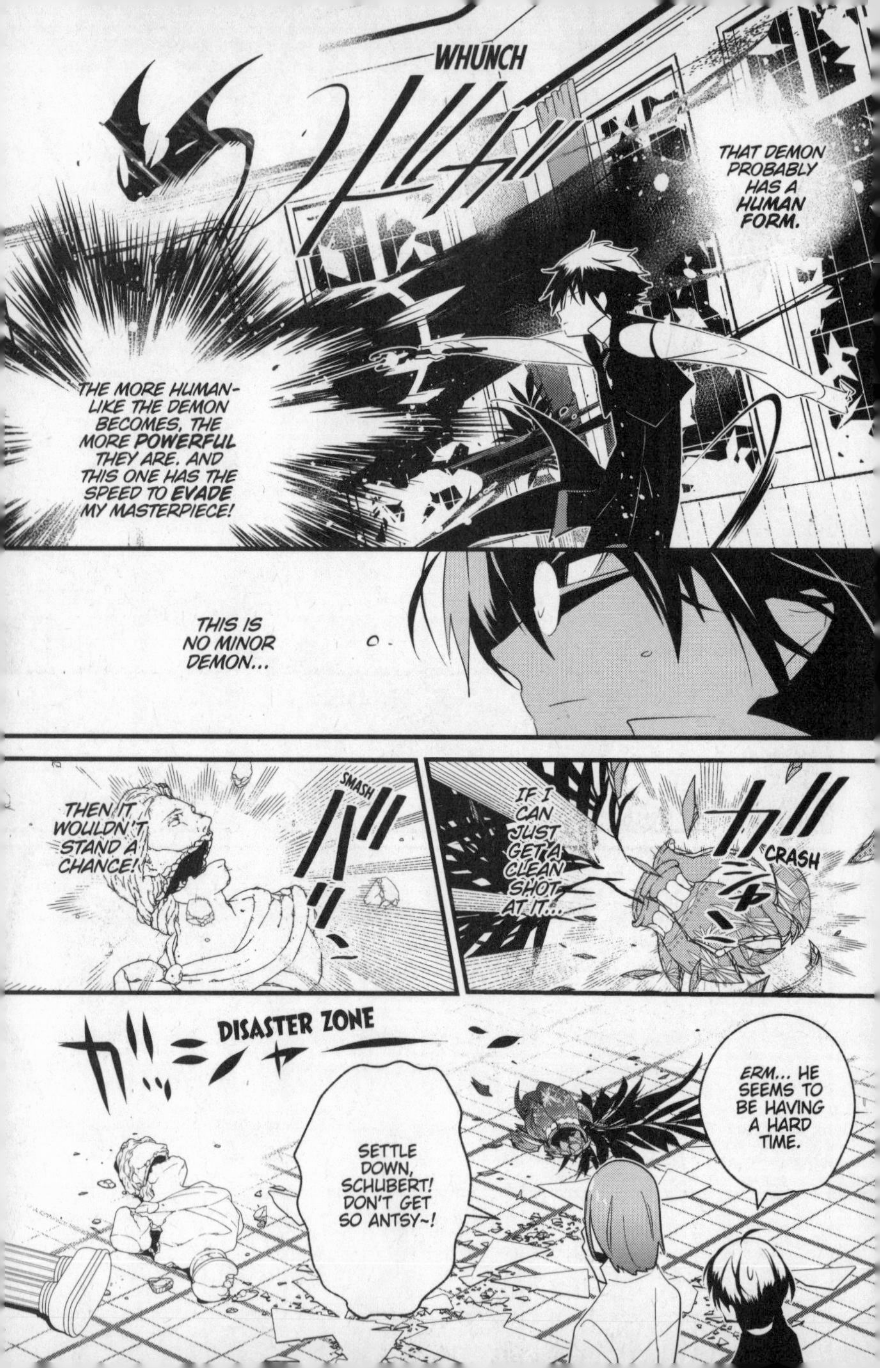
WHUNCH
THAT DEMON PROBABLY HAS A HUMAN FORM.
THE MORE HUMAN-LIKE THE DEMON BECOMES, THE MORE POWERFUL THEY ARE. AND THIS ONE HAS THE SPEED TO EVADE MY MASTERPIECE!
THIS IS NO MINOR DEMON...
IF I CAN JUST GET A CLEAN SHOT AT IT...
CRASH
SMASH
THEN IT WOULDN'T STAND A CHANCE!
ERM... HE SEEMS TO BE HAVING A HARD TIME.
SETTLE DOWN, SCHUBERT! DON'T GET SO ANTSY~!
DISASTER ZONE

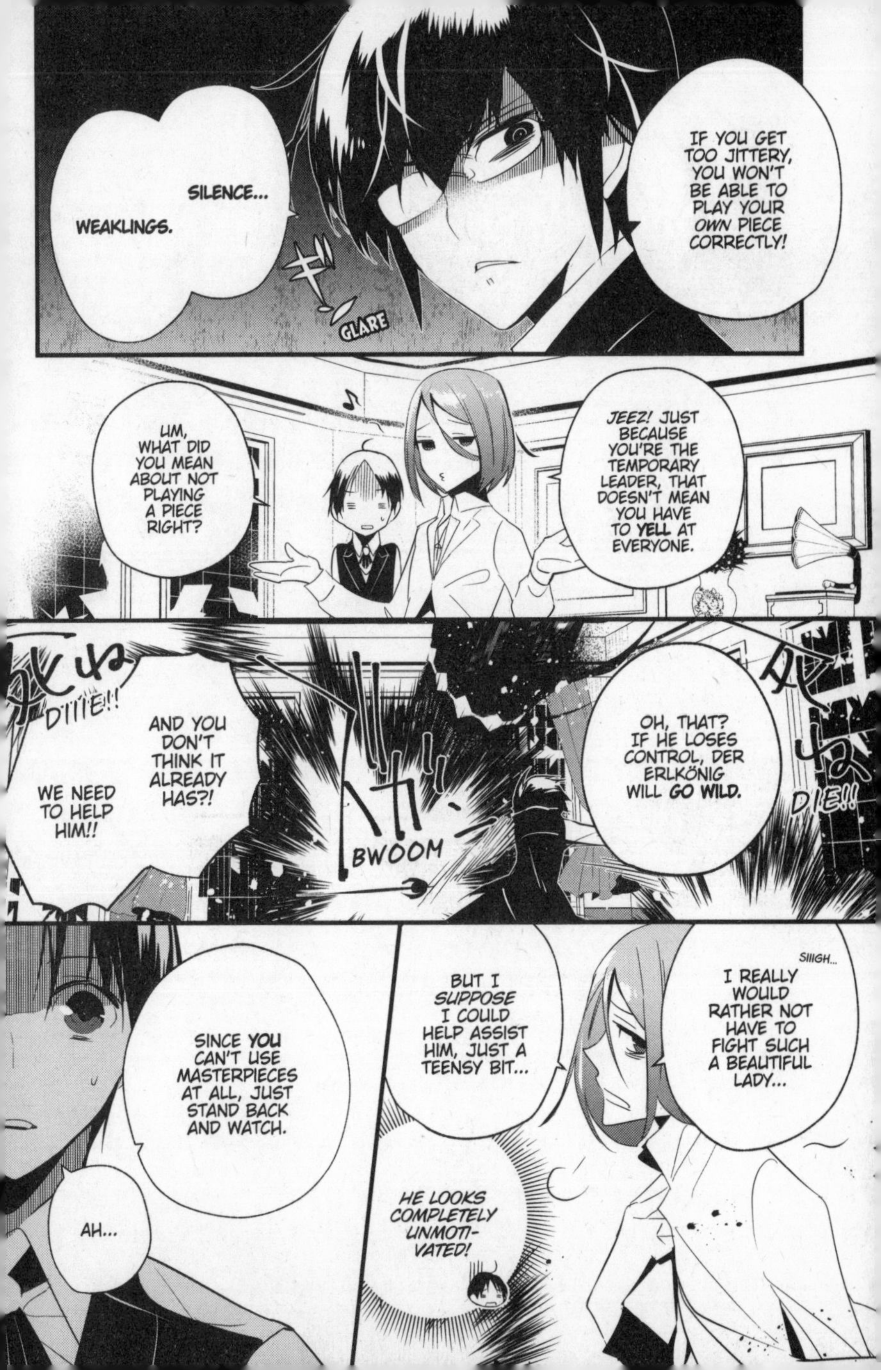
IF YOU GET TOO JITTERY, YOU WON'T BE ABLE TO PLAY YOUR *OWN* PIECE CORRECTLY!
SILENCE...
WEAKLINGS.
GLARE
JEEZ! JUST BECAUSE YOU'RE THE TEMPORARY LEADER, THAT DOESN'T MEAN YOU HAVE TO **YELL** AT EVERYONE.
UM, WHAT DID YOU MEAN ABOUT NOT PLAYING A PIECE RIGHT?
DIE!!
OH, THAT? IF HE LOSES CONTROL, DER ERLKÖNIG WILL **GO WILD.**
BWOOM
AND YOU DON'T THINK IT ALREADY HAS?!
WE NEED TO HELP HIM!!
DIIIE!!
SIIIGH...
I REALLY WOULD RATHER NOT HAVE TO FIGHT SUCH A BEAUTIFUL LADY...
BUT I *SUPPOSE* I COULD HELP ASSIST HIM, JUST A TEENSY BIT...
HE LOOKS COMPLETELY UNMOTI-VATED!
SINCE **YOU** CAN'T USE MASTERPIECES AT ALL, JUST STAND BACK AND WATCH.
AH...

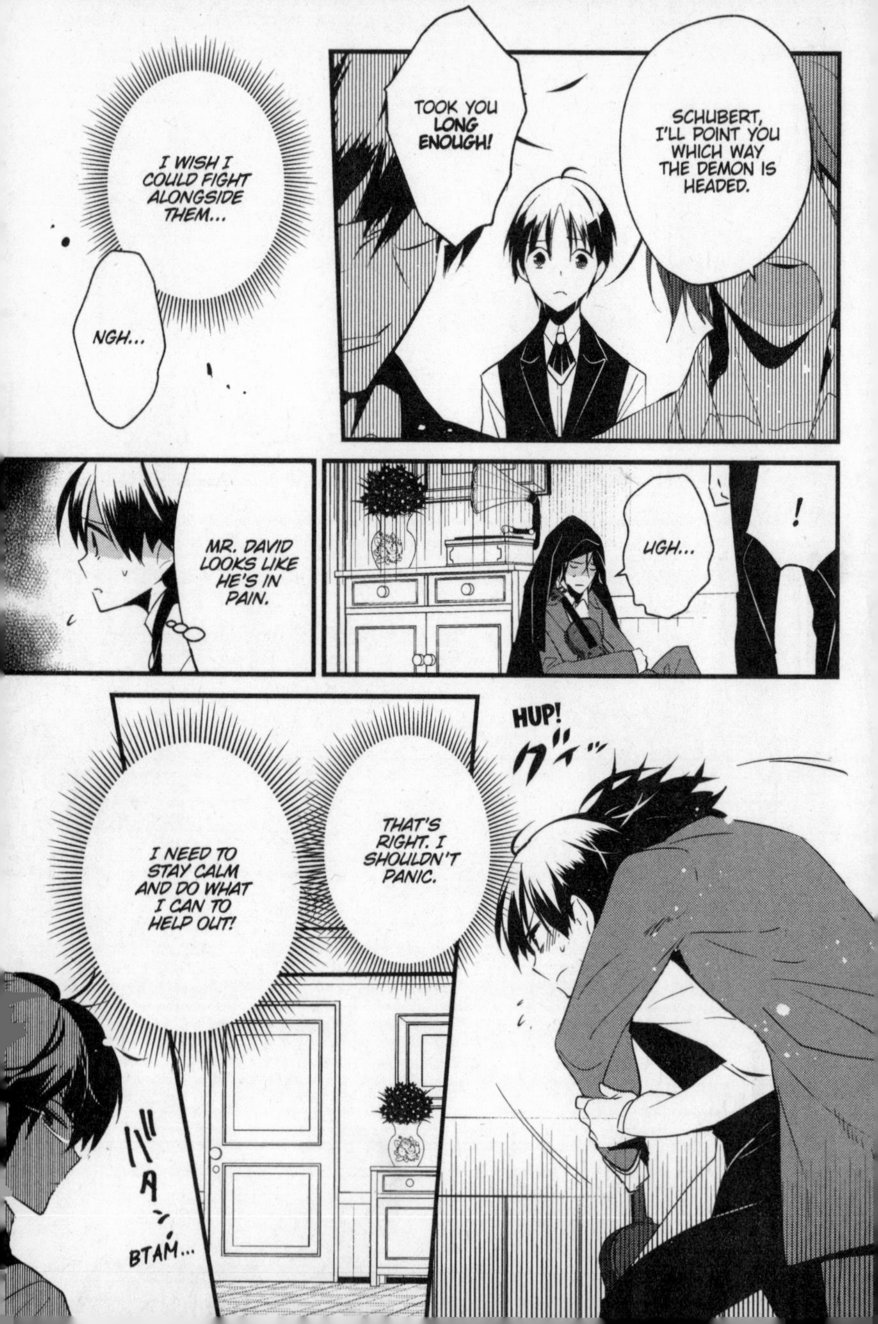
SCHUBERT, I'LL POINT YOU WHICH WAY THE DEMON IS HEADED.
TOOK YOU LONG ENOUGH!
I WISH I COULD FIGHT ALONGSIDE THEM...
NGH...
!
UGH...
MR. DAVID LOOKS LIKE HE'S IN PAIN.
HUP!
THAT'S RIGHT. I SHOULDN'T PANIC.
I NEED TO STAY CALM AND DO WHAT I CAN TO HELP OUT!
BTAM...

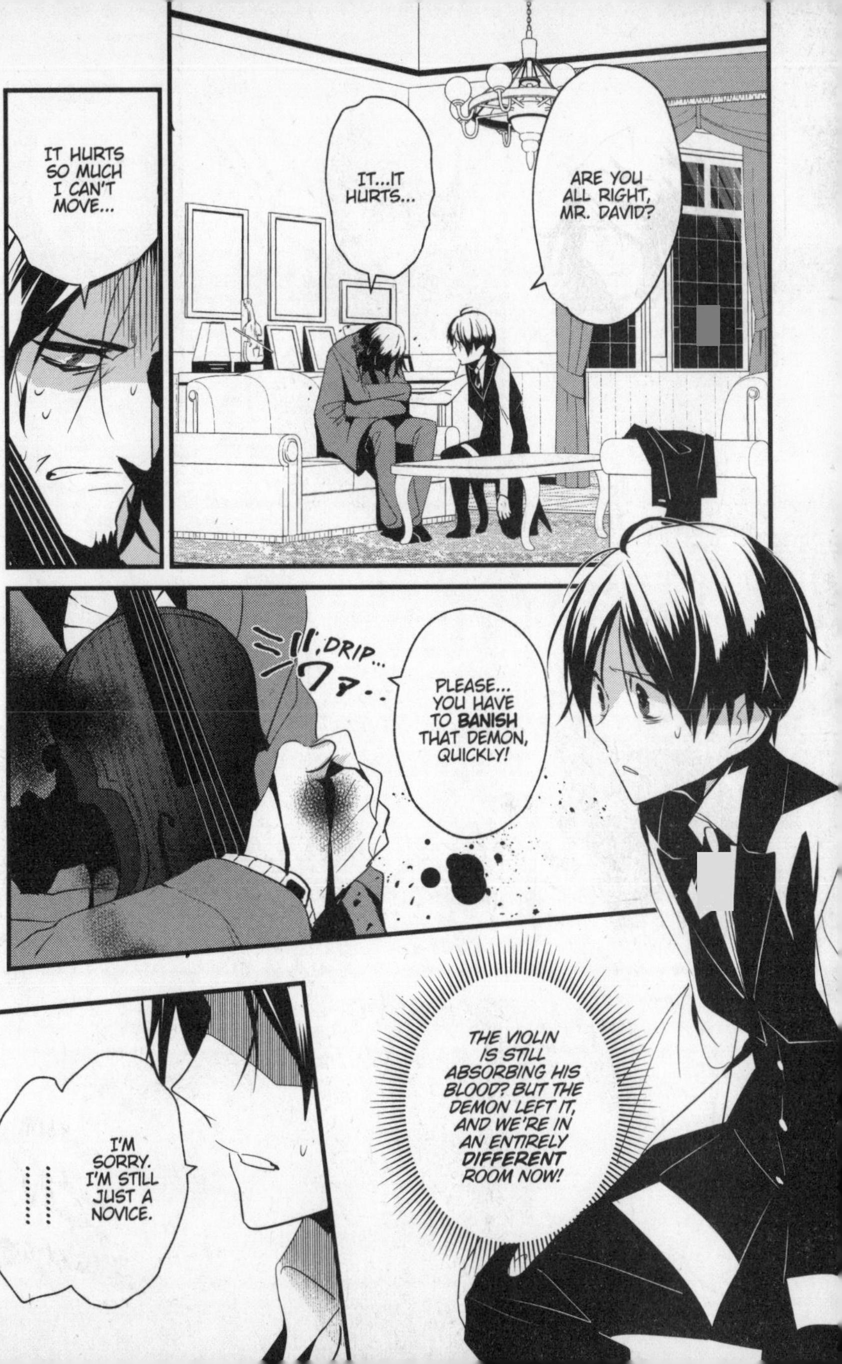
ARE YOU ALL RIGHT, MR. DAVID?
IT...IT HURTS...
IT HURTS SO MUCH I CAN'T MOVE...
DRIP...
PLEASE... YOU HAVE TO **BANISH** THAT DEMON, QUICKLY!
THE VIOLIN IS STILL ABSORBING HIS BLOOD? BUT THE DEMON LEFT IT, AND WE'RE IN AN ENTIRELY **DIFFERENT** ROOM NOW!
......
I'M SORRY. I'M STILL JUST A NOVICE.

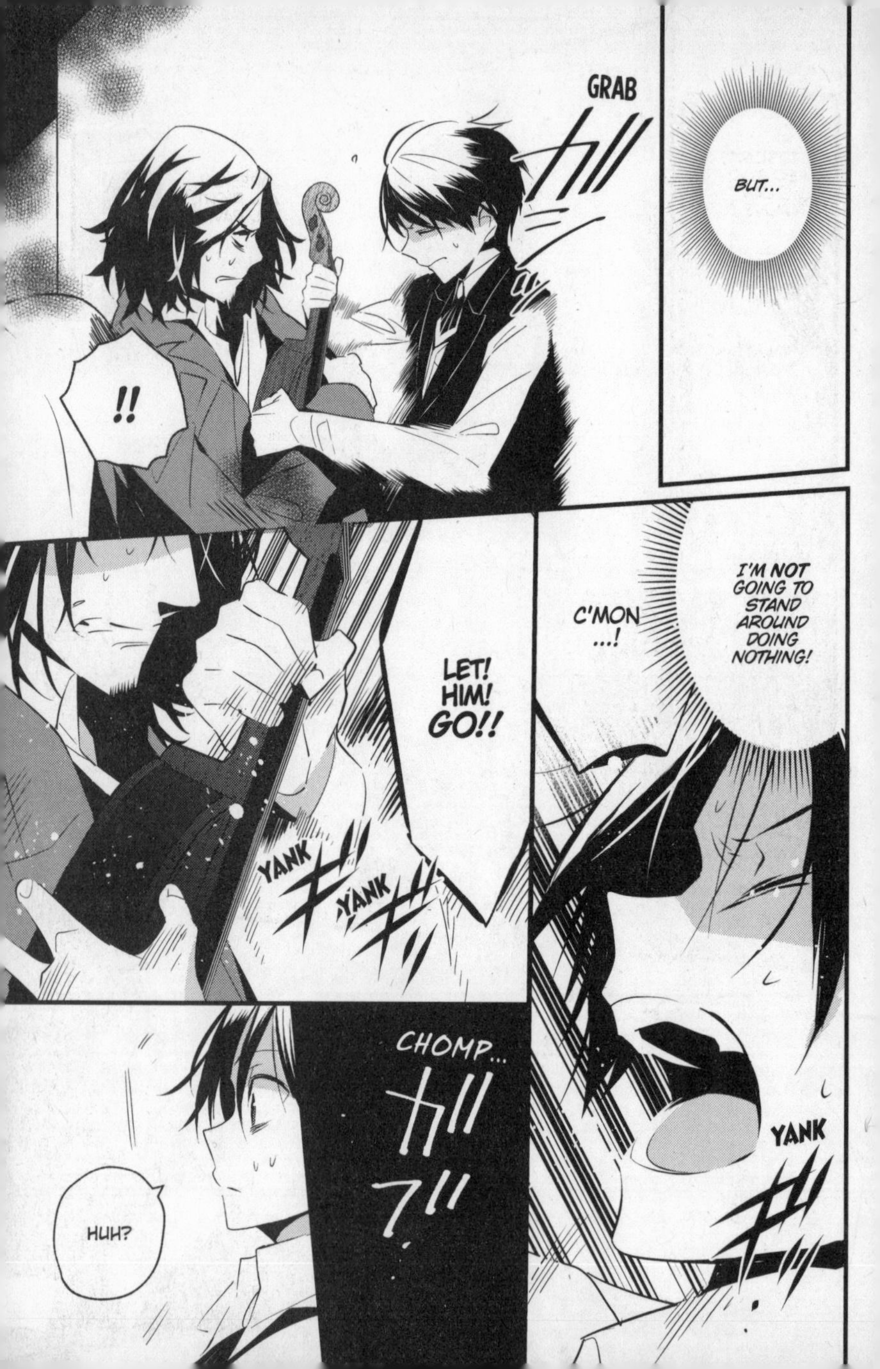
BUT...
GRAB
!!
I'M NOT GOING TO STAND AROUND DOING NOTHING!
C'MON ...!
YANK
LET! HIM! GO!!
YANK
YANK
CHOMP...
HUH?

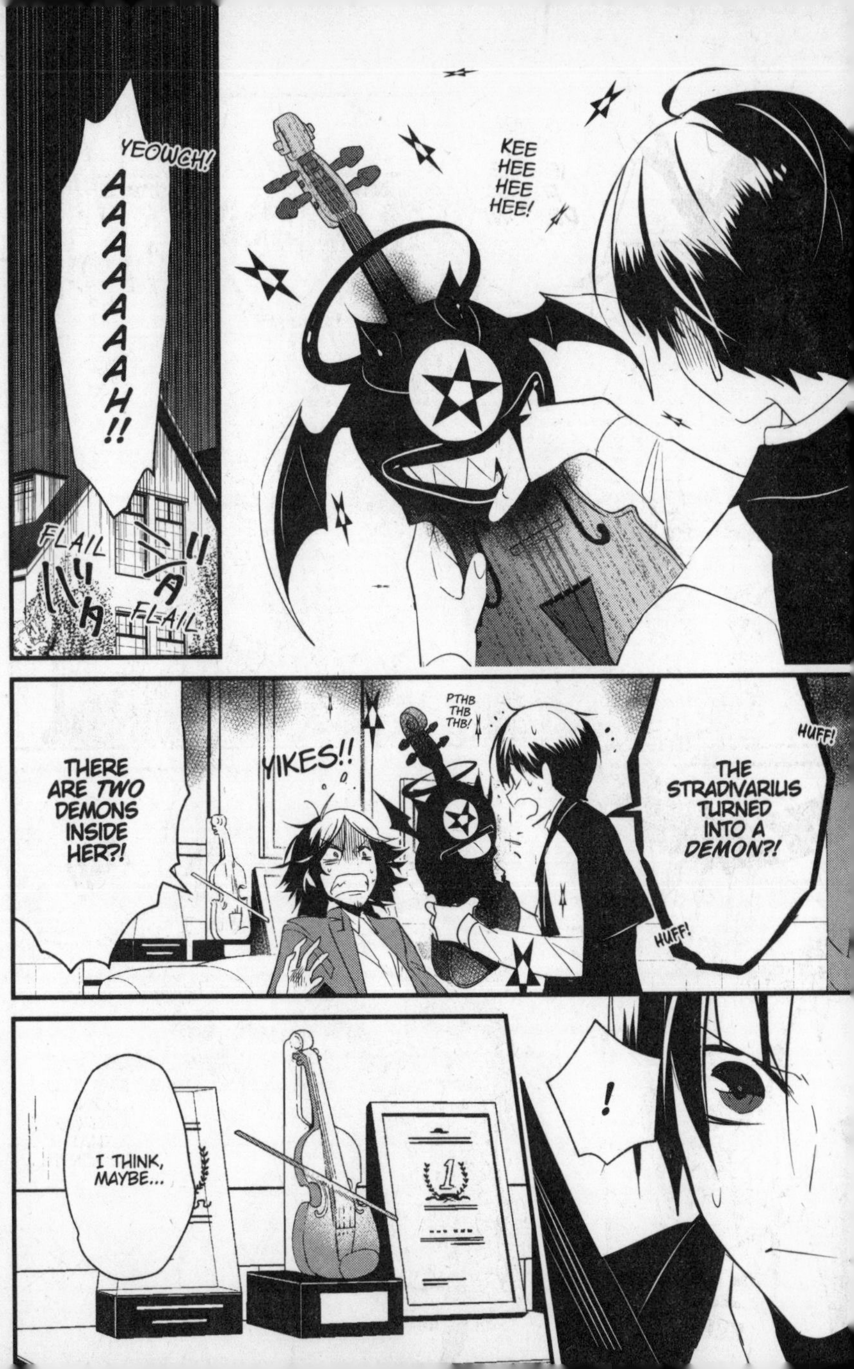
KEE HEE HEE HEE!
YEOWCH!
AAAAAAAAH!!
FLAIL
FLAIL
HUFF!
THE STRADIVARIUS TURNED INTO A *DEMON*?!
HUFF!
PTHB THB THB!
YIKES!!
THERE ARE *TWO* DEMONS INSIDE HER?!
!
I THINK, MAYBE...

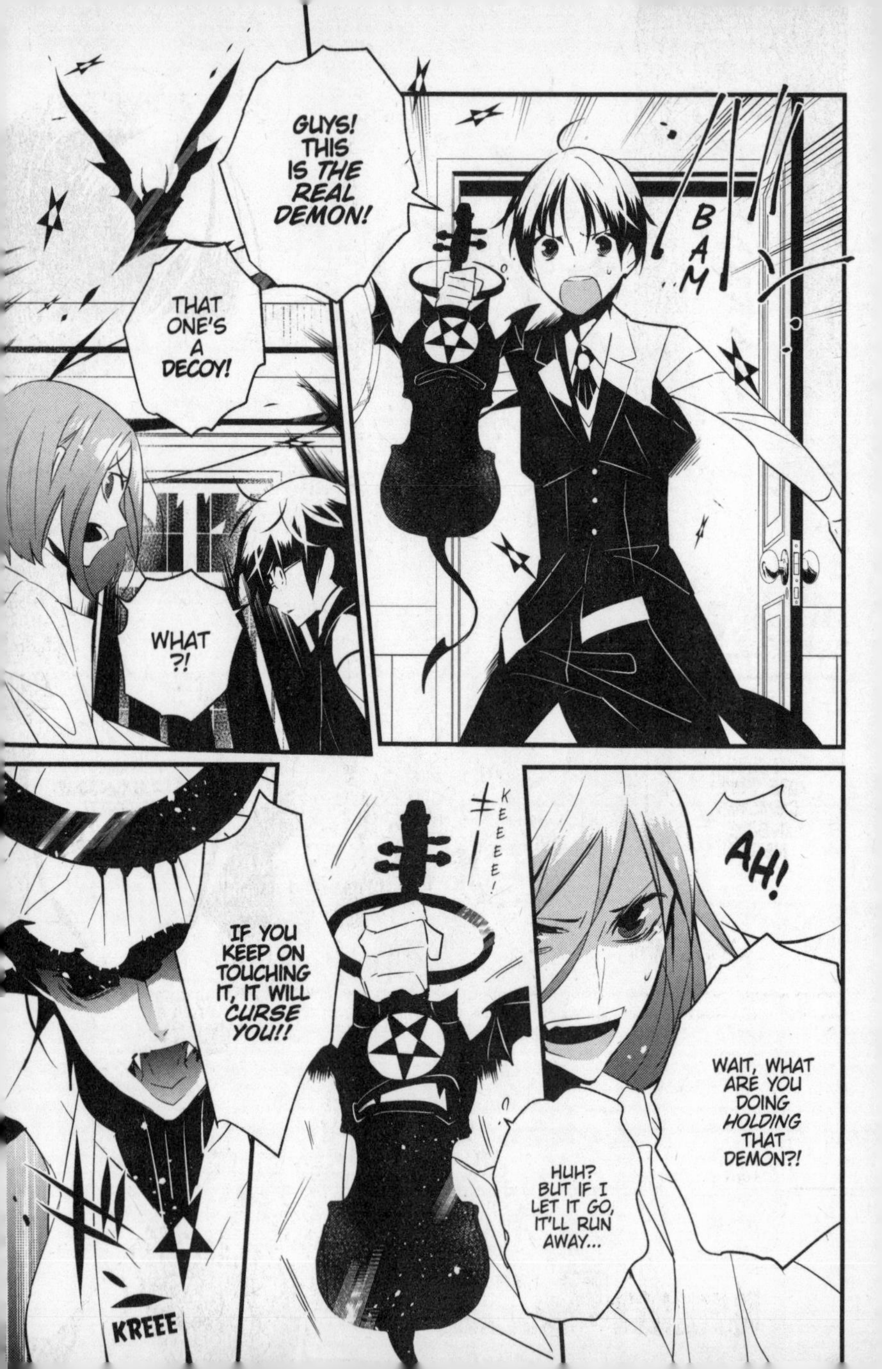
BAM
GUYS! THIS IS THE REAL DEMON!
THAT ONE'S A DECOY!
WHAT?!
AH!
WAIT, WHAT ARE YOU DOING HOLDING THAT DEMON?!
HUH? BUT IF I LET IT GO, IT'LL RUN AWAY...
KEEEE!
IF YOU KEEP ON TOUCHING IT, IT WILL CURSE YOU!!
KREEE

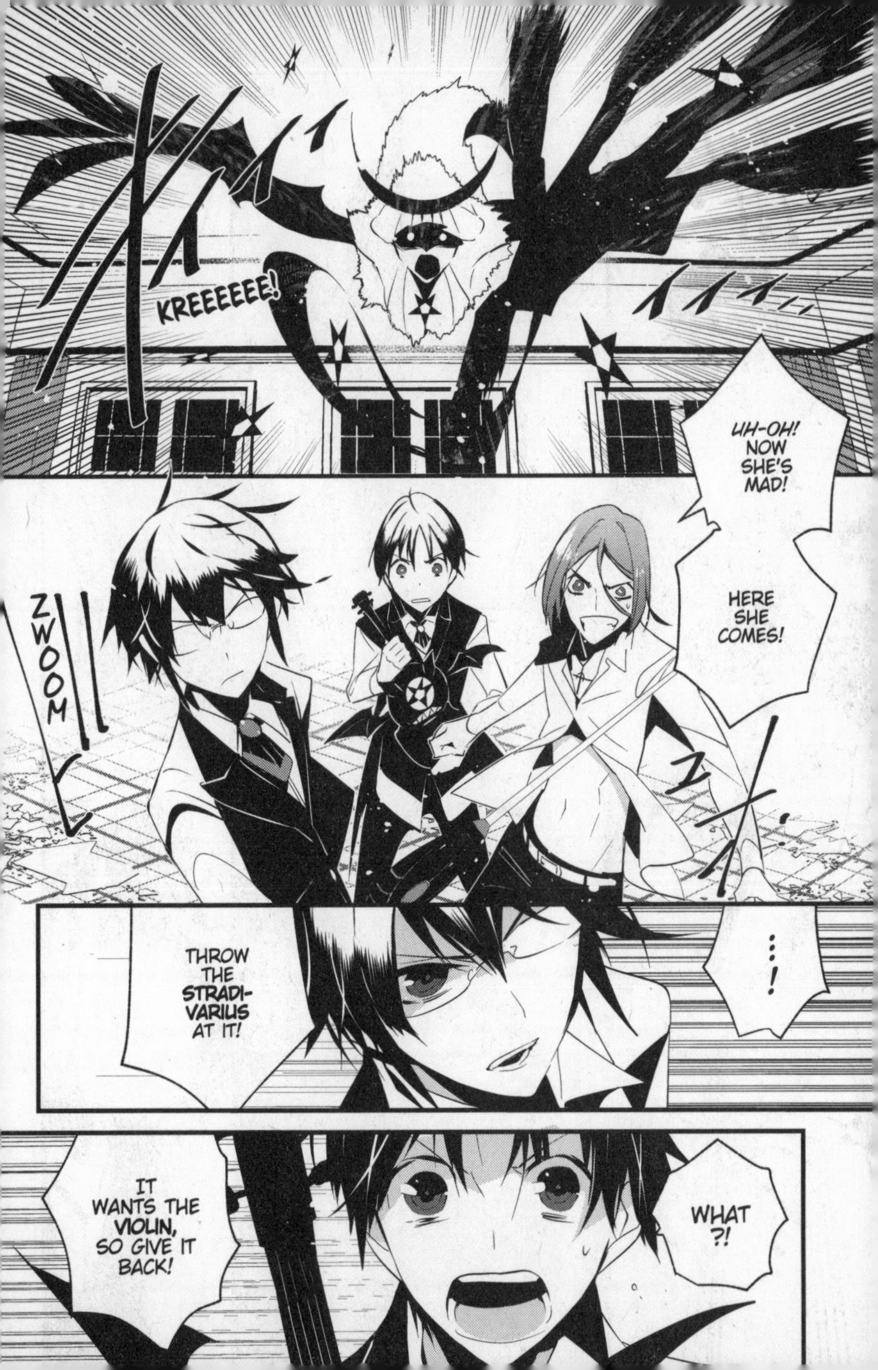
KREEEEEE!
UH-OH! NOW SHE'S MAD!
HERE SHE COMES!
ZWOOM
...!
THROW THE STRADI-VARIUS AT IT!
WHAT?!
IT WANTS THE VIOLIN, SO GIVE IT BACK!

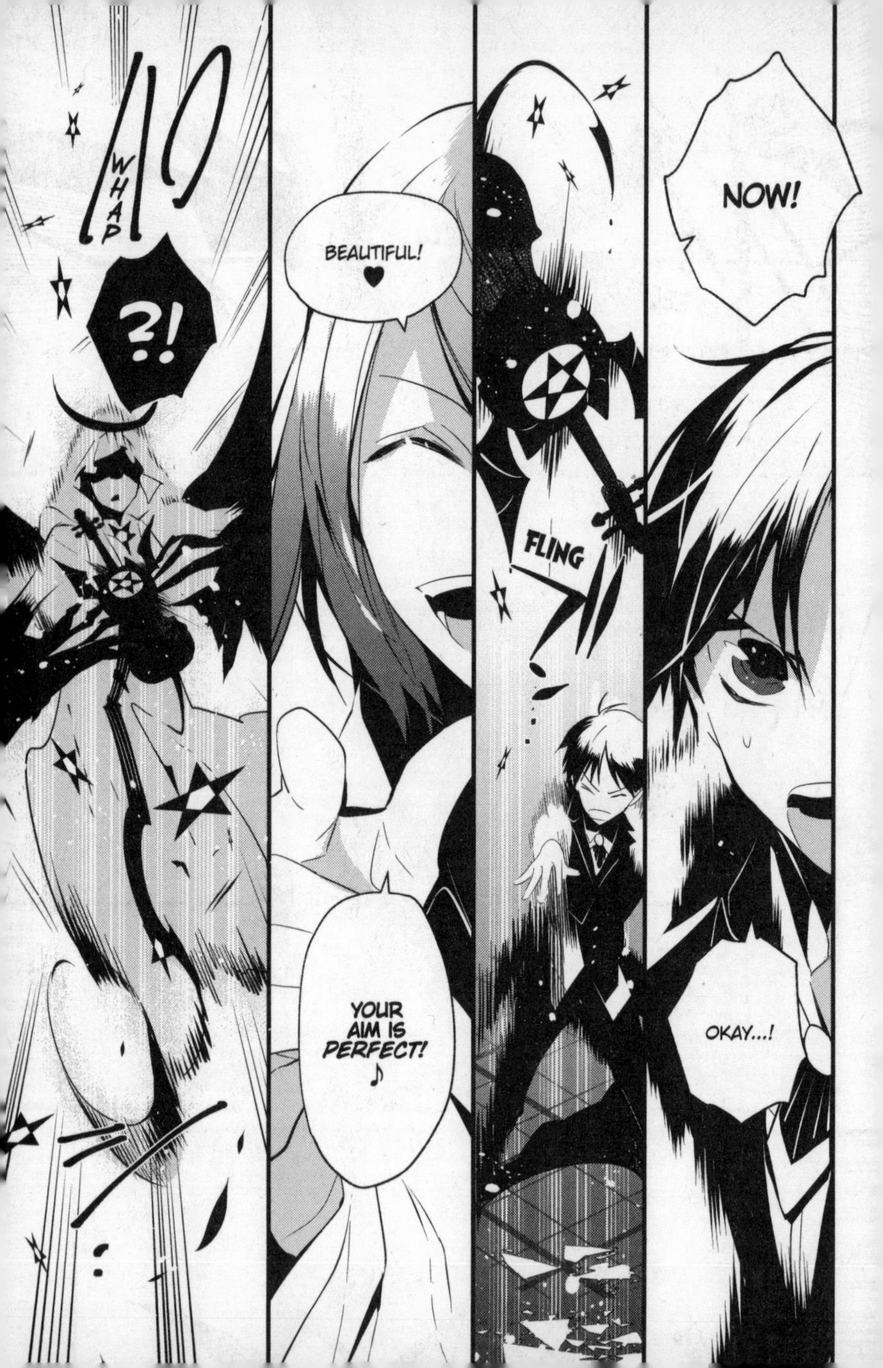
NOW!
OKAY...!
FLING
BEAUTIFUL! ♥
YOUR AIM IS PERFECT! ♪
WHAP
?!

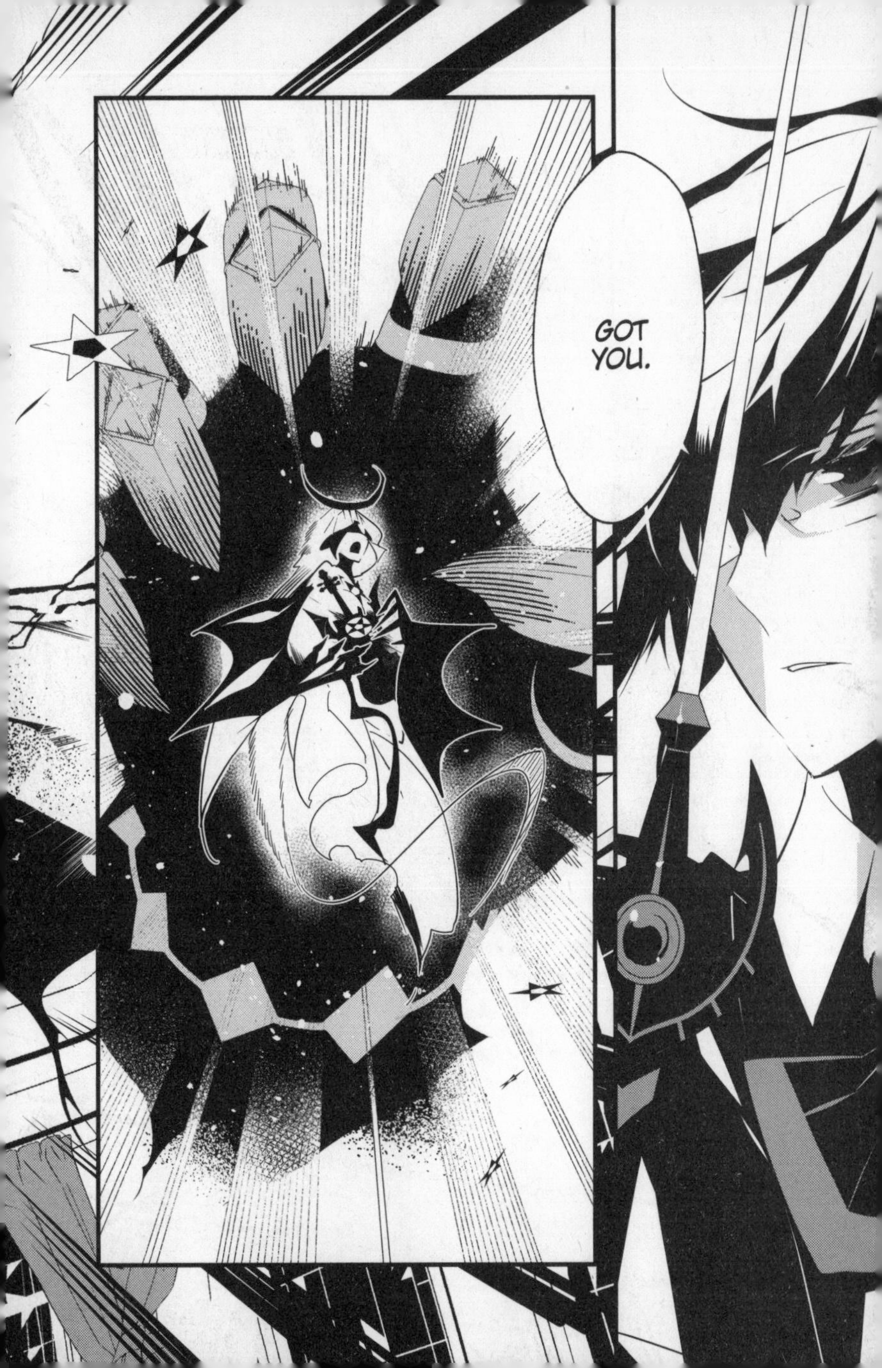
GOT YOU.

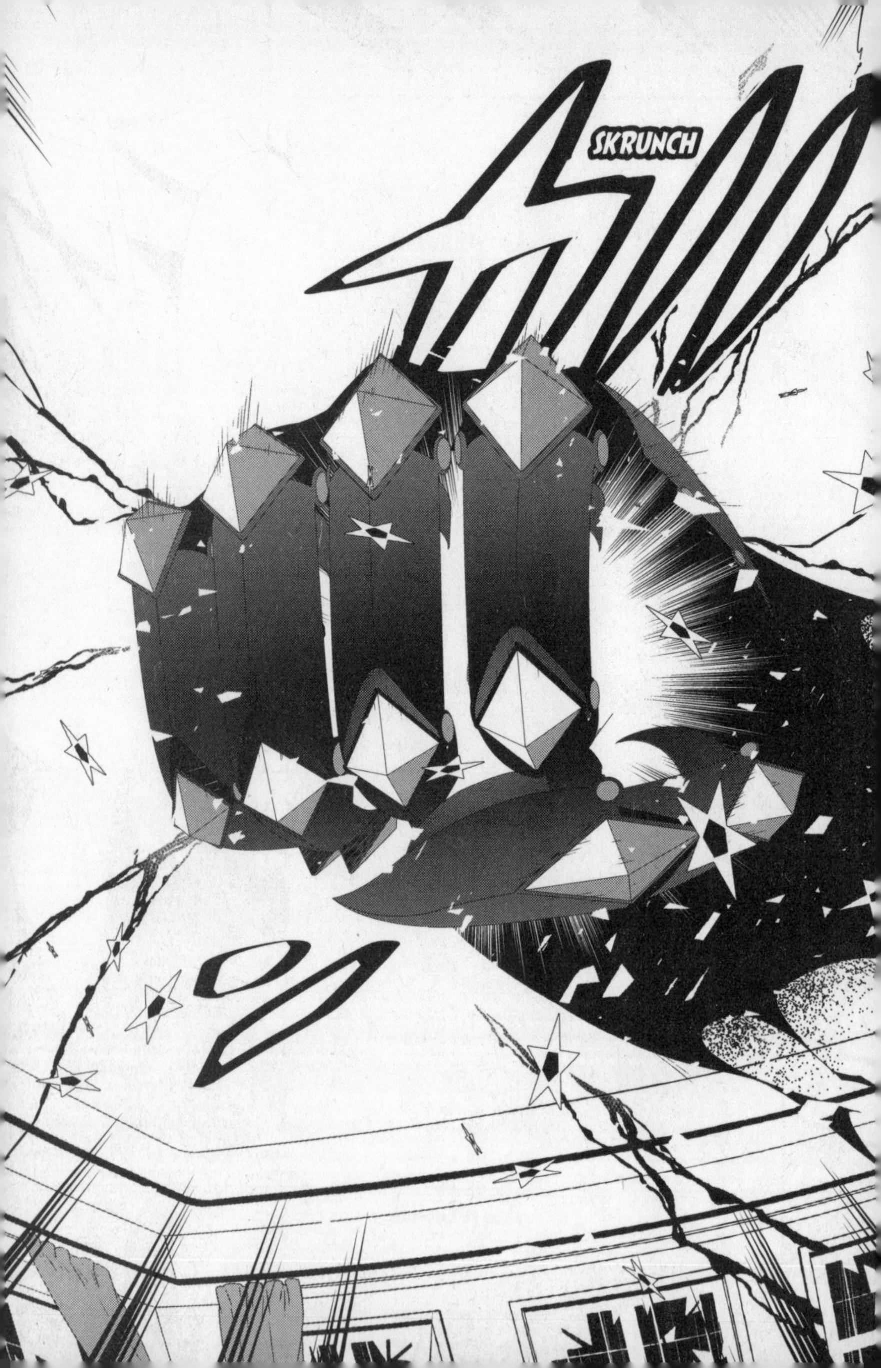
SKRUNCH

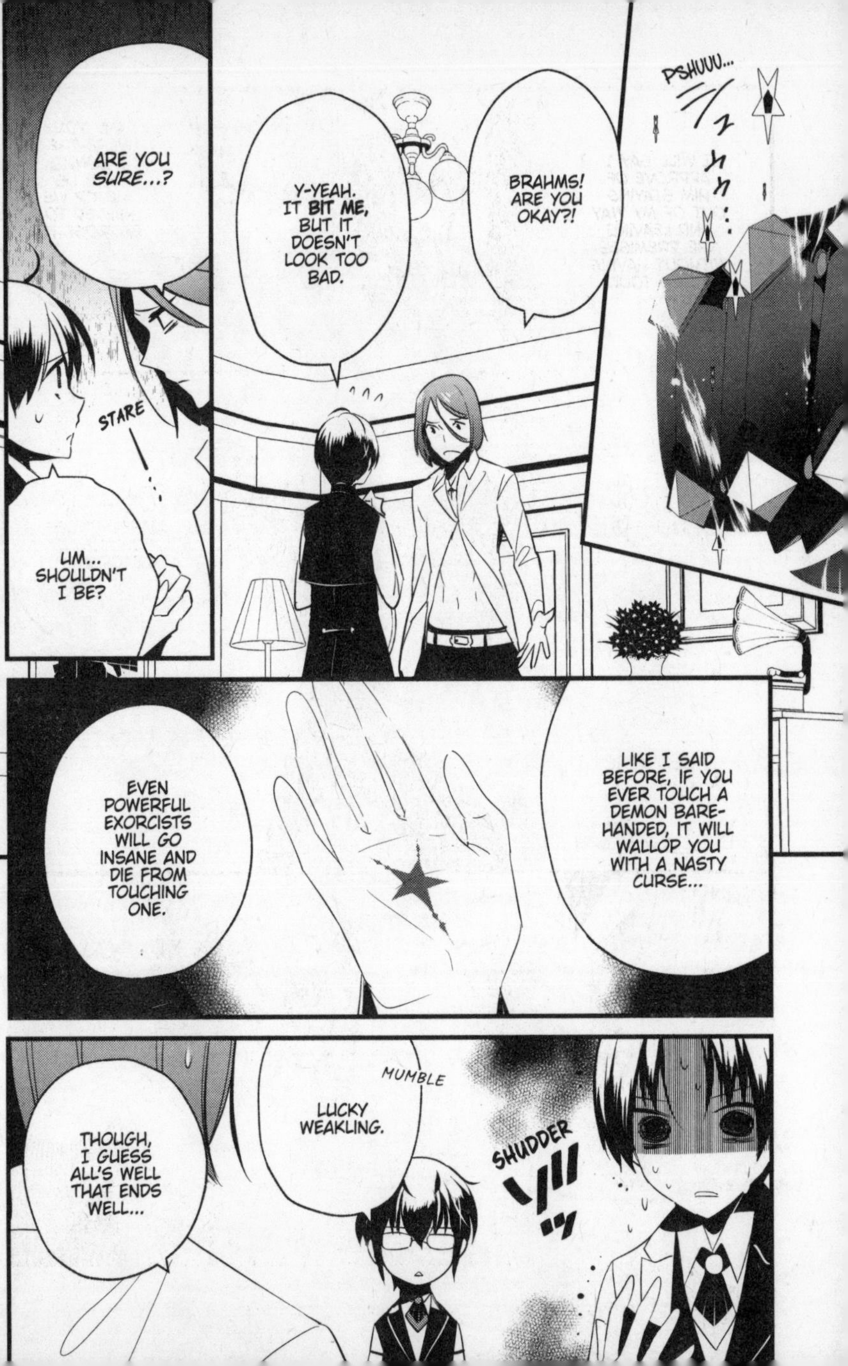
PSHUUU...
BRAHMS! ARE YOU OKAY?!
Y-YEAH. IT BIT ME, BUT IT DOESN'T LOOK TOO BAD.
ARE YOU SURE...?
STARE
UM... SHOULDN'T I BE?
LIKE I SAID BEFORE, IF YOU EVER TOUCH A DEMON BARE-HANDED, IT WILL WALLOP YOU WITH A NASTY CURSE...
EVEN POWERFUL EXORCISTS WILL GO INSANE AND DIE FROM TOUCHING ONE.
SHUDDER
MUMBLE
LUCKY WEAKLING.
THOUGH, I GUESS ALL'S WELL THAT ENDS WELL...

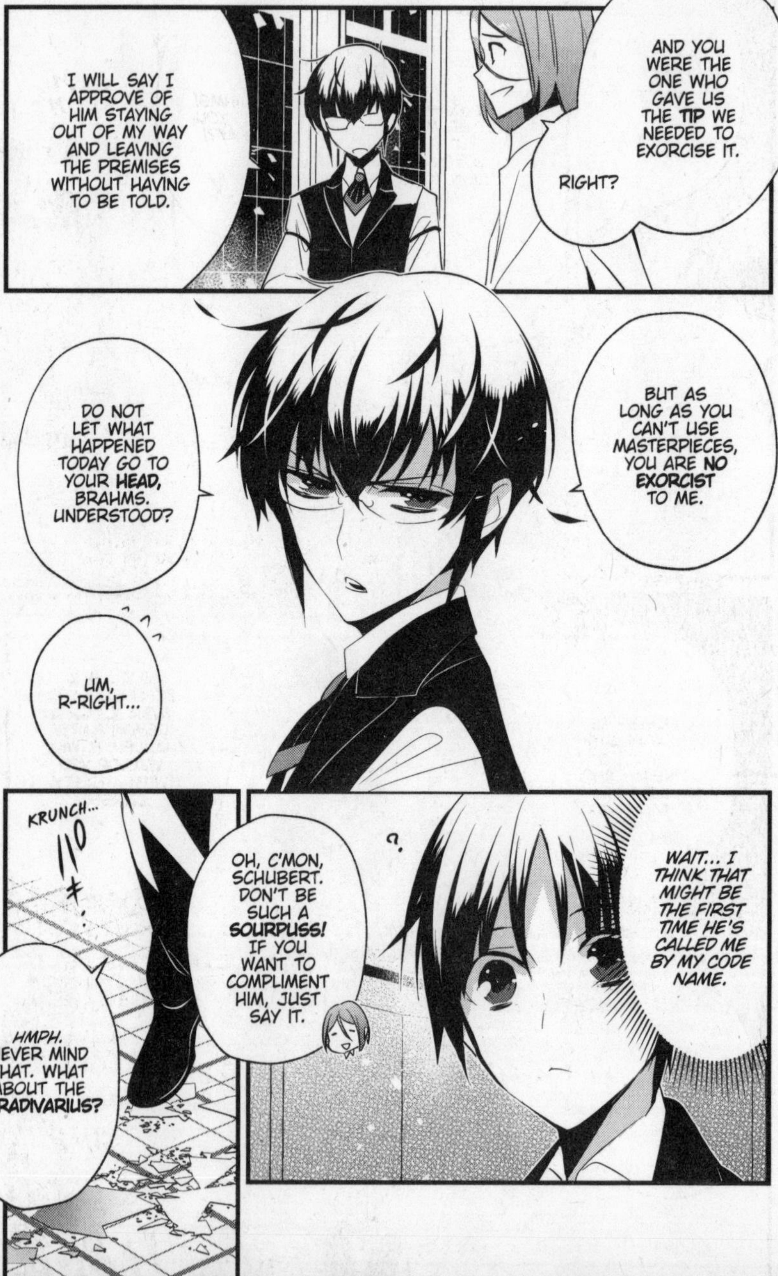
AND YOU WERE THE ONE WHO GAVE US THE TIP WE NEEDED TO EXORCISE IT.
RIGHT?
I WILL SAY I APPROVE OF HIM STAYING OUT OF MY WAY AND LEAVING THE PREMISES WITHOUT HAVING TO BE TOLD.
BUT AS LONG AS YOU CAN'T USE MASTERPIECES, YOU ARE NO EXORCIST TO ME.
DO NOT LET WHAT HAPPENED TODAY GO TO YOUR HEAD, BRAHMS. UNDERSTOOD?
UM, R-RIGHT...
WAIT... I THINK THAT MIGHT BE THE FIRST TIME HE'S CALLED ME BY MY CODE NAME.
KRUNCH...
OH, C'MON, SCHUBERT. DON'T BE SUCH A SOURPUSS! IF YOU WANT TO COMPLIMENT HIM, JUST SAY IT.
HMPH. NEVER MIND THAT. WHAT ABOUT THE STRADIVARIUS?

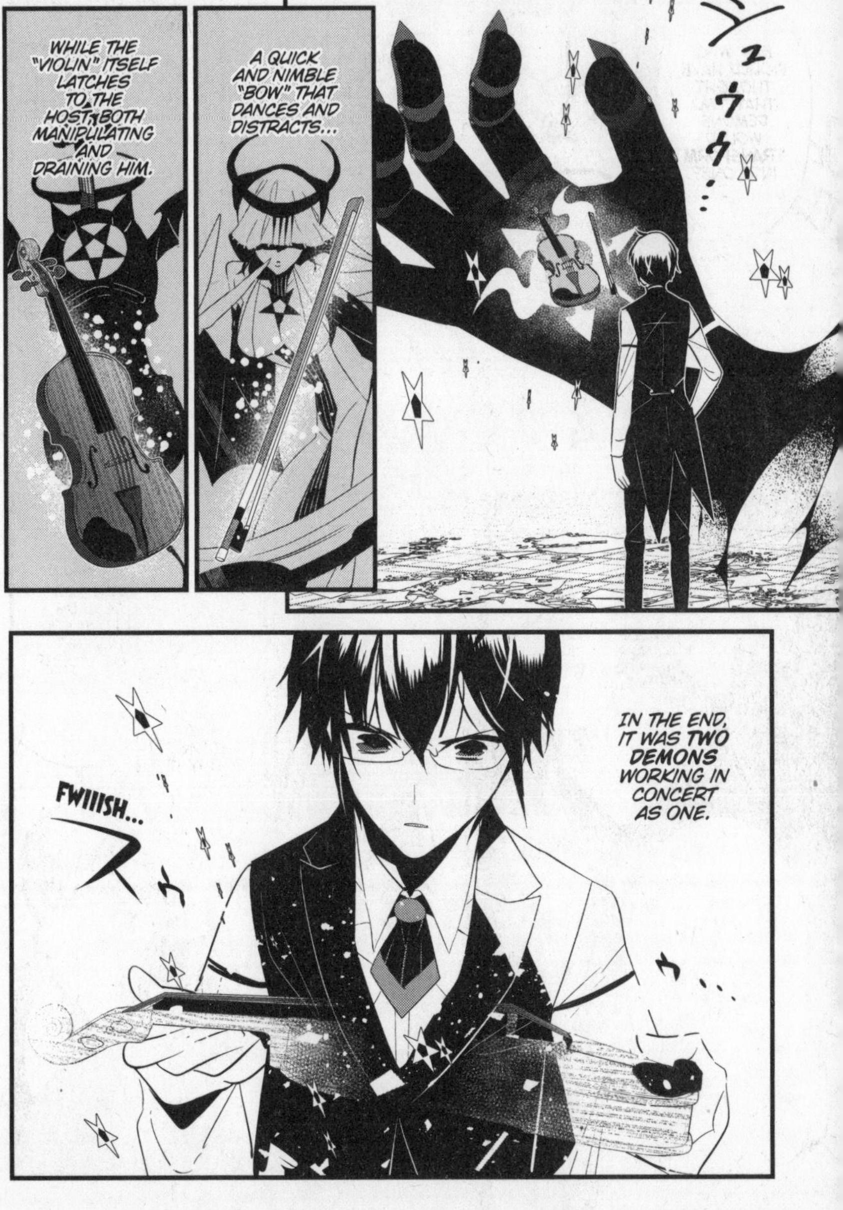
SHWUFF...
A QUICK AND NIMBLE "BOW" THAT DANCES AND DISTRACTS...
WHILE THE "VIOLIN" ITSELF LATCHES TO THE HOST, BOTH MANIPULATING AND DRAINING HIM.
IN THE END, IT WAS TWO DEMONS WORKING IN CONCERT AS ONE.
FWIIISH...

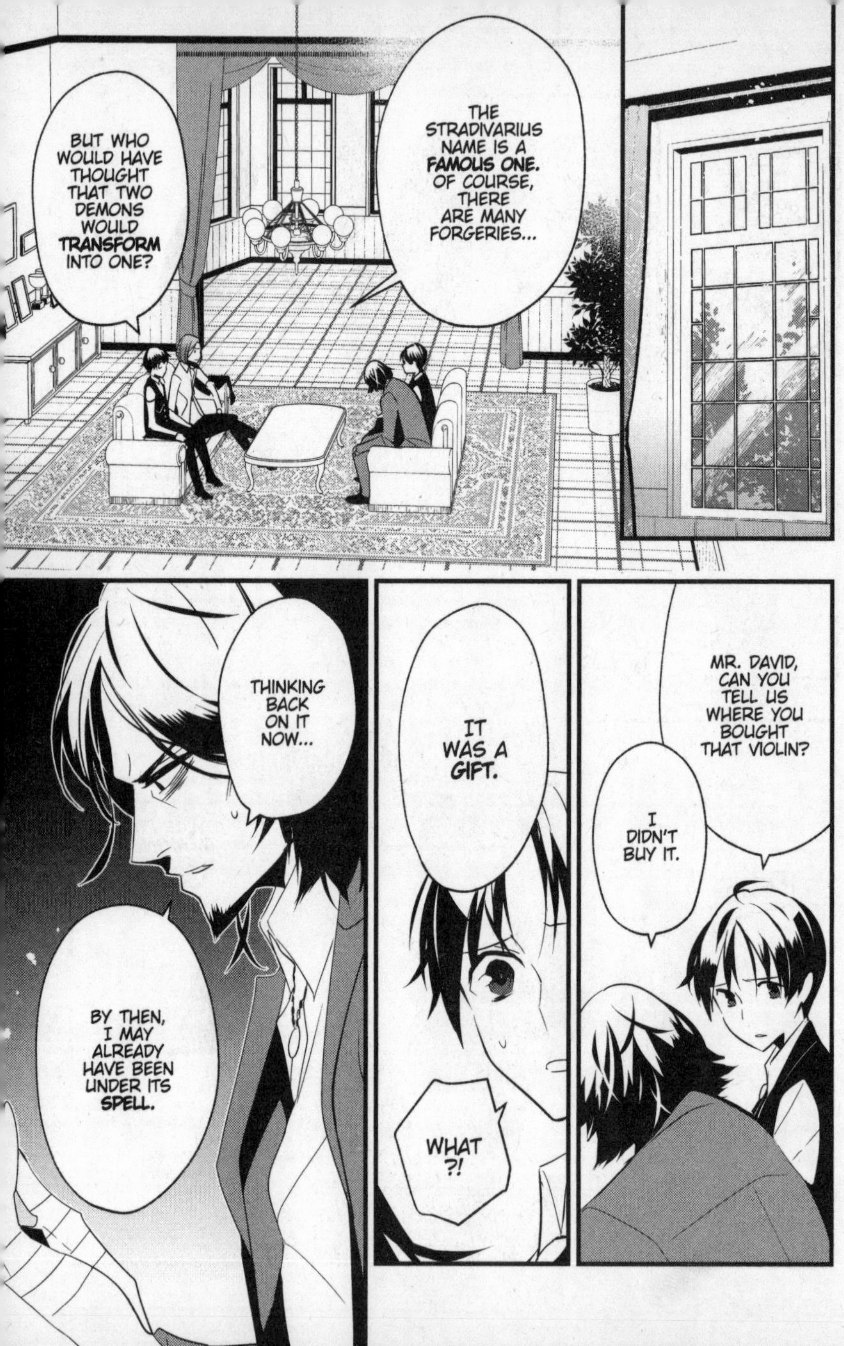
THE STRADIVARIUS NAME IS A **FAMOUS ONE.** OF COURSE, THERE ARE MANY FORGERIES...
BUT WHO WOULD HAVE THOUGHT THAT TWO DEMONS WOULD **TRANSFORM** INTO ONE?
MR. DAVID, CAN YOU TELL US WHERE YOU BOUGHT THAT VIOLIN?
I DIDN'T BUY IT.
IT WAS A **GIFT.**
WHAT?!
THINKING BACK ON IT NOW...
BY THEN, I MAY ALREADY HAVE BEEN UNDER ITS **SPELL.**

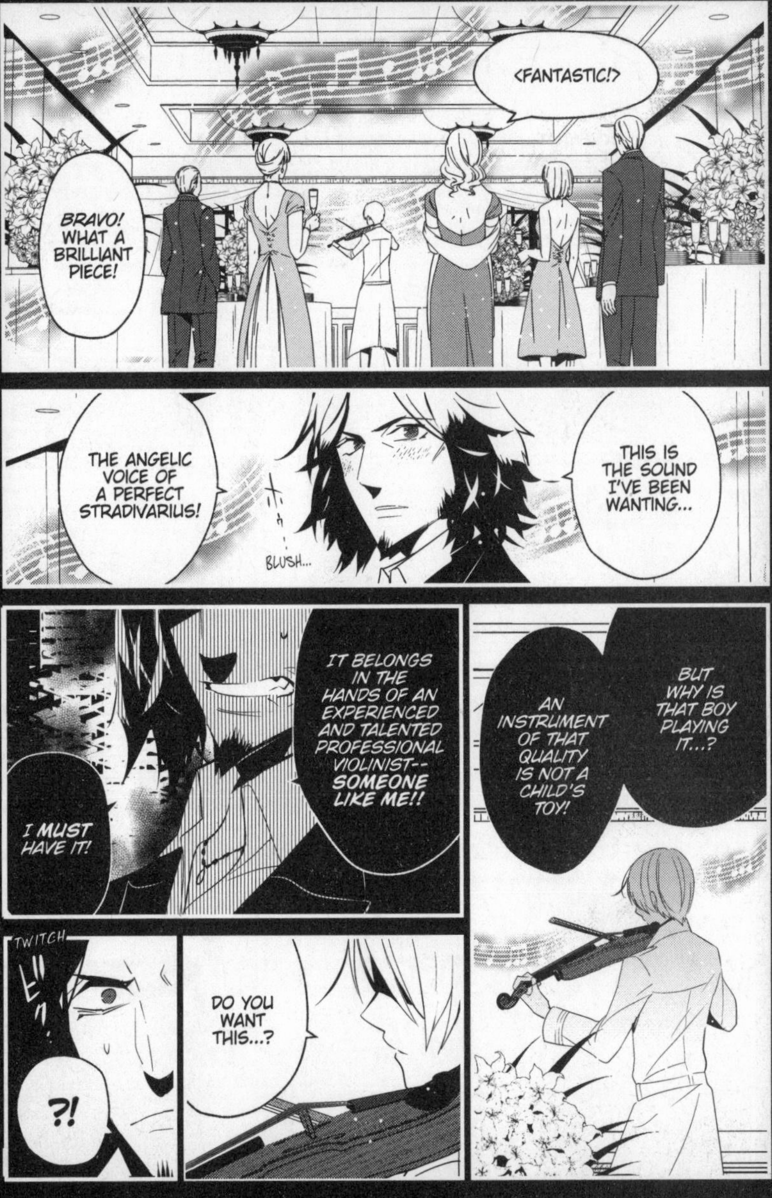
<FANTASTIC!>
BRAVO! WHAT A BRILLIANT PIECE!
THIS IS THE SOUND I'VE BEEN WANTING...
BLUSH...
THE ANGELIC VOICE OF A PERFECT STRADIVARIUS!
BUT WHY IS THAT BOY PLAYING IT...?
AN INSTRUMENT OF THAT QUALITY IS NOT A CHILD'S TOY!
IT BELONGS IN THE HANDS OF AN EXPERIENCED AND TALENTED PROFESSIONAL VIOLINIST-- SOMEONE LIKE ME!!
I MUST HAVE IT!
DO YOU WANT THIS...?
TWITCH
?!

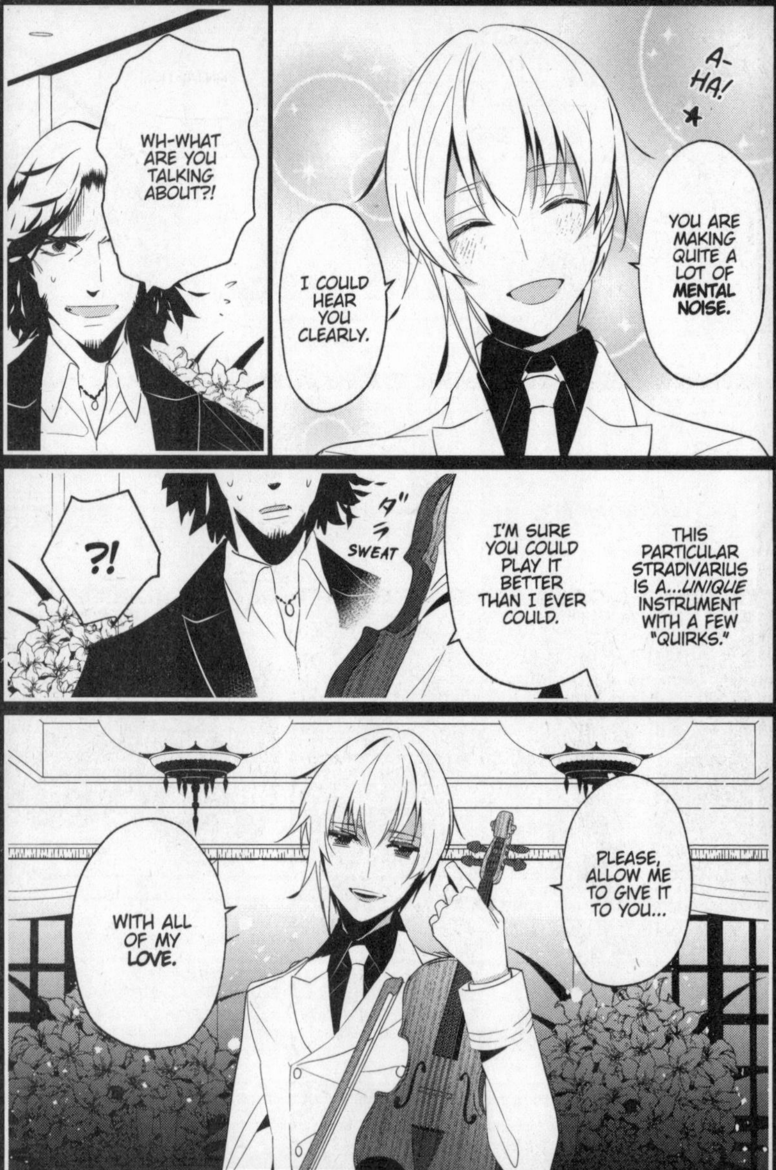
A-HA!
YOU ARE MAKING QUITE A LOT OF MENTAL NOISE.
I COULD HEAR YOU CLEARLY.
WH-WHAT ARE YOU TALKING ABOUT?!
THIS PARTICULAR STRADIVARIUS IS A...*UNIQUE* INSTRUMENT WITH A FEW "QUIRKS."
I'M SURE YOU COULD PLAY IT BETTER THAN I EVER COULD.
SWEAT
?!
PLEASE, ALLOW ME TO GIVE IT TO YOU...
WITH ALL OF MY LOVE.

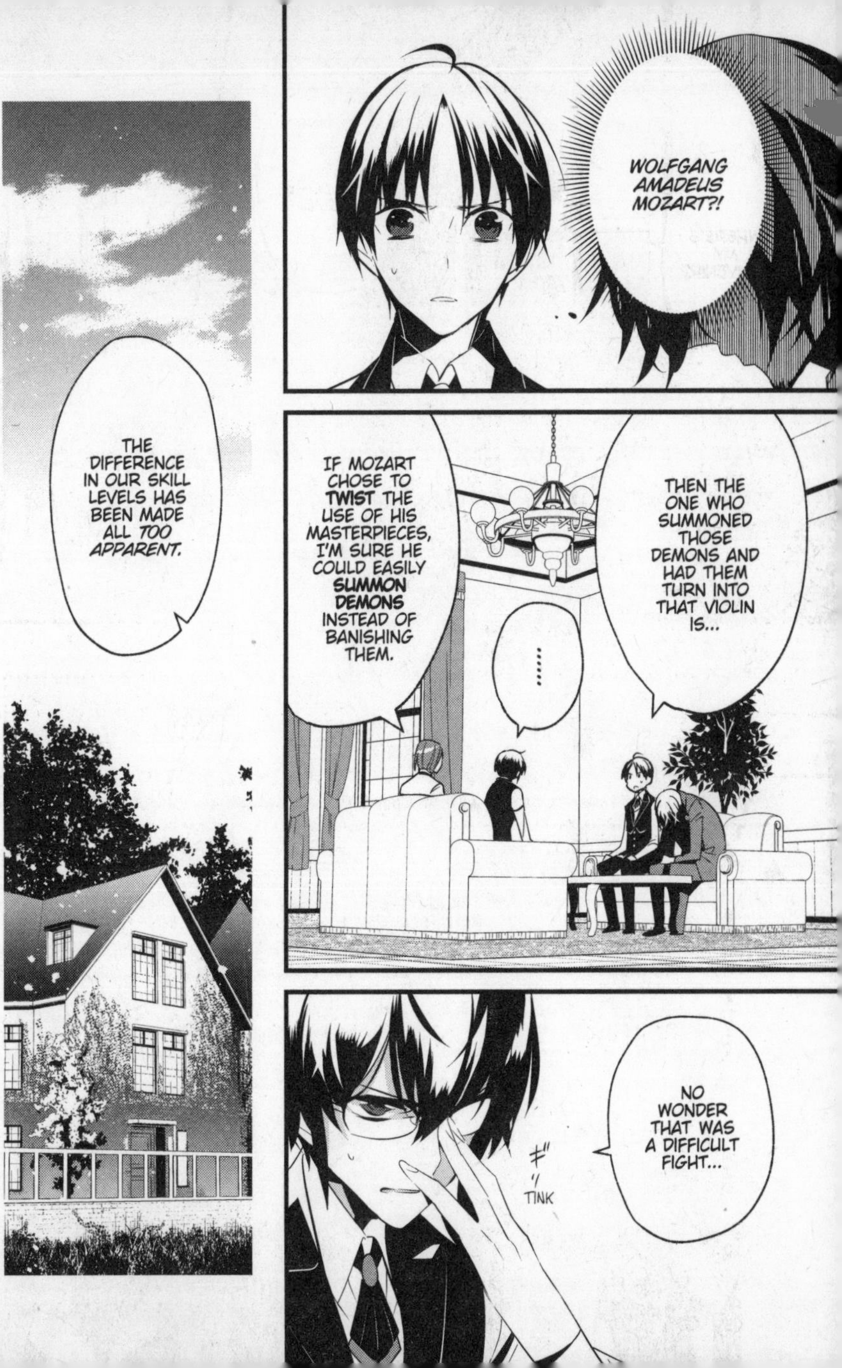
WOLFGANG AMADEUS MOZART?!
THEN THE ONE WHO SUMMONED THOSE DEMONS AND HAD THEM TURN INTO THAT VIOLIN IS...
IF MOZART CHOSE TO **TWIST** THE USE OF HIS MASTERPIECES, I'M SURE HE COULD EASILY **SUMMON DEMONS** INSTEAD OF BANISHING THEM.
......
NO WONDER THAT WAS A DIFFICULT FIGHT...
ギッ
TINK
THE DIFFERENCE IN OUR SKILL LEVELS HAS BEEN MADE ALL *TOO APPARENT.*

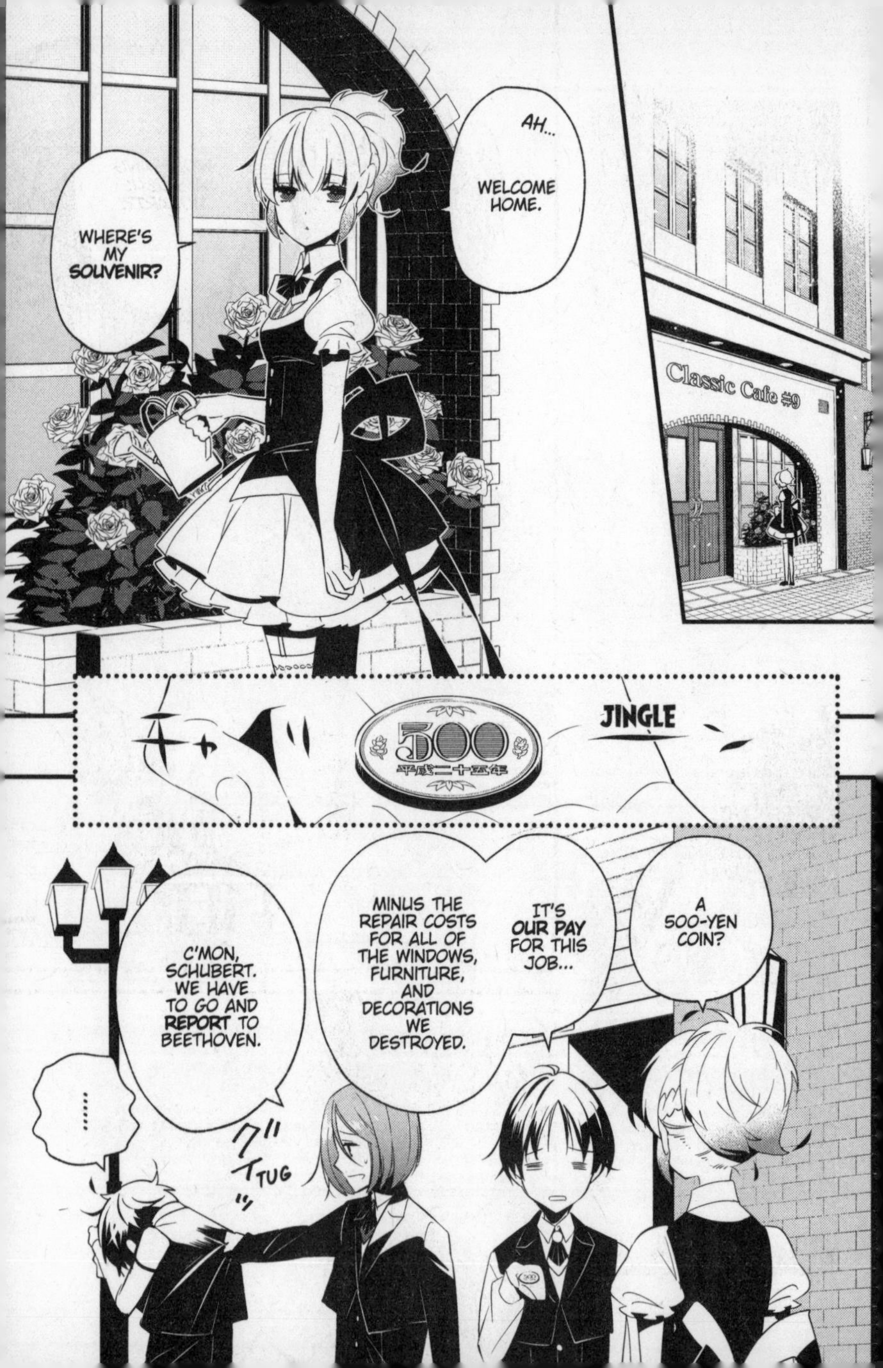
Classic Cafe #9
AH... WELCOME HOME.
WHERE'S MY SOUVENIR?
JINGLE
500
平成二十五年
A 500-YEN COIN?
IT'S **OUR PAY** FOR THIS JOB...
MINUS THE REPAIR COSTS FOR ALL OF THE WINDOWS, FURNITURE, AND DECORATIONS WE DESTROYED.
C'MON, SCHUBERT. WE HAVE TO GO AND **REPORT** TO BEETHOVEN.
......
グイッ TUG

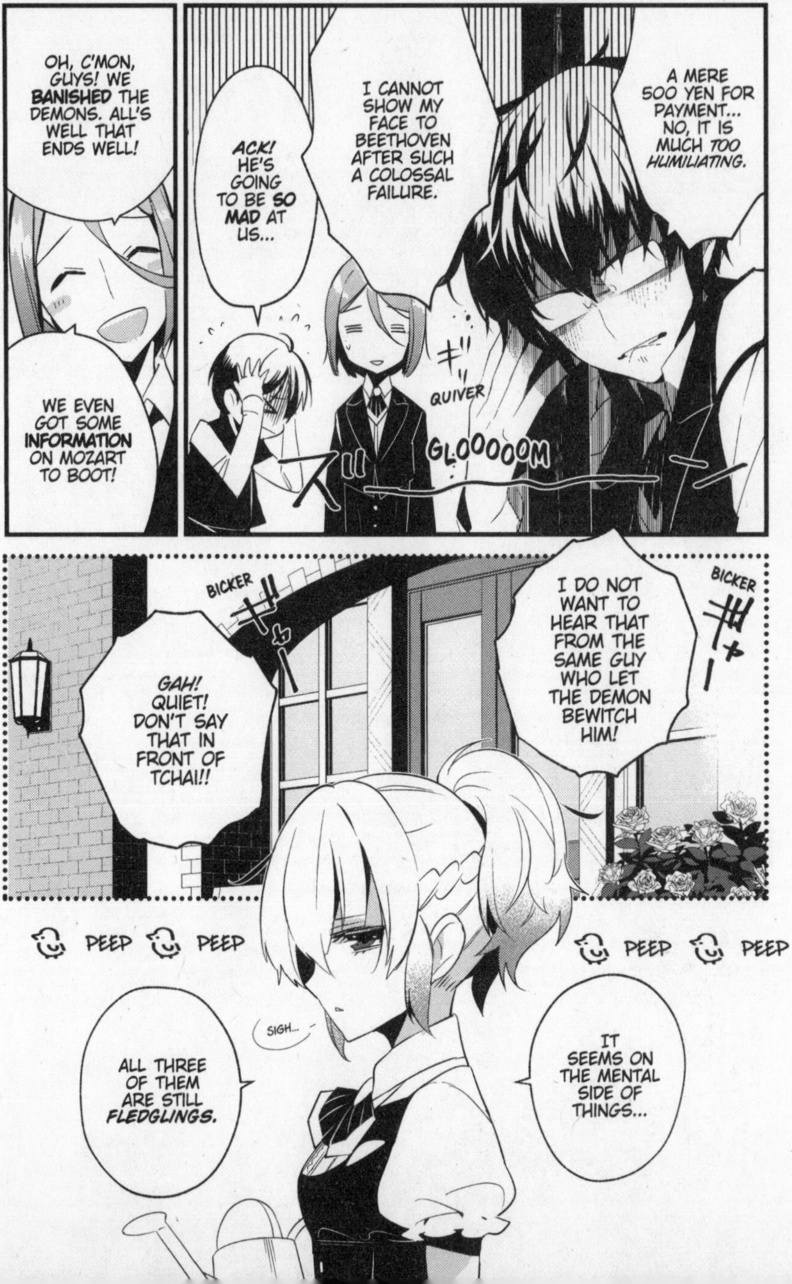
A MERE 500 YEN FOR PAYMENT... NO, IT IS MUCH TOO HUMILIATING.
I CANNOT SHOW MY FACE TO BEETHOVEN AFTER SUCH A COLOSSAL FAILURE.
ACK! HE'S GOING TO BE SO MAD AT US...
QUIVER
GLOOOOOM
OH, C'MON, GUYS! WE BANISHED THE DEMONS. ALL'S WELL THAT ENDS WELL!
WE EVEN GOT SOME INFORMATION ON MOZART TO BOOT!
BICKER
I DO NOT WANT TO HEAR THAT FROM THE SAME GUY WHO LET THE DEMON BEWITCH HIM!
GAH! QUIET! DON'T SAY THAT IN FRONT OF TCHAI!!
BICKER
PEEP PEEP
IT SEEMS ON THE MENTAL SIDE OF THINGS...
SIGH...
ALL THREE OF THEM ARE STILL FLEDGLINGS.
PEEP PEEP

Magia the Ninth

#10. Kinderszenen

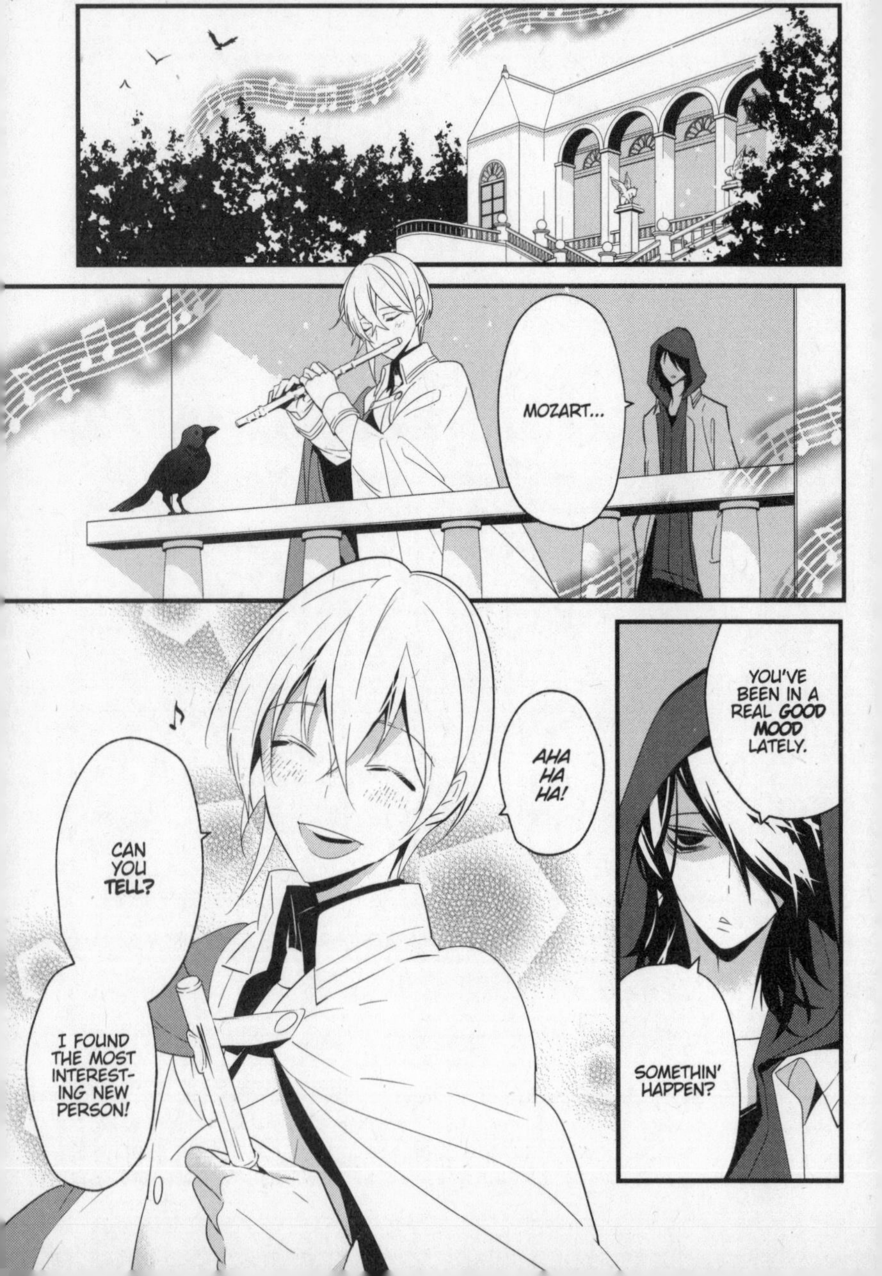
MOZART...
YOU'VE BEEN IN A REAL GOOD MOOD LATELY.
SOMETHIN' HAPPEN?
AHA HA HA!
CAN YOU TELL?
I FOUND THE MOST INTEREST-ING NEW PERSON!

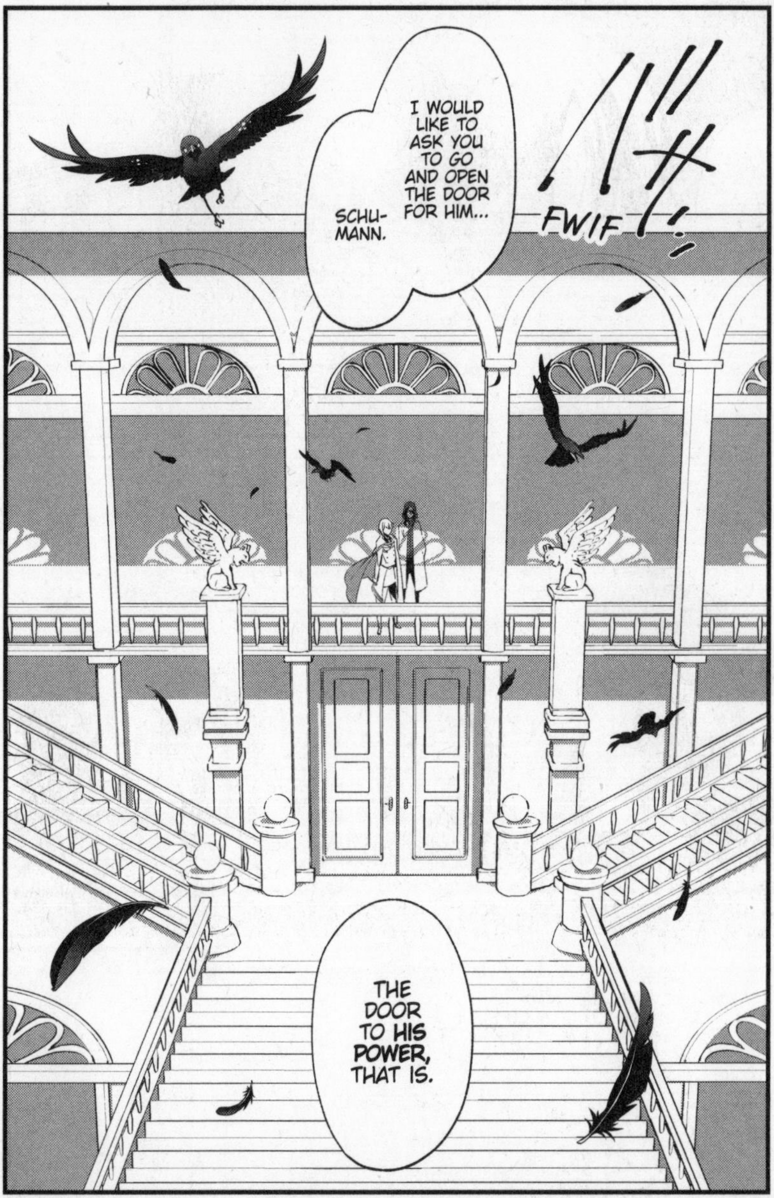
FWIF
I WOULD LIKE TO ASK YOU TO GO AND OPEN THE DOOR FOR HIM...
SCHU-MANN.
THE DOOR TO HIS POWER, THAT IS.

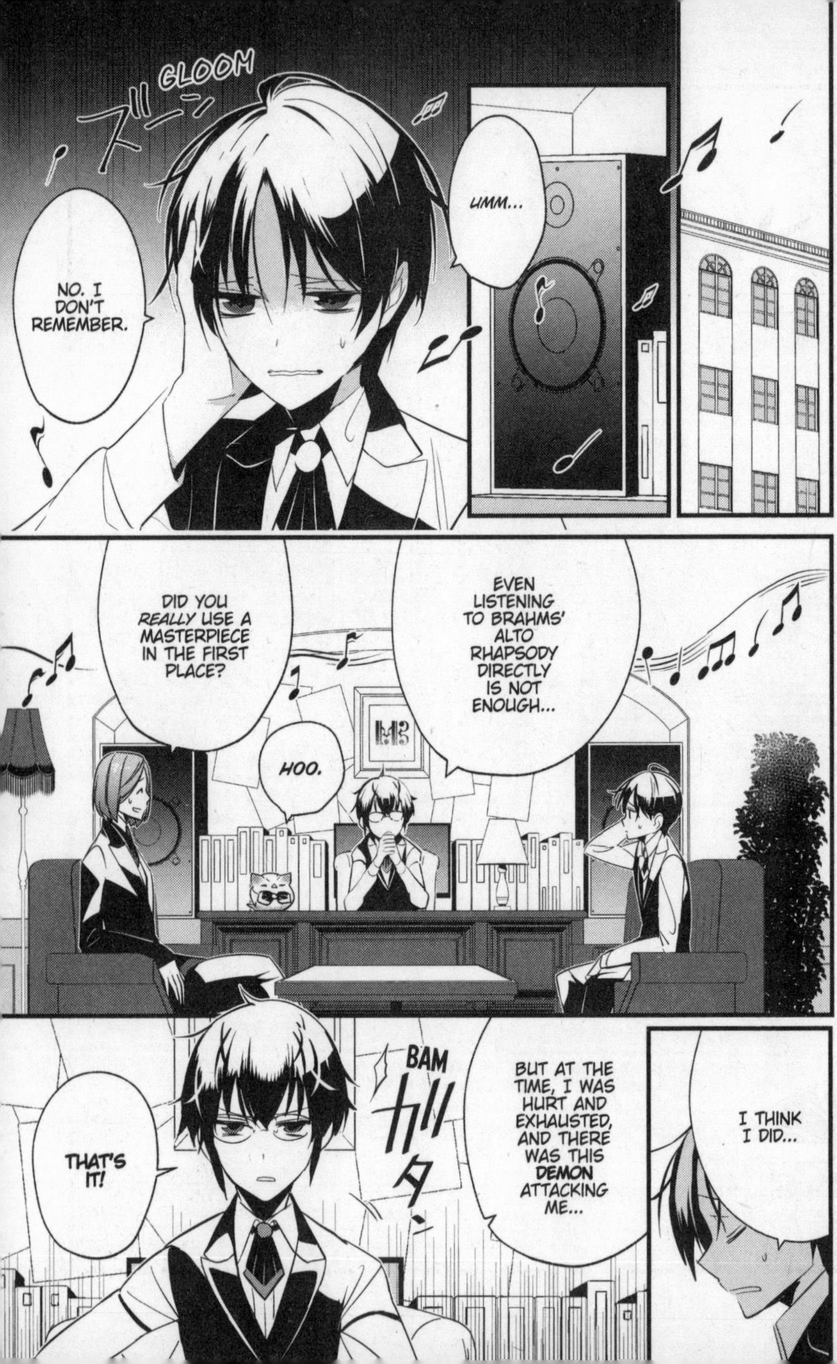
UMM...
GLOOM
NO. I DON'T REMEMBER.
EVEN LISTENING TO BRAHMS' ALTO RHAPSODY DIRECTLY IS NOT ENOUGH...
HOO.
DID YOU *REALLY* USE A MASTERPIECE IN THE FIRST PLACE?
I THINK I DID...
BUT AT THE TIME, I WAS HURT AND EXHAUSTED, AND THERE WAS THIS **DEMON** ATTACKING ME...
BAM
THAT'S IT!

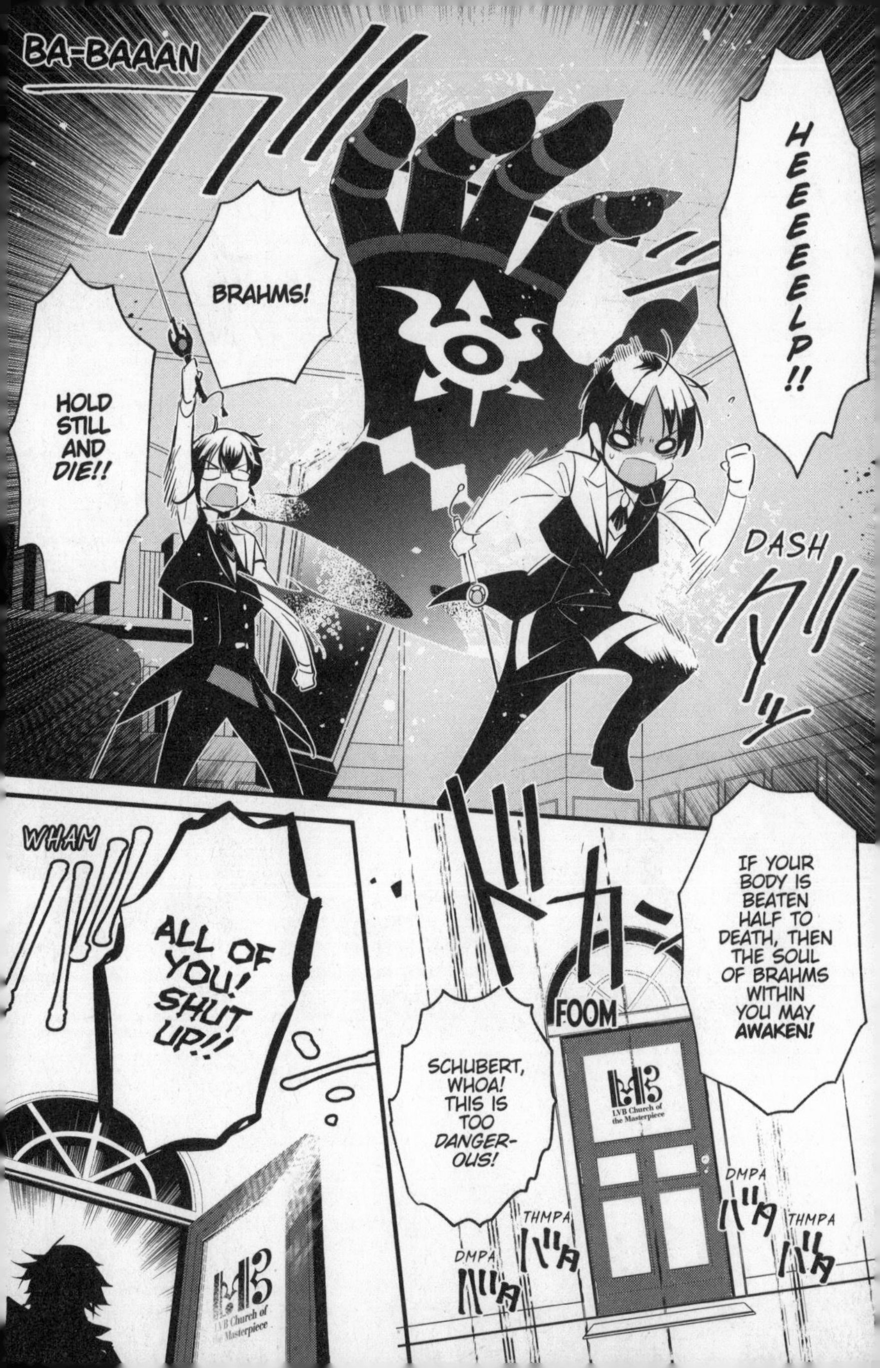
HEEEEEELP!!
BA-BAAAN
BRAHMS!
HOLD STILL AND DIE!!
DASH
IF YOUR BODY IS BEATEN HALF TO DEATH, THEN THE SOUL OF BRAHMS WITHIN YOU MAY AWAKEN!
FOOM
SCHUBERT, WHOA! THIS IS TOO DANGER-OUS!
LVB Church of the Masterpiece
DMPA
THMPA
THMPA
DMPA
WHAM
ALL OF YOU! SHUT UP!!
LVB Church of the Masterpiece

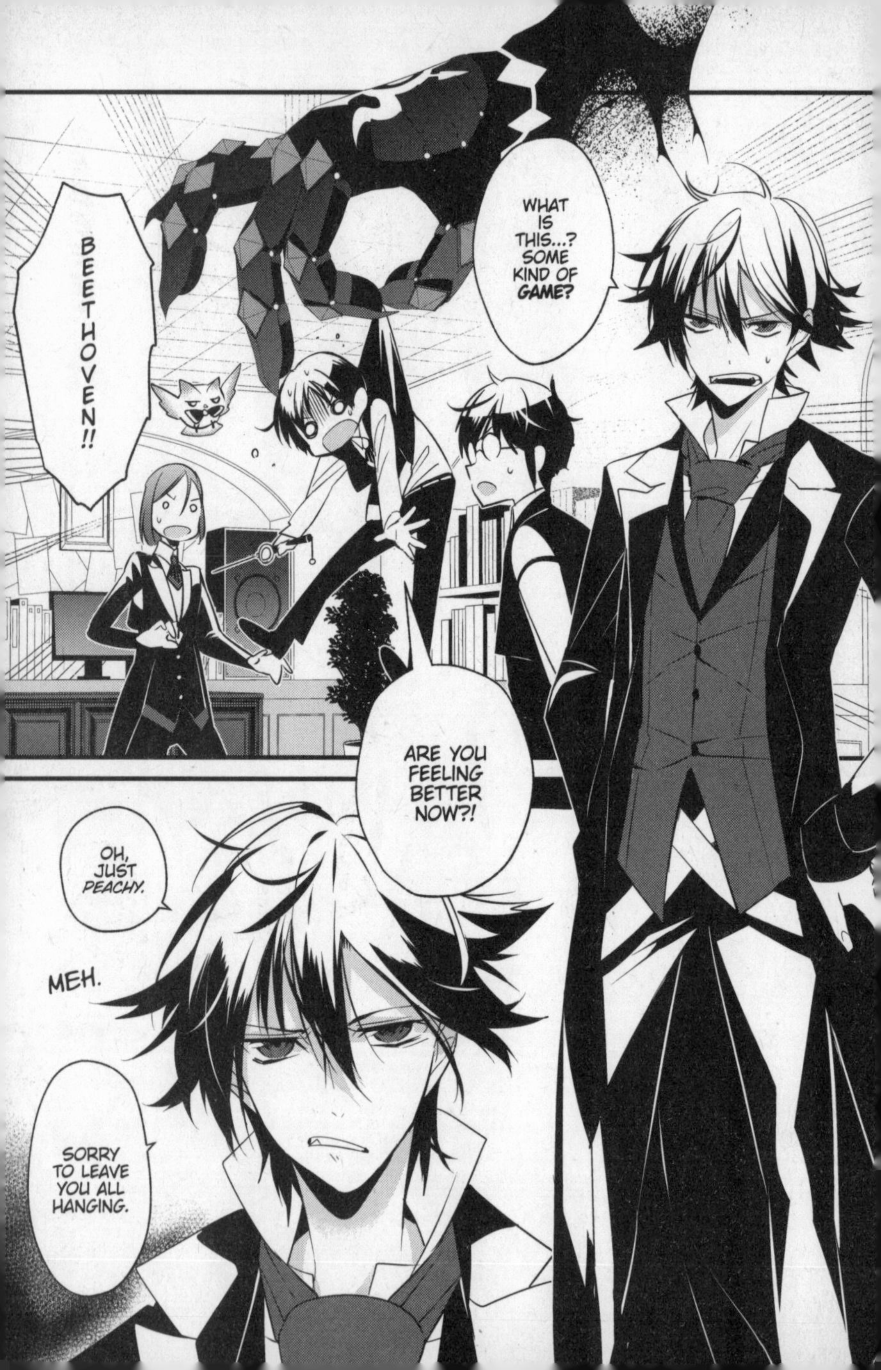
WHAT IS THIS...? SOME KIND OF GAME?
BEETHOVEN!!
ARE YOU FEELING BETTER NOW?!
OH, JUST PEACHY.
MEH.
SORRY TO LEAVE YOU ALL HANGING.

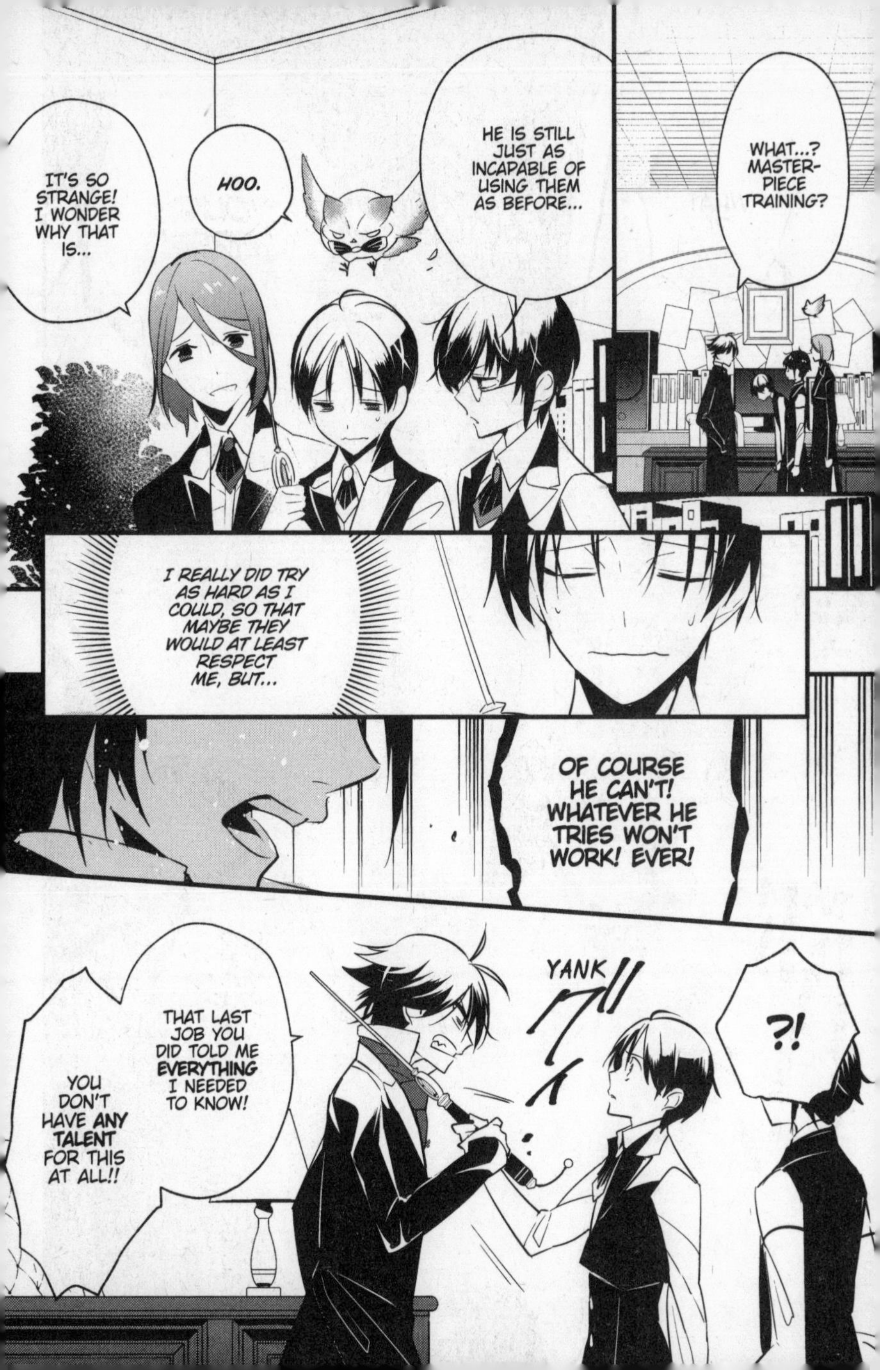

WHAT...? MASTER-PIECE TRAINING?
HE IS STILL JUST AS INCAPABLE OF USING THEM AS BEFORE...
HOO.
IT'S SO STRANGE! I WONDER WHY THAT IS...
I REALLY DID TRY AS HARD AS I COULD, SO THAT MAYBE THEY WOULD AT LEAST RESPECT ME, BUT...
OF COURSE HE CAN'T! WHATEVER HE TRIES WON'T WORK! EVER!
?!
YANK
THAT LAST JOB YOU DID TOLD ME **EVERYTHING** I NEEDED TO KNOW!
YOU DON'T HAVE **ANY TALENT** FOR THIS AT ALL!!

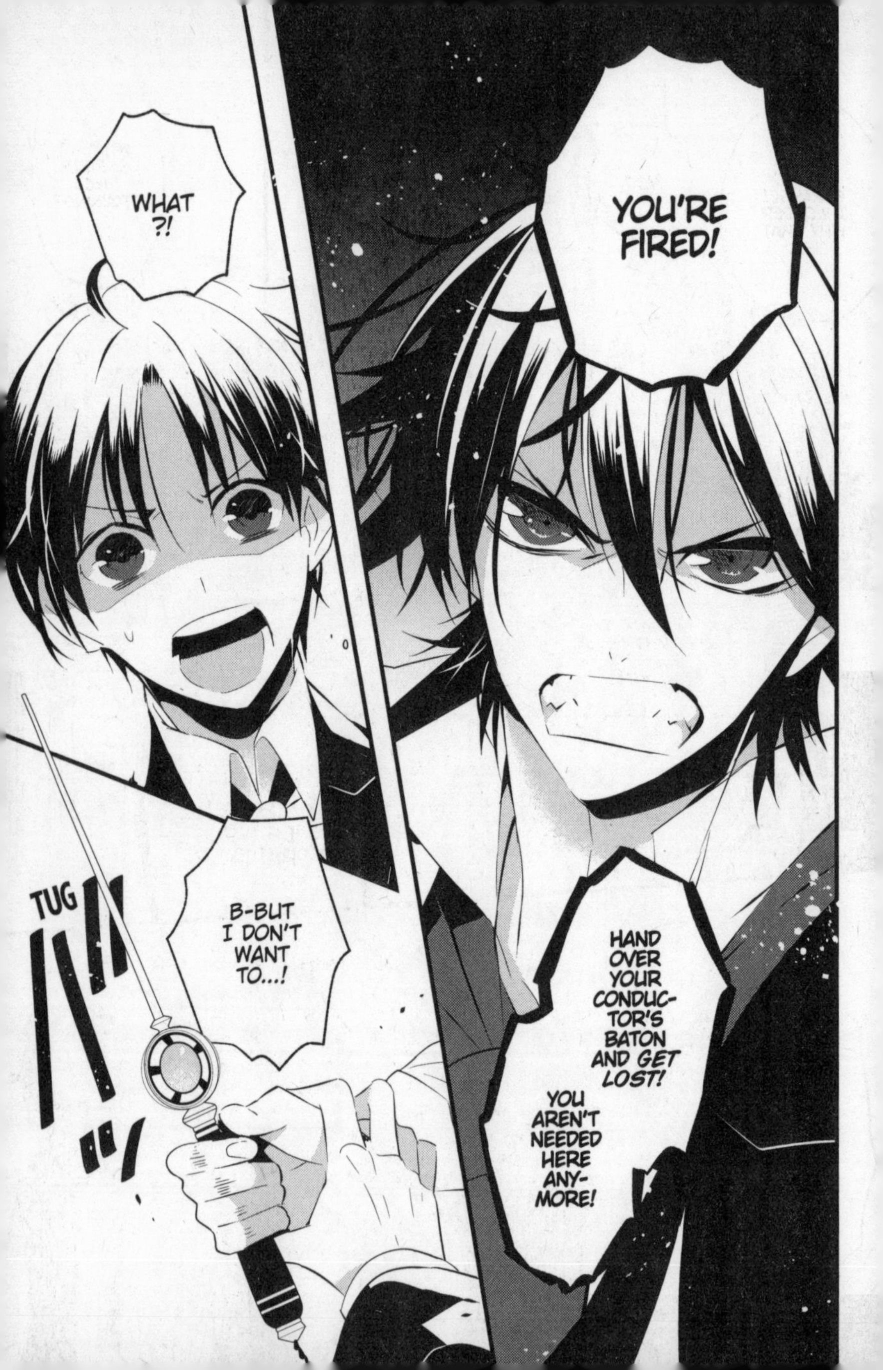
YOU'RE FIRED!
HAND OVER YOUR CONDUCTOR'S BATON AND GET LOST!
YOU AREN'T NEEDED HERE ANYMORE!
WHAT ?!
B-BUT I DON'T WANT TO...!
TUG

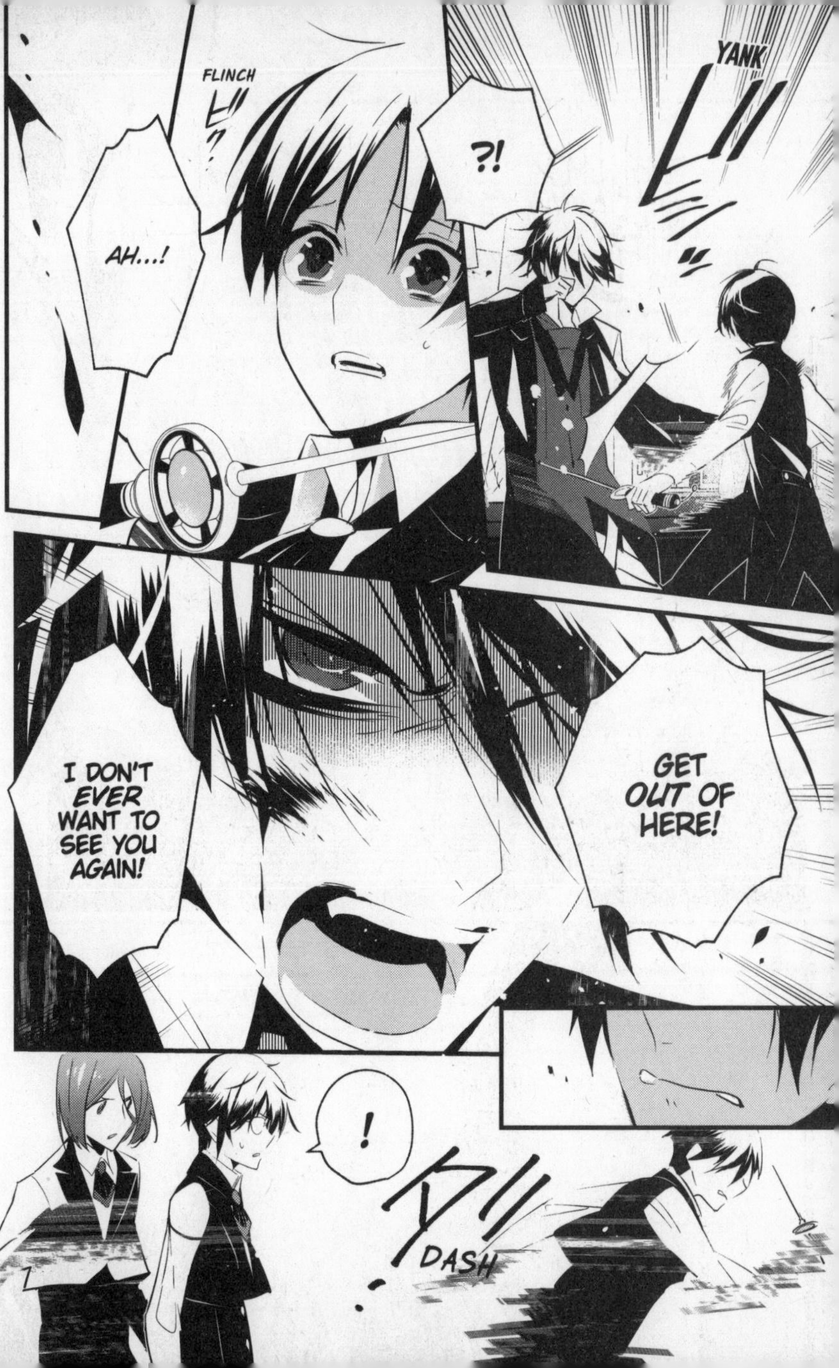
YANK
?!
FLINCH
AH...!
GET OUT OF HERE!
I DON'T EVER WANT TO SEE YOU AGAIN!
DASH
!

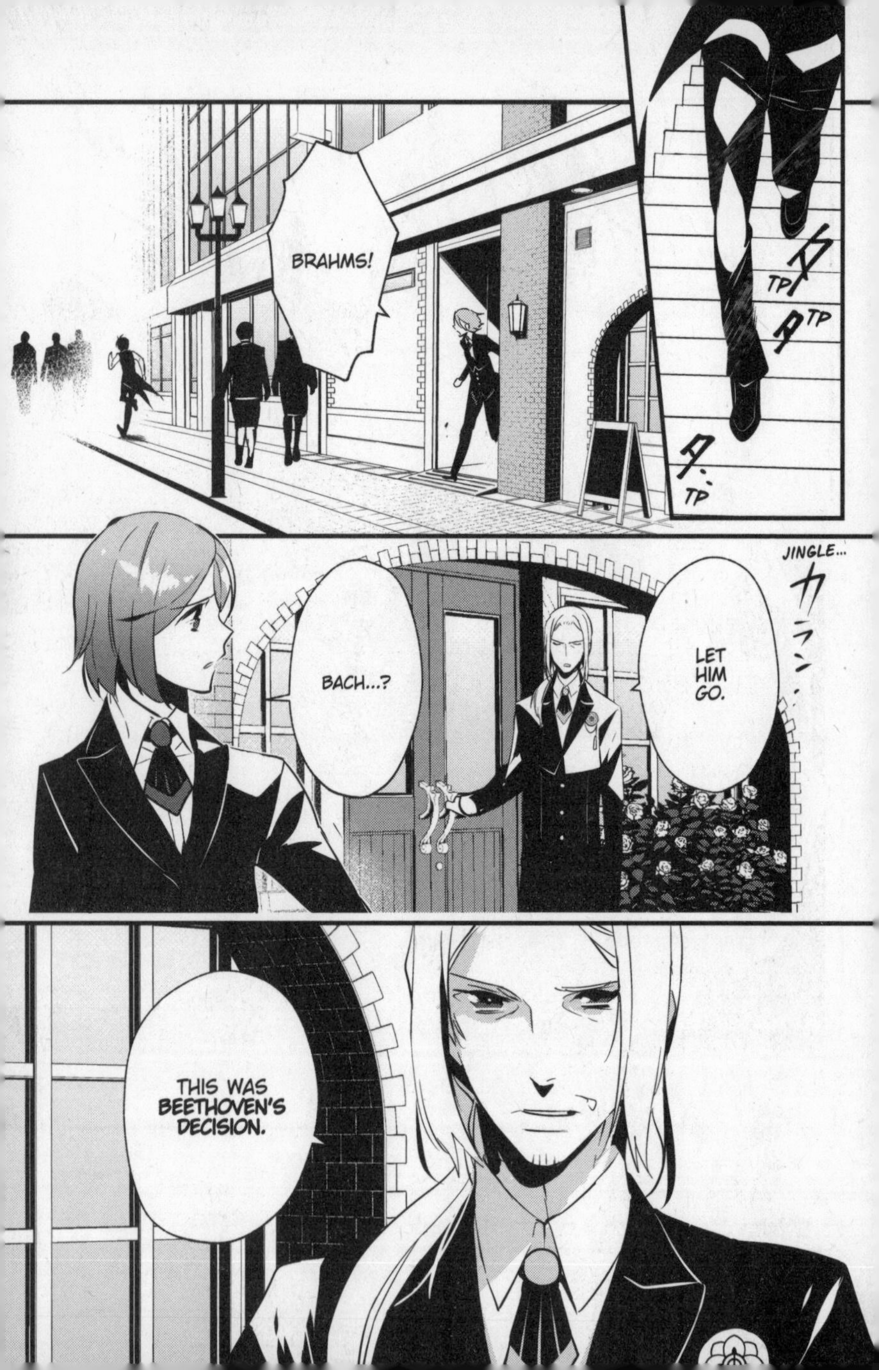

TP
TP
TP
BRAHMS!
JINGLE...
カラン
LET HIM GO.
BACH...?
THIS WAS BEETHOVEN'S DECISION.

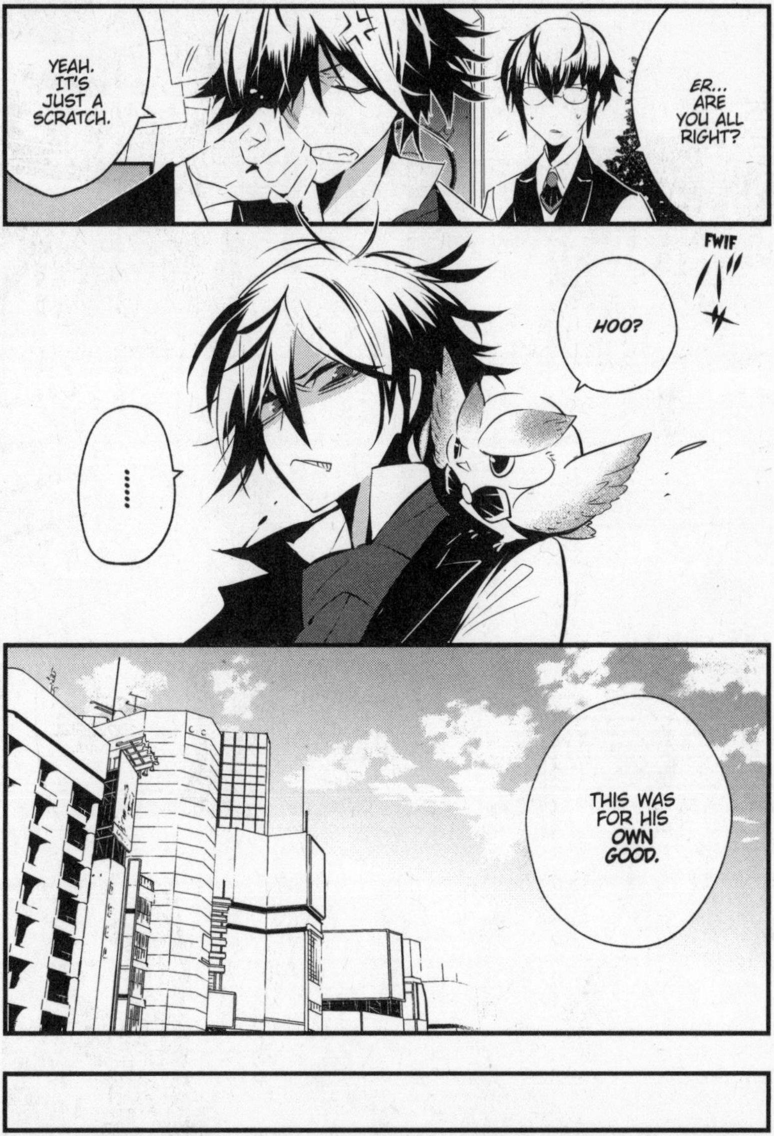
ER... ARE YOU ALL RIGHT?
YEAH. IT'S JUST A SCRATCH.
FWIF
HOO?
......
THIS WAS FOR HIS OWN GOOD.

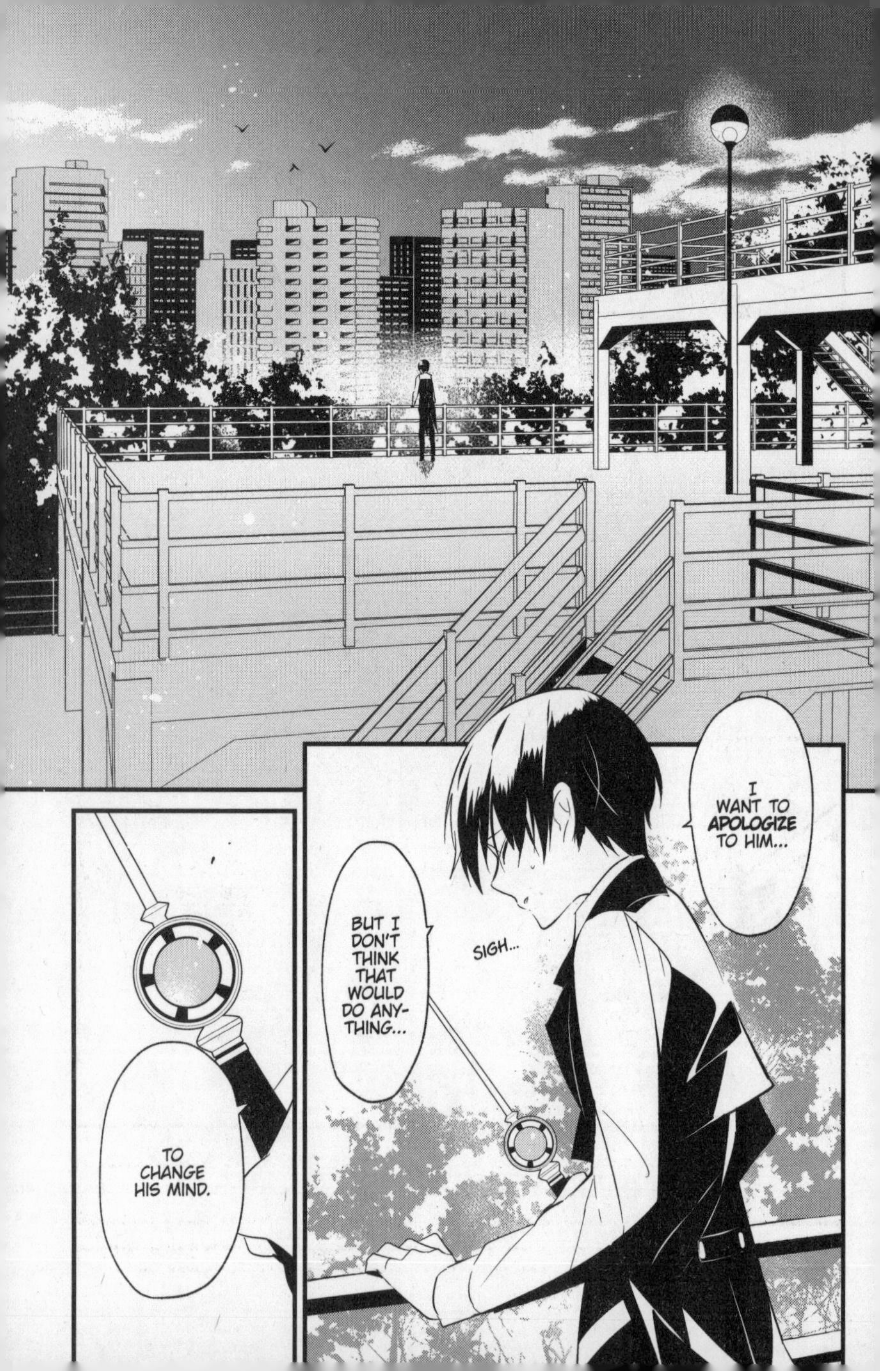
I WANT TO APOLOGIZE TO HIM...
SIGH...
BUT I DON'T THINK THAT WOULD DO ANYTHING...
TO CHANGE HIS MIND.

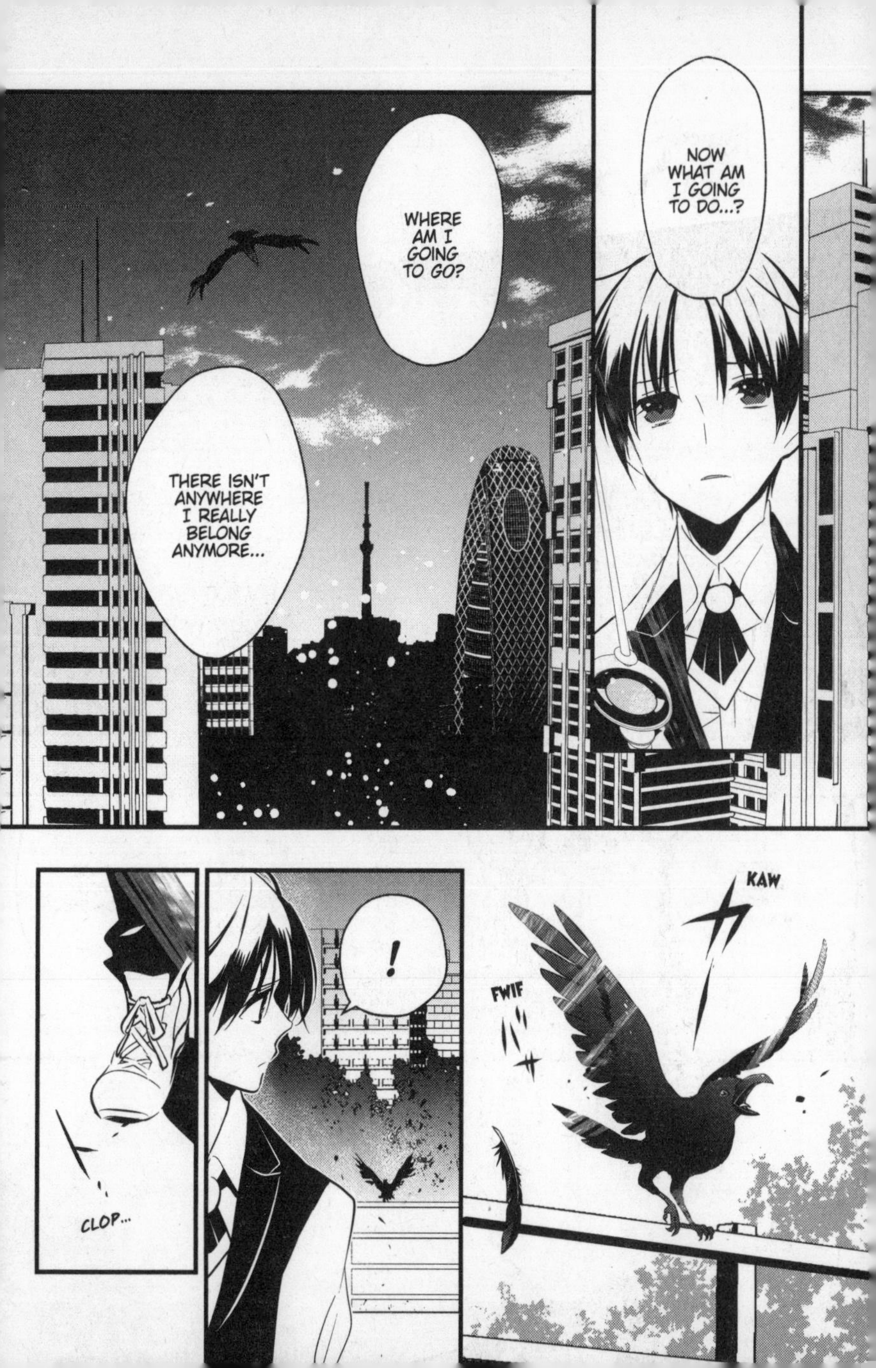
NOW WHAT AM I GOING TO DO...?
WHERE AM I GOING TO GO?
THERE ISN'T ANYWHERE I REALLY BELONG ANYMORE...
KAW
FWIF
!
CLOP...

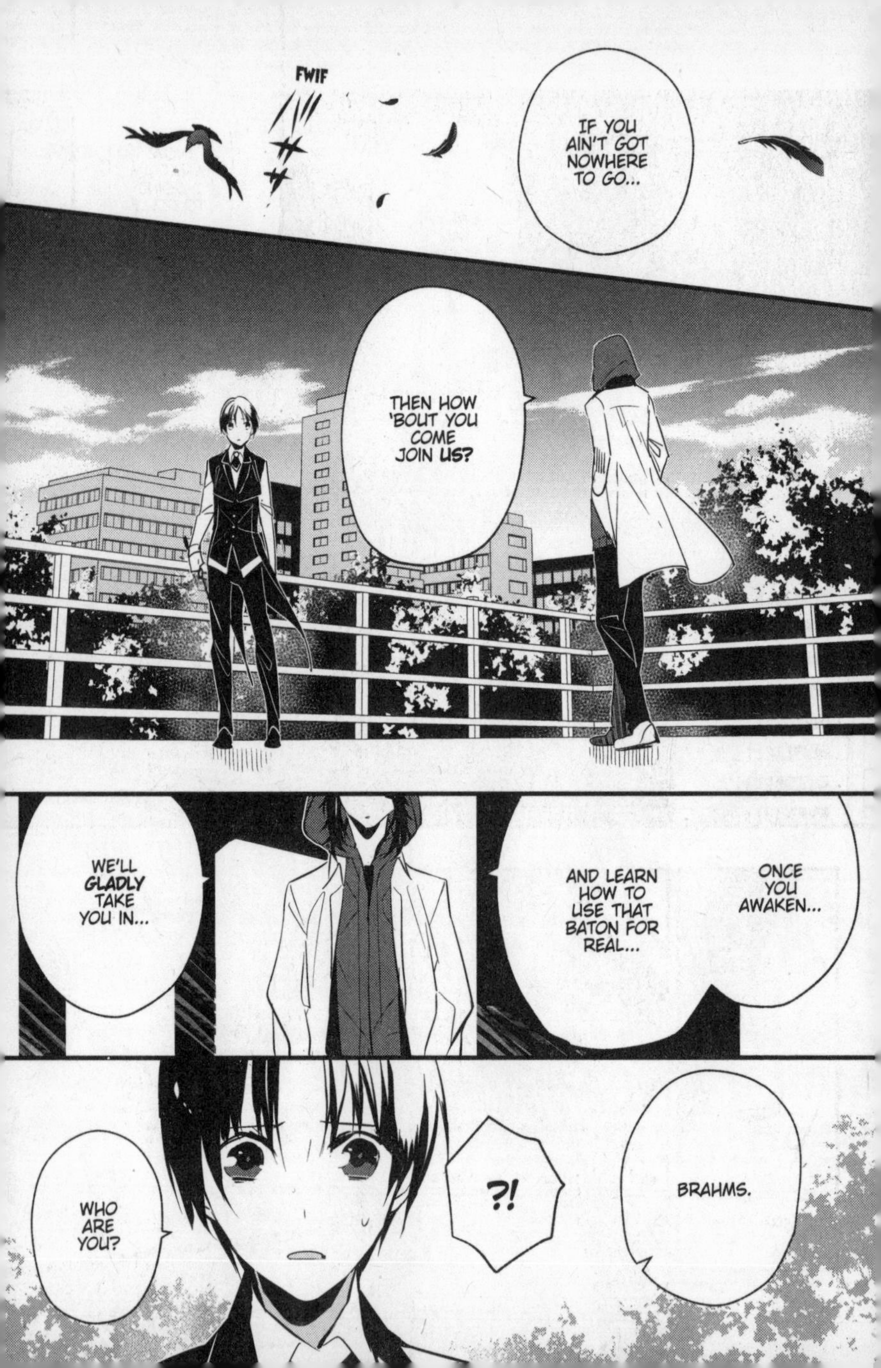
IF YOU AIN'T GOT NOWHERE TO GO...
FWIF
THEN HOW 'BOUT YOU COME JOIN US?
ONCE YOU AWAKEN...
AND LEARN HOW TO USE THAT BATON FOR REAL...
WE'LL GLADLY TAKE YOU IN...
BRAHMS.
?!
WHO ARE YOU?

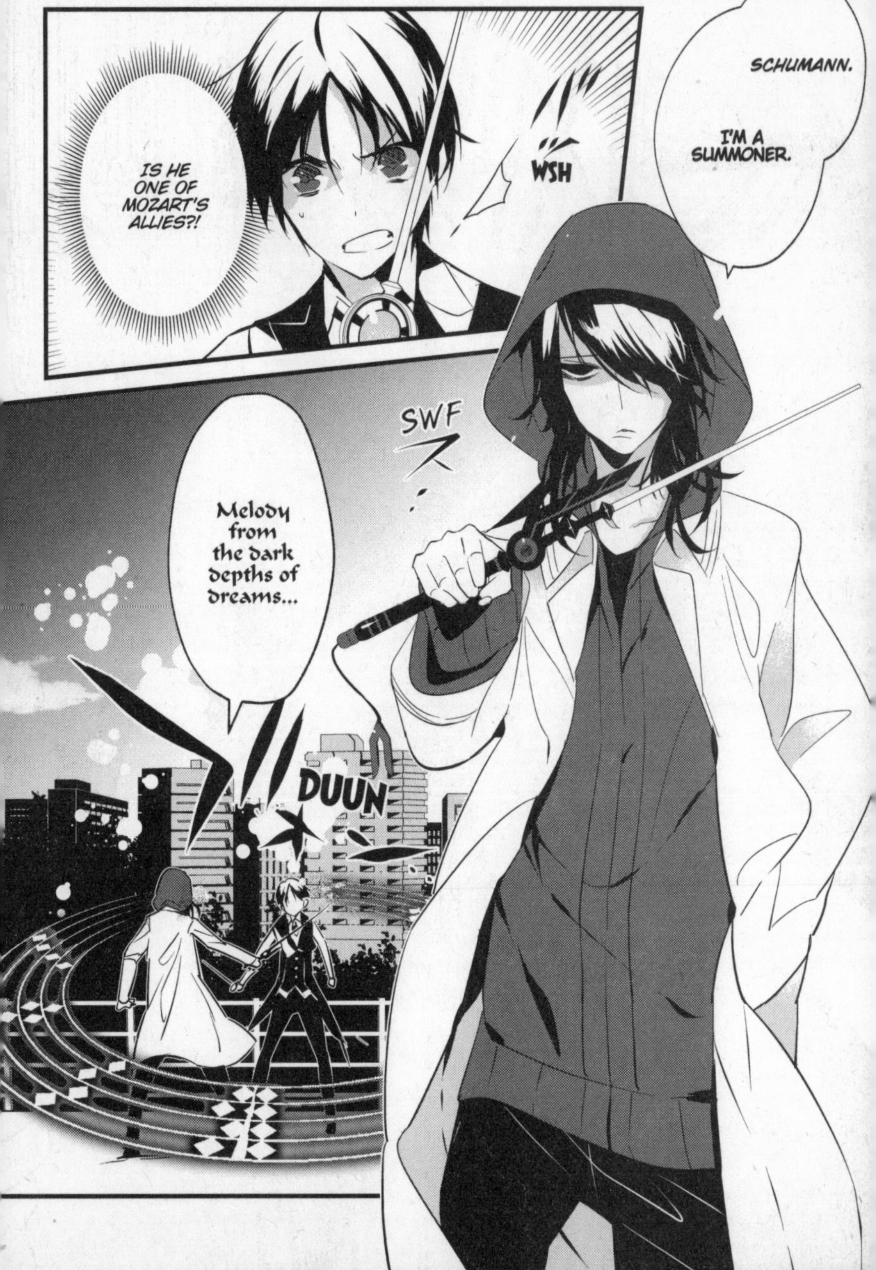
SCHUMANN.
I'M A SUMMONER.
WSH
IS HE ONE OF MOZART'S ALLIES?!
SWF
Melody from the dark depths of dreams...
DUUN

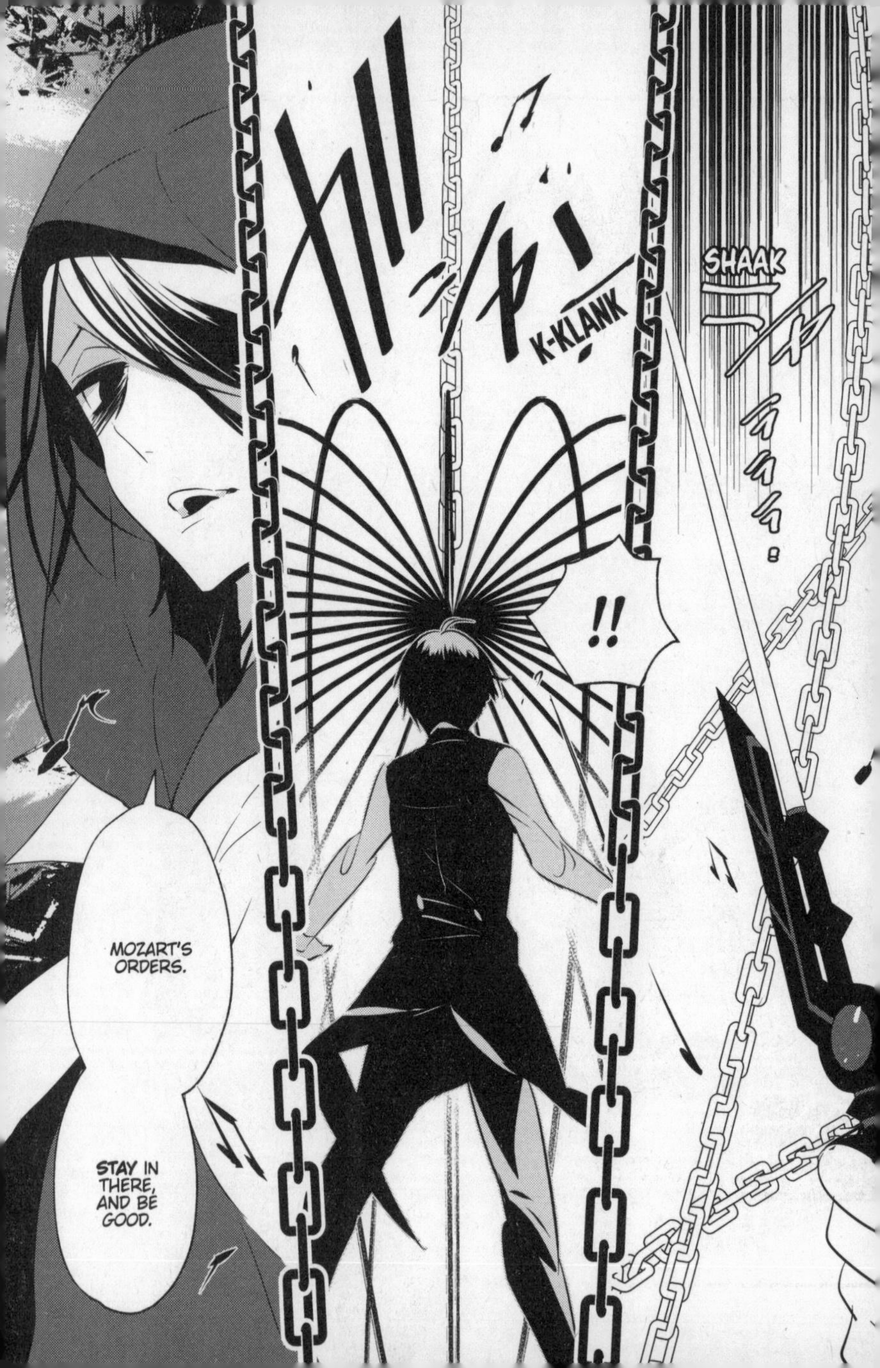
SHAAK
K-KLANK
!!
MOZART'S ORDERS.
STAY IN THERE, AND BE GOOD.

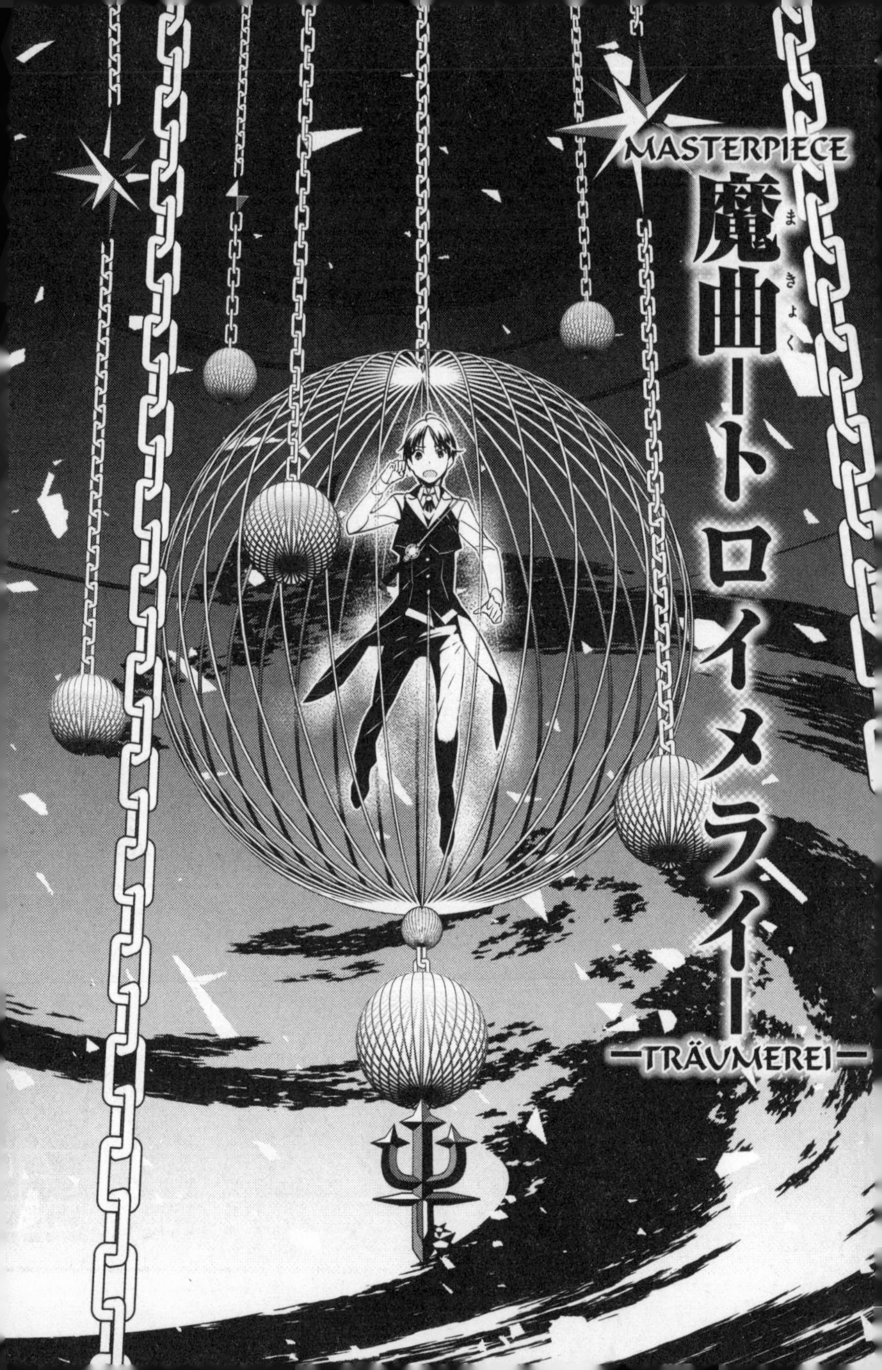
MASTERPIECE
魔曲(まきょく)―トロイメライ―
―TRÄUMEREI―

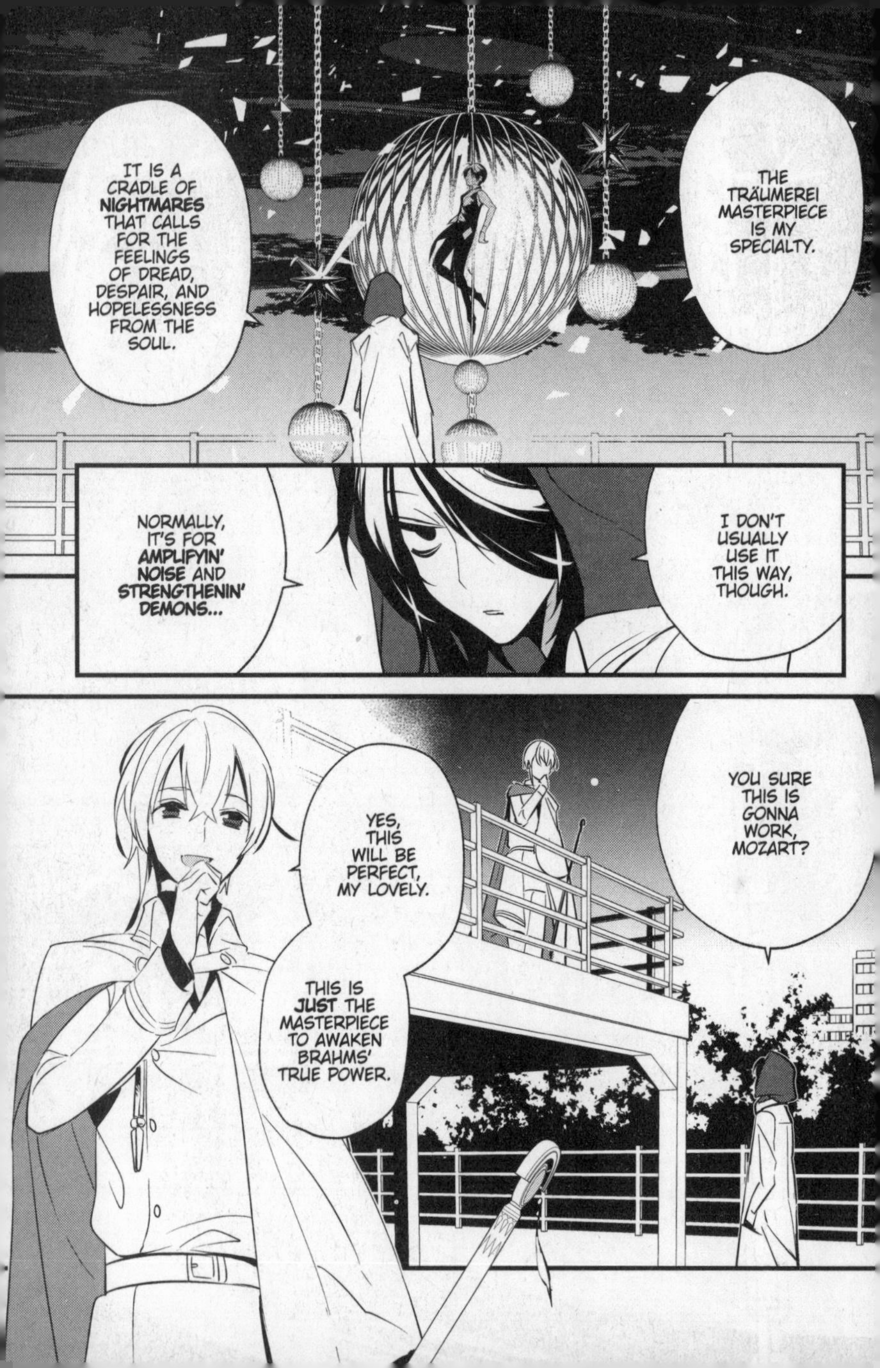
THE TRÄUMEREI MASTERPIECE IS MY SPECIALTY.
IT IS A CRADLE OF NIGHTMARES THAT CALLS FOR THE FEELINGS OF DREAD, DESPAIR, AND HOPELESSNESS FROM THE SOUL.
I DON'T USUALLY USE IT THIS WAY, THOUGH.
NORMALLY, IT'S FOR AMPLIFYIN' NOISE AND STRENGTHENIN' DEMONS...
YOU SURE THIS IS GONNA WORK, MOZART?
YES, THIS WILL BE PERFECT, MY LOVELY.
THIS IS JUST THE MASTERPIECE TO AWAKEN BRAHMS' TRUE POWER.

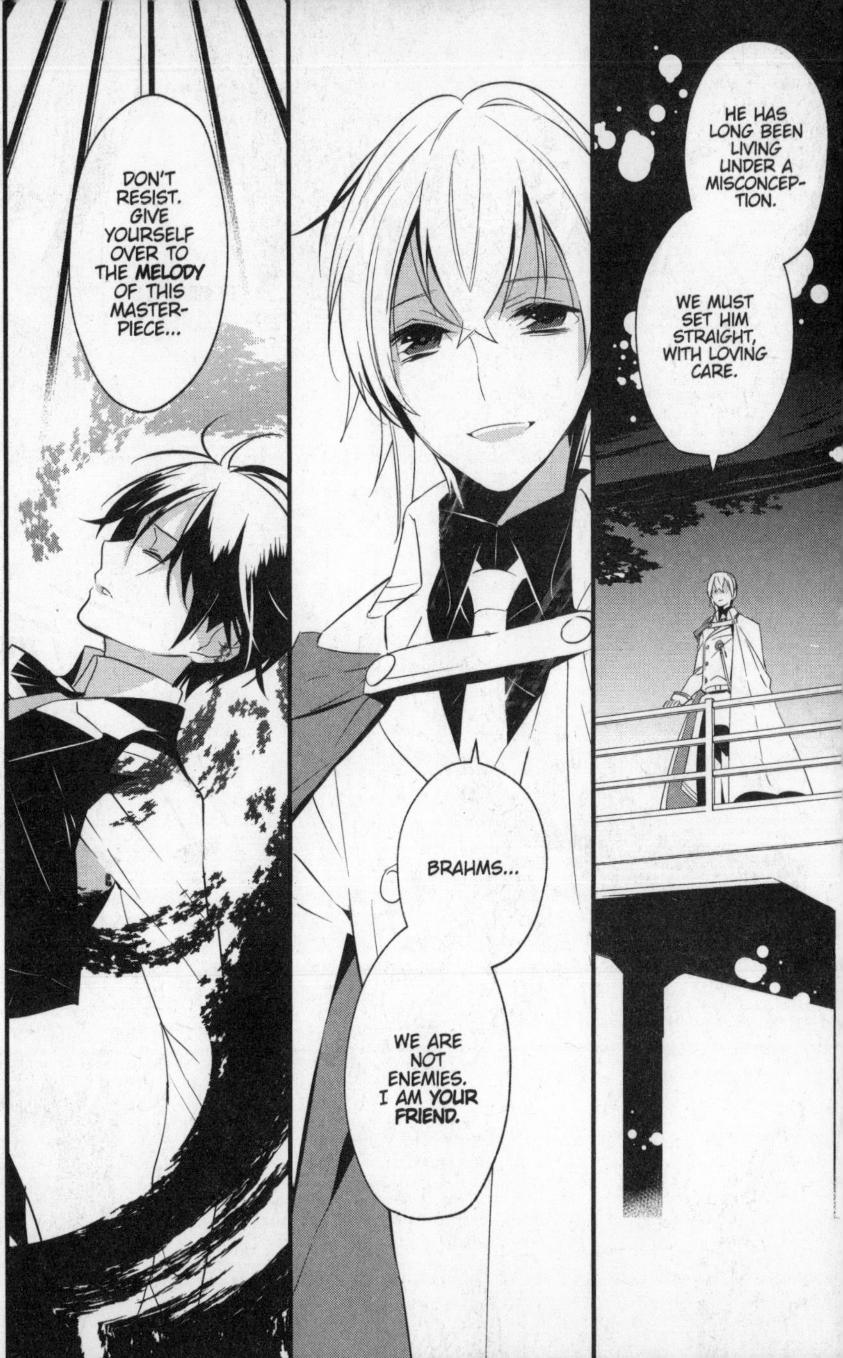
HE HAS LONG BEEN LIVING UNDER A MISCONCEPTION.
WE MUST SET HIM STRAIGHT, WITH LOVING CARE.
BRAHMS...
WE ARE NOT ENEMIES. I AM YOUR FRIEND.
DON'T RESIST. GIVE YOURSELF OVER TO THE MELODY OF THIS MASTERPIECE...

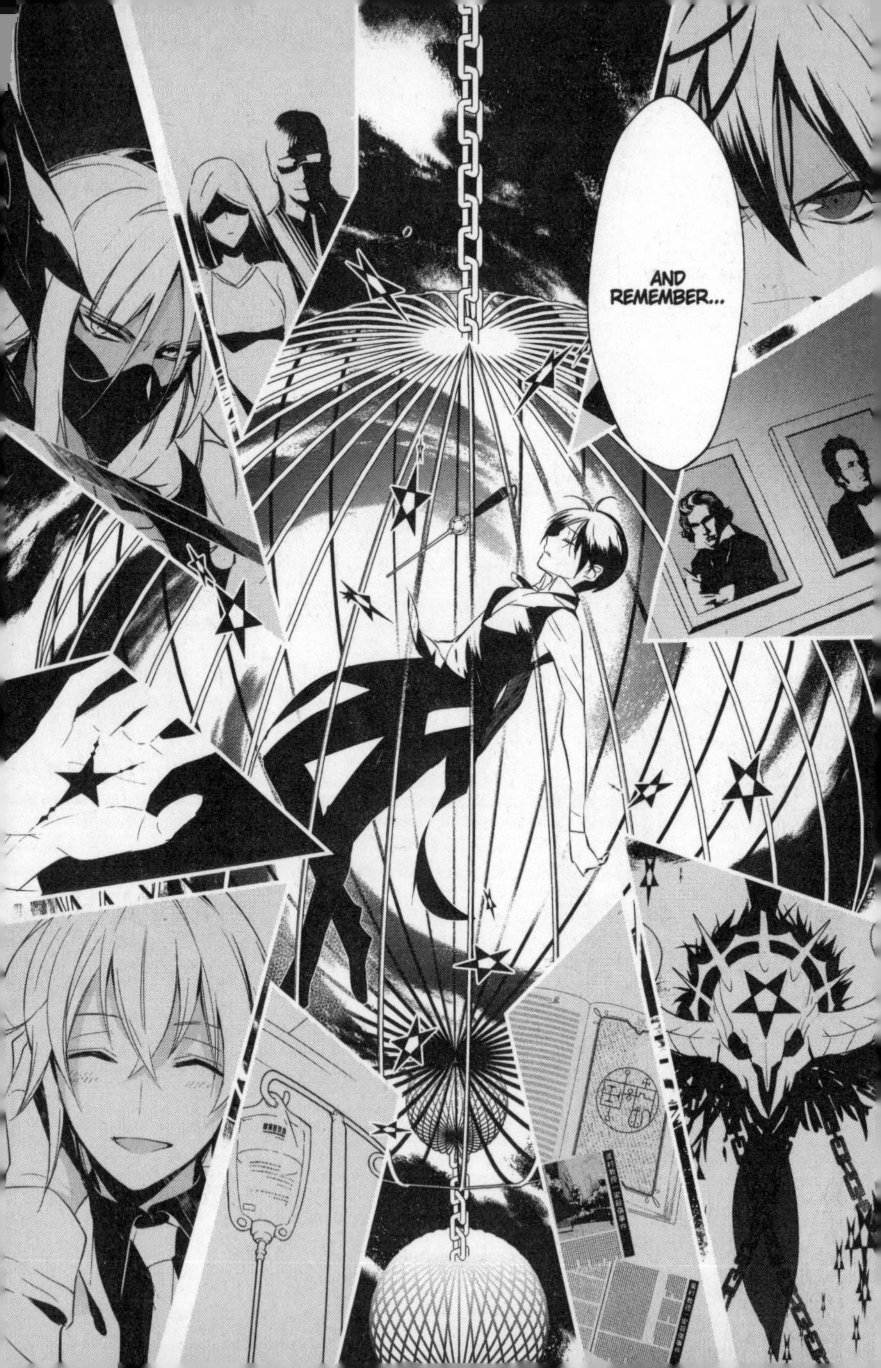
AND REMEMBER...

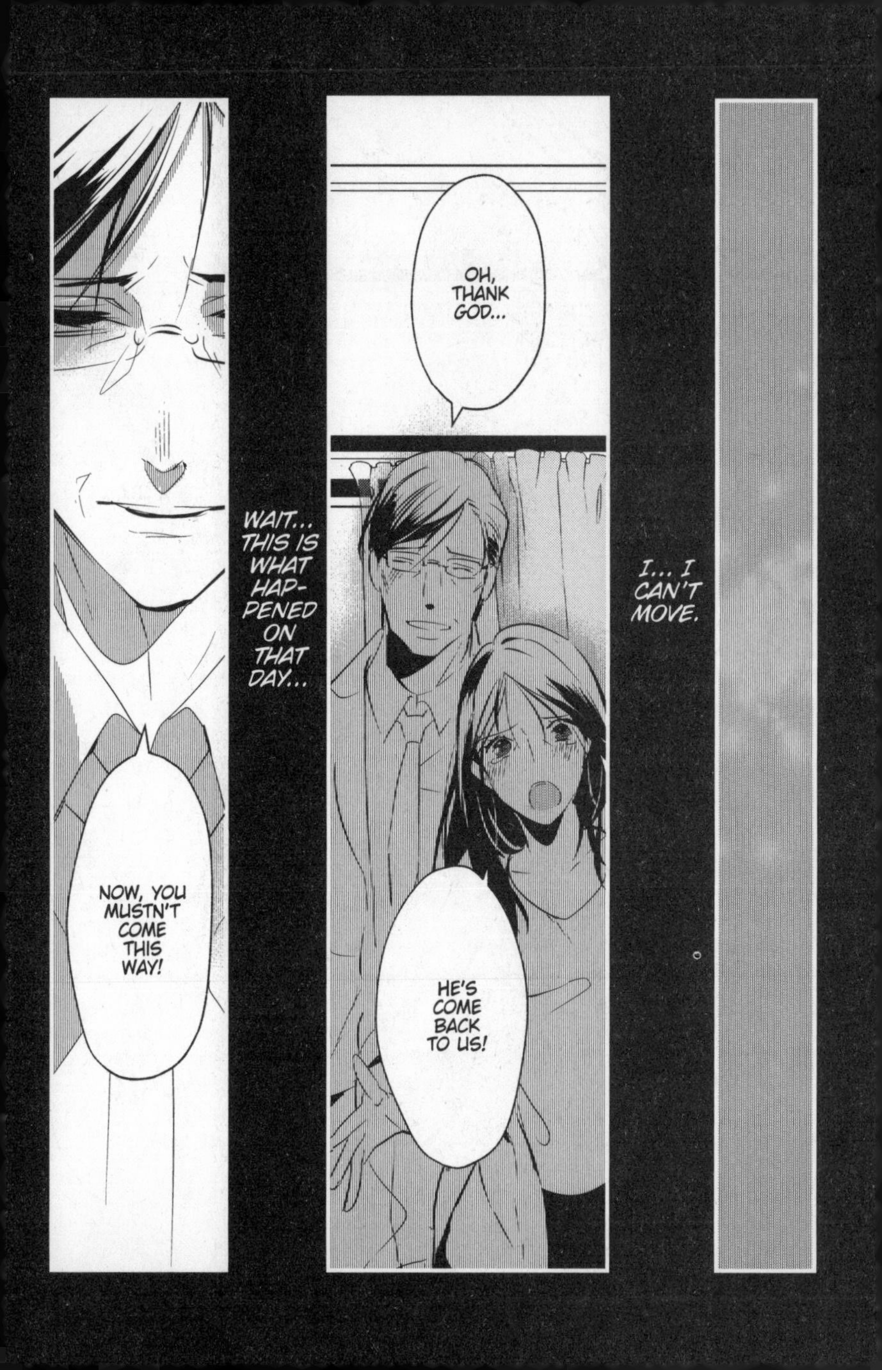
I... I CAN'T MOVE.
OH, THANK GOD...
HE'S COME BACK TO US!
WAIT... THIS IS WHAT HAPPENED ON THAT DAY...
NOW, YOU MUSTN'T COME THIS WAY!

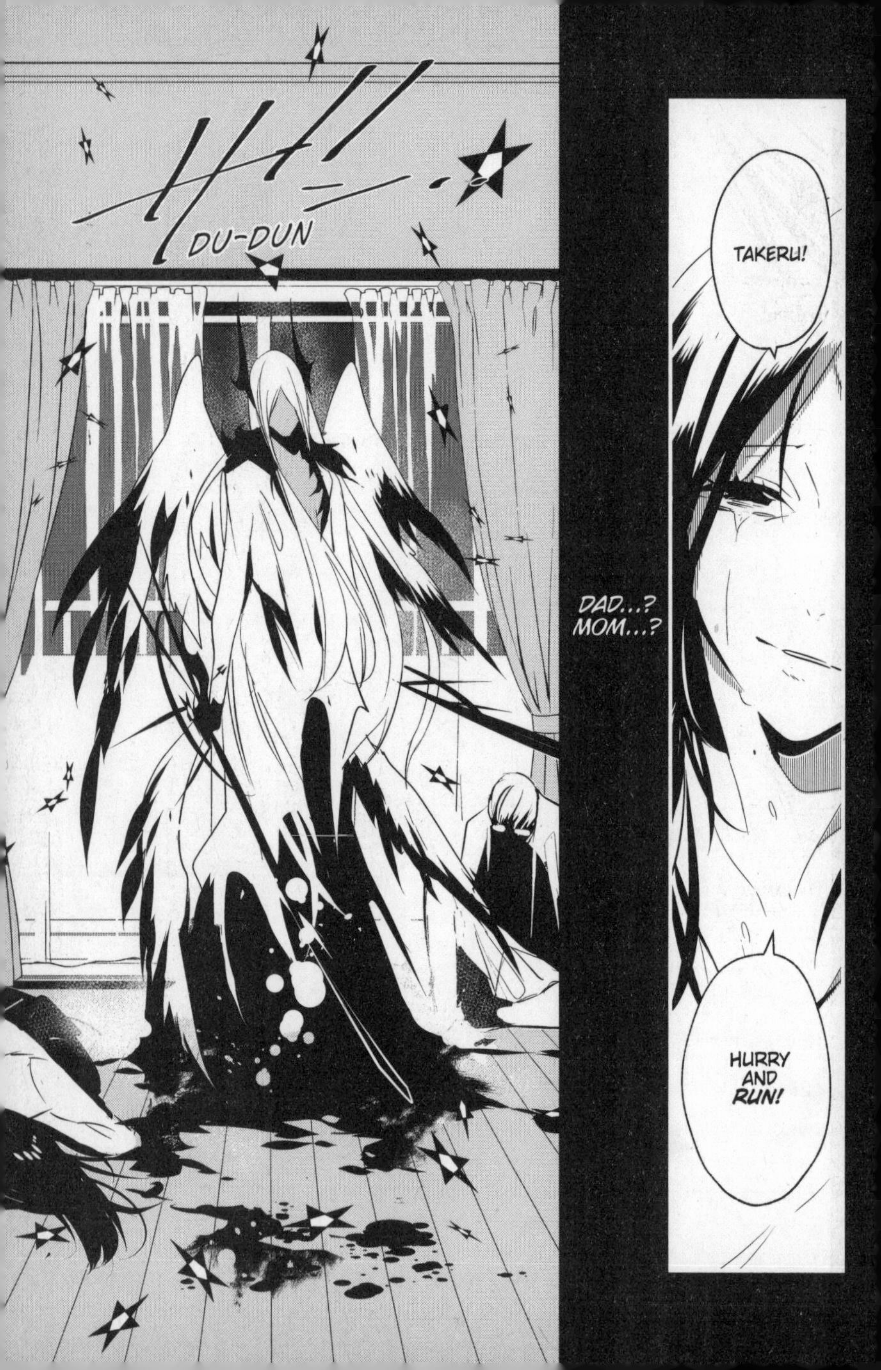
TAKERU!
HURRY AND RUN!
DAD...? MOM...?
DU-DUN

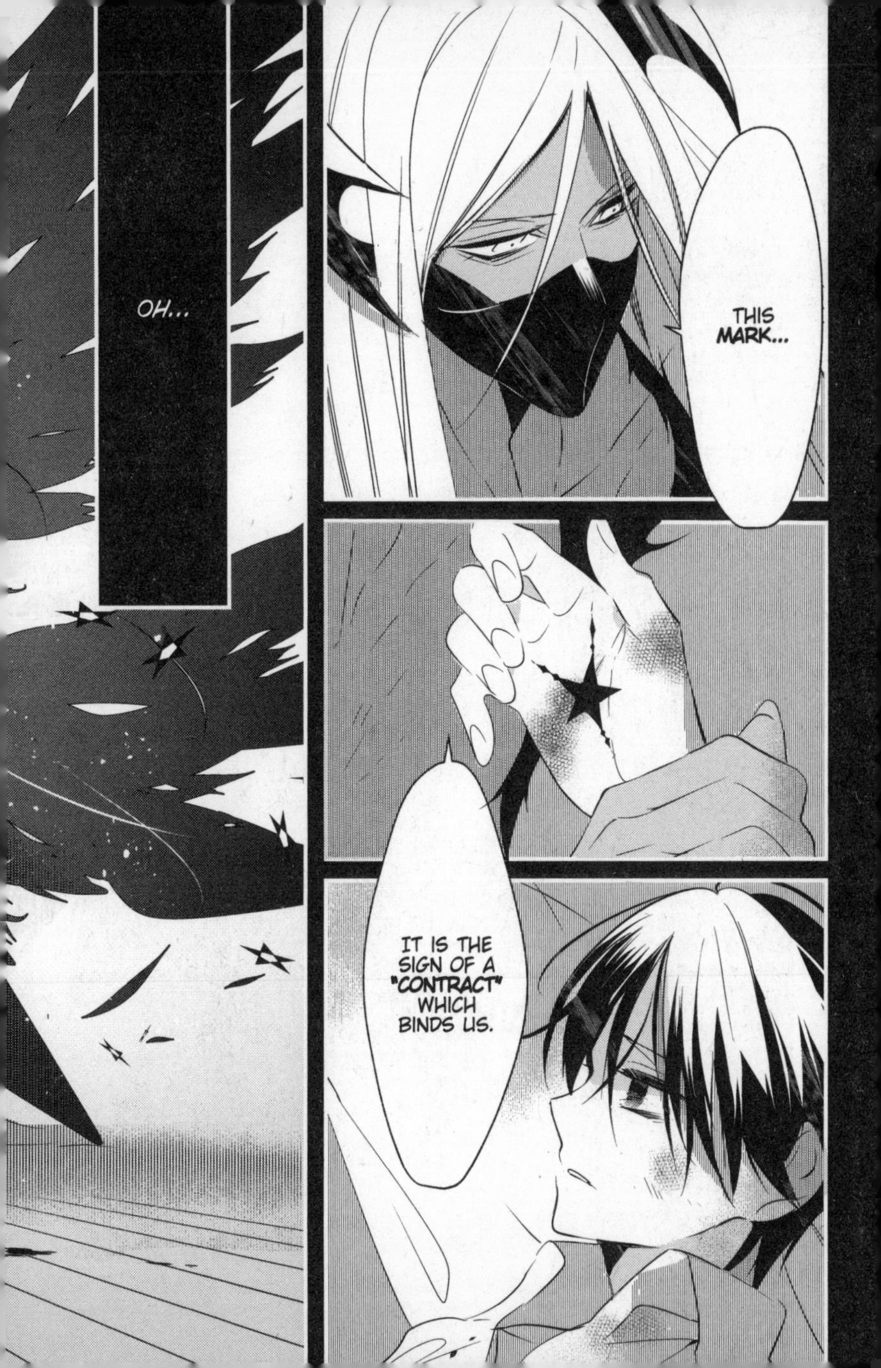
THIS MARK...
IT IS THE SIGN OF A "CONTRACT" WHICH BINDS US.
OH...

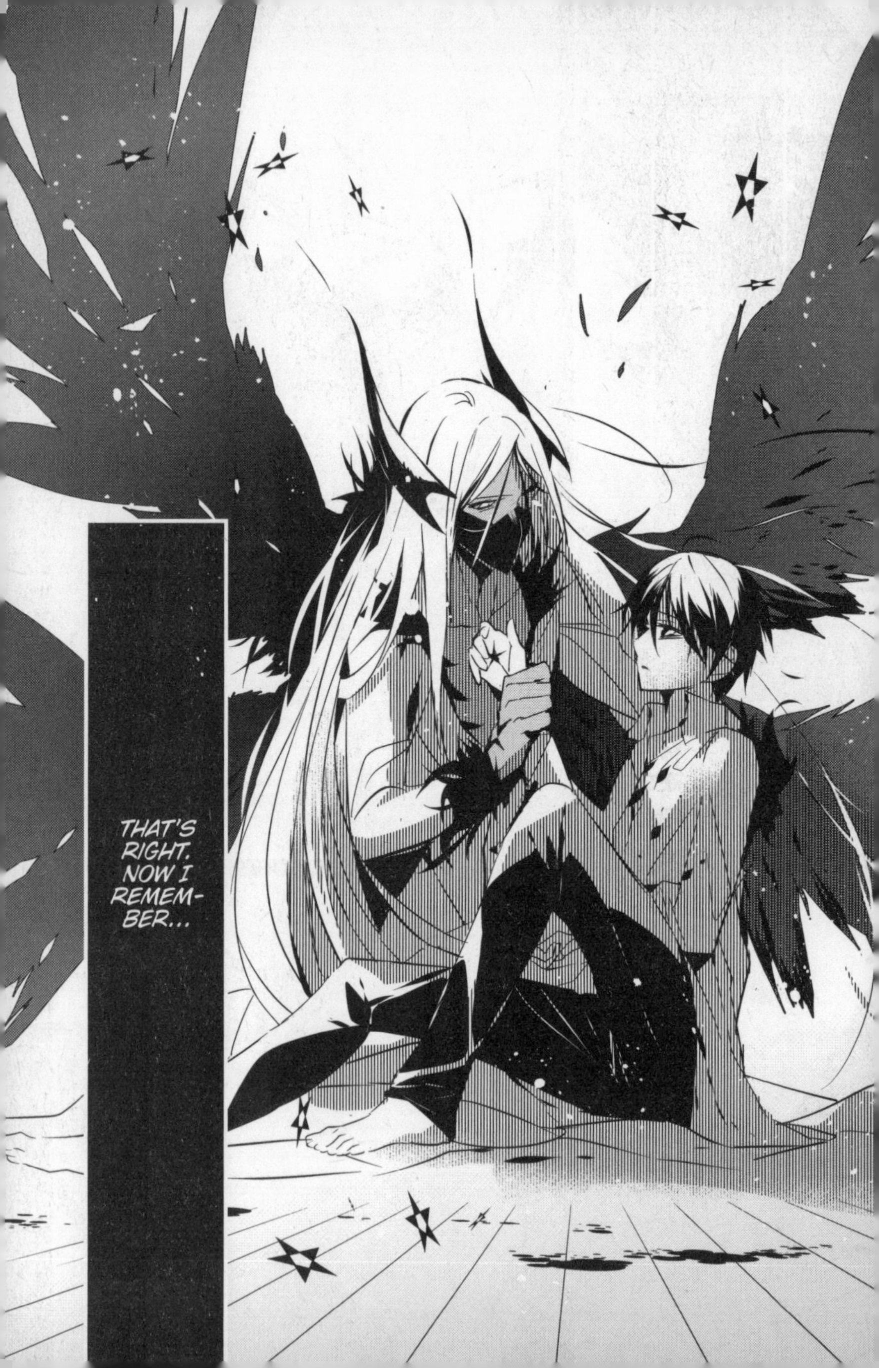
THAT'S RIGHT. NOW I REMEMBER...

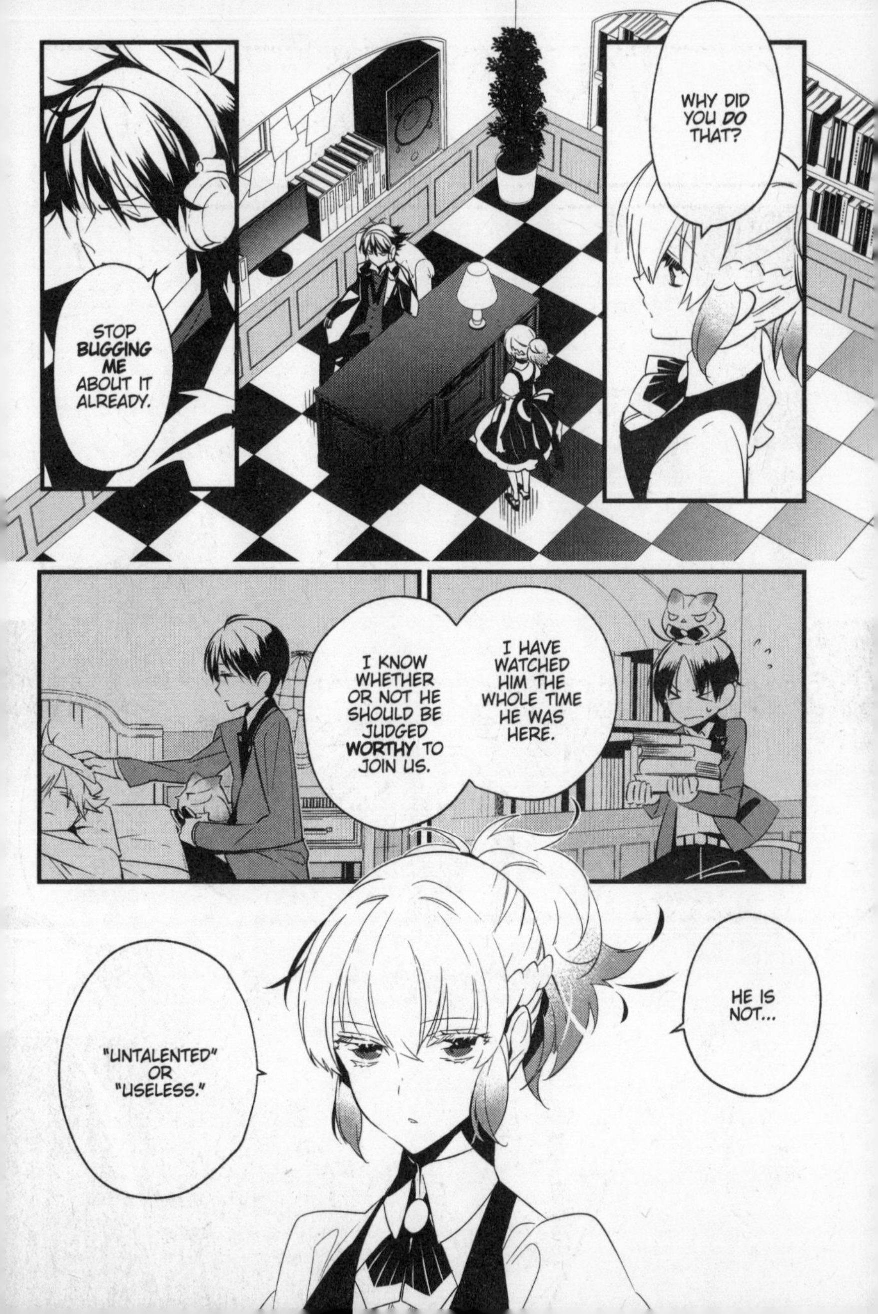
WHY DID YOU *DO* THAT?
STOP **BUGGING ME** ABOUT IT ALREADY.
I HAVE WATCHED HIM THE WHOLE TIME HE WAS HERE.
I KNOW WHETHER OR NOT HE SHOULD BE JUDGED **WORTHY** TO JOIN US.
HE IS NOT...
"UNTALENTED" OR "USELESS."

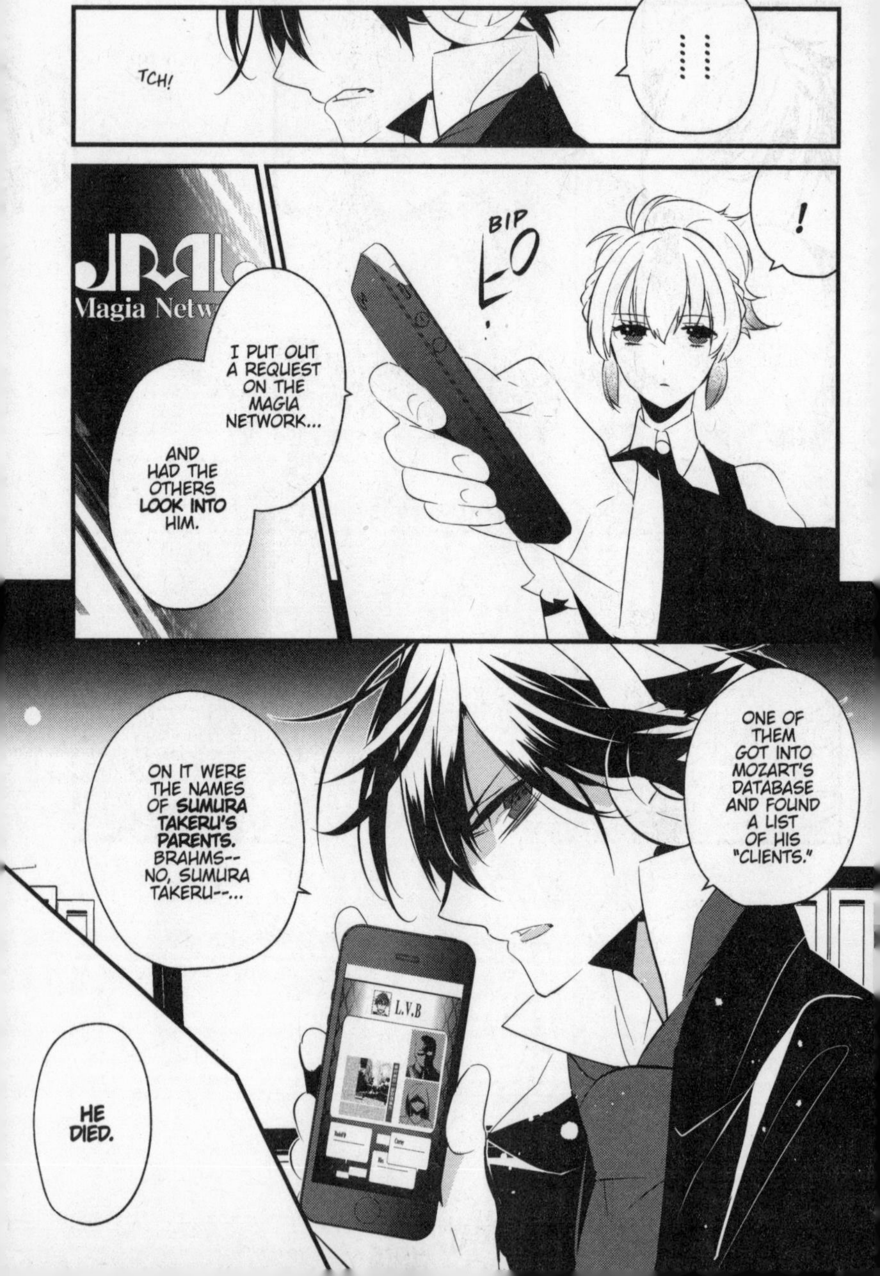
......
TCH!
!
BIP
I PUT OUT A REQUEST ON THE MAGIA NETWORK...
AND HAD THE OTHERS LOOK INTO HIM.
ONE OF THEM GOT INTO MOZART'S DATABASE AND FOUND A LIST OF HIS "CLIENTS."
ON IT WERE THE NAMES OF SUMURA TAKERU'S PARENTS. BRAHMS--NO, SUMURA TAKERU--...
L.V.B
HE DIED.

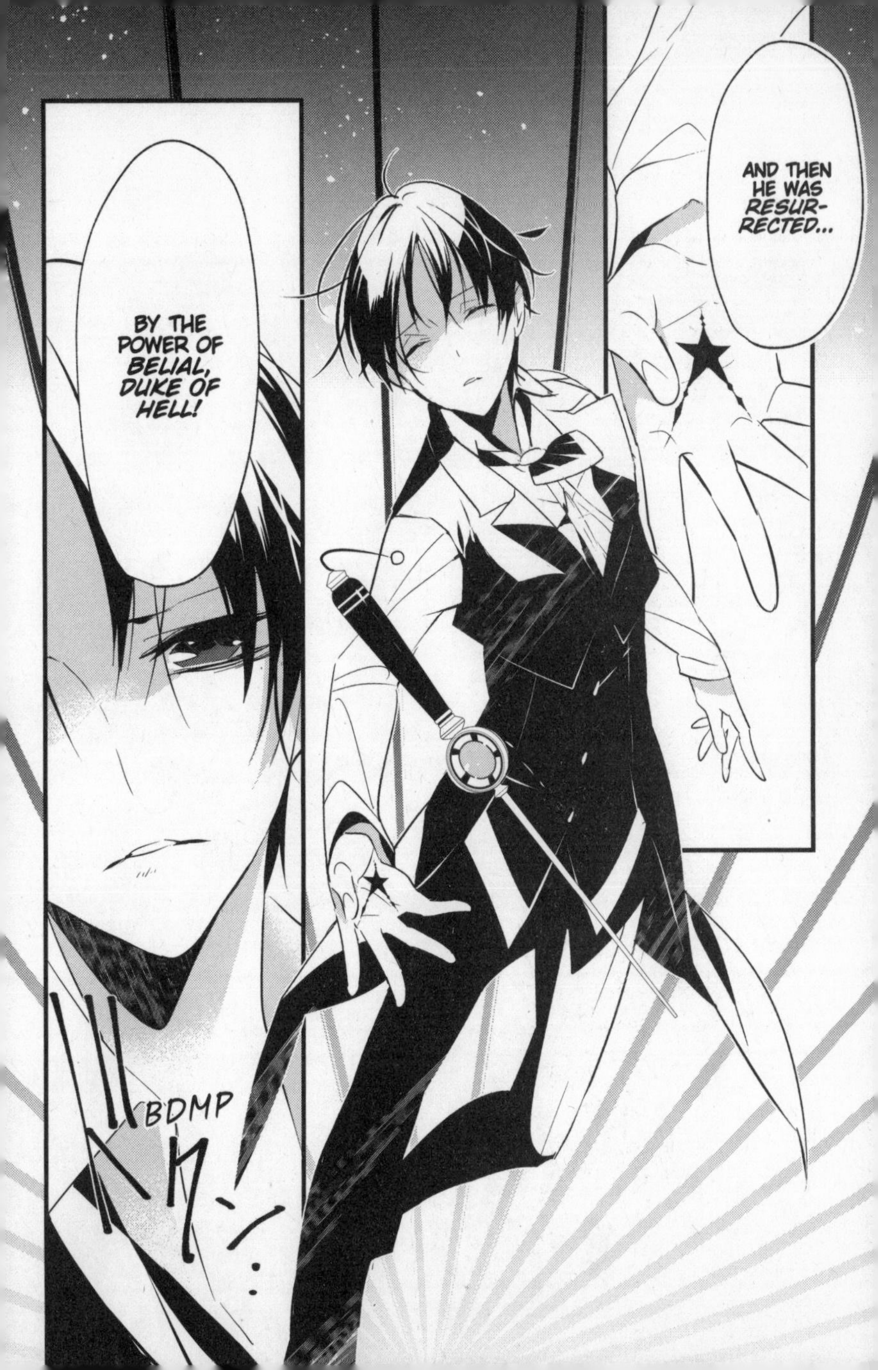
AND THEN HE WAS RESURRECTED...
BY THE POWER OF BELIAL, DUKE OF HELL!
BDMP

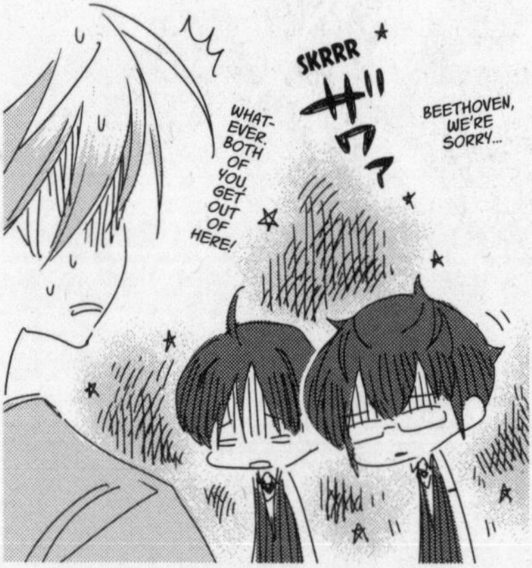
BEETHOVEN, WE'RE SORRY...
SKRRR
WHATEVER. BOTH OF YOU, GET OUT OF HERE!

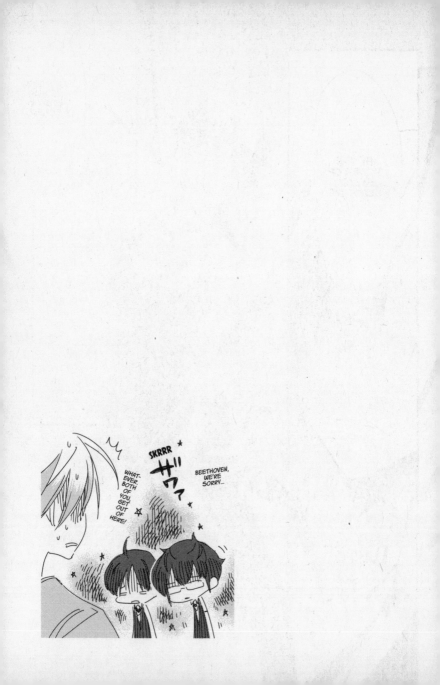

Magia the Ninth

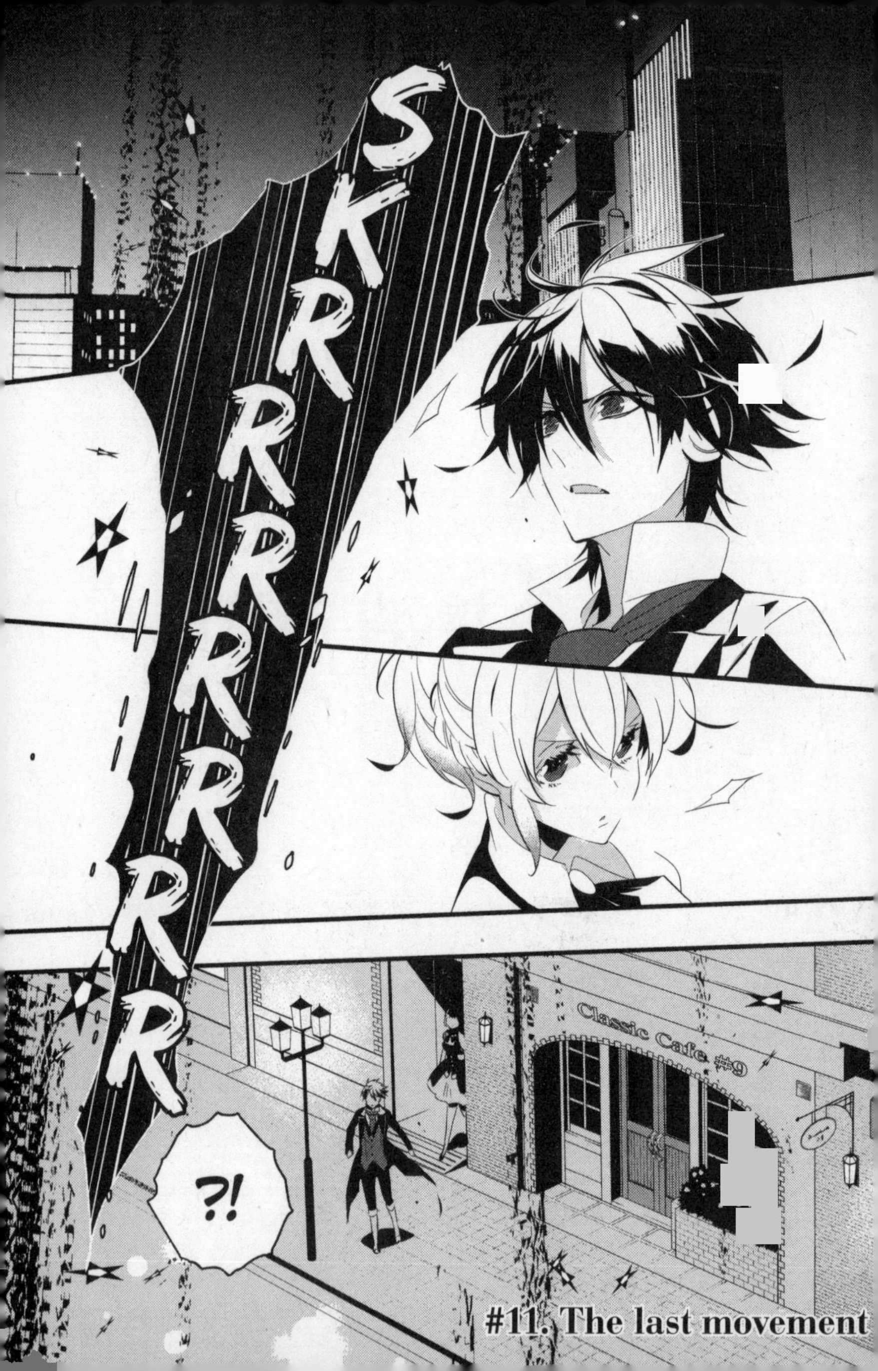
SKRRRRRRRR
?!
Classic Cafe #9
#11. The last movement

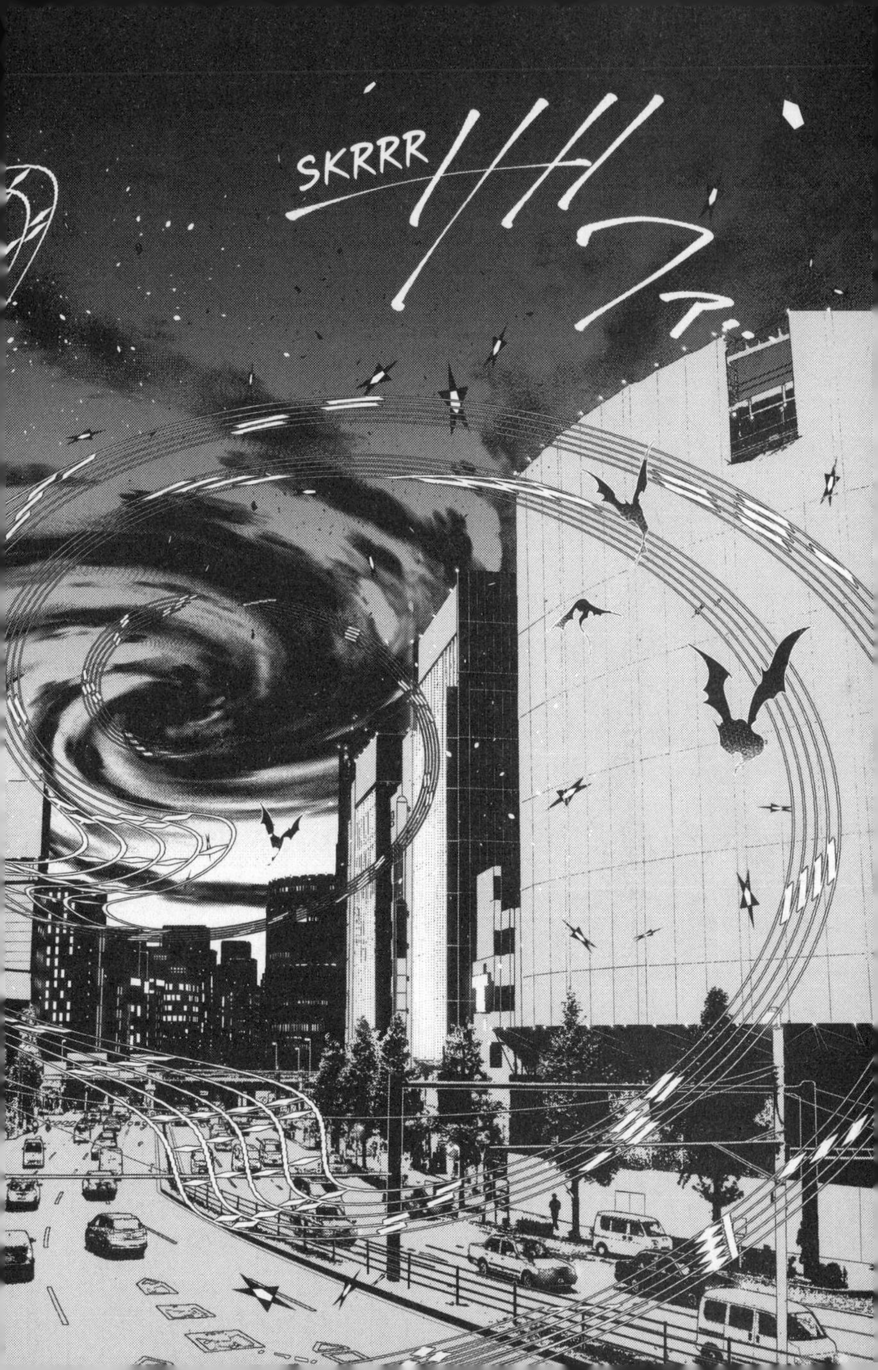
SKRRR

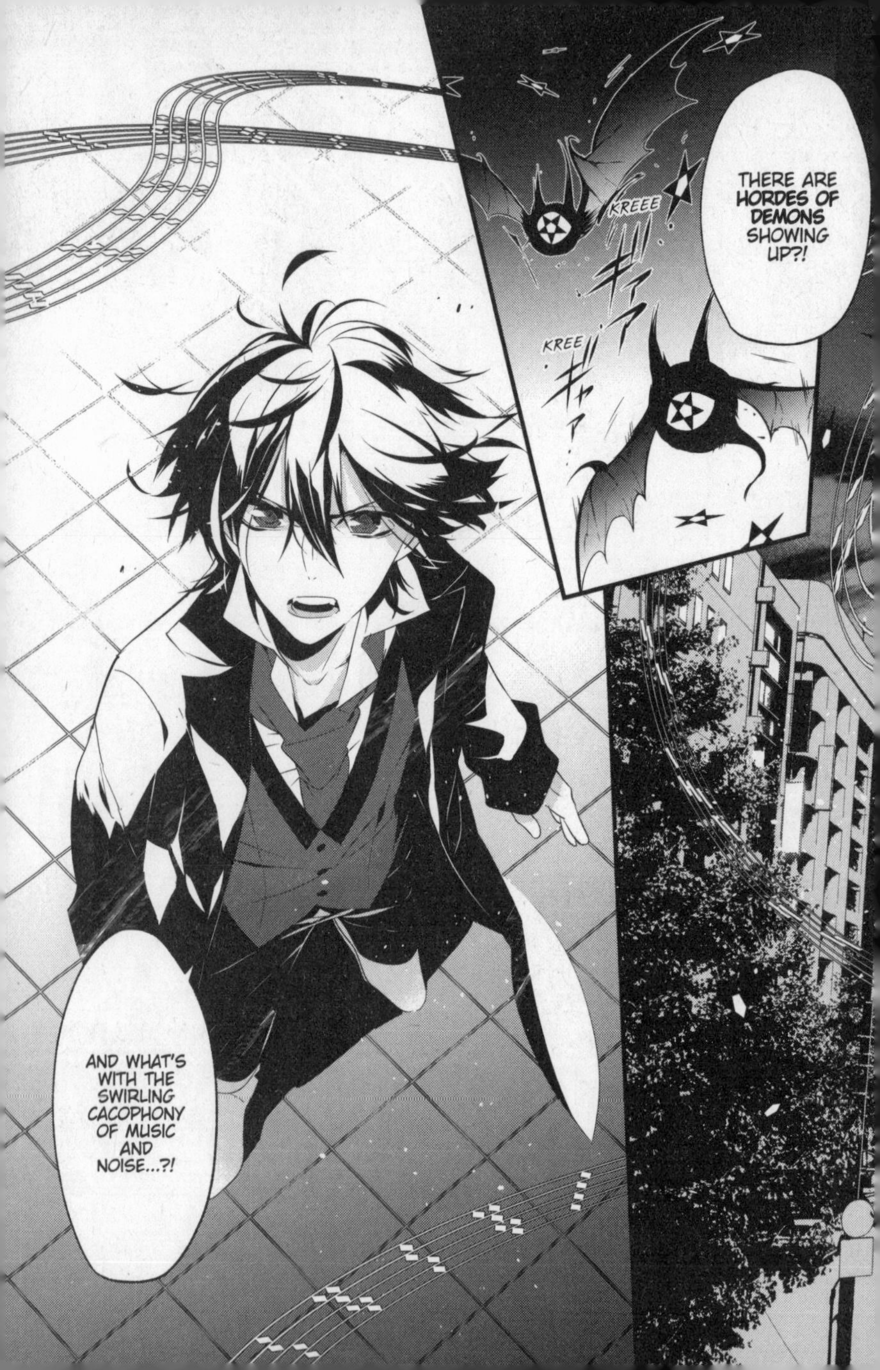
THERE ARE HORDES OF DEMONS SHOWING UP?!
KREEE
KREE
AND WHAT'S WITH THE SWIRLING CACOPHONY OF MUSIC AND NOISE...?!

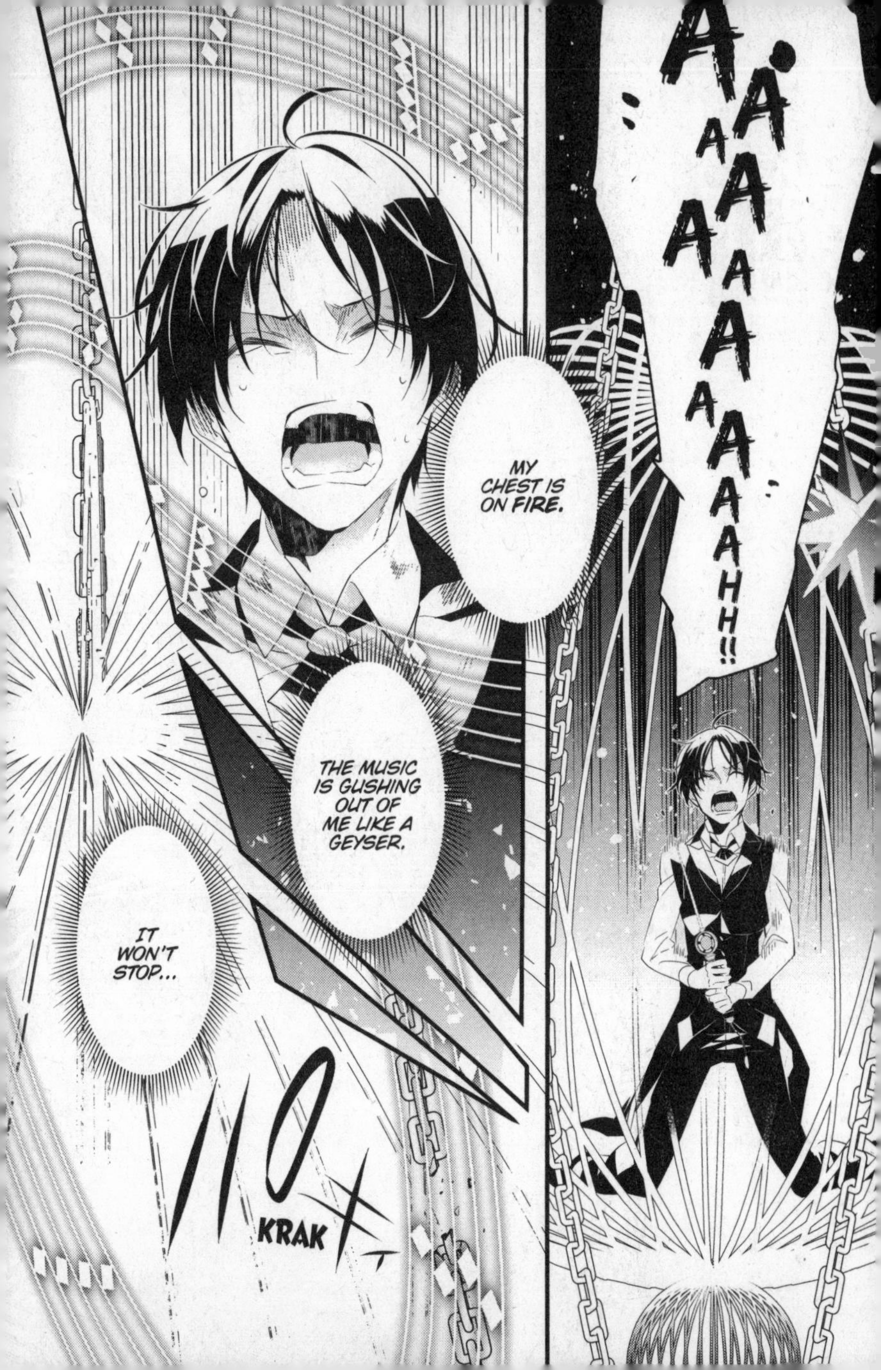
AAAAAAAAAAAAHH!!
MY CHEST IS ON FIRE.
THE MUSIC IS GUSHING OUT OF ME LIKE A GEYSER.
IT WON'T STOP...
KRAK

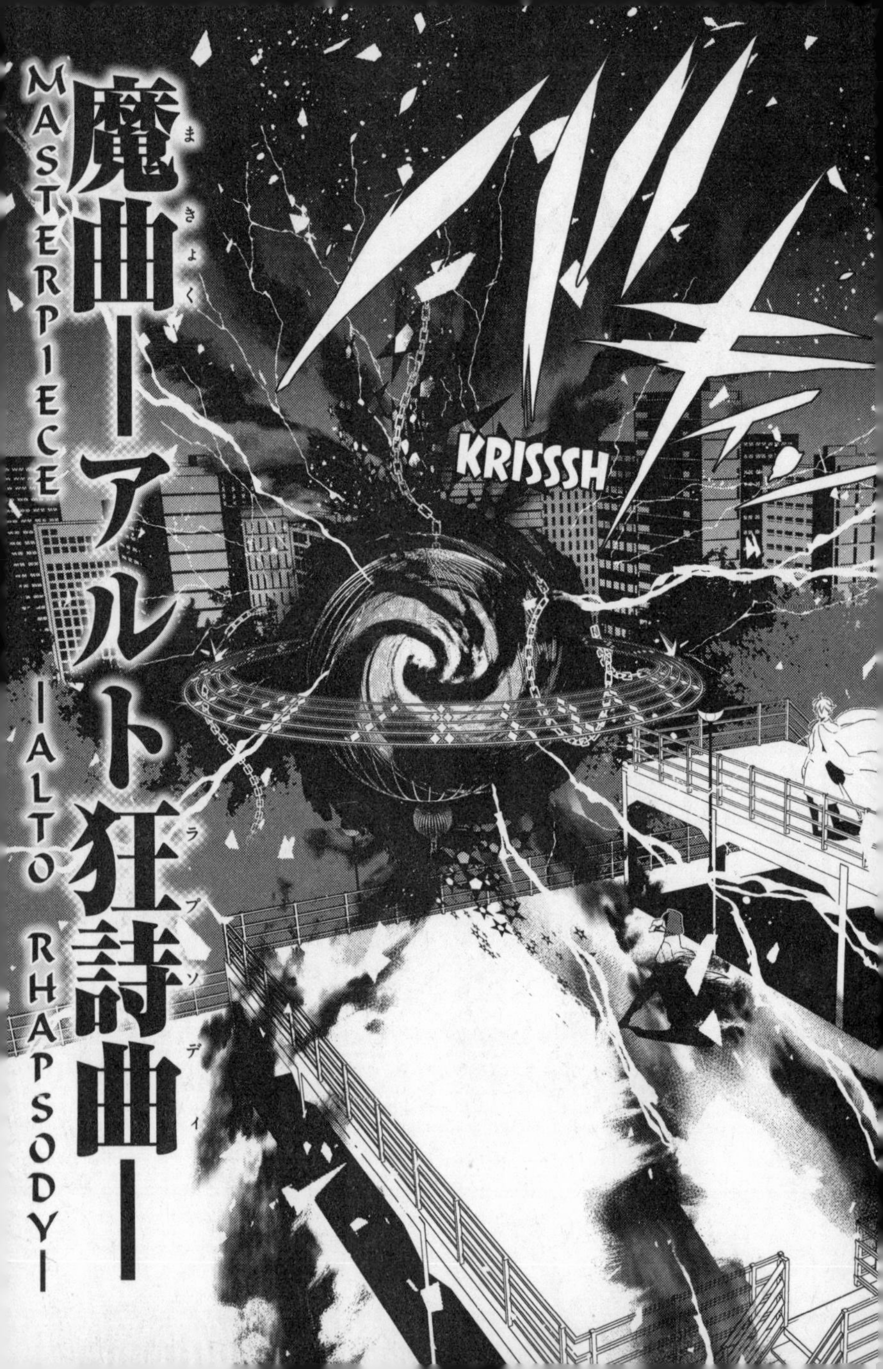
KRISSSH
魔曲ーアルト狂詩曲ー
MASTERPIECE –ALTO RHAPSODY–

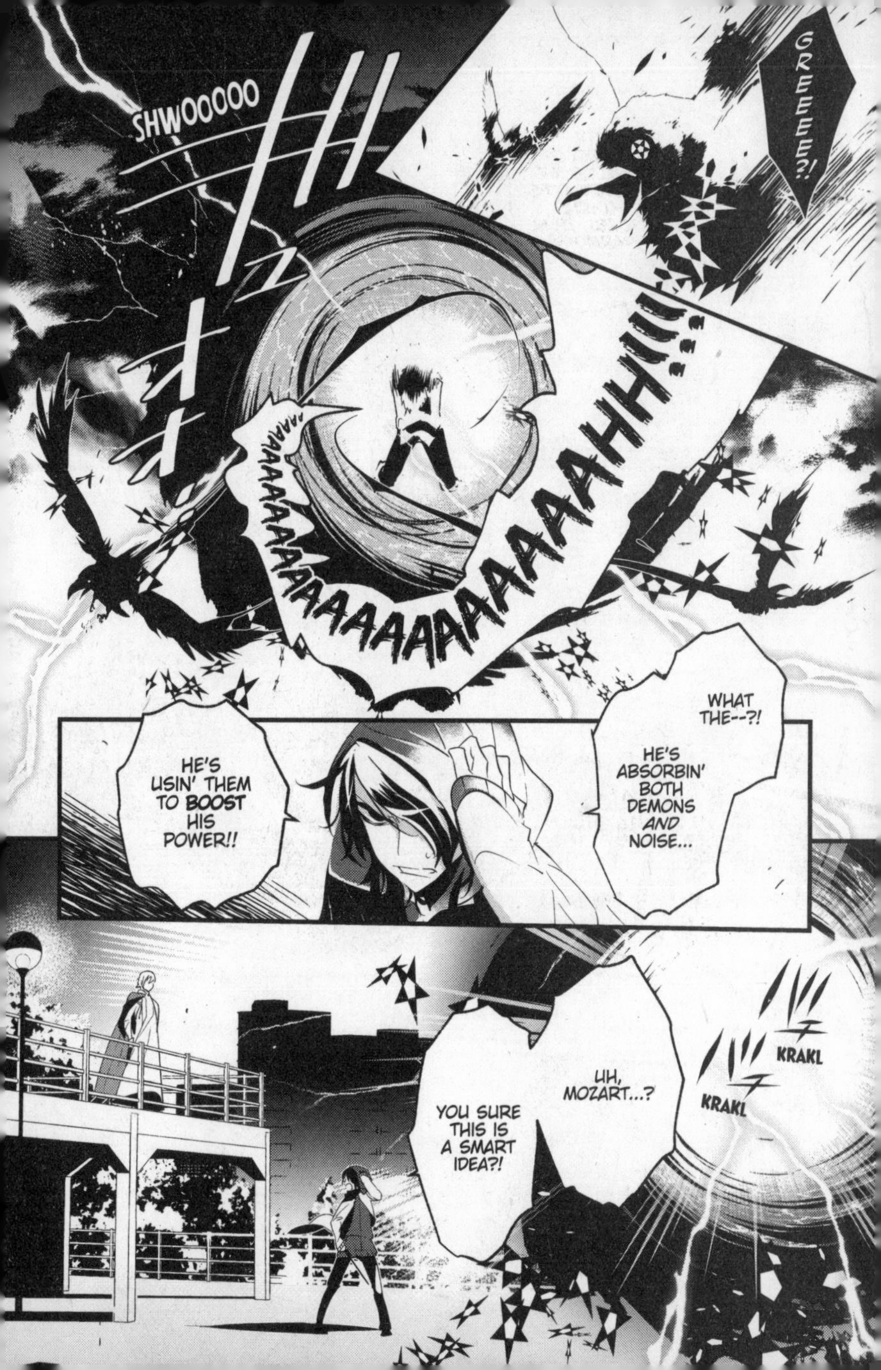
GREEEE?!
SHWOOOOO
AAAAAAAAAAAAAAAAAAAAAAAHH!!!!
WHAT THE--?!
HE'S ABSORBIN' BOTH DEMONS AND NOISE...
HE'S USIN' THEM TO BOOST HIS POWER!!
KRAKL
KRAKL
UH, MOZART...?
YOU SURE THIS IS A SMART IDEA?!

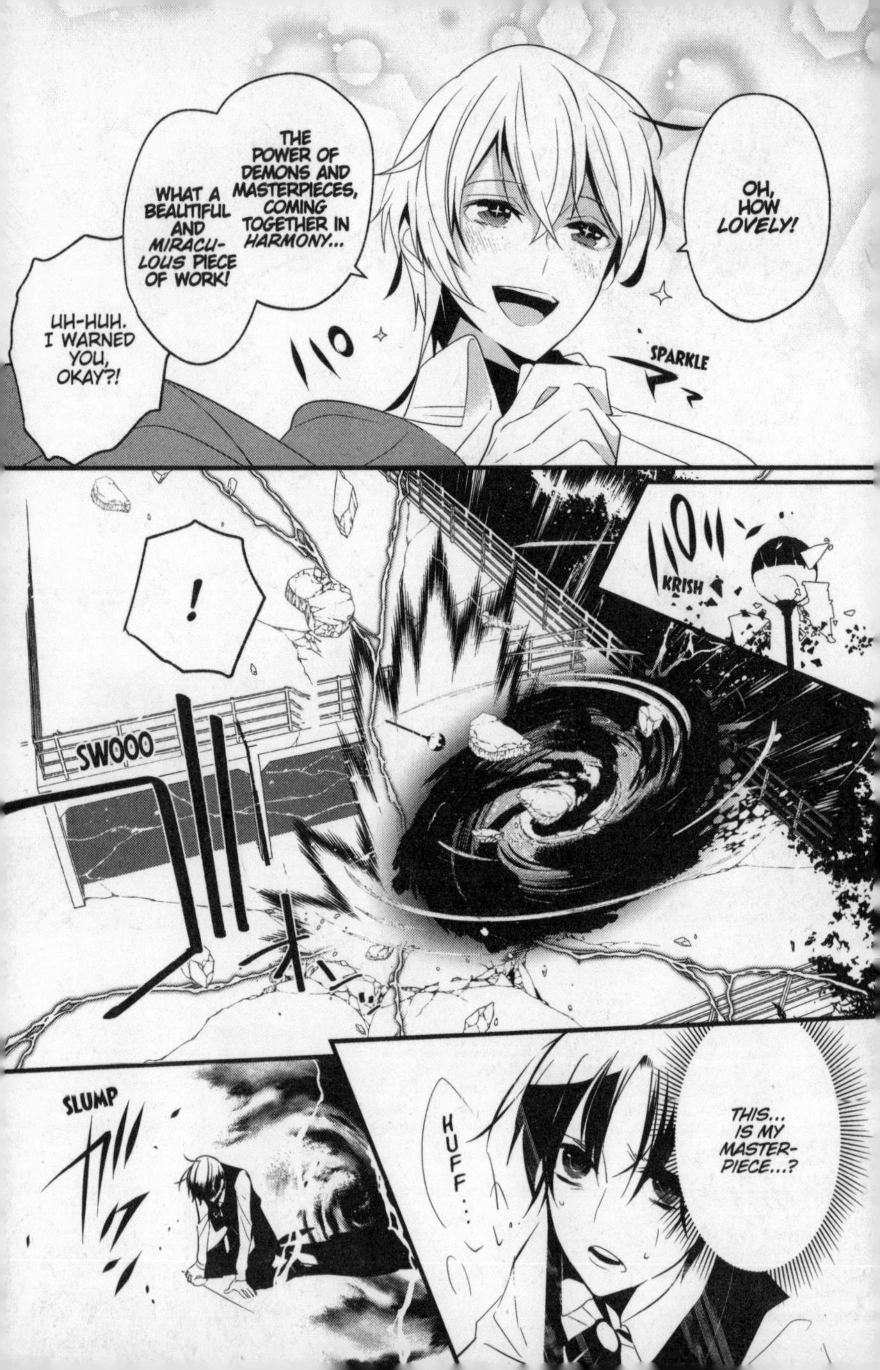
OH, HOW LOVELY!
THE POWER OF DEMONS AND MASTERPIECES, COMING TOGETHER IN HARMONY...
WHAT A BEAUTIFUL AND MIRACULOUS PIECE OF WORK!
SPARKLE
UH-HUH. I WARNED YOU, OKAY?!
KRISH
!
SWOOO
THIS... IS MY MASTERPIECE...?
HUFF...
SLUMP

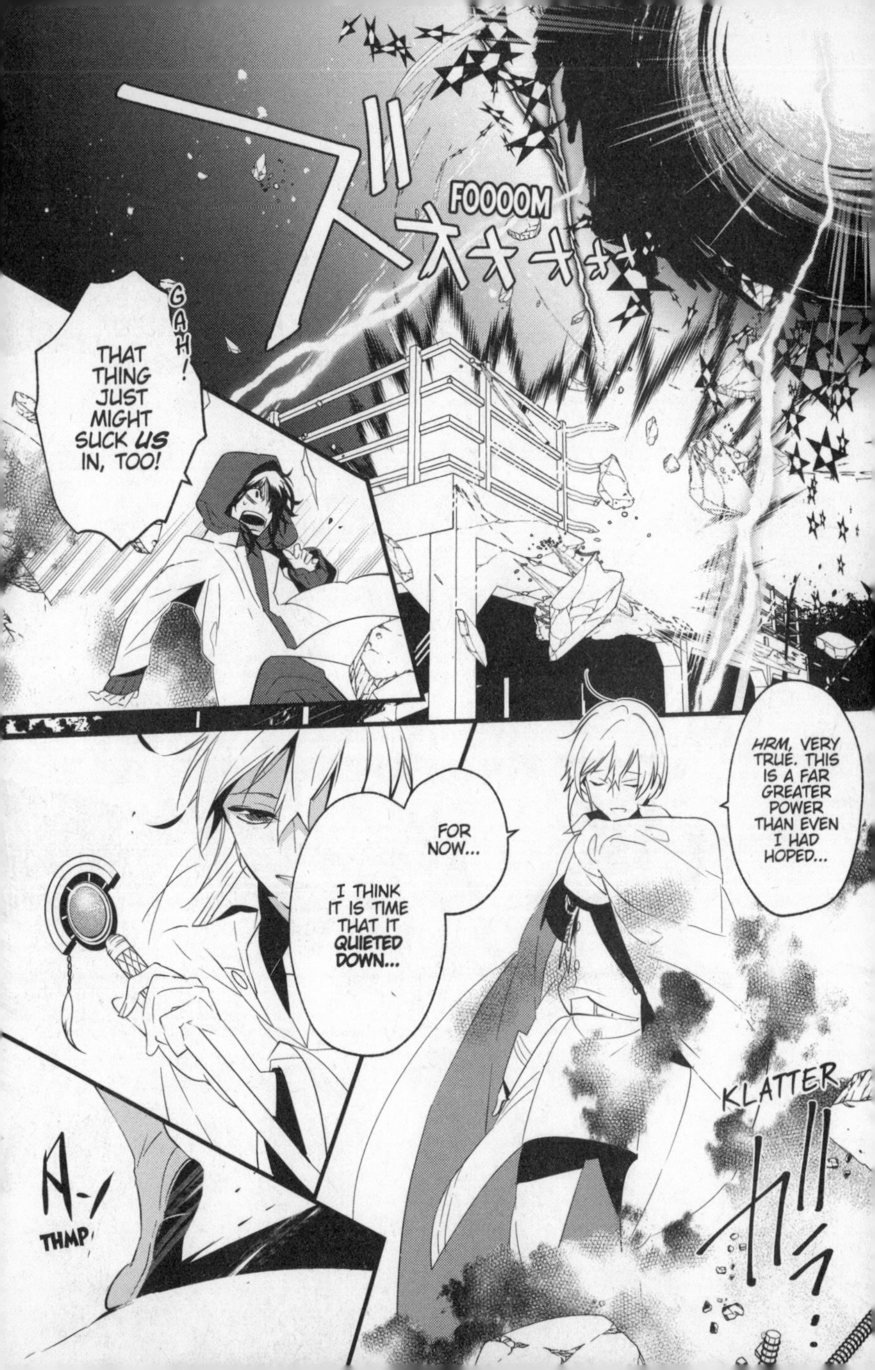
FOOOOM
GAH!
THAT THING JUST MIGHT SUCK *US* IN, TOO!
HRM, VERY TRUE. THIS IS A FAR GREATER POWER THAN EVEN I HAD HOPED...
FOR NOW...
I THINK IT IS TIME THAT IT **QUIETED DOWN...**
KLATTER
THMP

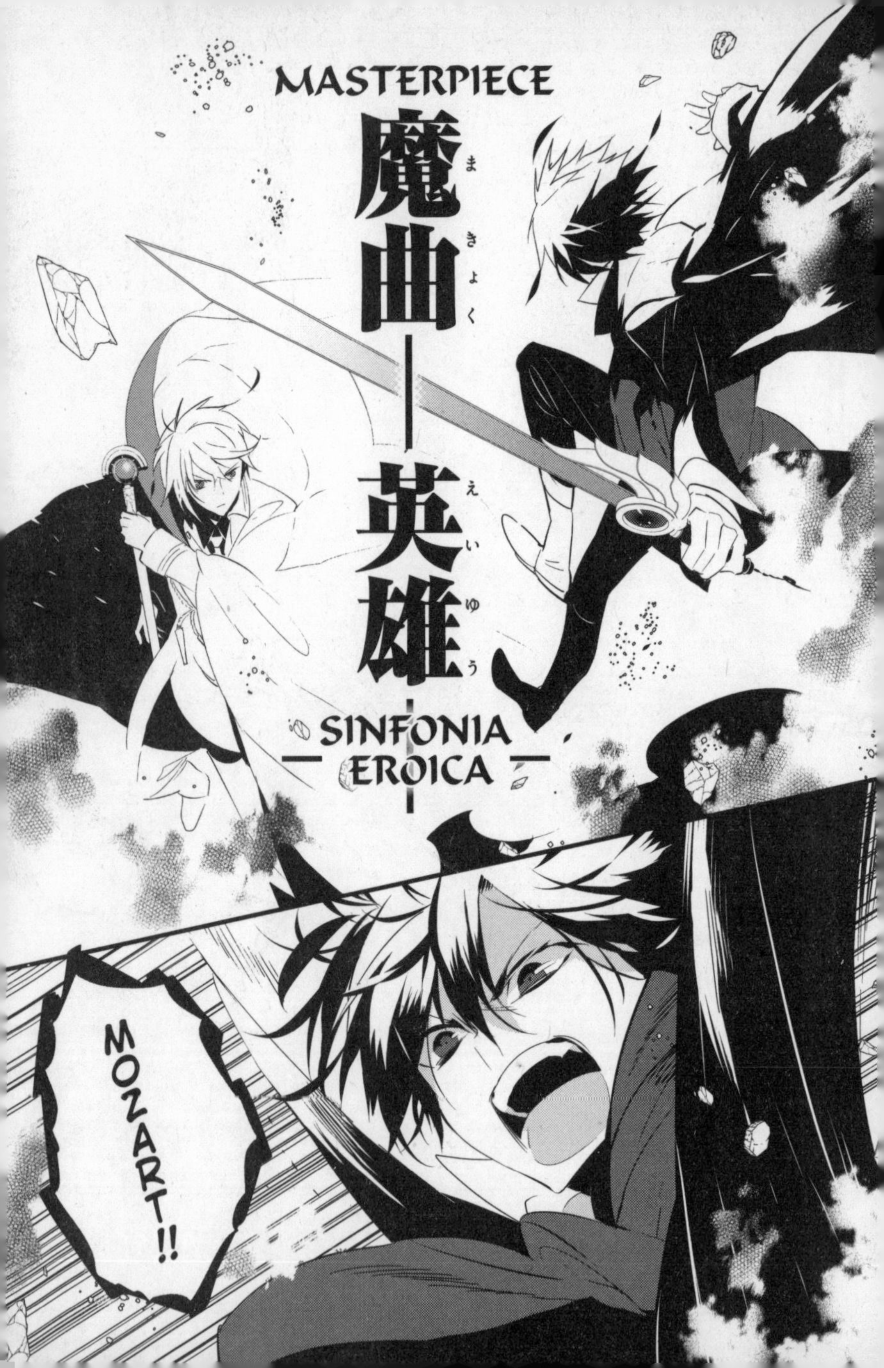
MASTERPIECE
魔曲 英雄
まきょく えいゆう
SINFONIA EROICA
MOZART!!

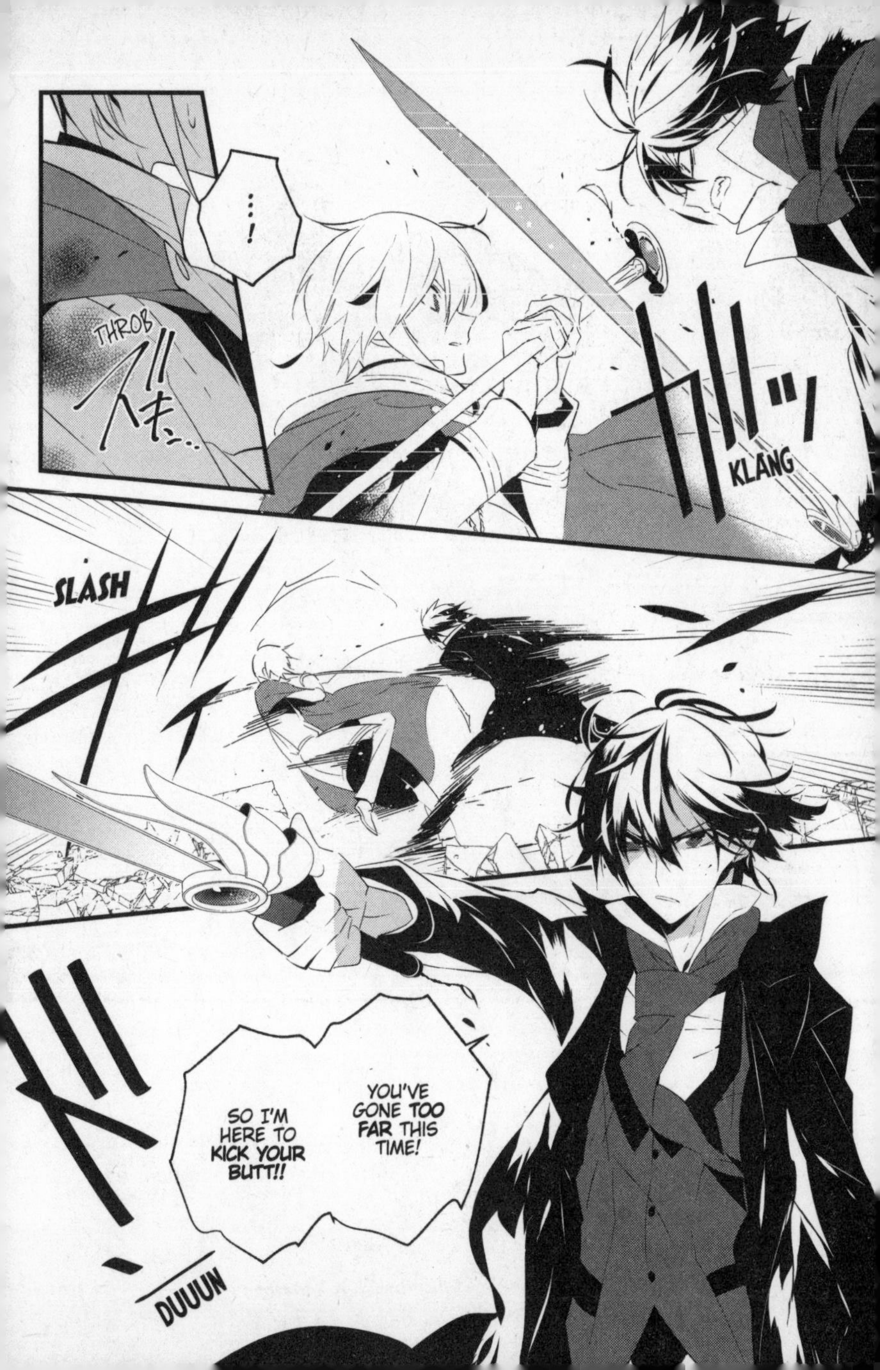
KLANG
...!
THROB
SLASH
YOU'VE GONE TOO FAR THIS TIME!
SO I'M HERE TO KICK YOUR BUTT!!
DUUUN

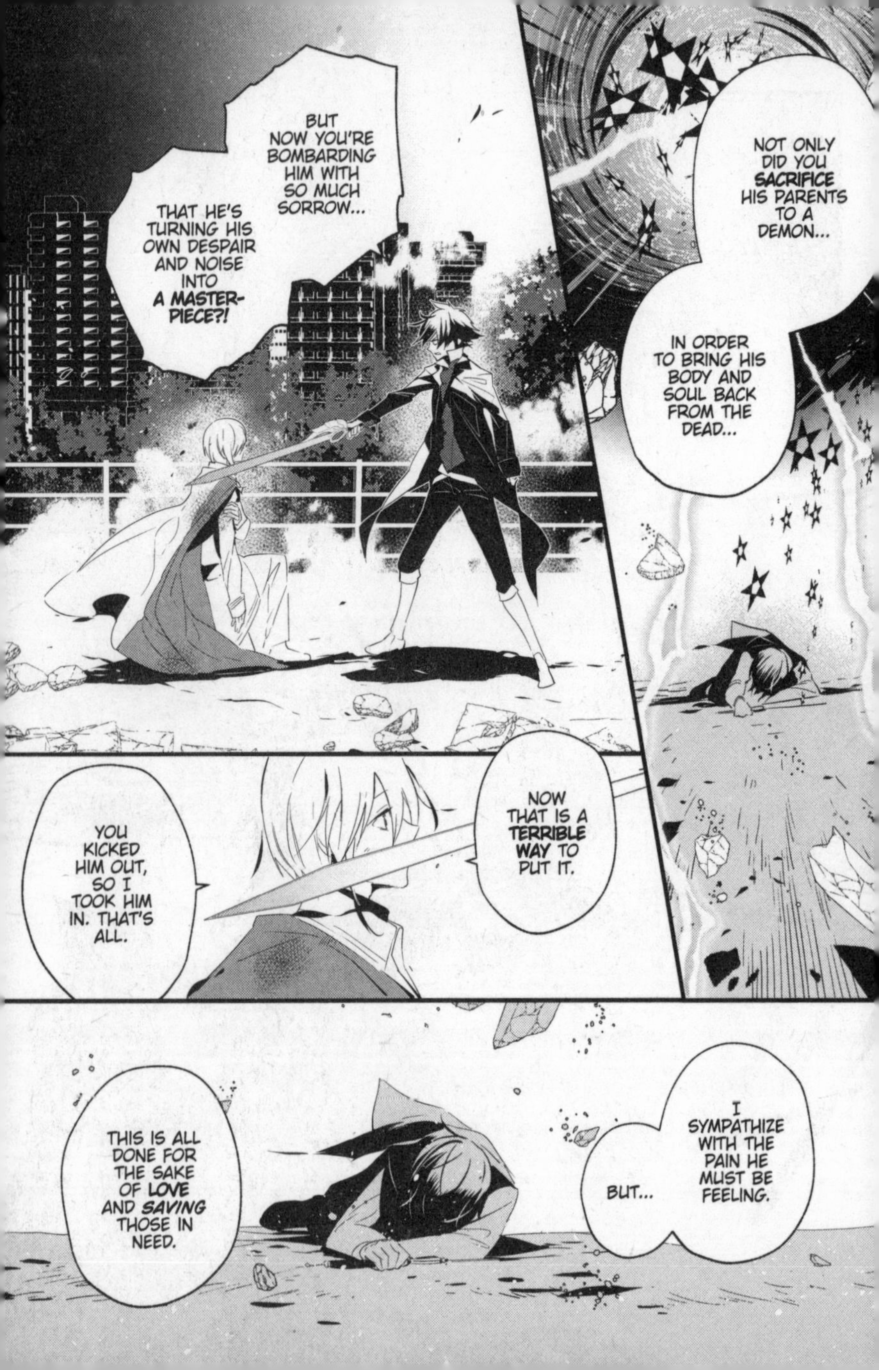

NOT ONLY DID YOU **SACRIFICE** HIS PARENTS TO A DEMON...
IN ORDER TO BRING HIS BODY AND SOUL BACK FROM THE DEAD...
BUT NOW YOU'RE BOMBARDING HIM WITH SO MUCH SORROW...
THAT HE'S TURNING HIS OWN DESPAIR AND NOISE INTO **A MASTER-PIECE?!**
NOW THAT IS A **TERRIBLE WAY** TO PUT IT.
YOU KICKED HIM OUT, SO I TOOK HIM IN. THAT'S ALL.
I SYMPATHIZE WITH THE PAIN HE MUST BE FEELING.
BUT...
THIS IS ALL DONE FOR THE SAKE OF **LOVE** AND ***SAVING*** THOSE IN NEED.

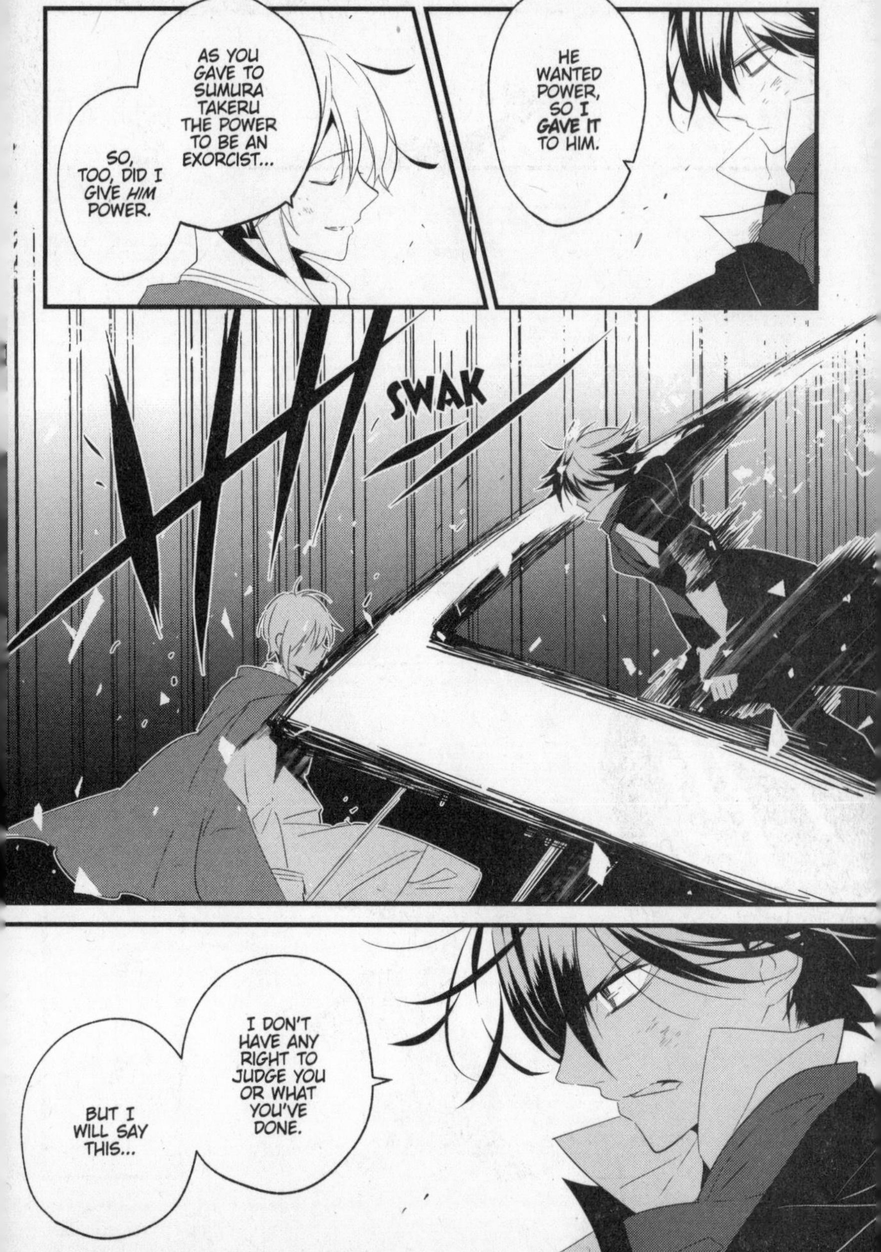
HE WANTED POWER, SO I GAVE IT TO HIM.
AS YOU GAVE TO SUMURA TAKERU THE POWER TO BE AN EXORCIST...
SO, TOO, DID I GIVE *HIM* POWER.
SWAK
I DON'T HAVE ANY RIGHT TO JUDGE YOU OR WHAT YOU'VE DONE.
BUT I WILL SAY THIS...

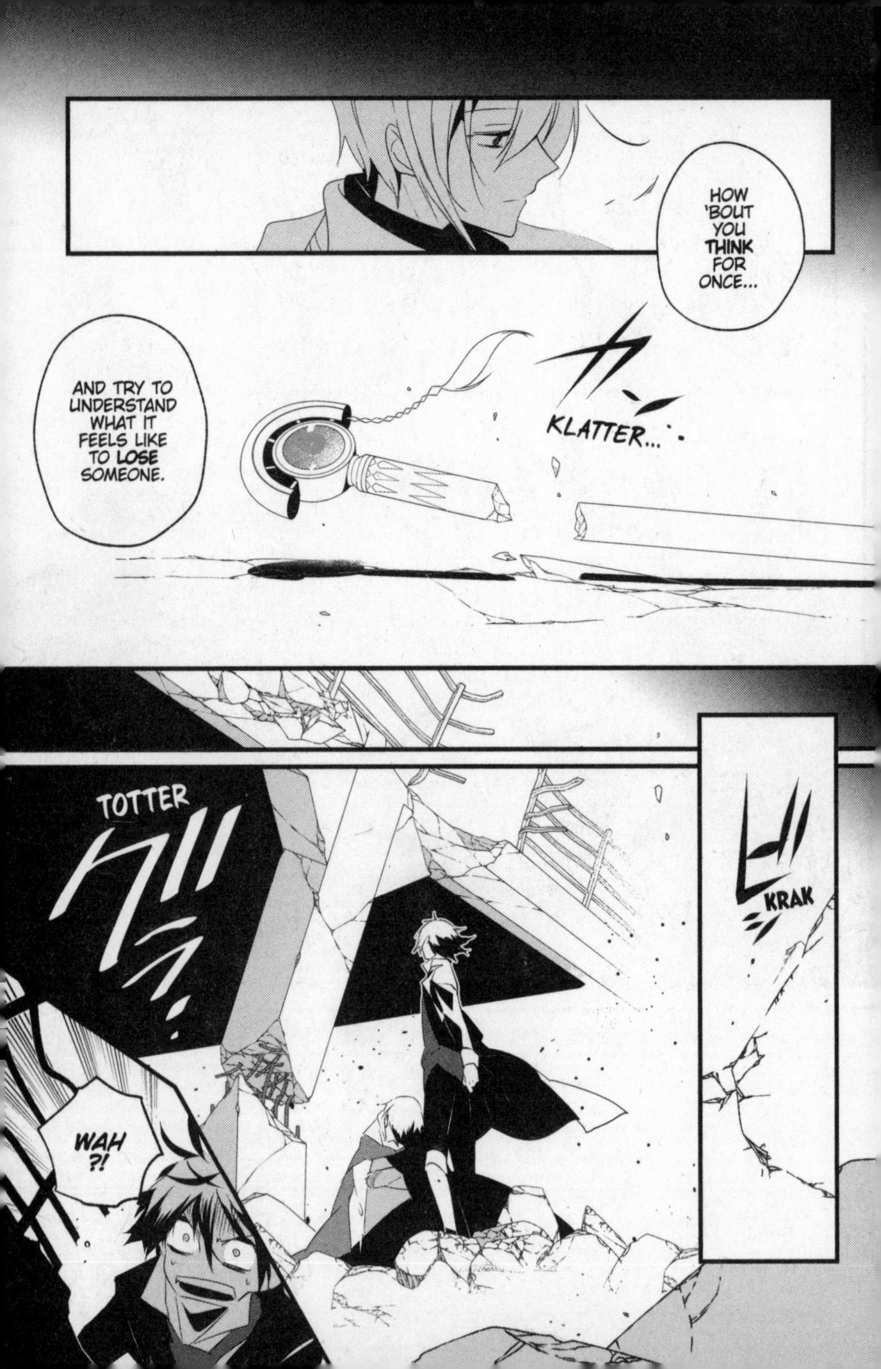
HOW 'BOUT YOU THINK FOR ONCE...
AND TRY TO UNDERSTAND WHAT IT FEELS LIKE TO LOSE SOMEONE.
KLATTER...
KRAK
TOTTER
WAH ?!

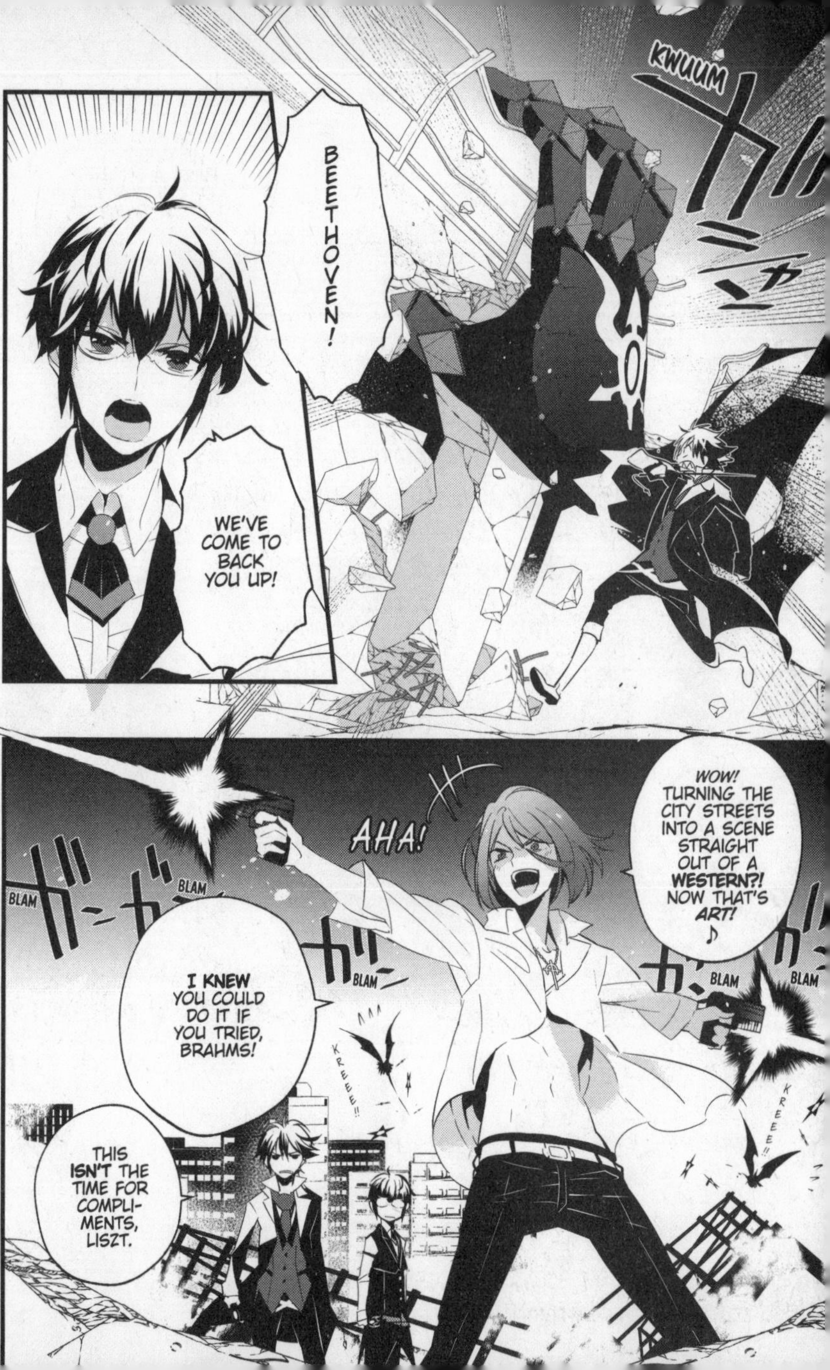
KWUUM
BEETHOVEN!
WE'VE COME TO BACK YOU UP!
WOW! TURNING THE CITY STREETS INTO A SCENE STRAIGHT OUT OF A WESTERN?! NOW THAT'S ART! ♪
AHA!
BLAM
BLAM
KREEE!!
BLAM
BLAM
BLAM
I KNEW YOU COULD DO IT IF YOU TRIED, BRAHMS!
KREEE!!
THIS ISN'T THE TIME FOR COMPLI-MENTS, LISZT.

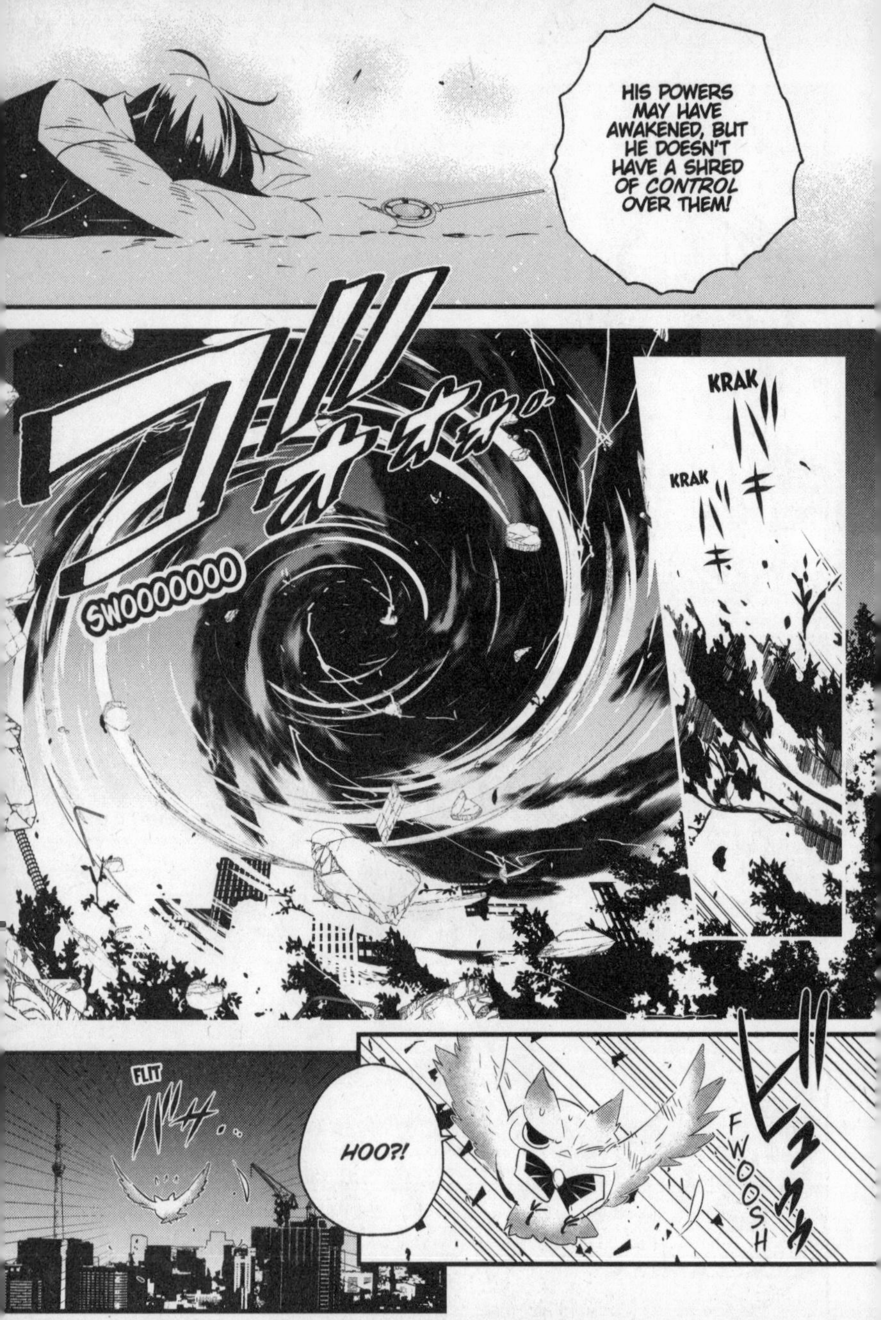
HIS POWERS MAY HAVE AWAKENED, BUT HE DOESN'T HAVE A SHRED OF CONTROL OVER THEM!
KRAK
KRAK
SWOOOOOOO
FWOOSH
HOO?!
FLIT

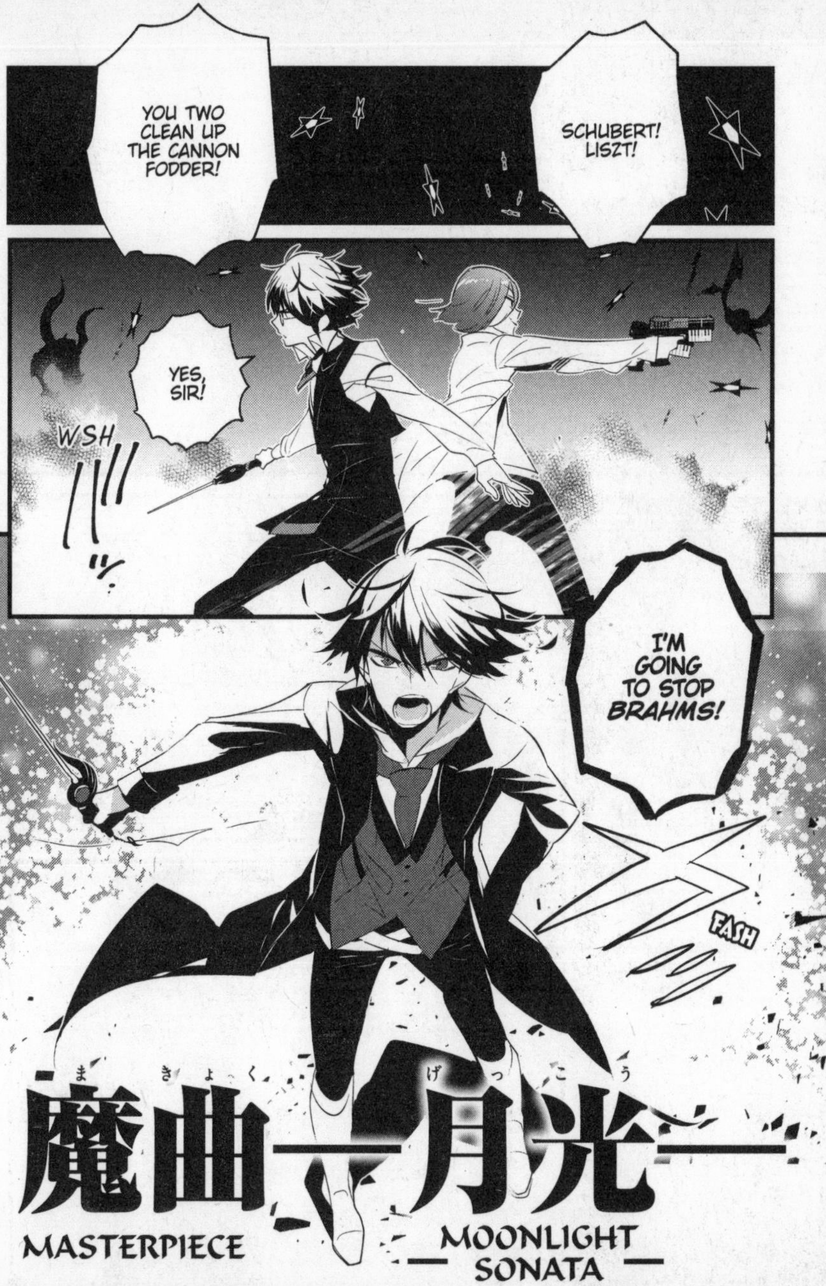
SCHUBERT! LISZT!
YOU TWO CLEAN UP THE CANNON FODDER!
YES, SIR!
WSH
I'M GOING TO STOP BRAHMS!
FASH
まきょく
魔曲
げっこう
月光
MASTERPIECE
MOONLIGHT SONATA

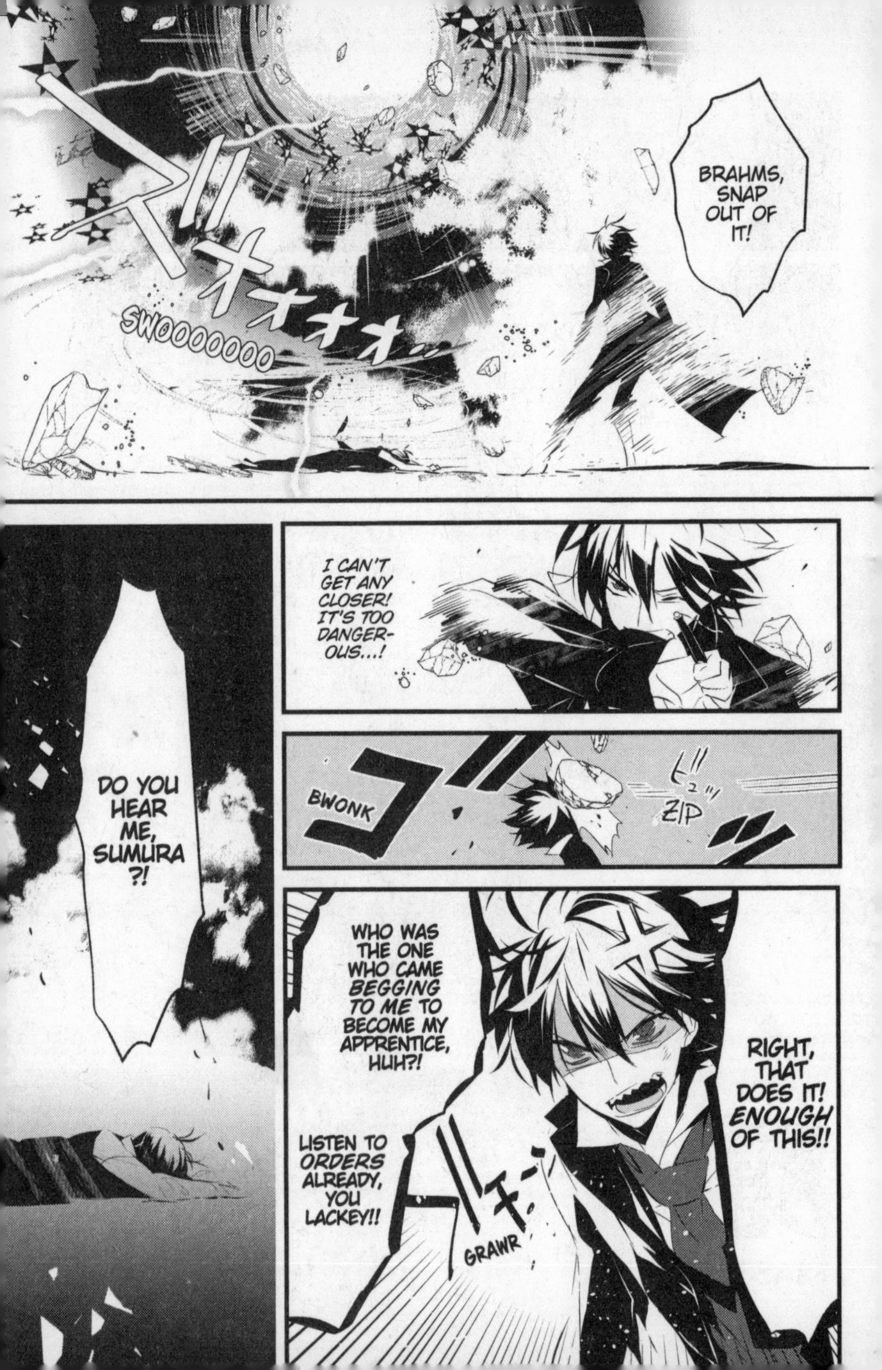
BRAHMS, SNAP OUT OF IT!
SWOOOOOOO
I CAN'T GET ANY CLOSER! IT'S TOO DANGER-OUS...!
ZIP
BWONK
RIGHT, THAT DOES IT! ENOUGH OF THIS!!
WHO WAS THE ONE WHO CAME BEGGING TO ME TO BECOME MY APPRENTICE, HUH?!
LISTEN TO ORDERS ALREADY, YOU LACKEY!!
GRAWR
DO YOU HEAR ME, SUMURA?!

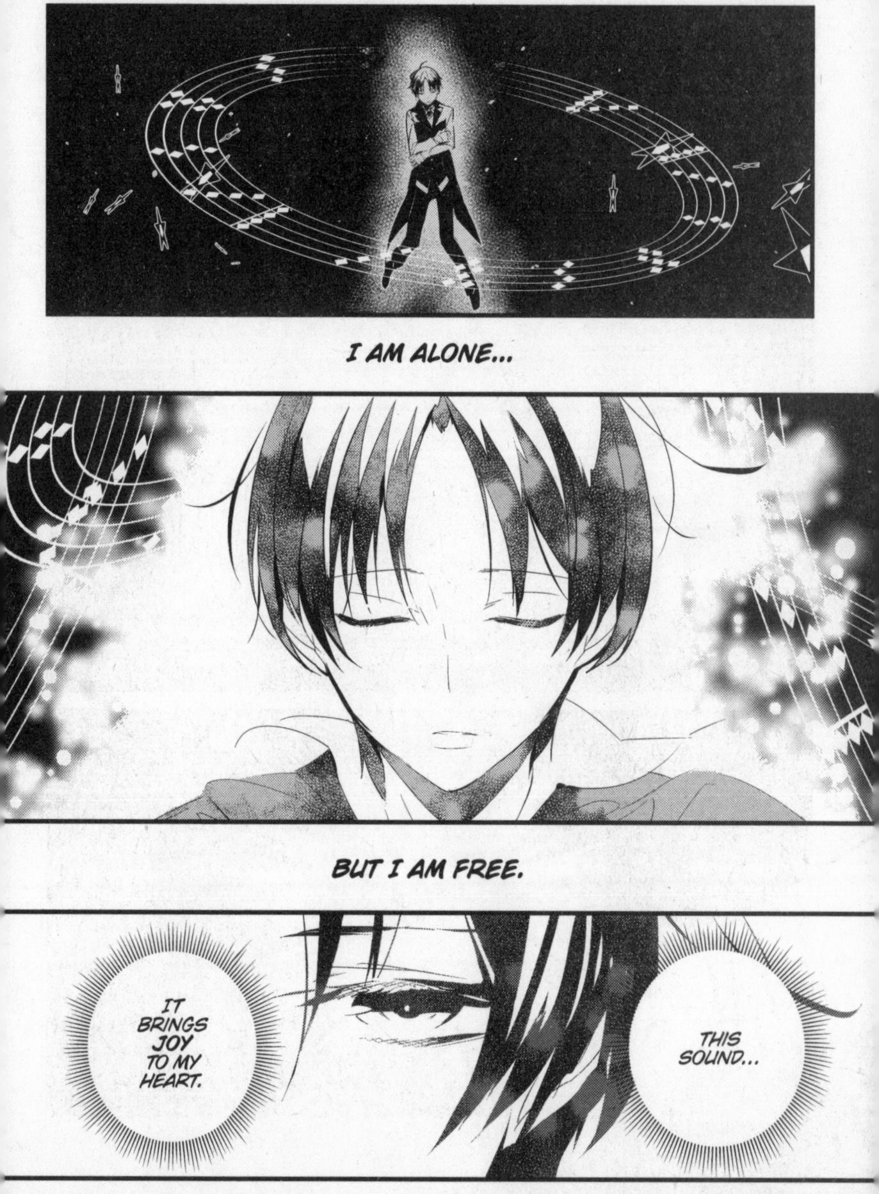
I AM ALONE...
BUT I AM FREE.
THIS SOUND...
IT BRINGS JOY TO MY HEART.

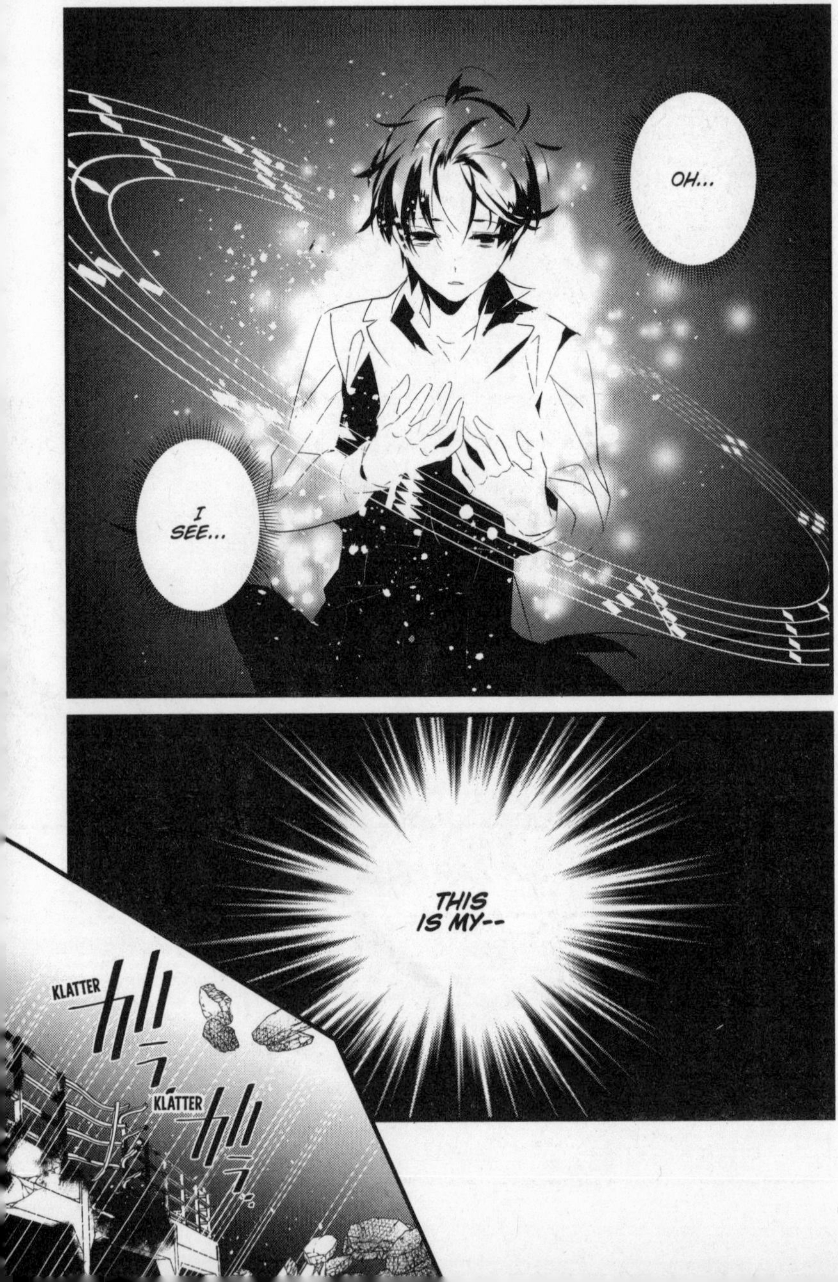
OH...
I SEE...
THIS IS MY--
KLATTER
KLATTER

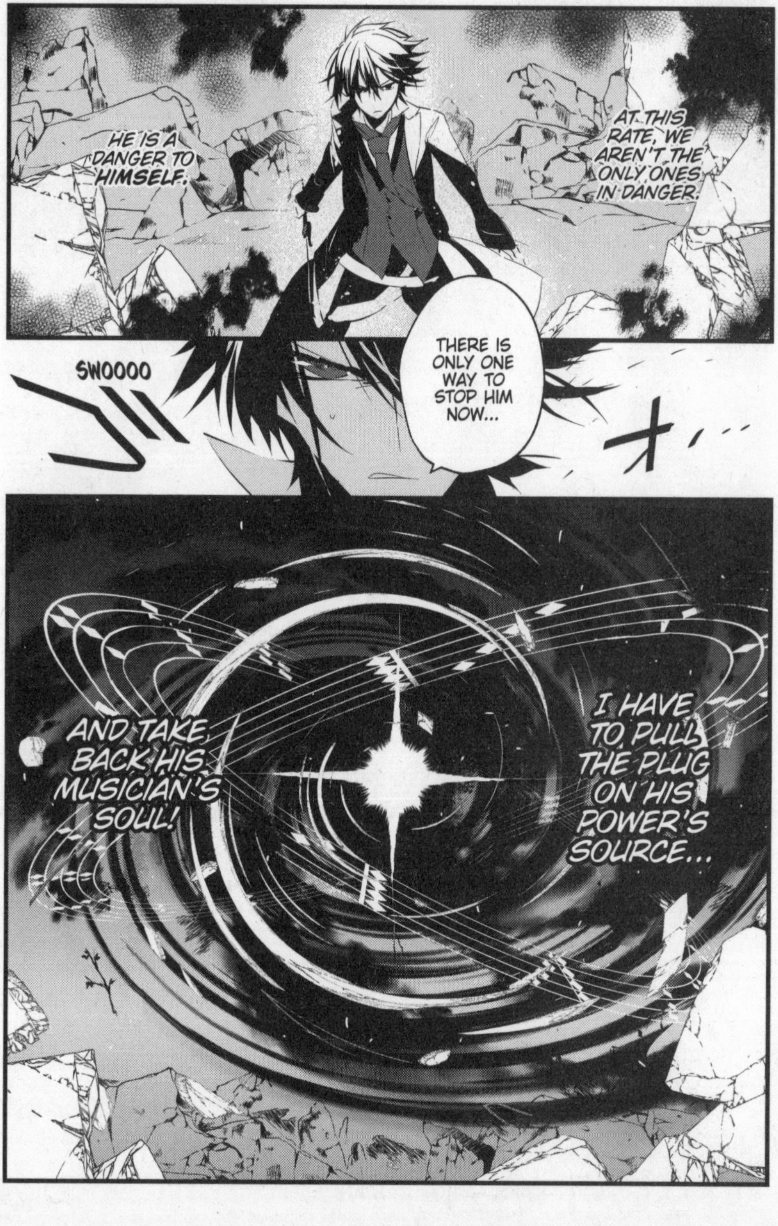
AT THIS RATE, WE AREN'T THE ONLY ONES IN DANGER.
HE IS A DANGER TO HIMSELF.
THERE IS ONLY ONE WAY TO STOP HIM NOW...
SWOOOO
I HAVE TO PULL THE PLUG ON HIS POWER'S SOURCE...
AND TAKE BACK HIS MUSICIAN'S SOUL!

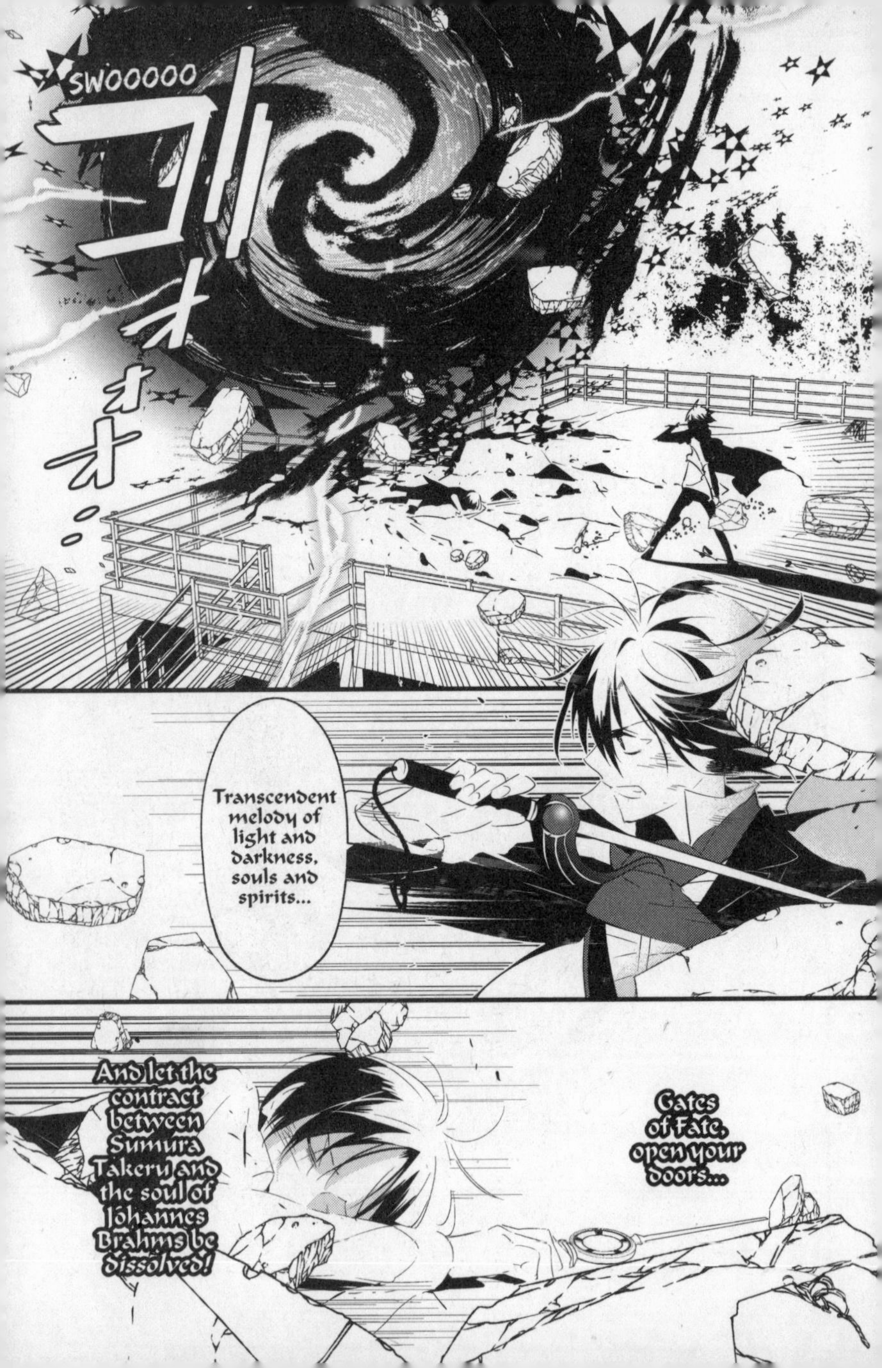
SWOOOOO
Transcendent melody of light and darkness, souls and spirits...
Gates of Fate, open your doors...
And let the contract between Sumura Takeru and the soul of Johannes Brahms be dissolved!

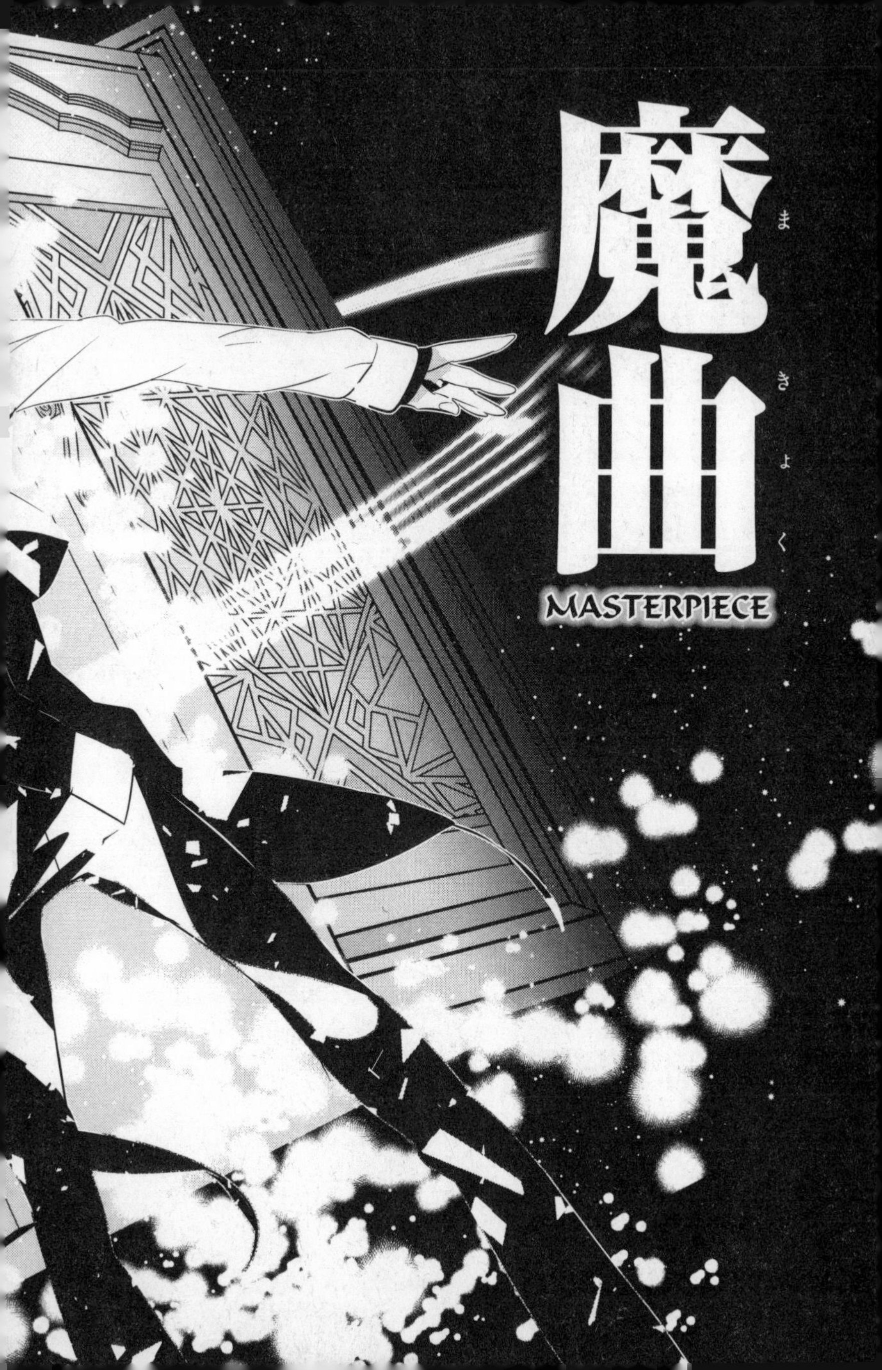
魔曲（まきょく）
MASTERPIECE

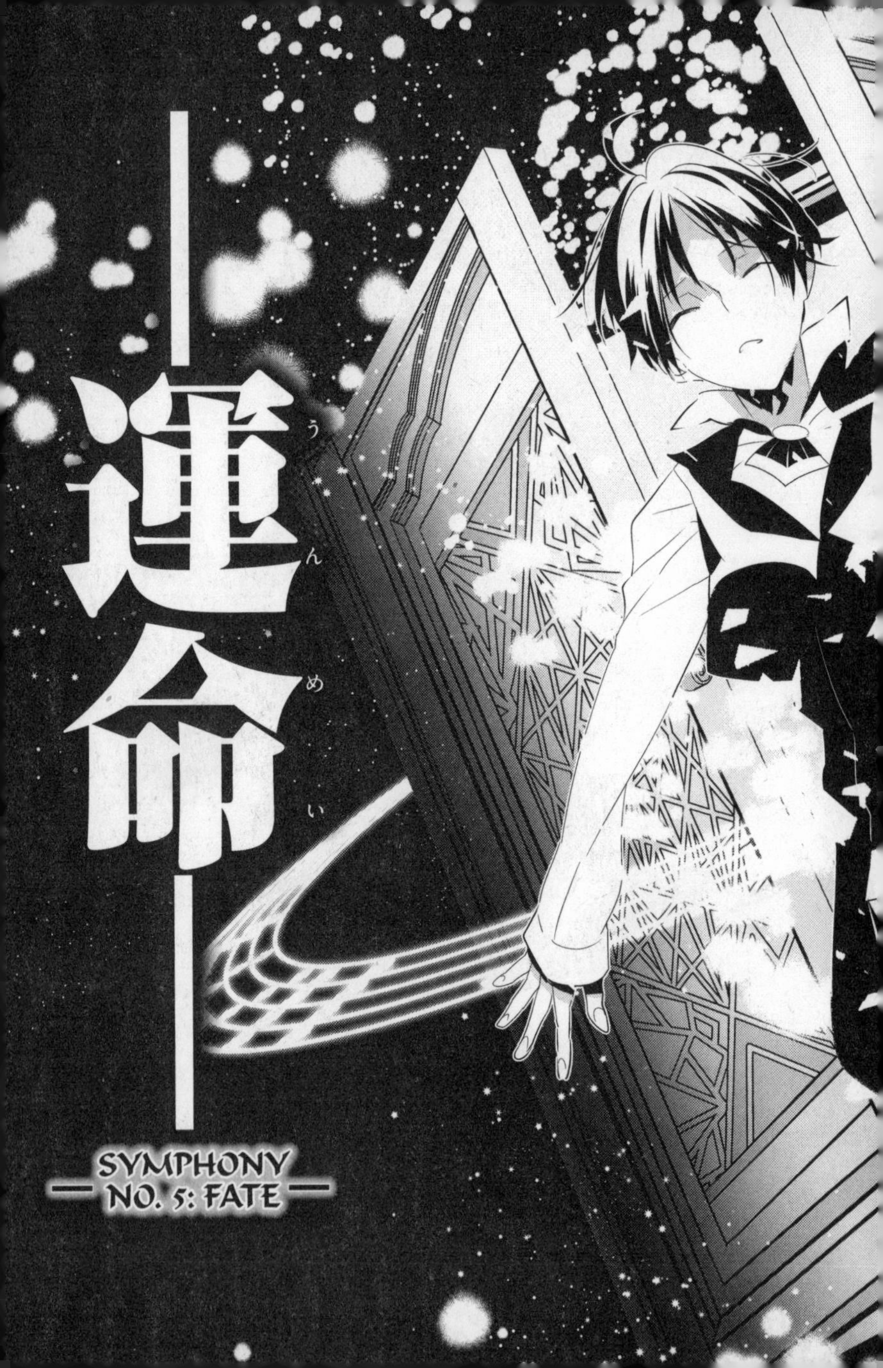
運命
うんめい
SYMPHONY
NO. 5: FATE

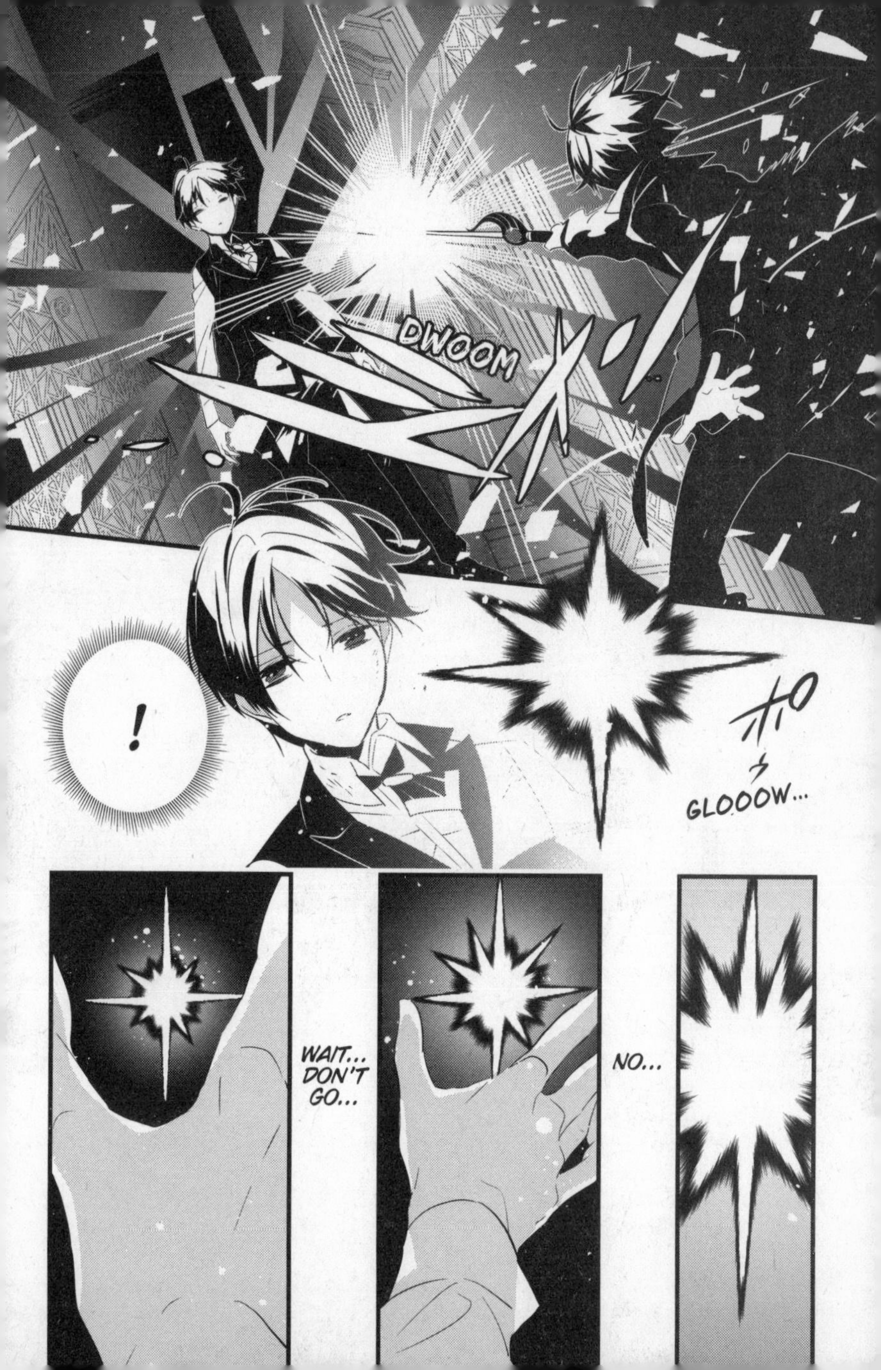
DWOOM
GLOOOW...
!
NO...
WAIT... DON'T GO...

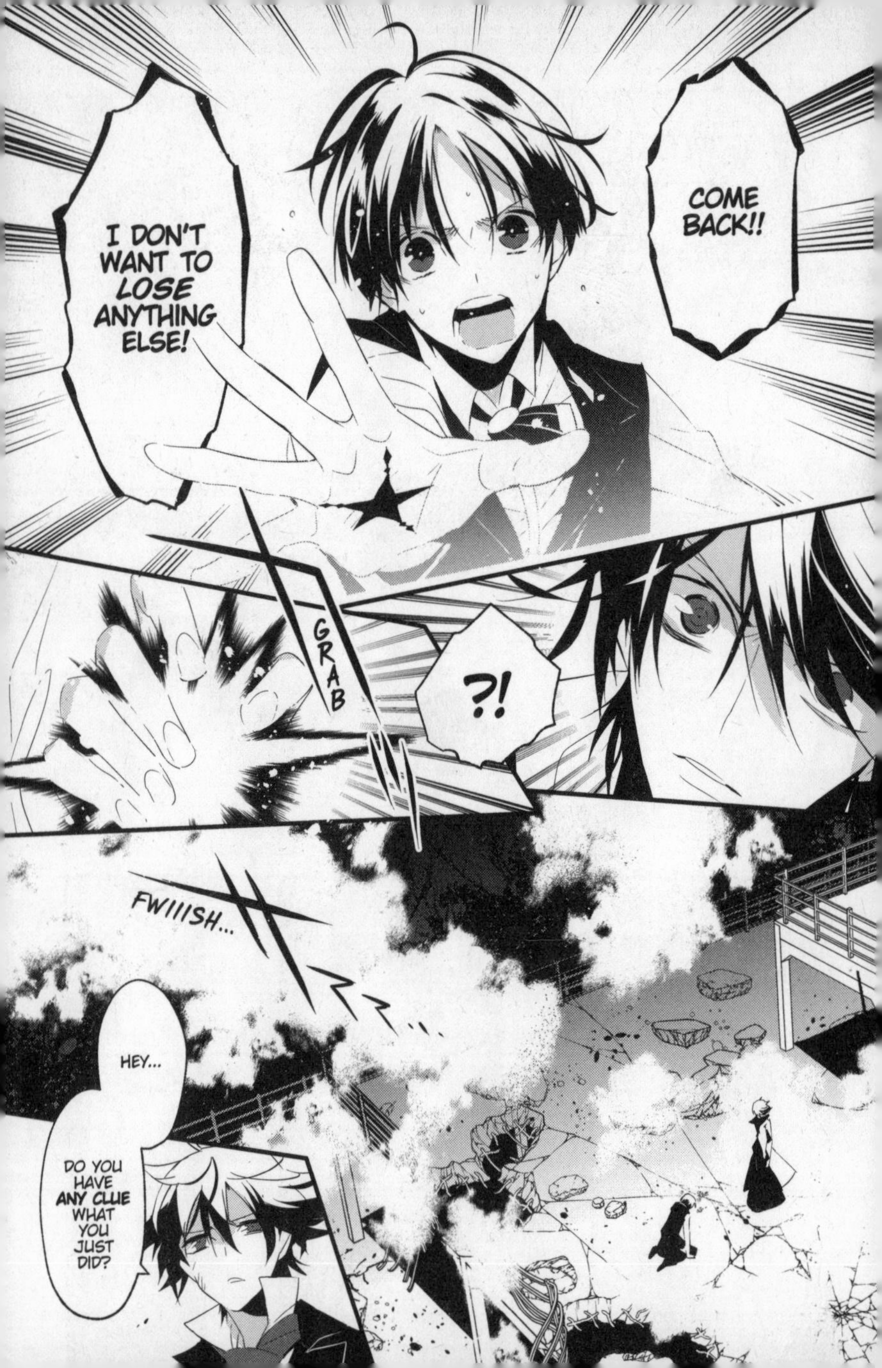
COME BACK!!
I DON'T WANT TO LOSE ANYTHING ELSE!
?!
GRAB
FWIIISH...
ZZ...
HEY...
DO YOU HAVE ANY CLUE WHAT YOU JUST DID?

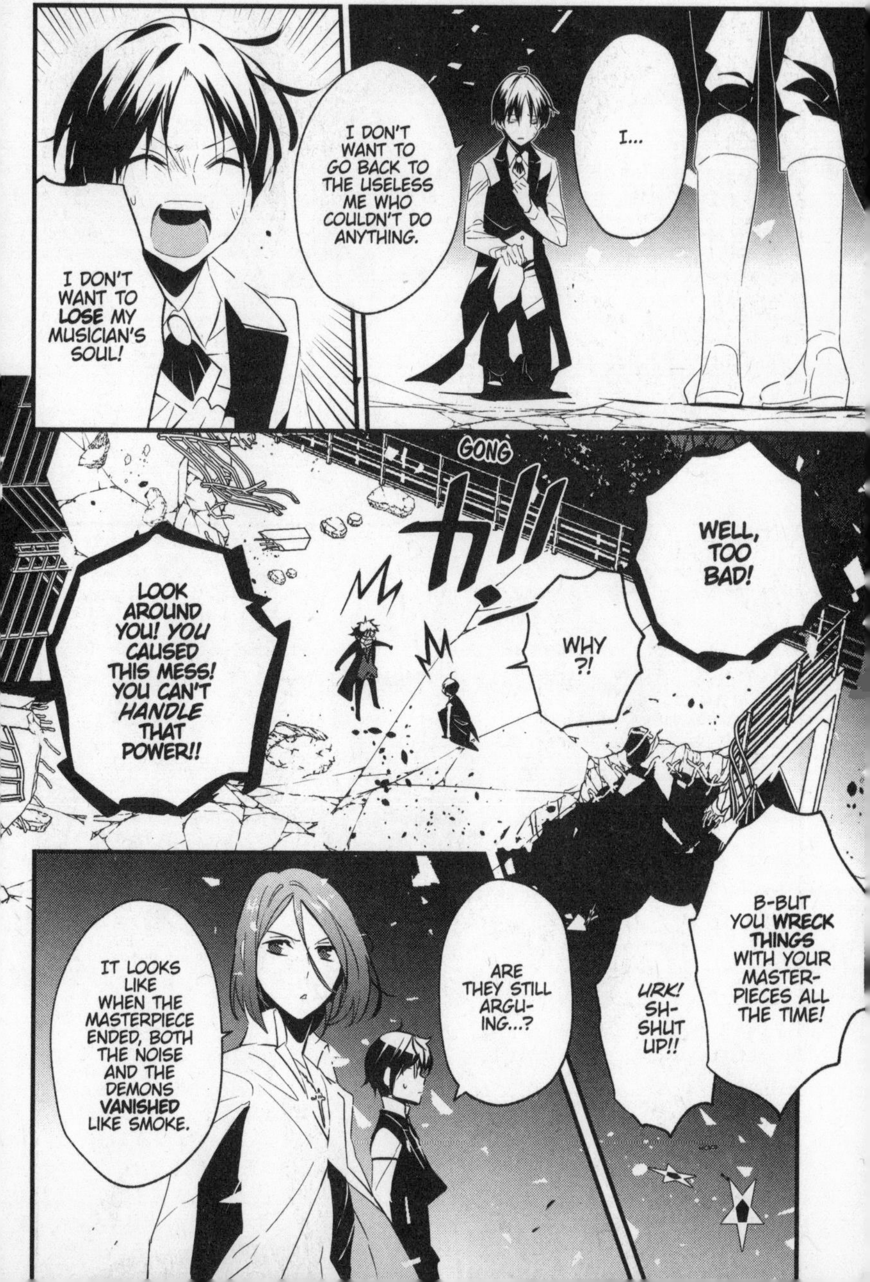
I...
I DON'T WANT TO GO BACK TO THE USELESS ME WHO COULDN'T DO ANYTHING.
I DON'T WANT TO LOSE MY MUSICIAN'S SOUL!
WELL, TOO BAD!
GONG
WHY ?!
LOOK AROUND YOU! YOU CAUSED THIS MESS! YOU CAN'T HANDLE THAT POWER!!
B-BUT YOU WRECK THINGS WITH YOUR MASTER-PIECES ALL THE TIME!
URK! SH-SHUT UP!!
ARE THEY STILL ARGU-ING...?
IT LOOKS LIKE WHEN THE MASTERPIECE ENDED, BOTH THE NOISE AND THE DEMONS VANISHED LIKE SMOKE.

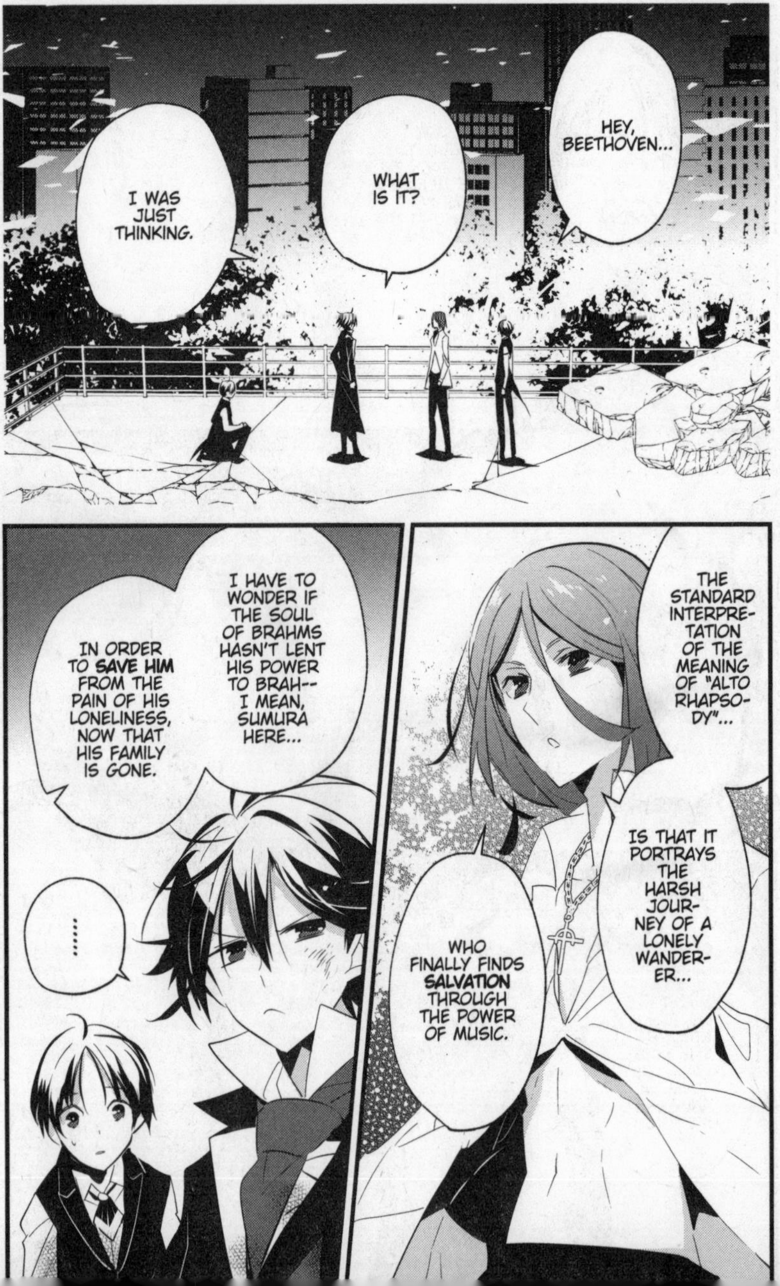
HEY, BEETHOVEN...
WHAT IS IT?
I WAS JUST THINKING.
THE STANDARD INTERPRETATION OF THE MEANING OF "ALTO RHAPSODY"...
IS THAT IT PORTRAYS THE HARSH JOURNEY OF A LONELY WANDERER...
WHO FINALLY FINDS SALVATION THROUGH THE POWER OF MUSIC.
I HAVE TO WONDER IF THE SOUL OF BRAHMS HASN'T LENT HIS POWER TO BRAH-- I MEAN, SUMURA HERE...
IN ORDER TO SAVE HIM FROM THE PAIN OF HIS LONELINESS, NOW THAT HIS FAMILY IS GONE.
......

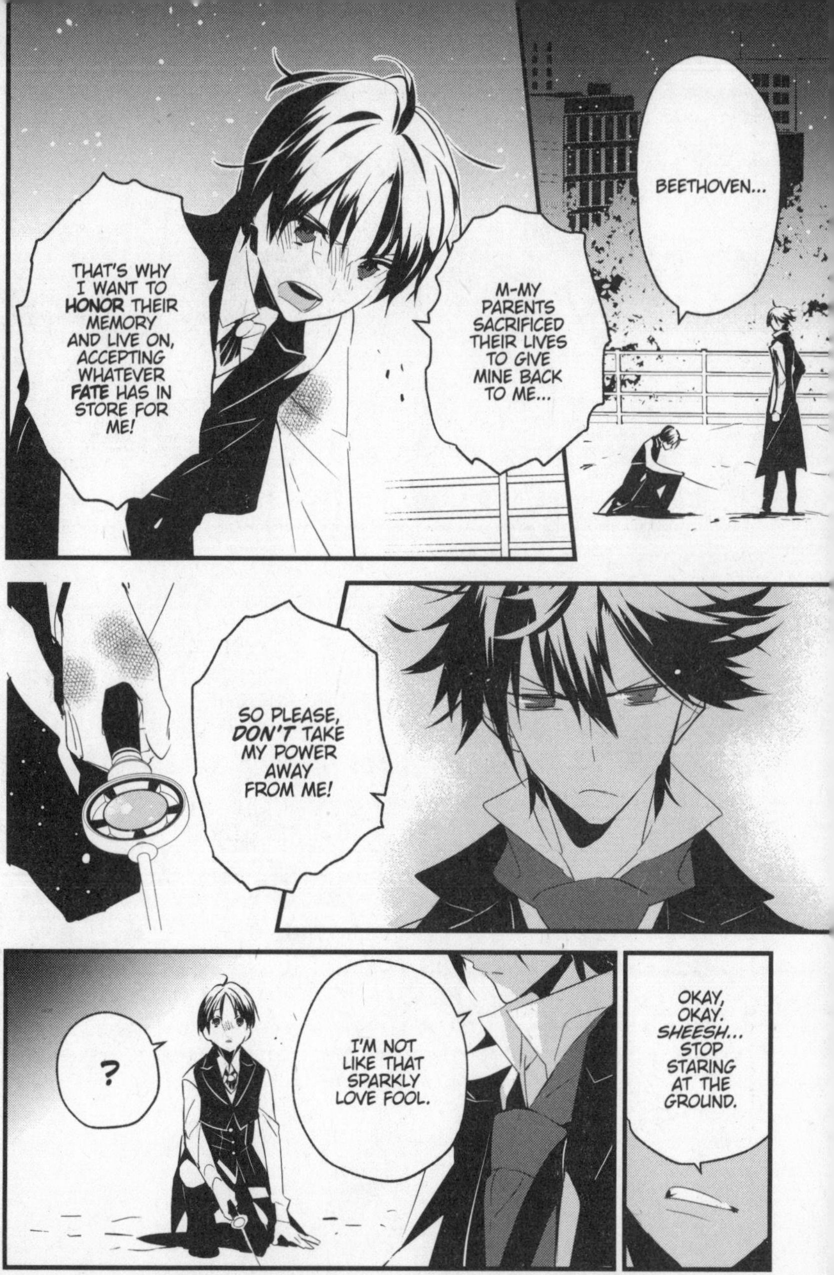
BEETHOVEN...
M-MY PARENTS SACRIFICED THEIR LIVES TO GIVE MINE BACK TO ME...
THAT'S WHY I WANT TO **HONOR** THEIR MEMORY AND LIVE ON, ACCEPTING WHATEVER **FATE** HAS IN STORE FOR ME!
SO PLEASE, ***DON'T*** TAKE MY POWER AWAY FROM ME!
OKAY, OKAY. ***SHEESH...*** STOP STARING AT THE GROUND.
I'M NOT LIKE THAT SPARKLY LOVE FOOL.
?

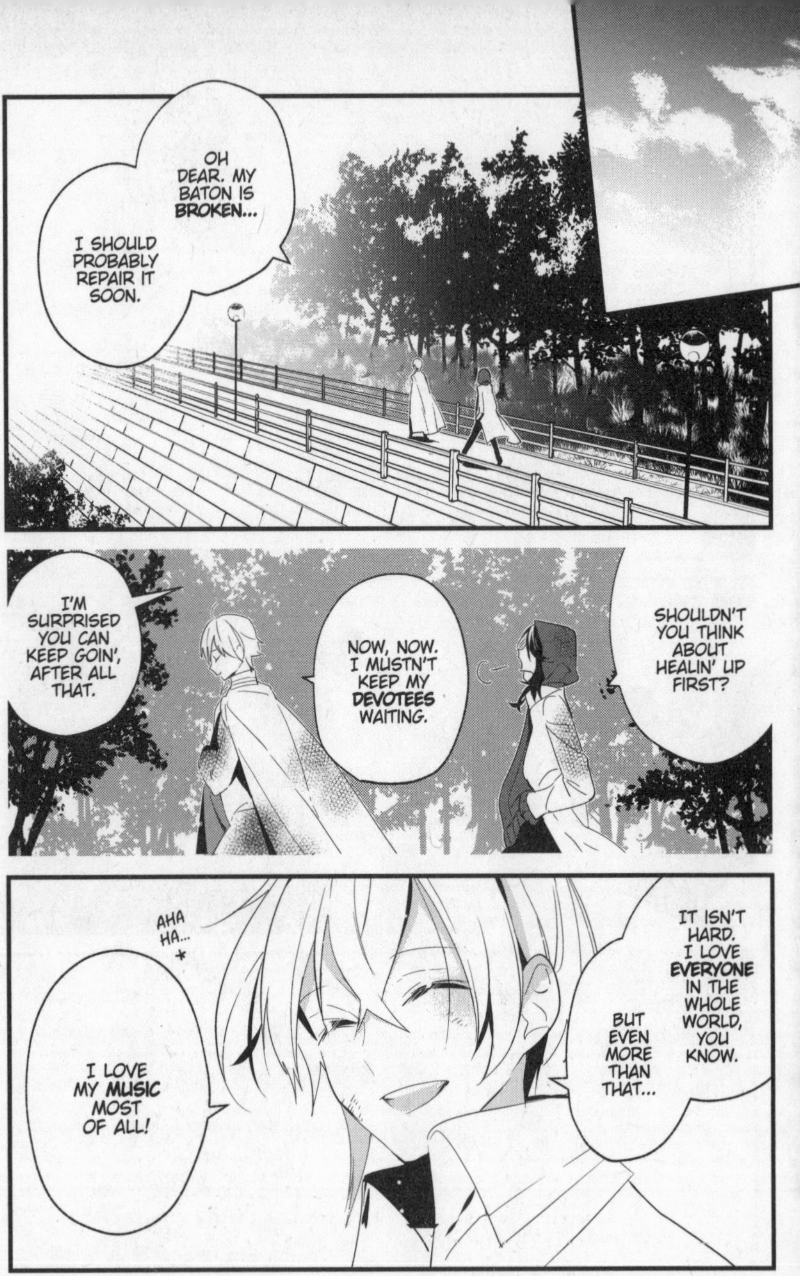
OH DEAR. MY BATON IS BROKEN...
I SHOULD PROBABLY REPAIR IT SOON.
SHOULDN'T YOU THINK ABOUT HEALIN' UP FIRST?
NOW, NOW. I MUSTN'T KEEP MY DEVOTEES WAITING.
I'M SURPRISED YOU CAN KEEP GOIN', AFTER ALL THAT.
IT ISN'T HARD. I LOVE EVERYONE IN THE WHOLE WORLD, YOU KNOW.
BUT EVEN MORE THAN THAT...
AHA HA...
I LOVE MY MUSIC MOST OF ALL!

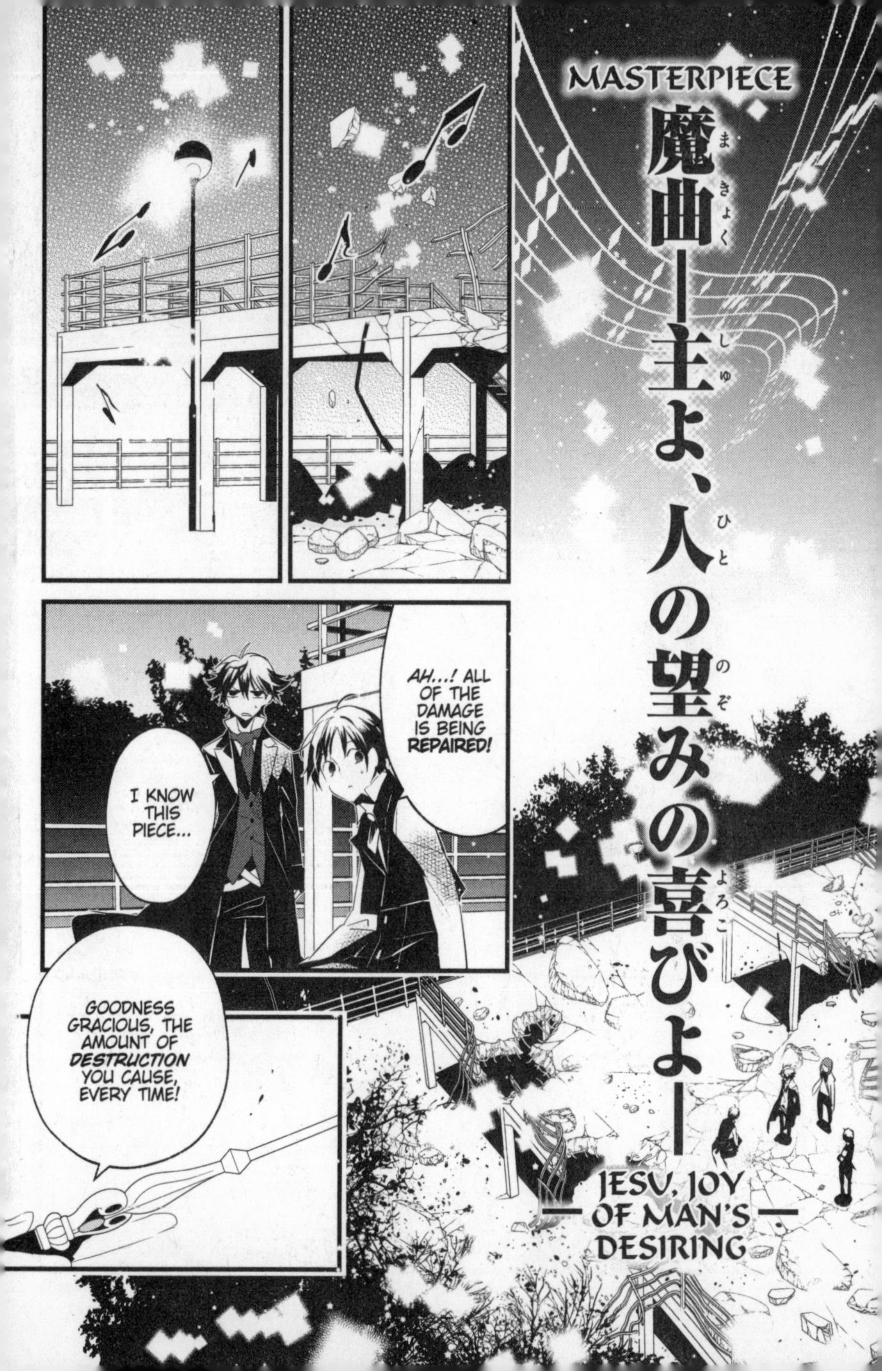
MASTERPIECE
魔曲―主よ、人の望みの喜びよ―
JESU, JOY OF MAN'S DESIRING
AH...! ALL OF THE DAMAGE IS BEING REPAIRED!
I KNOW THIS PIECE...
GOODNESS GRACIOUS, THE AMOUNT OF DESTRUCTION YOU CAUSE, EVERY TIME!

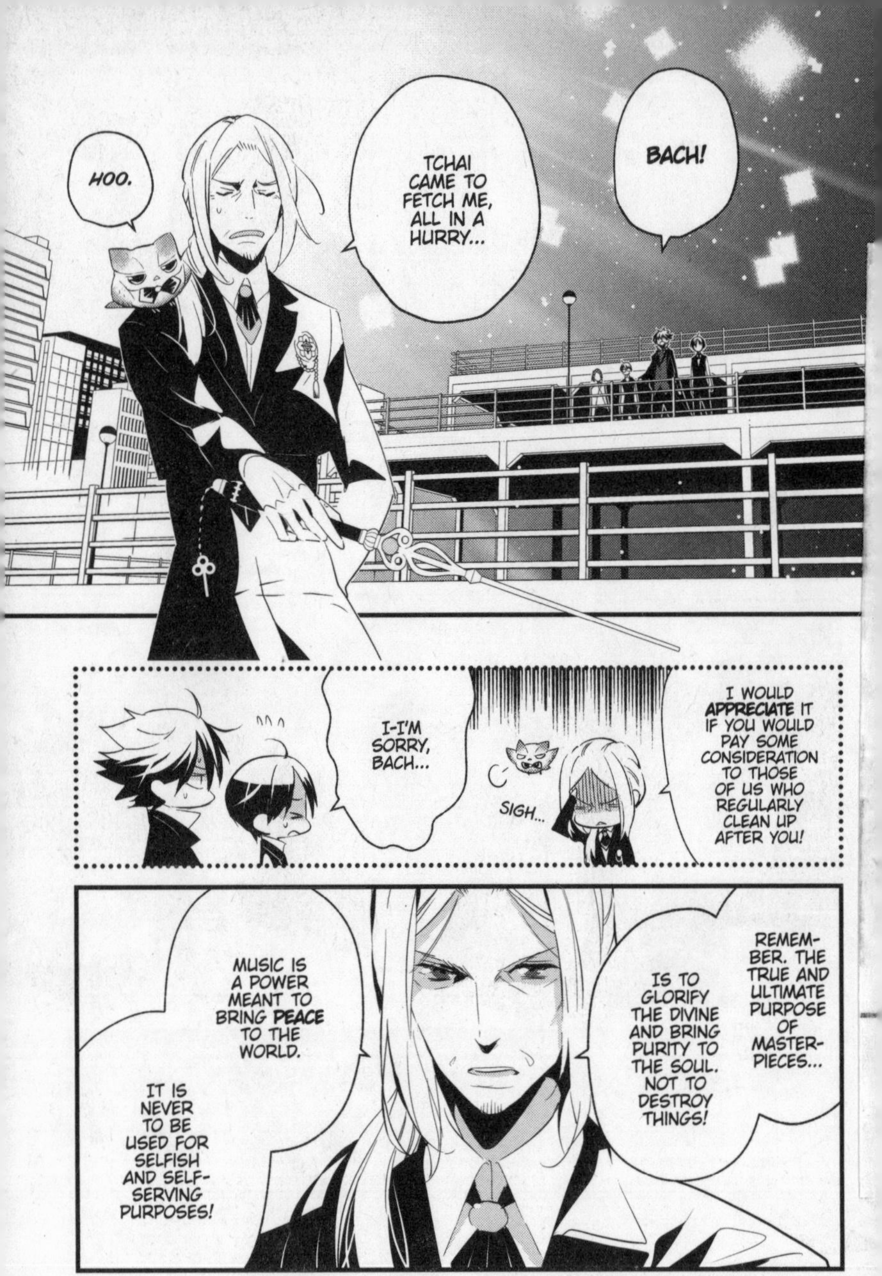
BACH!
TCHAI CAME TO FETCH ME, ALL IN A HURRY...
HOO.
I WOULD APPRECIATE IT IF YOU WOULD PAY SOME CONSIDERATION TO THOSE OF US WHO REGULARLY CLEAN UP AFTER YOU!
SIGH...
I-I'M SORRY, BACH...
REMEMBER. THE TRUE AND ULTIMATE PURPOSE OF MASTERPIECES...
IS TO GLORIFY THE DIVINE AND BRING PURITY TO THE SOUL. NOT TO DESTROY THINGS!
MUSIC IS A POWER MEANT TO BRING PEACE TO THE WORLD.
IT IS NEVER TO BE USED FOR SELFISH AND SELF-SERVING PURPOSES!

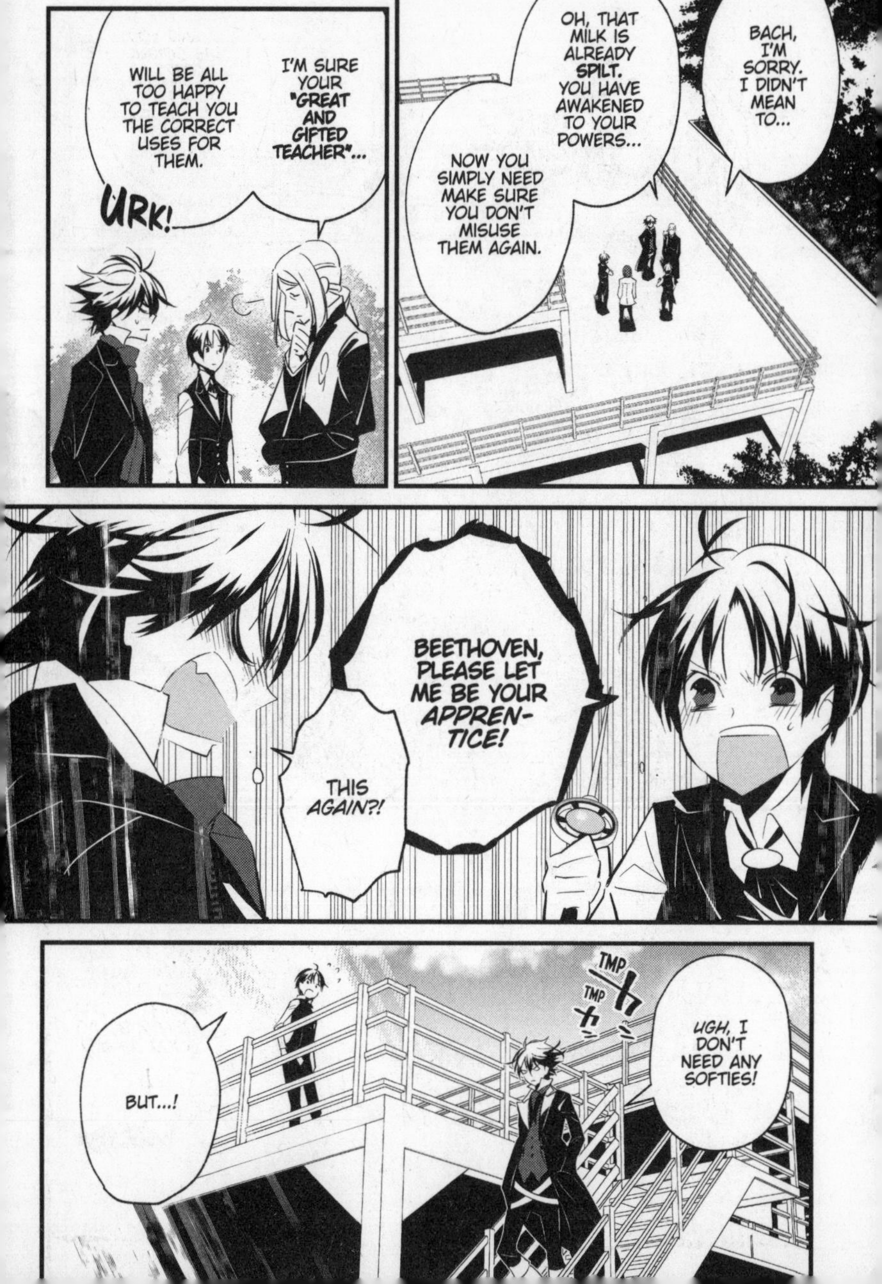
BACH, I'M SORRY. I DIDN'T MEAN TO...
OH, THAT MILK IS ALREADY SPILT. YOU HAVE AWAKENED TO YOUR POWERS...
NOW YOU SIMPLY NEED MAKE SURE YOU DON'T MISUSE THEM AGAIN.
I'M SURE YOUR "GREAT AND GIFTED TEACHER"...
WILL BE ALL TOO HAPPY TO TEACH YOU THE CORRECT USES FOR THEM.
URK!
BEETHOVEN, PLEASE LET ME BE YOUR APPREN-TICE!
THIS AGAIN?!
TMP
TMP
UGH, I DON'T NEED ANY SOFTIES!
BUT...!

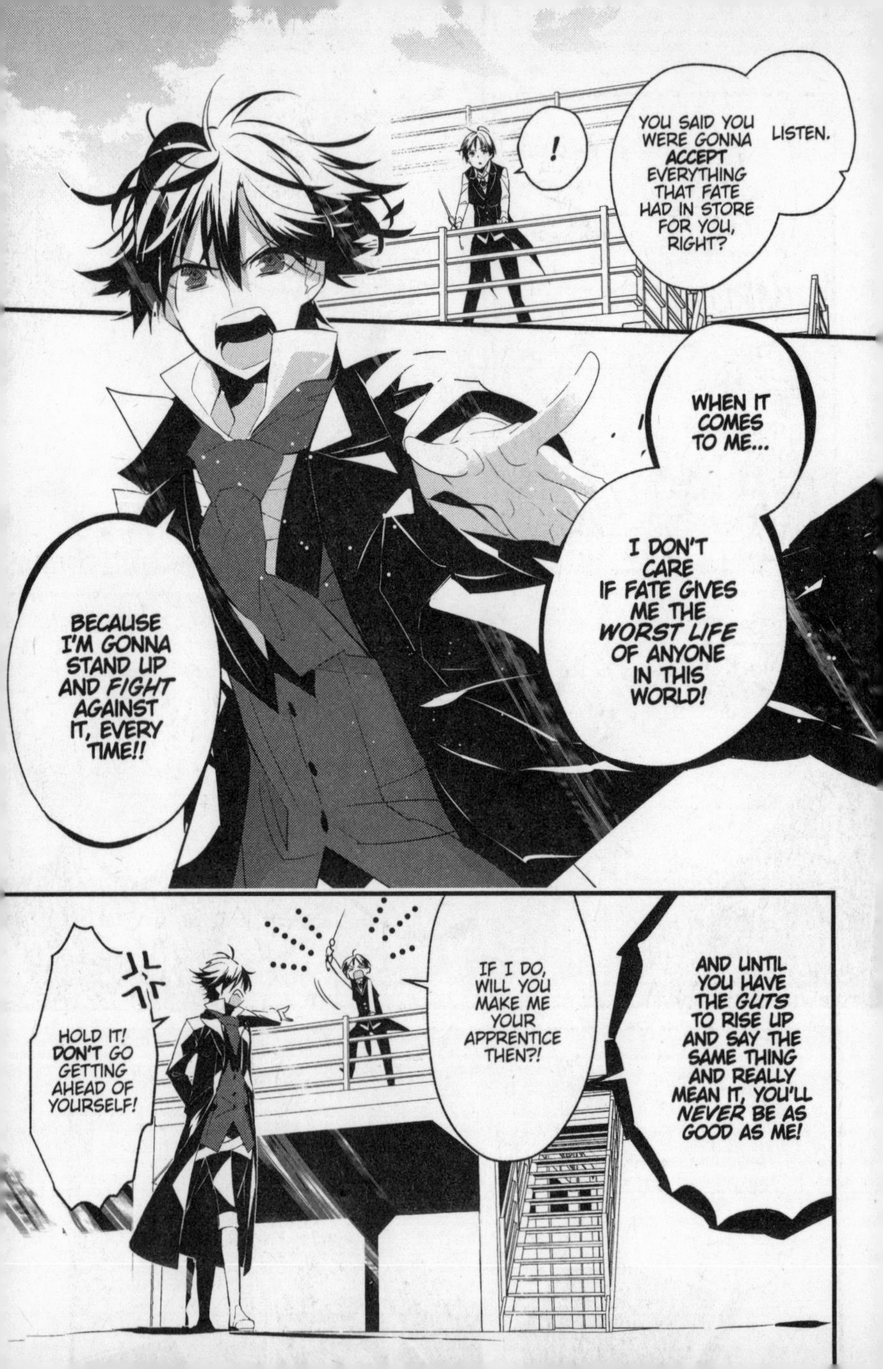
LISTEN.
YOU SAID YOU WERE GONNA ACCEPT EVERYTHING THAT FATE HAD IN STORE FOR YOU, RIGHT?
!
WHEN IT COMES TO ME...
I DON'T CARE IF FATE GIVES ME THE WORST LIFE OF ANYONE IN THIS WORLD!
BECAUSE I'M GONNA STAND UP AND FIGHT AGAINST IT, EVERY TIME!!
AND UNTIL YOU HAVE THE GUTS TO RISE UP AND SAY THE SAME THING AND REALLY MEAN IT, YOU'LL NEVER BE AS GOOD AS ME!
IF I DO, WILL YOU MAKE ME YOUR APPRENTICE THEN?!
HOLD IT! DON'T GO GETTING AHEAD OF YOURSELF!

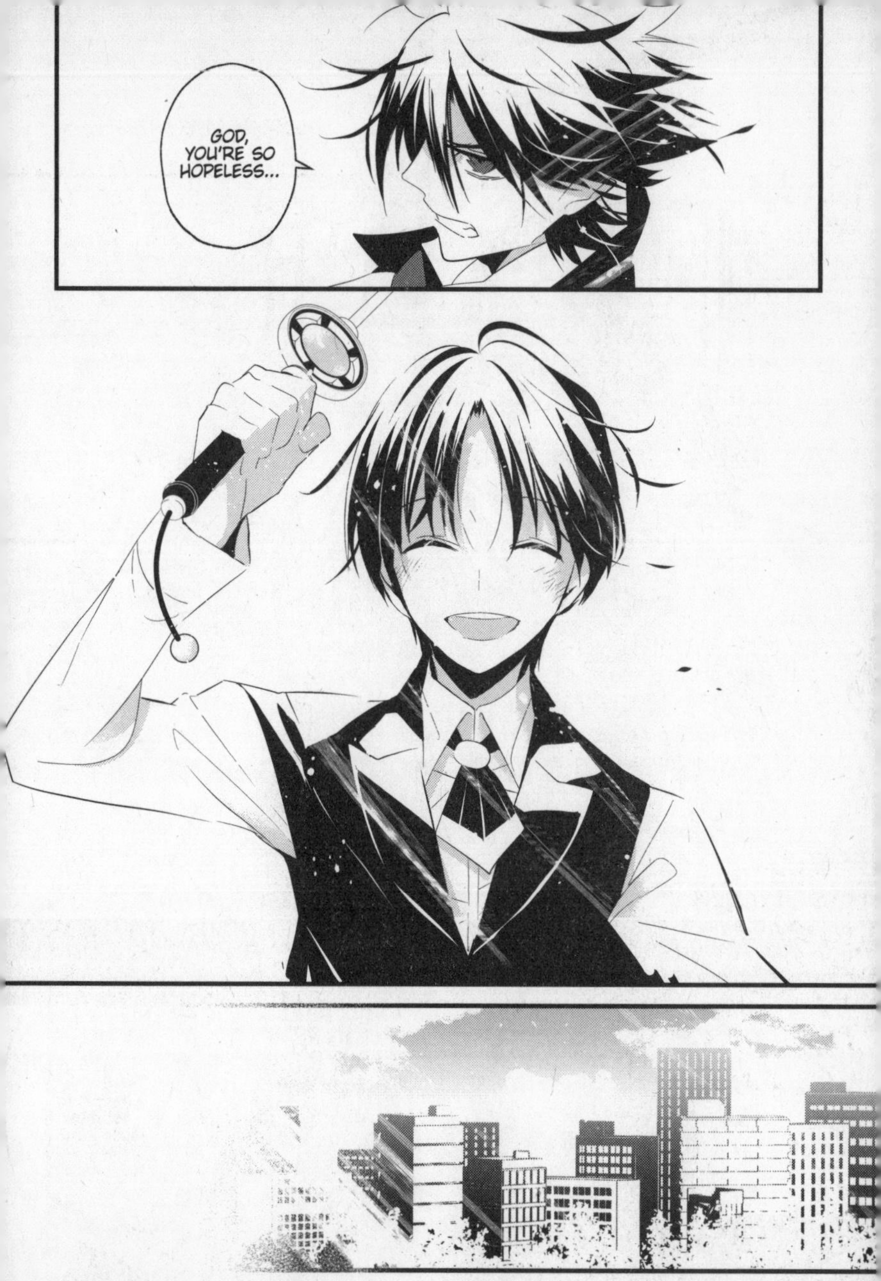
GOD, YOU'RE SO HOPELESS...

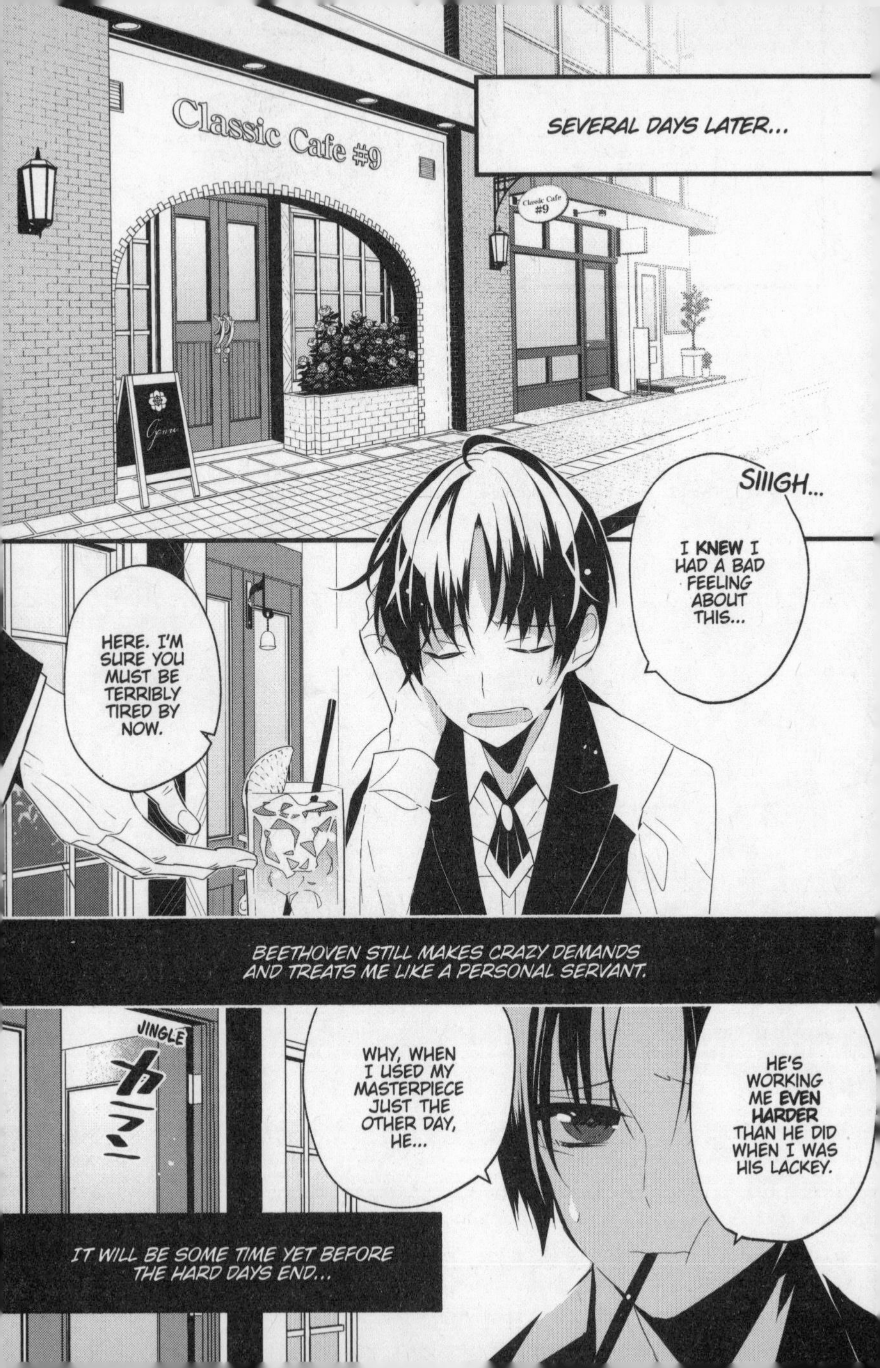
SEVERAL DAYS LATER...
Classic Cafe #9
Classic Cafe #9
SIIIGH...
I KNEW I HAD A BAD FEELING ABOUT THIS...
HERE. I'M SURE YOU MUST BE TERRIBLY TIRED BY NOW.
BEETHOVEN STILL MAKES CRAZY DEMANDS AND TREATS ME LIKE A PERSONAL SERVANT.
HE'S WORKING ME EVEN HARDER THAN HE DID WHEN I WAS HIS LACKEY.
WHY, WHEN I USED MY MASTERPIECE JUST THE OTHER DAY, HE...
JINGLE
IT WILL BE SOME TIME YET BEFORE THE HARD DAYS END...

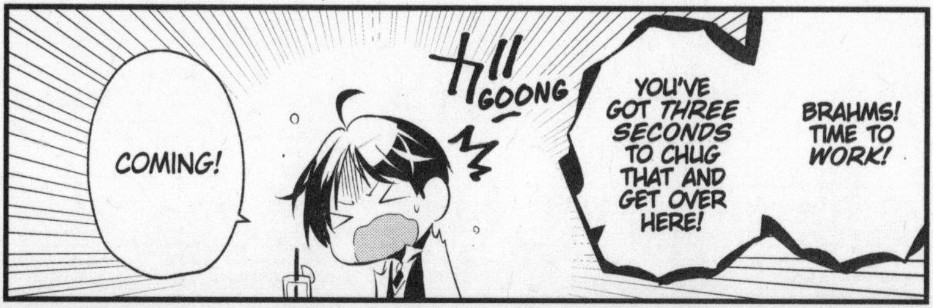
BRAHMS! TIME TO WORK!
YOU'VE GOT THREE SECONDS TO CHUG THAT AND GET OVER HERE!
GOONG
COMING!

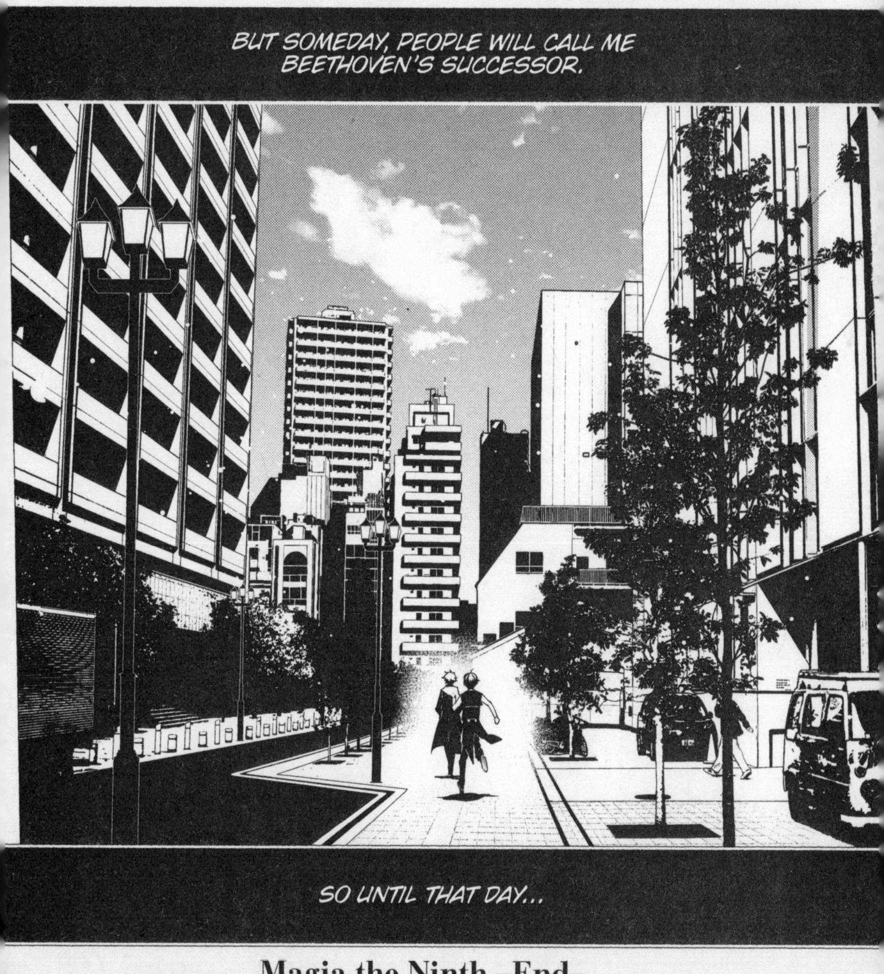
BUT SOMEDAY, PEOPLE WILL CALL ME BEETHOVEN'S SUCCESSOR.
SO UNTIL THAT DAY...

Magia the Ninth –End–

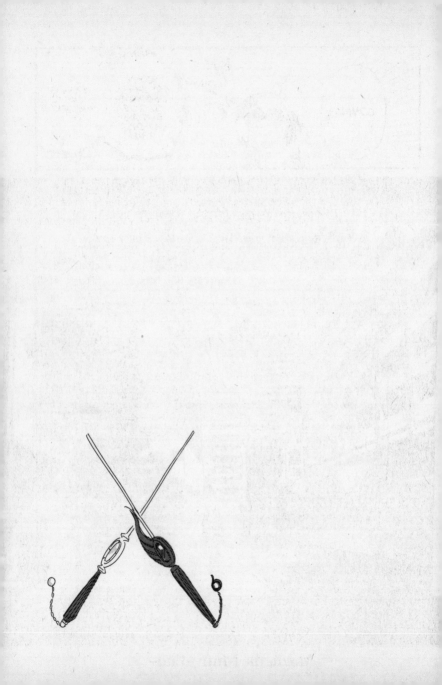

Thank you very much for reading *Magia the Ninth.* It is sad that this story must come to a close so quickly, but I am thankful for all the love and support I have received from all of you fans. Even now that the story is over, I'm still receiving comments and fan letters, and that makes me feel all warm inside. Perhaps sometime, somewhere, I will have the opportunity to draw the characters of *Magia the Ninth* again. When my next new work comes out, I hope all of you will stop by to see me again!

A Notice About My Pen Name

As of 2016, my pen name will change from Ichiya Sazanami to...

さざなみ MISA SAZANAMI

漣ミサ

Please keep that in mind in the future.

The reason I decided to change my pen name stems mostly from how difficult people found it to read the original one. Thus I decided to switch it to something much easier to understand. Though only the first name is changing, I plan to take this as a chance to redouble my efforts and make even better works in the future. I hope to see you all again! (Sazanami)

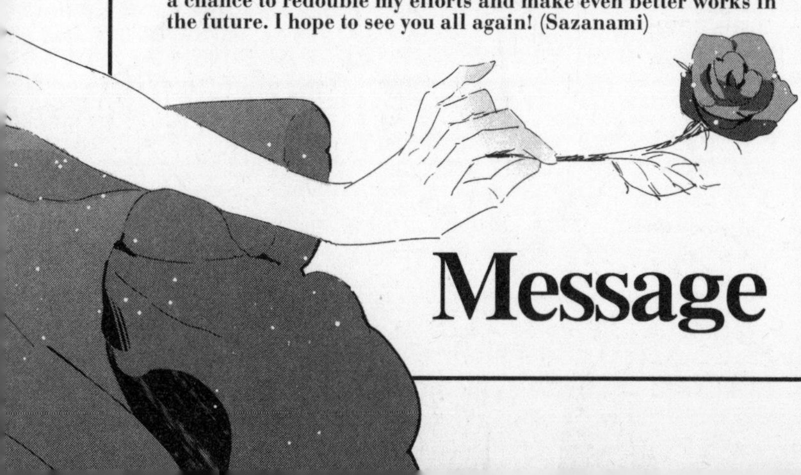

Message

Special Thanks

KOUYOU SATSUKI-SAN

OUKA YAKAGI-SAN

KIMAMA-SAN

YUTSUKI INUMURA-SAN

MY EDITOR

HIROKI HORIE-SAN (DIRECTOR)

DANYUMI-SAN (COVER DESIGN)

and you!

Sazanami Yokiyo

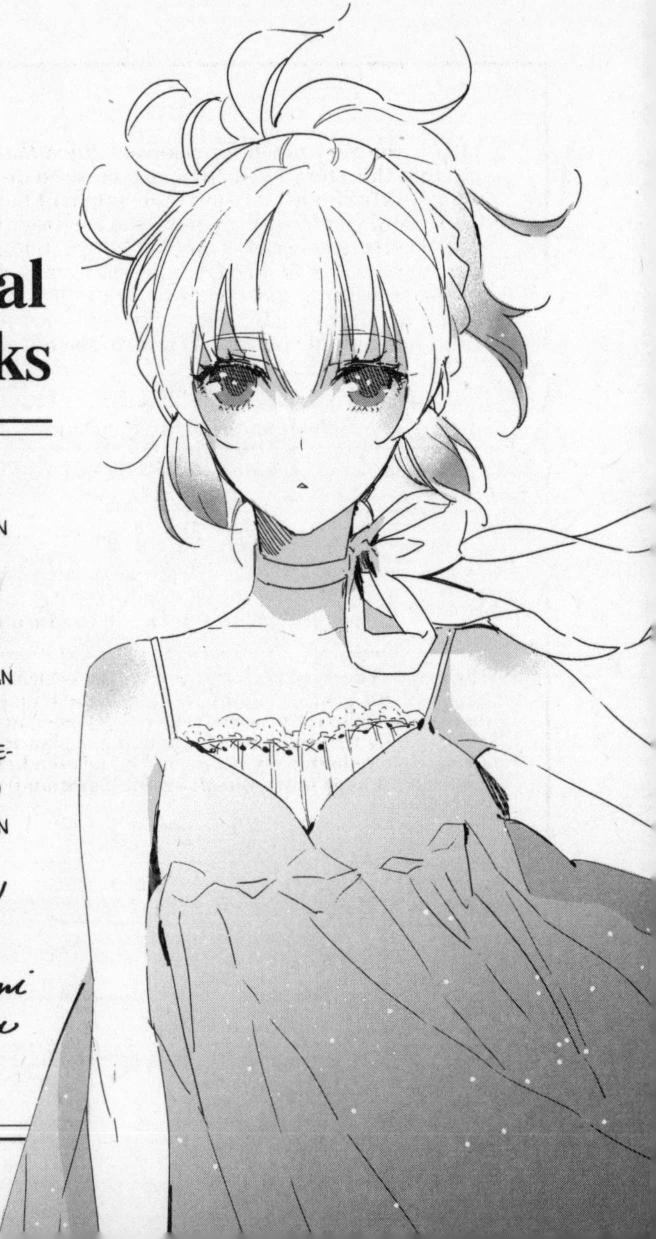

Magia The ninth

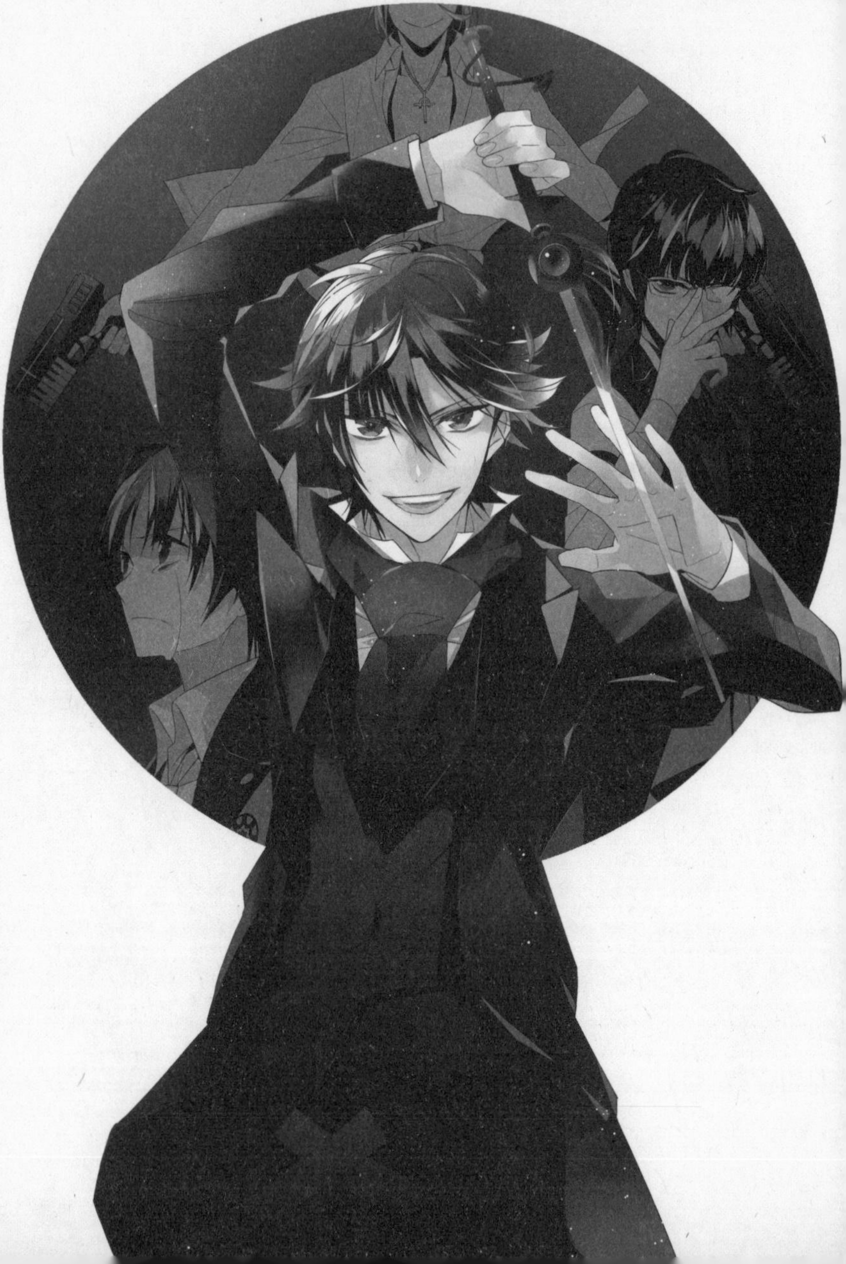

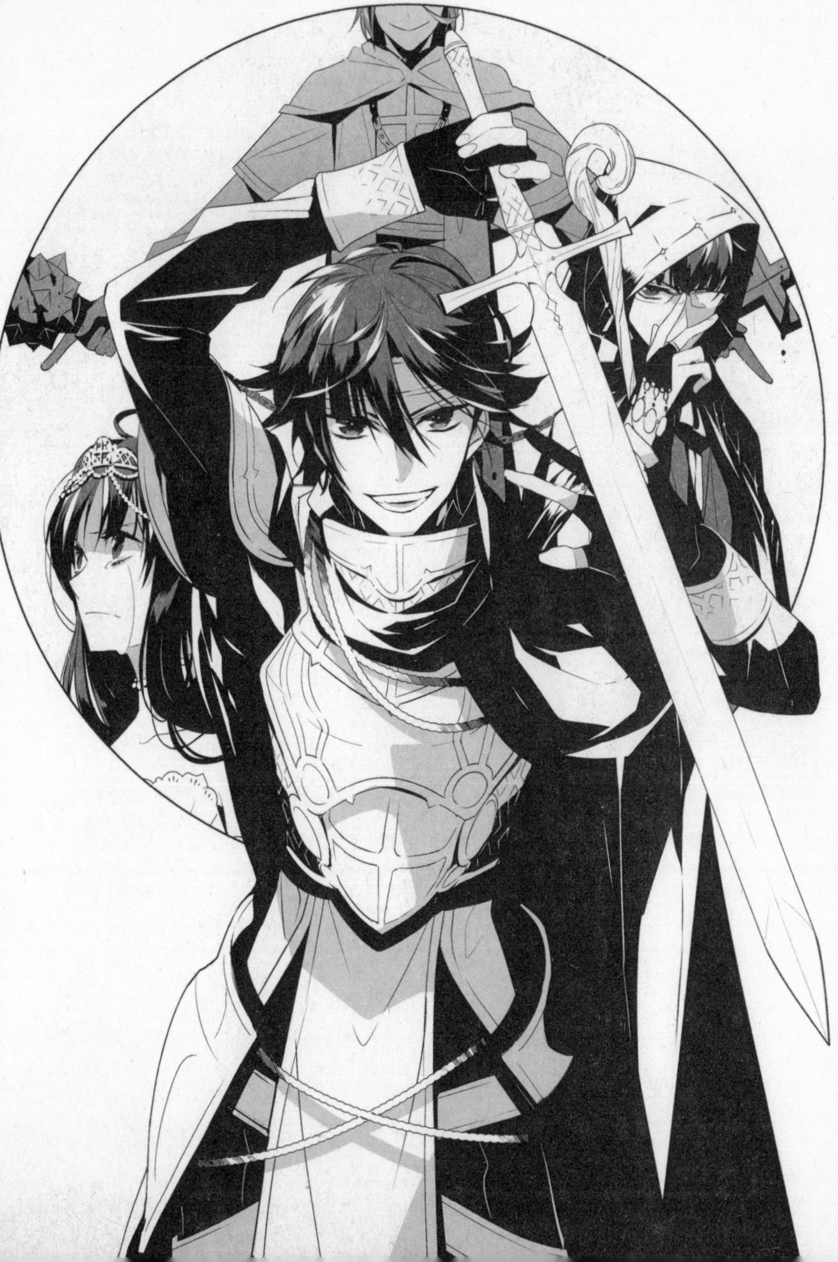

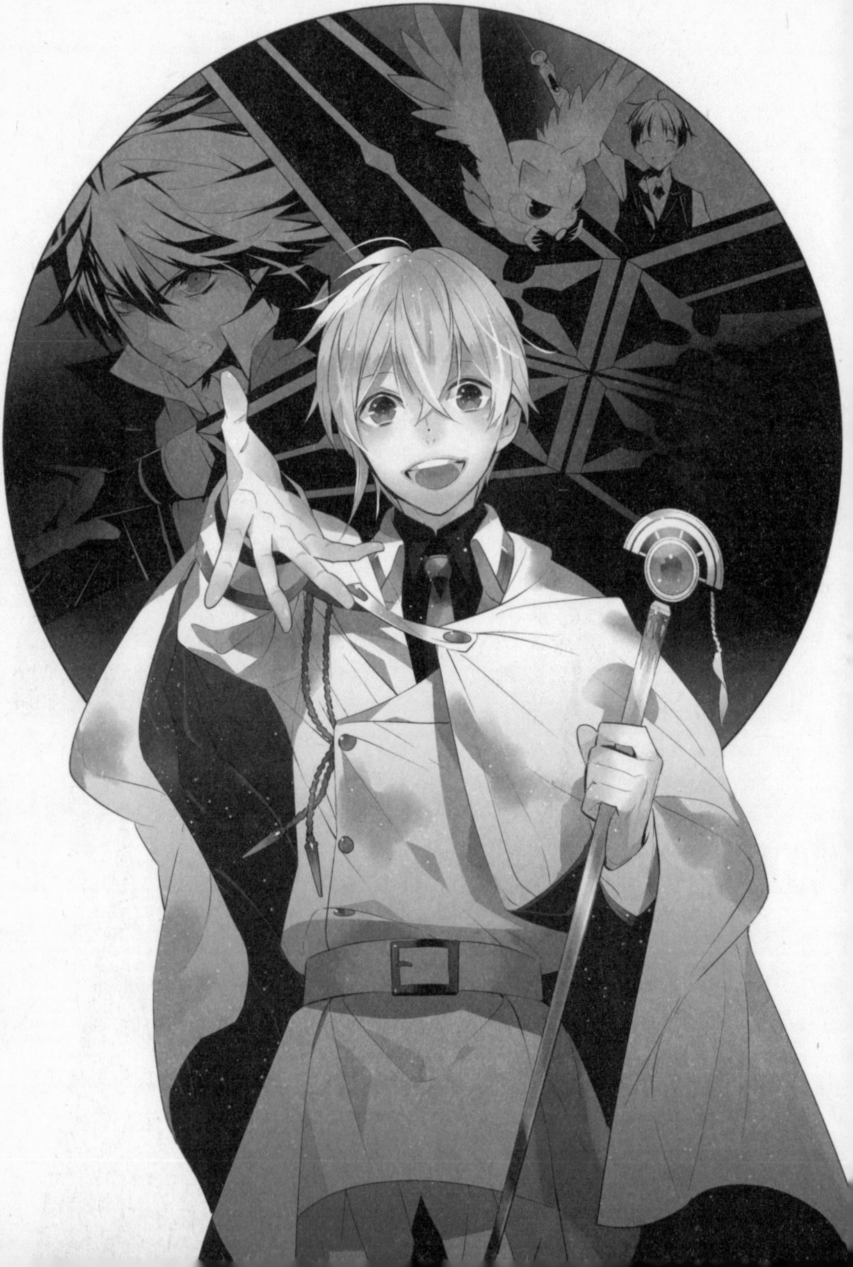

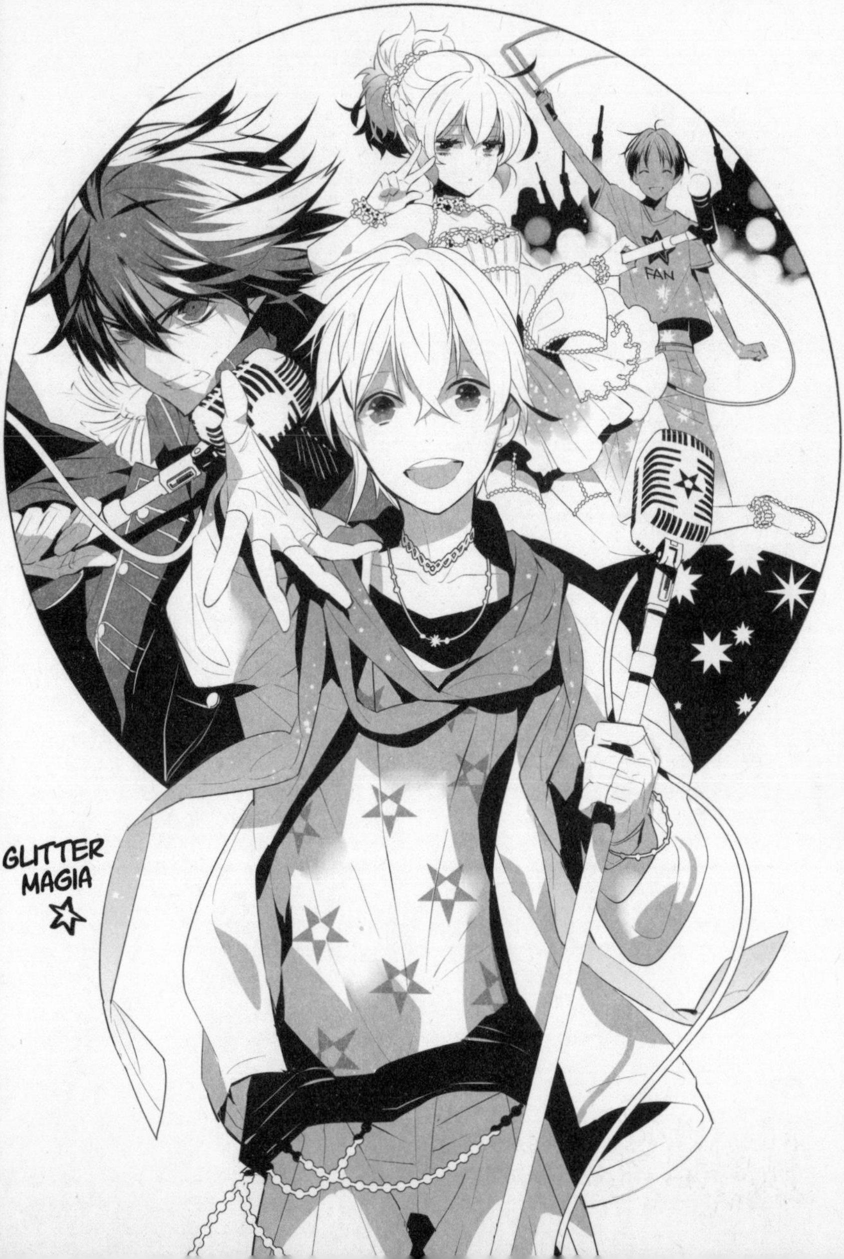
FAN
GLITTER MAGIA

Magia the Ninth

Magia the Ninth